The Politics and Economics of Indonesia's Natural Resources

Resources for the Future (RFF) improves environmental and natural resource policymaking worldwide through independent social science research of the highest caliber. Founded in 1952, RFF pioneered the application of economics as a tool for developing more effective policy about the use and conservation of natural resources. Its scholars continue to employ social science methods to analyze critical issues concerning pollution control, energy policy, land and water use, hazardous waste, climate change, biodiversity, and the environmental challenges of developing countries.

RFF Press supports the mission of RFF by publishing book-length works that present a broad range of approaches to the study of natural resources and the environment. Its authors and editors include RFF staff, researchers from the larger academic and policy communities, and journalists. Audiences for publications by RFF Press include all of the participants in the policymaking process — scholars, the media, advocacy groups, NGOs, professionals in business and government, and the public.

The **Institute of Southeast Asian Studies (ISEAS)** was established as an autonomous organization in 1968. It is a regional centre dedicated to the study of socio-political, security and economic trends and developments in Southeast Asia and its wider geostrategic and economic environment.

The Institute's research programmes are the Regional Economic Studies (RES, including ASEAN and APEC), Regional Strategic and Political Studies (RSPS), and Regional Social and Cultural Studies (RSCS).

ISEAS Publications, an established academic press, has issued more than 1,000 books and journals. It is the largest scholarly publisher of research about Southeast Asia from within the region. ISEAS Publications works with many other academic and trade publishers and distributors to disseminate important research and analyses from and about Southeast Asia to the rest of the world.

The Politics and Economics of Indonesia's Natural Resources

Edited by
Budy P. Resosudarmo

RFF PRESS
RESOURCES FOR THE FUTURE

INSTITUTE OF SOUTHEAST ASIAN STUDIES
Singapore

First published in Singapore in 2005 by
ISEAS Publications
Institute of Southeast Asian Studies
30 Heng Mui Keng Terrace
Pasir Panjang
Singapore 119614

E-mail: publish@iseas.edu.sg
http://bookshop.iseas.edu.sg

First published in the United States of America in 2006 by
Resources for the Future
1616 P Street NW
Washington, DC 20036-1400
USA

The responsibility for facts and opinions in this publication rests exclusively with the
authors and their interpretations do not necessarily reflect the views or the policy of the
Institute or its supporters.

Library of Congress Cataloguing-in-Publication Data

The politics and economics of Indonesia's natural resources / edited by Budy P.
   Resosudarmo.
      p. cm. – (Indonesia update series)
   Includes bibliographical references and index.
   ISBN 1-933115-25-4 (pbk.)
         1. Natural resources—Indonesia. 2. Environmental policy—Indonesia. 3.
         Indonesia—Economic policy. I. Resosudarmo, Budy P. II. Series.

HC447.5.P65   2006
333.709598 — dc22

Copy-edited and typeset by Beth Thomson and Sue Mathews
Indexed by Angela Grant

The Politics and Economics of Indonesia's Natural Resources

The Politics and Economics of Indonesia's Natural Resources

Edited by

Budy P. Resosudarmo

CONTENTS

Tables   vii
Figures   ix
Contributors   xi
Acknowledgments   xiii
Glossary   xv
Preface: Looking Back to Move Forward, by Emil Salim   xxi

1   Introduction   1
     Budy P. Resosudarmo

PART I   Recent Political and Economic Developments

2   Politics: Indonesia's Year of Elections and the End of the
     Political Transition   13
     Edward Aspinall

3   The Economy: High Growth Remains Elusive   31
     Ross H. McLeod

**PART II   Globalisation, Decentralisation and Sustainable
             Development**

4   Indonesia in a Changing Global Environment   53
     Warwick J. McKibbin

5   International Trade and the Natural Resource 'Curse'
     in Southeast Asia: Does China's Growth Threaten Regional
     Development?   71
     Ian Coxhead

6   Unfinished Edifice or Pandora's Box? Decentralisation and
     Resource Management in Indonesia   92
     *James J. Fox, Dedi Supriadi Adhuri and Ida Aju Pradnja
     Resosudarmo*

7   Does Indonesia have the Balance Right in Natural Resource
     Revenue Sharing?   109
     Armida S. Alisjahbana

8   Development Performance and Future Scenarios in the
     Context of Sustainable Utilisation of Natural Resources   125
     Iwan J. Azis and Emil Salim

PART III   Sectoral Challenges

9   Oligarchy in the Timber Markets of Indonesia:
     From Apkindo to IBRA to the Future of the Forests   145
     Paul K. Gellert

10   If Only Fish Could Vote: The Enduring Challenges of Coastal
     and Marine Resources Management in Post-*reformasi* Indonesia 162
     Ian M. Dutton

11   Petroleum Paradox: The Politics of Oil and Gas   179
     Francisia S.S.E. Seda

PART IV   Illegal Extractions and Conflicts

12   Illegal Logging in Indonesia: Myth and Reality   193
     Krystof Obidzinski

13   Illegal Coalmining in West Sumatra: Access and Actors in
     the Post-Soeharto Era   206
     Erwiza Erman

14   Local Government and Environmental Conservation in
     West Java   216
     Joan Hardjono

PART V   Laws and Institutions

15   New Legal Initiatives for Natural Resource Management in
     a Changing Indonesia: The Promise, the Fear and the Unknown   231
     Jason M. Patlis

16   Institutional Transformation for Better Policy Implementation
     and Enforcement   248
     Isna Marifa

References   259
Index   283

TABLES

2.1   Results of the 1999 and 2004 DPR elections (selected groups)   15

2.2   Results of the 2004 presidential elections   17

3.1   IBRA's cumulative fund remittance to the government, 1999/2000 – end 2003   44

5.1   Southeast Asian countries' trade with China and ranking of China among their trading partners, 1990–2003   77

5.2   Southeast Asian competition with China in the US market, 1990–2000   78

5.3   RCA values for China and Southeast Asia   80

5.4   Correlation coefficients of RCA measures between China and Southeast Asian economies, 1989–2003   84

6.1   Regional fisheries and species overexploitation   97

6.2   Forestry revenue-sharing scheme   101

7.1   Natural resource revenue-sharing arrangements before and after decentralisation   112

7.2   Variation in revenue per capita of districts by source of revenue, fiscal years 2000 and 2002   118

16.1   National-level agencies involved in setting policies affecting natural resources   250

FIGURES

3.1	Consumer and share prices, exchange rate and inflation, 2003–04	32
3.2	Monetary policy's non-relationship with GDP	33
3.3	Investment, 1997–2004	36
3.4	Major sectors' shares of GDP, 1994–2004	38
3.5	Trends in labour force structure, 1986–2003	40
3.6	Real minimum wages relative to the 1997 average (selected provinces)	41
3.7	Growth rates of major non-oil/gas exports, 1996–2003	42
3.8	Real bank deposits by selected regions, 1992–2004	48
4.1	Real GDP growth in selected OECD countries and Asia, 1992–2004	54
4.2	Industrial production in Asia, 1999–2005	55
4.3	Current account balance in selected countries, 1995–2004	57
4.4	Investment in selected countries, 1995–2003	58
4.5	Relative trends in energy consumption in Indonesia, 1980–2000	59
4.6	Energy consumption in Indonesia by source, 1980–2000	60
4.7	Relative trends in carbon dioxide emissions in Indonesia, 1980–2000	61
4.8	Change in forest area by type, 1990–2000	63
5.1	RCA differences, Indonesia minus China	82
5.2	RCA differences, Vietnam minus China.	83
7.1	Oil and gas revenue as a share of domestic revenue, 1969/70–2003	111

7.2   Average fiscal capacity per capita of oil/gas and non-oil/gas-producing districts before and after decentralisation   116

7.3   Fiscal capacity per capita of selected oil/gas-producing districts before and after decentralisation   117

7.4   Routine and development expenditures of oil/gas and non-oil/gas-producing cities and districts before and after decentralisation   119

7.5   Development expenditures of oil/gas and non-oil/gas-producing districts before and after decentralisation   120

8.1   The ESE triangle: Indonesia's economic, social and environmental development performance   130

8.2   Trends in real GDP, 2000–20   133

8.3   Trends in the price index, 2000–20   135

8.4   Trends in the current account deficit, 2000–20   136

8.5   Trends in the Gini index, 2000–20   137

8.6   Trends in employment, 2000–20   138

8.7   Trends in the poverty line, 2000–20   139

8.8   Trends in incomes of the poor, 2000–20   139

9.1   Export value of forest products, 1990–2002   148

CONTRIBUTORS

Dedi Supriadi Adhuri
Scientist, Research Center for Social and Cultural Studies, Indonesian
Institute of Sciences, Jakarta

Armida S. Alisjahbana
Professor, Faculty of Economics, Padjadjaran University, Bandung

Edward Aspinall
Lecturer, Department of Chinese and South-East Asian Studies and
Department of History, Faculty of Arts, University of Sydney, Sydney

Iwan J. Azis
Professor, Department of City and Regional Planning, and Johnson Graduate
School of Management, Cornell University, Ithaca, and Faculty of Economics,
University of Indonesia, Jakarta

Ian Coxhead
Professor, Department of Agricultural and Applied Economics, University of
Wisconsin, Madison

Ian M. Dutton
Director, Conservation Measures Group, The Nature Conservancy,
Washington DC

Erwiza Erman
Scientist, Research Center for Regional Resources, Indonesian Institute of
Sciences, Jakarta

James J. Fox
Professor and Director, Research School of Pacific and Asian Studies,
Australian National University, Canberra

Paul K. Gellert
Assistant Professor, Department of Development Sociology and Southeast
Asia Program, Cornell University, Ithaca

Joan Hardjono
Independent researcher, Bandung

Isna Marifa
Director, PT Qipra Galang Kualita Environmental Training and Consulting,
Jakarta

Warwick J. McKibbin
Professor, Economics Division, Research School of Pacific and Asian Studies,
and Director, Centre for Applied Macroeconomic Analysis, Australian
National University, Canberra, and Professorial Fellow, Lowy Institute for
International Policy, Sydney

Ross H. McLeod
Senior Fellow, Economics Division, Research School of Pacific and Asian
Studies, Australian National University, Canberra

Krystof Obidzinski
Research Fellow, Center for International Forestry Research, Bogor

Jason M. Patlis
Senior Legal Advisor, Coastal Resources Management Project, Jakarta

Budy P. Resosudarmo
Fellow, Economics Division, Research School of Pacific and Asian Studies,
Australian National University, Canberra

Ida Aju Pradnja Resosudarmo
PhD candidate, School of Resources, Environment and Society, Faculty of
Science, Australian National University, Canberra

Emil Salim
Professor, Faculty of Economics, University of Indonesia, Jakarta

Francisia S.S.E. Seda
Lecturer, Department of Sociology, Faculty of Social and Political Sciences,
University of Indonesia, Jakarta

ACKNOWLEDGMENTS

This book is a result of the Indonesia Update conference held on 24–25 September 2004 at the Australian National University (ANU) on the theme 'Natural resources in Indonesia: The economic, political and environmental challenges'. There are a number of organisations and people that I would like to thank for making the conference and the publication of this book possible.

The Australian Agency for International Development (AusAID) was the principal financial sponsor of the conference and of this book. The Nature Conservancy, Cornell University, the Center for International Forestry Research and BHP Billiton Indonesia also contributed financially to support the participation of some of the speakers. As in previous years, the 2004 Indonesia Update conference received generous support from the Research School of Pacific and Asian Studies (RSPAS) at the ANU. James Fox, the Director of RSPAS, has been a major source of encouragement, especially for work on the environment and natural resources in Indonesia, which is a particular area of his personal research interest. Within RSPAS, the Division of Economics, headed by Warwick McKibbin and Hal Hill, provided moral and material help directly and through the division's Indonesia Project; the Department of Political and Social Change provided administrative assistance; and the National Institute of Asia and the Pacific funded the promotional aspects of the conference. Without the financial support of these organisations, the conference and this volume would not have materialised. I thank them for their contributions.

My gratitude goes to Cathy Haberle, Trish van der Hoek and Liz Drysdale of the Indonesia Project, who were the main actors behind the success of the conference. I thank Alison Ley of the Department of Political and Social Change who organised the Speakers' Dinner; Catharina Williams for her assistance with the media; and a group of ANU students, all of whose names I do not have the space to list here, for their help with the organisation and the practicalities of the conference. I also want to thank my colleagues in the Indonesia Project, Chris Manning, Hal Hill and Ross McLeod, for their suggestions and consistent support before, during and since the conference. Their support in both substantive and practical matters helped me a great deal in convening the conference and preparing the book.

I would like to thank all the speakers and moderators who took part in the Indonesia Update conference as well as those who contributed to this book. As usual the conference proved to be a valuable forum for the exchange of ideas and dissemination of information, much of which is encompassed in this book. My appreciation also goes to the reviewers of the various chapters in this book: Jean Aden, Timothy Brown, Daju Indira Dharmapatni, Julian Disney, Achmad Fauzy, Greg Fealy, Brian Fegan, Anton Gunawan, Ariel Heryanto, Hal Hill, Frank Jotzo, Chris Manning, Ross McLeod, Lesley Potter and Ida Aju Pradnja Resosudarmo.

I particularly thank Beth Thomson and Sue Mathews for their excellent work in copy editing, designing and typesetting this book. Finally, my appreciation goes to Triena Ong of the Institute for Southeast Asian Studies for her assistance and support in publishing this latest volume in the Indonesia Update series.

Budy P. Resosudarmo
April 2005

I dedicate this book to
my wife, Daju Omang, and
my children, Dhika, Yana and Sesa

GLOSSARY

adat	norm/tradition/custom
ADB	Asian Development Bank
Amdal	Analisis Mengenai Dampak Lingkungan (Environmental Impact Analysis)
ANU	Australian National University
APBD	Anggaran Pendapatan dan Belanja Daerah (local government budget)
APBN	Anggaran Pendapatan dan Belanja Negara (central government budget)
APHI	Asosiasi Pengusaha Hutan Indonesia (Indonesian Association of Forest Concessionaires)
Apkasi	Asosiasi Pemerintah Kabupaten Seluruh Indonesia (Association of Indonesian Districts/District Heads)
Apkindo	Asosiasi Panel Kayu Indonesia (Indonesian Plywood Producers' Association)
ASEAN	Association of South East Asian Nations (Indonesia, Malaysia, the Philippines, Singapore, Thailand, Brunei Darussalam, Cambodia, Laos, Myanmar and Vietnam)
Asmindo	Asosiasi Industri Permebelan dan Kerajinan Indonesia (Indonesian Association of Furniture and Handcraft Industry)
ATC	Agreement on Textiles and Clothing
AusAID	Australian Agency for International Development
Badan Legislatif	Legislation Board
banjir kap	intensive traditional/manual logging
Bapedal	Badan Pengendalian Dampak Lingkungan (Environmental Impact Management Agency)

Bappeda	Badan Perencanaan Pembangunan Daerah (Regional Development Planning Board)
Bappenas	Badan Perencanaan Pembangunan Nasional (National Development Planning Agency)
BI	Bank Indonesia
BIN	Badan Intelijen Negara (National Intelligence Agency)
BPN	Badan Pertanahan Nasional (National Land Agency)
BPS	Badan Pusat Statistik (Statistics Indonesia, the Central Statistics Agency, formerly Central Bureau of Statistics)
BRIK	Badan Revitalisasi Industri Kehutanan (Wood Industry Revitalisation Agency)
Bulog	Badan Urusan Logistik (the national food logistics agency)
bupati	head of a *kabupaten* (district)
CDM	Clean Development Mechanism (of the Kyoto Protocol)
CGI	Consultative Group on Indonesia
Coremap	Coral Reef Rehabilitation and Management Program
CoW	contract of work
CPUE	catch per unit effort
cukong	financial backer
DAK	Dana Alokasi Khusus (Specific Purpose Fund or Specific Allocation Grant to regions)
DAK–DR	Dana Alokasi Khusus–Dana Reboisasi (specific purpose fund for reforestation)
Dana Pembangunan Daerah	Regional Development Fund
dana perimbangan	equalisation funds (to regions)
Dana Reboisasi	Reforestation Fund
Dati I	Daerah Tingkat I (first-level region, that is, province)
Dati II	Daerah Tingkat II (second-level region/district, that is, *kabupaten/kota*)
datuk	the *adat* (traditional) leader in a Minang family clan
DAU	Dana Alokasi Umum (General Allocation Fund, General Purpose Fund, or fiscal equalisation transfer to regions)
DIK	Daftar Isian Kegiatan (routine expenditures)
DIP	Daftar Isian Proyek (list of budgeted technical projects; regional development spending)
DPD	Dewan Perwakilan Daerah (Council of Regional Representatives)
DPR	Dewan Perwakilan Rakyat (People's Representative Council, Indonesia's national parliament)
DPRD	Dewan Perwakilan Rakyat Daerah (Regional People's Representative Council)

DR	Dana Reboisasi (Reforestation Fund)
ESE triangle	economic–social–environmental triangle
EU	European Union
FDI	foreign direct investment
GAM	Gerakan Aceh Merdeka (Free Aceh Movement)
GDP	gross domestic product
Golkar	Golongan Karya (the state political party under the New Order, and one of the major post-New Order parties)
GRDP	gross regional domestic product
GT	gross tonnes
GTAP	Global Trade Analysis Project
HPH	Hak Pengusahaan Hutan (large-scale forest harvesting concession rights)
HPHH	Hak Pemungutan Hasil Hutan (small-scale forest harvesting concession rights)
IBRA	Indonesian Bank Restructuring Agency
IHPH	Iuran Hak Pengusahaan Hutan (forest concession licence fee)
IHPHH	Ijin Hak Pemungutan Hasil Hutan (forest product harvest concession royalty)
ijin pinjam pakai	borrowing permit (literally, 'borrowed use' permit)
IMF	International Monetary Fund
Inpres	Instruksi Presiden (Presidential Instruction)
IPHHK	Ijin Pemungutan Hasil Hutan Kayu (timber extraction permit)
IPK	Ijin Pemanfaatan Kayu (timber utilisation permit)
IPPK	Ijin Pemungutan dan Pemanfaatan Kayu (timber extraction and utilisation permit)
IRRI	International Rice Research Institute
ITTO	International Tropical Timber Organization
IUPHHK	Ijin Usaha Pemanfaatan Hasil Hutan Kayu (timber utilisation permit)
ijin lokasi	location permit
ijin pemanfaatan tanah	land use permit
JSX	Jakarta Stock Exchange
kabupaten	district, regency
kandep	*kantor departemen* (*kabupaten*-level office of a central government ministry)
kanwil	*kantor wilayah* (provincial-level office of a central government ministry)
kappersil	a small logging concession permit based on PP 1/1957

kecamatan	subdistrict
Kepmen	Keputusan Menteri (Ministerial Decision)
Keppres	Keputusan Presiden (Presidential Decision/Decree)
KFDC	Kalimantan Forestry Development Corporation
KKN	*korupsi, kolusi, nepotisme* (corruption, collusion, nepotism)
Koalisi Kebangsaan	Nationhood Coalition
kota	city, municipality
krismon	*krisis moneter* (monetary crisis)
KUD	Koperasi Unit Desa (village unit cooperatives)
LIPI	Lembaga Ilmu Pengetahuan Indonesia (Indonesian Institute of Sciences)
LNG	liquefied natural gas
LPEM	Lembaga Penyelidikan Ekonomi dan Masyarakat (Institute for Economic and Social Research, University of Indonesia)
MFA	Multi-fibre Arrangement
MPA	marine protected area
MPI	Masyarakat Perhutanan Indonesia (Indonesian Forestry Society)
MPR	Majelis Permusyawaratan Rakyat (People's Consultative Assembly)
MREP Project	Marine Resources Evaluation and Planning Project
New Order	the Soeharto era, 1965–98
NGO	non-government organisation
NIC	newly industrialised country
NRKK	Nanyo Ringyo Kabushiki Kaisha (a Japanese logging company)
NTT	Nusa Tenggara Timur (East Nusa Tenggara)
NU	Nahdlatul Ulama (traditionalist Islamic organisation)
OECD	Organisation for Economic Co-operation and Development
OPEC	Organization of the Petroleum Exporting Countries
opkoop	buying up of timber
PAD	Pendapatan Asli Daerah (locally derived revenue)
PAN	Partai Amanat Nasional (National Mandate Party, a modernist Muslim party associated with Amien Rais)
PBB	Pajak Bumi dan Bangunan (land and building tax)
PBB	Partai Bulan Bintang (Crescent Moon and Star Party, a *shariah*-oriented modernist Islamic party)
PBR	Partai Bintang Reformasi (Star Reform Party, a PPP splinter group)

PD	Partai Demokrat (Democrat Party, the vehicle for Susilo Bambang Yudhoyono)
PDI	Partai Demokrasi Indonesia (Indonesian Democracy Party)
PDI-P	Partai Demokrasi Indonesia – Perjuangan (Indonesian Democratic Party of Struggle, the vehicle for Megawati Sukarnoputri)
PDS	Partai Damai Sejahtera (Prosperous Peace Party, a Christian party)
peraturan	regulation, implementing decree
Peraturan Pemerintah	government regulation
Peraturan Presiden	Presidential Decree
Perda	Peraturan Daerah (regional government by-law)
Perhutani	state-owned forestry company
Perpu	Peraturan Pemerintah Pengganti Undang-Undang (Government Regulation in Lieu of Legislation)
Pertamina	Perusahaan Pertambangan Minyak dan Gas Bumi Negara (Indonesia's state-owned oil company)
pesantren	Islamic school
PJP	Pola Umum Pembangunan Jangka Panjang (long-term development plan)
PKB	Partai Kebangkitan Bangsa (National Awakening Party, aligned to Nahdlatul Ulama)
PKPB	Partai Karya Peduli Bangsa (Care for the Nation Functional Party, a Soeharto nostalgia party)
PKS	Partai Keadilan Sejahtera (Prosperous Justice Party, an urban, puritanical Islamist party, preceded by its forerunner, Partai Keadilan in 1999)
POLRI	Polisi Republik Indonesia (Indonesian National Police)
PP	Peraturan Pemerintah (Government Decree or Regulation)
PPP	Partai Persatuan Pembangunan (United Development Party, an Islamic party led by Hamzah Haz)
PPP	purchasing power parity
preman	extortionist, standover criminal
Prolegnas	Program Legislatif Nasional (Priority List for the National Legislative Program)
PSC	production-sharing contract
PSDH	Provisi Sumber Daya Hutan (Forestry Royalty)
PTPN	Perseroan Terbatas (PT) Perkebunan Nusantara (government plantation company)
Puskesmas	Pusat Kesehatan Masyarakat (community health centre)
putra daerah	local inhabitant

RCA	revealed comparative advantage
reformasi	reform
Repelita	Rencana Pembangunan Lima Tahun (Five-year Development Plan)
retribusi	local government levy or charge
RKT	Rencana Kerja Tahunan (annual working plan)
RSPAS	Research School of Pacific and Asian Studies (ANU)
RTRW	Rencana Tata Ruang Wilayah (regional spatial plan)
SBY	(President) Susilo Bambang Yudhoyono
SDO	Subsidi Daerah Otonom (Autonomous Region Subsidy)
SITC	Standard International Trade Classification
SK	Surat Keputusan (government decision/decree)
SK	Surat Keterangan (letter of instruction)
SKSHH	Surat Keterangan Sahnya Hasil Hutan (certificate of validity of forest products)
SP-Bun	Serikat Pekerja Perkebunan (Plantation Workers Union)
SPM	Standar Pelayanan Minimal (minimum performance standards)
sumber daya alam	natural resources
surat keputusan	government decree
TAP MPR	decrees of the MPR
TNI	Tentara Nasional Indonesia (Indonesian National Army)
TPTI	Tebang Pilih Tanam Indonesia (Indonesian Selective Cutting and Replanting System)
undang-undang	law
UNDP	United Nations Development Programme
US	United States
USAID	United States Agency for International Development
wilayah	region
wilayah laut	maritime area
WTO	World Trade Organization
yayasan	private charitable foundation

Currencies

$	US dollar
Rp	rupiah

PREFACE:
LOOKING BACK TO MOVE FORWARD

Emil Salim

What is the important fact about Indonesian development in the last 30 years? The fact is that it has not followed a path that leads to sustainable development. Indonesia's development has been heavily dependent on natural resource extractions. Renewable resources such as water, forests, fisheries and other biological resources have been exploited beyond their ability to regenerate and will continue to diminish in the years ahead. Reliance on non-renewable resources and such activities as mining, minerals and fossil fuels cannot be sustained for ever. Clearly, the whole process of national development has not been sustainable. The question is: why and how has this situation occurred?

Let me go back to the situation 30 years ago. When we Indonesians started to formulate our development policies in 1966–67, there was little mention of environmental issues anywhere in the world; in particular, there was little mention of the links between development and the environment. Accordingly, when we began to draw up a national development plan in 1968, our focus was solely on economic development.

Up till the early 1970s, international development conferences tended to focus on single-track economic development involving infrastructure, agriculture and other primary sectors – so-called 'normal' economic development. In 1972, the United Nations held a Conference on the Human Environment in Stockholm. At the Stockholm conference, something new emerged: the environment. Most developing country delegations to the conference were economists who knew a lot about economics but nothing about the environment. What was this environmental issue about? Those of us from the developing countries knew the tune but we did not know the words of the song!

It is also important to note that, at around the time of the Stockholm conference, developing countries were campaigning for countries of the North to provide as much as 0.7 per cent of their GDP in aid to the South. Hence developing countries, including Indonesia, thought that the Stockholm conference was only a scheme by the North to impose a new condition, related to aid, on the South. So we did nothing.

Subsequently, Indonesia entered a new stage of development after experiencing an oil bonanza. Instinctively we felt that the proceeds should be used for poverty alleviation. Revenue from the oil bonanza funded the Inpres program of presidential grants for village development, rural development, village schools and so on. But we were still not sure what we should do with this animal called the environment. In 1978 the Indonesian government established a Ministry of the Environment, and I was appointed minister. The first agency that I visited in this capacity was the World Bank, which had a vice-president for Asia. I asked him, 'What is this environmental issue? How do we translate that into development policy?' The reply was, 'We are the World Bank; we are a financial institution; we don't have enough staff members to deal with issues like the environment'. Clearly, at that time mainstream development did not take account of the environment.

However, I was referred to Mr James Lee, one of the few experts in the World Bank dealing with the environment at that time. He taught me what the environment was all about and how there is an environmental argument in debates about development. I began to understand how the environment fits into the picture, but I was still not absolutely clear about the linkage between development and the environment. Mr Lee suggested that I talk to NGOs such as Friends of the Earth and the Environmental Defense Fund. I asked them a simple question: 'What the hell is "environment"? How do we reconcile the environment and development?' After several discussions with Friends of the Earth and the Environmental Defense Fund, I noticed that civil society's thinking on the issue of the need to integrate environment and development was already much more advanced than that of formal institutions, including international institutions like the World Bank.

Let me now move on to the 1980s and 1990s. What was the 'religion' at that time? It was the 'Washington Consensus': governments of developing countries were too deeply involved in development and should pull out; the private sector should do the job. The philosophy was that governments must undertake privatisation and that countries must rely upon the market.

For Indonesia, the message was clear: we must adopt a market paradigm, and the private sector should dominate the market. Indonesia embraced the Washington Consensus and its corollary that we should deregulate state enterprises. We did everything possible in that direction. Mind you, we were very high-spirited and enthusiastic in doing so. We even deregulated the financial market! Meanwhile, environmental issues were becoming more and more significant.

Do readers remember *Our Common Future* (WCED 1987) and the 1992 Rio conference?[1] Suddenly there were two conflicting trends. On one side, there was economic development *a là* the Washington Consensus: let the market prevail and encourage privatisation. On the other side, there was the message from the Rio conference: the need for sustainable development and a focus on environmental development. Wait a minute! There is a conflict here. The Rio conference told us that there is a problem with the market, namely market failure. The depletion of natural resources was not accounted for. Environmental externalities as a consequence of development processes were not internalised. There was something wrong with the rigid economic approach.

Can people imagine what was in the minds of developing countries? On the one hand, we had listened to the World Bank talking about the role of the market economy. On the other hand, suddenly there was another perspective: sustainable development that took the environment and market failure into account. Developing countries were in complete confusion, though we understood the need to maintain the environment.

For me in Indonesia, the main problem in translating this need into development policy was as follows. Around the world at that time, the only indicators of development were economic ones; there were no indicators to measure the condition or quality of the environment and whether the environment was getting better or worse. Environmental indicators were considered irrelevant.

Let me give an example of this type of approach. When we went to the aid consortium Inter-Governmental Group on Indonesia[2] we were asked, 'What is your rate of growth? What is your budget deficit? What is your tax collection rate? What is your investment rate?' We were not asked any questions about the environment. As the country's Minister of the Environment, I felt a bit out of place. Further problems arose during cabinet sessions. When the Environment Minister raised his hand, the Industry Minister would always say, 'Up goes the price'. The main perception in cabinet at the time was that taking the environment into account would always lead to higher prices. Hence there was little action on environmental sustainability.

I became a kind of public relations spokesman. I was invited to various conferences throughout the world to speak about development and the environment in Indonesia, and always emphasised that the environment was important in our country. All these speeches were given in a spirit of goodness and glory – with the idea that improving the environment was important and beneficial for Indonesia and that Indonesian laws on the environment were very good too. Nobody attacked my remarks, since I always said, 'According to Indonesia's laws on the environment, this is what Indonesia wants to do' or 'According to the presidential decree, this is what we are willing to do'. Nobody asked 'Is Indonesia actually doing it?' Hence, I was conveniently free from critique.

The turning point occurred when the financial crisis hit in 1997–98 and it became clear that our development policies must have been flawed. Other developing countries also shared this perception. Do readers remember the

Summit of the Americas in Santiago, Chile, in April 1998? All of a sudden the Washington Consensus was reviewed and attacked by the developing countries. The outcome was the 'Santiago Consensus' that market failures need to be recognised, that the government needs to correct the market, that the financial market needs to be reviewed and studied, and that environmental factors should be taken into account – including the depletion of resources and the need to internalise externalities. Hence, the environment became an important factor in economics.

For Indonesia, it was too late. We had already suffered. We had a disastrous financial crisis, soaring unemployment, a steep drop in the human development index, a high index of perceived corruption, accelerated deterioration of the environment, shrinking natural resources, increased illegal resource extraction and a serious weakening of governance. From 1998 to 2004, Indonesia's development was accompanied by great soul searching as we asked what had gone wrong and what we must do in the future.

We now understand the need to reform the total development strategy of Indonesia and to achieve triple-track development – not only economic development but also social and environmental development. But how do we do this? What model can we use? Indonesia has now installed a new government under the leadership of Susilo Bambang Yudhoyono. Our strategy for future development should focus on four issues.

First, we need good governance, because market failure requires government intervention and government intervention requires good governance. Good governance itself requires three important changes: public sector reform, better service delivery, and better laws and better enforcement of laws.

Second, we need to repair and improve infrastructure. This should include not only economic infrastructure such as roads but also social infrastructure such as schools. And let us concentrate on infrastructure for the poor, not infrastructure such as shopping malls, though these are now very popular in Indonesia.

Third, we need a pro-poor policy. Why not recognise the informal sector? Why not get the informal sector into the mainstream of development? Why not improve services to the poor? Why not create productive employment?

Fourth, development should not be only government-led: there is a need for other stake-holders to be partners in development. Development should involve government, civil society and business in a balanced triangular partnership in which all play an equal role. Civil society must become a countervailing power to business and government.

This ideal situation seems impossible to achieve. However, the recent election has shown that the people are against the ruling elite – that is, the established political elite. They are also against established big businesses that, in cooperation with the political elite, through money politics, want to dictate who should be elected and who should not. In brief, in this election we have seen a revolt of the person on the street, of civil society. That is why it is important that the new government should work with civil society and improve and stimulate its development.

In summary, I foresee that the concept of sustainable development will now comprise economic, social and environmental considerations supported by government, business and civil society. This book is a major step in understanding the challenges of sustainable development embracing two frameworks: the economic–social–environment framework and the government–business–civil society framework. The focus this time is forestry, fisheries and mining. Equipped with a better understanding of likely challenges and opportunities, I believe that, by adopting these two frameworks, we will succeed in the implementation of our development processes.

NOTES

1   United Nations Conference on Environment and Development, Rio de Janeiro, 3–14 June 1992.
2   This was an international group of lenders established in 1967 by the Netherlands to coordinate multilateral aid to Indonesia. In 1992, it was replaced by the Consultative Group on Indonesia.

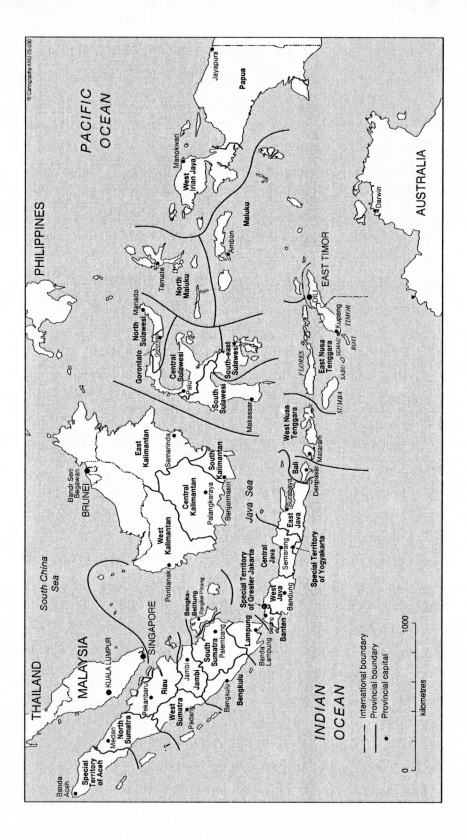

1 INTRODUCTION

Budy P. Resosudarmo

The fall of President Soeharto provided the impetus for the transformation from an authoritarian society to a more democratic one in Indonesia, and for the move from a highly centralised towards a much more decentralised system of government. These transformations offered the prospect that Indonesia would be able to manage its natural resources better, and achieve a long-term development path that embraced both resource sustainability and equity.

Thus far, however, the radical changes that have taken place in Indonesia have created an environment of political uncertainty, inconsistent laws and regulations, weak law enforcement, a weak governmental system and insecurity of land tenure. The immediate effects have been to increase the number of conflicts between various levels of government, local communities and companies carrying out natural resource extraction activities, increase the level of corruption in local areas, and increase the number of local taxes and local natural resource extraction licences. The management of natural resources in the country may not have worsened, but neither has it improved.

BACKGROUND

Indonesia is a massive archipelago stretching between the Indian and Pacific oceans and linking the continents of Asia and Australia. It is a diversified country both in terms of its population and in terms of its natural resources. In 2004 Indonesia had a population of approximately 230 million consisting of around 350 ethnic groups. Most of these groups have their own language and customary (*adat*) laws, regulations and norms. The two largest ethnic groups are the Javanese (45 per cent of the population) and the Sundanese (14 per cent). The population is growing at an annual rate of about 1.5 per cent. The majority of

Indonesians – 61 per cent – live in Java and Bali, which together have a land area comprising only around 7 per cent of Indonesia. Another 21 per cent live in Sumatra (27 per cent of Indonesia), while the remaining 18 per cent inhabit Sulawesi, Kalimantan, Nusa Tenggara, Maluku and Papua – the greater part of Indonesia in terms of land area. The majority of the population is Muslim (88 per cent). Nevertheless other religions and denominations are represented; Protestants comprise 5 per cent of the population, Catholics 3 per cent and Hindus 2 per cent.

It is well known that Indonesia has abundant natural resources such as oil, gas and minerals as well as rich and very diverse forest and marine resources. Oil and gas are found in Aceh, Riau, South Sumatra and East Kalimantan. Mineral ores such as copper and gold are abundant in Papua, coal in most of Kalimantan and West Sumatra, tin on the island of Bangka, and nickel in South Sulawesi and North Maluku.

Indonesia's vast rainforests account for over 50 per cent of the tropical forests in the Southeast Asian region and more than 10 per cent of the world's total tropical forests (Barbier 1998). In terms of area, the country's tropical forests are third only to those of Brazil and Congo (Zaire). In them are found extremely diverse flora and fauna with abundant nutrients and untapped medicinal potential. Indonesia also carries the world's largest remaining mangrove forests and has the largest area of coral reefs of any country. Indonesia's waters are among the most productive of all tropical seas. The Banda–Flores Sea, for instance, lies at the heart of global marine biodiversity (Dutton et al. 2001); nowhere else on earth is there a comparable diversity of marine resources (see Chapter 10 by Dutton).[1]

Forest and marine resources have always been important for Indonesia. At least 20 million Indonesians depend on the forests for their livelihood (Sunderlin et al. 2000). Similarly, millions of Indonesians have been, and continue to be, dependent on marine resources in one way or another. Fish stocks in Indonesian waters provide a source of income and livelihood for at least 5 million fishers. Fish provide more than 60 per cent of the animal protein intake of the average Indonesian and are the only affordable source of protein for the majority of the population (Bailey 1988).

The exploitation of Indonesia's natural resources intensified greatly after Soeharto came to power in 1966–67. The president was quick to realise the potential of the country's abundant forests, oil, gas and minerals for development. Realising that large-scale resource extraction could be performed only with the involvement of foreign companies, he enacted three important laws in the first year of his presidency. These were Law 1/1967 on foreign investment, which provided clear procedures for foreign operations in Indonesia along with generous tax concessions for foreign companies; Law 5/1967 on forestry, which put all forests under the control of the state;[2] and Law 11/1967 on mining, inferring that all lands within the Republic of Indonesia could be used for mining. These three laws effectively made all of the country's natural resources available for extraction by large-scale operations with a foreign investment component.[3]

Soeharto's policy turned out to be effective. Within a few years several multinational companies were carrying out natural resource extraction in Indonesia, their operations protected by his regime, which was then virtually politically unchallenged. During the 1970s, several major foreign companies became involved in oil extraction. During this period, oil became Indonesia's main export commodity and the country's major source of government revenue. In the 1980s, the role of oil in the Indonesian economy declined while that of other natural resource products, such as liquefied natural gas (LNG), copper, gold and timber, increased. By the mid-1990s, Indonesia had become the world's largest exporter of LNG and hardwood plywood,[4] the second largest producer of tin (after China), the third largest exporter of thermal coal (after Australia and South Africa) and the third largest exporter of copper (after the United States and Chile).[5] It also produced significant quantities of gold, nickel and forest products other than hardwood plywood. During the 1990s, oil and gas contributed approximately 30 per cent of the country's total exports (Kuncoro and Resosudarmo 2004), minerals and related products 19 per cent[6] and forest products 10 per cent (Simangunsong 2004).

It is important to note that while natural resource revenues were the main engine of economic growth during the 1970s and remain of critical importance to the Indonesian economy, since the 1980s the non-natural resource-based sector, particularly labour-intensive, export-oriented industry, has taken over as the main generator of economic growth. The Indonesian economy grew at an annual rate of about 7 per cent from the early 1970s to the mid-1990s, while the number of people living below the poverty line declined from around 40 per cent in the early 1970s to below 15 per cent in the mid-1990s.[7] Nevertheless, these statistics cannot hide the fact that Indonesia remained a poor nation.

The exploitation of natural resources has not been without problems. One of the major problems concerned the granting of rights to exploit Indonesia's natural resources. Extraction rights were mainly given to individuals or companies that were close to Soeharto, and that played a key role in strengthening his regime (see Chapter 9 by Gellert and Chapter 11 by Seda). The granting of rights was not based on considerations of resource sustainability or of a fair return (of benefits) to the general public. The result was a sharp acceleration in cases of environmental degradation (see Chapter 6 by Fox, Adhuri and Resosudarmo, Chapter 8 by Azis and Salim and Chapter 10 by Dutton).[8] As the years went by, there was mounting criticism of the government for its failure to ensure that resource utilisation benefited most of the population, for its failure to control the rate of exploitation of mineral reserves and for its failure to protect the interests of future generations. Conflicts between local communities and large natural resource extraction companies increased and intensified as the perception strengthened that while it was local resources and local land that was being exploited, local communities were receiving little or no benefit from these activities (see Chapter 8 by Azis and Salim).

By the mid-1990s, two major criticisms with regard to natural resource extraction had reached their peak among the general public: the skewed distribution of benefits and the unsustainability of the rate of extraction. Many also believed that as long as Soeharto remained in power and as long as Indonesia was unable to move to a more democratic society, these problems of natural resource management would persist.

In 1997 Indonesia, like other nations in the East Asian region, was engulfed by a severe economic crisis. The crisis shattered the economy, prompting social unrest and creating a volatile political situation. Many Indonesians, particularly the elites, questioned Soeharto's credibility in governing the country. In May 1998, after a massive riot in Jakarta and widespread demonstrations in major cities across the country, Soeharto was forced to step down from the presidency after 32 years in power.

The fall of Soeharto created an opportunity for Indonesia to foster the development of a more democratic society, in a process often referred to as *reformasi*. In the political arena, Laws 2/1999 and 31/2002 allowed the establishment of new political parties with clearly defined rights to compete in elections.[9] The enactment of Laws 3/1999 and 12/2003 paved the way for the two democratic elections that were held in 1999 and 2004. These elections were conducted remarkably smoothly, with relatively few cases of violence or electoral fraud. In the April 2004 general election, 11 of the 24 participating parties succeeded in gaining seats in parliament for their candidates. Later in the same year, Indonesians elected their president and vice-president directly for the first time. The two rounds of presidential elections held in July and September 2004 went extremely well, with Susilo Bambang Yudhoyono and Jusuf Kalla being elected president and vice-president. More importantly, there is now a balance of political power between the president and parliament and among political parties (see Chapter 2 by Aspinall), a balance that had been lacking under Soeharto.

Another change that has transformed Indonesia was the adoption in 2001 of a much more decentralised system of government. This was achieved through the enactment of Law 22/1999 on local government and Law 25/1999 on fiscal balancing between the central and regional governments. In 2001, authority for all but a few areas of governance was transferred from the central government to districts and municipalities, including authority for agriculture, industry, trade and investment, education, health and natural resource management (Alm, Aten and Bahl 2001). The main goal of the decentralisation policy was to give the regions a greater say in the development and growth of their own localities, thus giving them the capacity to fulfil their growth potential and distribute more of the benefits of economic growth to their residents. The new policy also sought to resolve the longstanding tensions between some regions and the central government over the unfair distribution of benefits from natural resource extraction, by giving resource-rich regions a greater share of the revenue generated by their own natural resources.

On the face of it, these rapid changes in the political and governmental landscape should have provided an opportunity for Indonesia to adopt a long-term development path that would embrace both resource sustainability and equity. This book examines exactly this issue, that is, whether or not *reformasi* and decentralisation have improved the management of the country's natural resources, particularly in the mining, fisheries and forestry sectors. Indeed, the main goal of the book is to provide a greater understanding of the current problems in managing Indonesia's natural resources.

THE GLOBAL ECONOMY AND CHINA'S DEVELOPMENT

Macroeconomic indicators suggest that the Indonesian economy has performed reasonably well in the last few years. Output has been growing at an annual rate of approximately 4.8 per cent. GDP has returned to the pre-crisis level, although per capita income is still 4 per cent below the 1997 level because Indonesia's population has increased. Inflation fell from about 15 per cent in early 2002 to below 5 per cent in February 2004. International reserves have been growing steadily and the government's fiscal policy is considered relatively prudent. However, this improvement in economic performance has not been without challenges, particularly since investment has not bounced back to its pre-crisis level (see Chapter 3 by McLeod).

The recent improvement in the global economy has affected Indonesia positively, while also creating some setbacks for the economy. The impact of the increasing world price of oil, for example, has been mixed. Because Indonesia exports oil, higher oil prices have generated higher revenues for the country. On the other hand, the government policy of subsidising domestic fuel prices puts severe pressure on the country's fiscal position and reduces the incentive to improve efficiency in fuel use. If this policy is maintained, domestic demand for fuel will increase rapidly, causing Indonesia's emissions of carbon dioxide to rise (see Chapter 4 by McKibbin). The rapid increase in domestic demand for fuel also reduces the net gain to Indonesia from oil exports (Resosudarmo and Tanujaya 2002).

A second issue concerns the balance of trade between Asia and the United States. The balance of trade is tilted towards Asia, inducing large capital outflows from Asia to the United States. If this trend continues, investment in Indonesia is unlikely to recover quickly (see Chapter 4 by McKibbin). A slow rate of investment, particularly in the manufacturing sector, would push the country to rely even more on the production of natural resources, increasing the pressure on Indonesia's mineral reserves, forest cover and marine resources.

A third issue relates to China's high growth, huge inflows of foreign direct investment and rapid expansion in world trade over the last several years. The rapid pace of development in China is at the same time both threatening and promising for Indonesian exports. It is threatening because China and Indonesia compete in the same export markets, in areas such as garments, textiles and footwear. It is promising because China is also increasing its imports, providing an opportunity for Indonesia to export more of its products, particularly primary products, to China. Hence Indonesia can expect to experience a negative terms of trade effect for manufacturing and a positive terms of trade effect for primary sectors such as forest products, including logs, lumber and woodchips (see Chapter 5 by Coxhead and Chapter 9 by Gellert). If Indonesia is not cautious, the increased pressure on Indonesia's natural resources caused by demand from China will lead to even more unsustainable levels of extraction.

REFORMASI, DECENTRALISATION AND NATURAL RESOURCES

In some respects, *reformasi* and the implementation of decentralisation have improved Indonesia's ability to respond to natural resource-related issues. For example, the new political environment has created opportunities for government to formulate better laws and regulations related to natural resource management; allowed local communities and local governments to have a greater say in the management of natural resources in their areas; and enabled the exposure of conflicts and mismanagement of natural resources through the media and parliamentary debates. A fairer system for the sharing of natural resource revenue between the central government and local governments is now in place, ensuring that local communities enjoy a larger portion of the benefits of natural resource extraction (see Chapter 7 by Alisjahbana).

But these changes have also generated challenges, including an environment of political uncertainty, inconsistent laws and regulations, weak law enforcement, a weak governmental system and insecurity of land tenure (see Chapter 6 by Fox, Adhuri and Resosudarmo, Chapter 9 by Gellert, Chapter 14 by Hardjono and Chapter 15 by Patlis). In general, it is possible to identify four important immediate effects of *reformasi* and the implementation of the decentralisation policy.

The first is the intensified disharmony among various levels of government. There has been an increase in conflicts between the central government and local governments, particularly in cases or sectors where the centre wishes to assert its dominance. The resistance of the central government to the erosion of its authority is apparent in its limited commitment to many aspects of the decentralisation process (see Chapter 6 by Fox, Adhuri and Resosudarmo, Chapter 7 by Alisjahbana and Chapter 15 by Patlis). There has also been an increase in disputes among local governments, particularly in cases where the relevant laws and regulations are ambiguous. Especially common are jurisdictional disputes over natural resources that lie on provincial/district borders (see Chapter 13 by Erman and Chapter 14 by Hardjono). In addition, sectoral government departments are coming into conflict, particularly over the designation of land use. An obvious example is the dispute between the Forestry and Mining Ministries over the right to mine in protection forests (see Chapter 15 by Patlis and Chapter 16 by Marifa).

The second immediate effect of *reformasi* and decentralisation has been to increase the number of disputes involving local communities over the right to exploit natural resources. These disputes tend to be of two types. The first occurs between local communities and the state or a large natural resource company, and typically concerns the ownership of land that the local people, based on *adat* law, claim or reclaim as theirs. Usually the government has given a company sole authority to extract natural resources in the area (see Chapter 13 by Erman). The second type of dispute occurs among local communities themselves as they compete to gain a higher share of the benefits of local natural resources. Given the ambiguity of laws and regulations, the increase in natural resource extraction by locals and the heightened interest in surveillance of local resources, it is not surprising that the number of disputes among local communities has increased (see Chapter 6 by Fox, Adhuri and Resosudarmo and Chapter 13 by Erman).

The third immediate effect has been to alter the nature of corruption. The era of centralised politics has disappeared, to be replaced by a system in which power and authority are far more diffused. The centralised nature of corruption – a one-stop shop for the giving and receiving of favours – has gone, to be replaced by a more fragmented bribe collection system. Under the new system, central government officials, ministry officials, local government officials, the military, the police and members of the national and local legislatures are all demanding bribes (see Chapter 11 by Seda and Chapter 9 by Gellert). Closely linked to this bribe collection system is the flourishing activity of illegal extraction of natural resources (see Chapter 12 by Obidzinski and Chapter 13 by Erman).

The fourth immediate effect has been for local governments to succumb to the strong temptation to raise revenues in the form of nuisance taxes and natural resource extraction licences (see Chapter 6 by Fox, Adhuri and Resosudarmo and Chapter 15 by Patlis). The primary argument for the application of such taxes and licences is that local governments face increasing expenditure responsibilities. Local governments are gratified that *reformasi* and the decentralisation process have given them the authority to make decisions affecting their own local jurisdictions, but they also tend to feel overwhelmed by their new responsibilities. These include several tasks that were formerly the responsibility of the central government, such as the payment of all civil servant salaries (including those of several million central government employees reassigned to regional positions) and the provision of extensive public services in their regions. Among the latter are primary and secondary education, health clinics, local and regional roads, water supply and sewerage (see Chapter 7 by Alisjahbana). However, local governments also have 'other' motivations for the proliferation of taxes and extraction licences, including those associated with corrupt behaviour by some local officers (see Chapter 6 by Fox, Adhuri and Resosudarmo, Chapter 12 by Obidzinski and Chapter 13 by Erman).

One might conclude that, although *reformasi* and decentralisation held out the promise of better management of the country's natural resources and of a move to a more sustainable development path, in practice this has not been the case. Indonesia continues to lose its valuable natural resources at a rapid and unsustainable pace.

THE ORGANISATION OF THE BOOK

This book is divided into five parts. Part I gives an account of recent political and economic developments in Indonesia (see Chapter 2 by Aspinall and Chapter 3 by McLeod). It provides the foundation for later discussion of the issues of natural resources and sustainable development.

Part II discusses issues related to globalisation, decentralisation and sustainable development. It begins by providing readers with an overview of current developments in the global economy and trends in international trade as well as their implications for the Indonesian economy and natural resource utilisation (see Chapter 4 by McKibbin and Chapter 5 by Coxhead). Chapter 6 by Fox, Adhuri and Resosudarmo analyses major issues related to *reformasi*, decentralisation, and natural resource extraction and management. Chapter 7 by Alisjahbana offers a critical and robust analysis of the current arrangements for sharing natural resource revenue between the centre and the regions. Despite the complex nature of the arrangements and their calculation, such an analysis is important because this was one of the main incentives for the ·regions to have a decentralised system of government. Part II closes with a discussion of the prospects for Indonesia to move to a more sustainable development path (see Chapter 8 by Azis and Salim).

Part III considers current challenges in the management of Indonesia's natural resources, particularly forestry, fisheries, oil and gas (see Chapter 9 by Gellert, Chapter 10 by Dutton and Chapter 11 by Seda). In addition to explaining the obstacles and difficulties in managing resources, these chapters describe the historical background of extraction activities in these sectors.

Part IV deals with illegal extraction and conflicts. Chapter 12 by Obidzinski examines major issues related to illegal logging, Chapter 13 by Erman discusses illegal mining in West Sumatra, and Chapter 14 by Hardjono illustrates how conflicts among local governments and between local governments and local communities have surfaced since the implementation of the decentralisation policy.

The final part of the book, Part V, focuses on the law and institutional problems related to natural resources. Chapter 15 by Patlis analyses current issues related to the enactment of new laws and offers some ideas for the way forward. Chapter 16 by Marifa suggests some directions for institutional transformation to achieve better management of the country's natural resources.

NOTES

1 See Resosudarmo and Subiman (2003) for a comprehensive review of biodiversity in Indonesia.
2 Under this law, 70 per cent of Indonesia's land area came under the control of the forestry department.
3 The basic agrarian law, Law 5/1960, also supported Soeharto's policy of large-scale natural resource exploitation through foreign investment. It specified that in cases of conflict between the state and local communities over land use, national interests would prevail.
4 See Barnes (1995) and World Forest Institute at <http://www.worldforestry.org/wfi/trade-5.htm>.
5 See Global InfoMine at <http://www.infomine.com/countries/indonesia.asp>.
6 See Global InfoMine at <http://www.infomine.com/countries/indonesia.asp>.
7 See Badan Pusat Statistik (BPS) at <http://www.bps.go.id/index.shtml>.
8 See also Resosudarmo, Subiman and Rahayu (2000) and Resosudarmo and Subiman (2003).
9 Previously Soeharto had restricted the number of political parties or groupings that could contest elections to just three. Golkar (Golongan Karya) was the political vehicle of the regime; it was a 'functional group' and was never officially declared a party. All the Islamic parties were merged into the United Development Party (PPP), while the nationalist and Christian parties were forced to amalgamate under the banner of the Indonesian Democracy Party (PDI).

PART I

Recent Political and
Economic Developments

2   POLITICS: INDONESIA'S YEAR OF ELECTIONS AND THE END OF THE POLITICAL TRANSITION

Edward Aspinall

When Indonesia's long-time authoritarian ruler Soeharto was overthrown in May 1998, the country embarked on a period of tumultuous political change. Governments rose and fell, dramatic reform of virtually all major state institutions began, new political movements proliferated, and violent conflicts broke out in several parts of the archipelago. The year 2004, I contend in this survey, marks the end of this period of rapid political flux. The lengthy electoral cycle that dominated the year's politics demonstrated that Indonesia's new political system is settling solidly into place. The April legislative election was the second to be held since the fall of Soeharto, and it passed remarkably smoothly, with relatively little violence or electoral fraud. The direct presidential elections that followed in two rounds in July and September realised one of the major promises of the *reformasi* era: for the first time in Indonesia's history, the population directly elected its head of state.

In place of the unpredictability and turmoil of the immediate post-Soeharto period, we now see the advent of an era of what might be called 'normalised' democratic politics, characterised by the atomisation of voters, greater fluidity of political affiliation, dominance of professional strata, modern techniques and big money. The media and the politics of personality and image dominate, exemplified by the election as president of arguably the most media-savvy politician of his generation, Susilo Bambang Yudhoyono. The very orderliness of the election, including the sense of alienation and boredom felt by many voters, confirmed that elections are seen by the majority as the sole legitimate means to change government. No major political force seriously questioned the legitimacy of the 2004 elections or threatened to overturn their results. Developments outside the electoral arena confirm the general picture; for instance, the various communal and other violent conflicts that marked the immediate post-Soeharto years continued to decline in intensity.

All of this does not mean that Indonesia's politics will become static or even that underlying sources of political tension have been resolved. It certainly does not mean that some sort of idealised system of democratic governance has arrived. Previous political updates (Crouch 2003; Jones 2004) have noted that entrenched vested interests permeate Indonesia's major institutions and have substantially frustrated reform, including reform in key areas – for example, overcoming corruption, reforming the judiciary and re-ordering civil–military relations. The following survey suggests that this pattern continues. Moreover, although the elections succeeded in formal terms, they also confirmed in power a layer of former Soeharto-era bureaucrats and political operators whose reconsolidation was first noted in the immediate post-Soeharto period (Hadiz 2003; Malley 2003). Even the new president, although presenting himself as an advocate of change and reform, was a leading member of the Soeharto-era political elite. The political architecture that is now settling into place does not signal an end to ongoing battles over reform. But the era of dramatic post-Soeharto political restructuring is drawing to an end.

ELECTIONS: DISILLUSIONMENT, FRAGMENTATION AND COALITION BUILDING

Indonesia's seven months of elections indicated some apparently contradictory trends. Voters registered significant dissatisfaction with the political establishment, but the polls also produced continuity. The much-anticipated authoritarian backlash did not eventuate, but reformist forces failed to dominate. There was increased political fragmentation, but this was tempered by strong trends toward coalition-building.

The first election, on 5 April, was for members of legislative bodies. Indonesia's approximately 150 million voters elected 550 members of the People's Representative Council (DPR), the national legislature, as well as thousands of members of provincial and district legislatures. Table 2.1 gives a summary of the national legislative results. People also voted for members of the newly created Council of Regional Representatives (DPD).

Parties that won more than 3 per cent of the vote in the elections for the DPR could nominate candidates for president and vice-president. Direct presidential elections were the major innovation brought to Indonesia's political system by constitutional reform in 2002. Following furious bargaining among potential candidates and party power-brokers, five tickets advanced to the first round of presidential voting on 5 July. The plurality winner was the retired general Susilo Bambang Yudhoyono, who until March had been Coordinating Minister for Political and Security Affairs in Megawati's cabinet. Popularly known as SBY, he ran alongside the leading Golkar politician, Jusuf Kalla. Coming second was

Table 2.1   Results of the 1999 and 2004 DPR elections (selected groups)

Party	1999		2004	
	% of vote	Seats	% of vote	Seats
Golkar (former party of Soeharto regime)	22.4	120	21.6	128
PDI-P (Indonesian Democratic Party of Struggle, Megawati's vehicle)	33.7	154	18.5	109
PKB (National Awakening Party, aligned to Nahdlatul Ulama)	12.6	51	10.6	52
PPP (United Development Party, an Islamic party led by Hamzah Haz)	10.7	59	8.2	58
PD (Democrat Party, the vehicle for SBY)	–	–	7.5	57
PKS (Prosperous Justice Party, an urban, puritanical Islamist party, preceded by its forerunner, Partai Keadilan, in 1999)	1.4	6	7.3	45
PAN (National Mandate Party, a modernist Muslim party associated with Amien Rais)	7.1	35	6.4	52
PBB (Crescent Moon and Star Party, a *shariah*-oriented modernist Islamic party)	1.9	13	2.6	11
PBR (Star Reform Party, a PPP splinter group headed by Zainuddin MZ)	–	–	2.4	13
PDS (Prosperous Peace Party, a Christian party)	–	–	2.1	12
PKPB (Care for the Nation Functional Party, a Soeharto nostalgia party)	–	–	2.1	2
TNI–POLRI (Indonesian National Army and Indonesian National Police)	–	38[a]	–	–
Total		476[b]		539[b]

– = not applicable
a   Appointed seats.
b   Of 550 seats altogether in the DPR.
Source: Komisi Pemilihan Umum (General Elections Commission).

the incumbent, Megawati Sukarnoputri, who had chosen as her vice-presidential partner Hasyim Muzadi, the head of the mass Islamic organisation Nahdlatul Ulama (NU). These two pairs advanced to the final round on 20 September, when SBY secured a handsome victory, wining 60.9 per cent of the vote to Megawati's 39.1 per cent. He won in most provinces, picking up the votes of most people who supported the other candidates in the first round (Table 2.2).

Voters entered the year in a mood of general dissatisfaction with the performance of the government and virtually the entire political class. By mid-2004, Indonesia's long period of economic crisis and stagnation was entering its eighth year. Opinion polls revealed that basic economic and welfare issues like employment, high prices and education rated very high as concerns for voters. Voters were also deeply angry about the persistence of corruption among politicians, and the press continued to report many corruption scandals involving politicians, especially those in provincial and district legislatures. A few weeks before the final round of the presidential vote, data from the attorney-general's office indicated that 352 members of regional legislatures had been named as suspects or were already charged in cases of corruption involving misuse of local budgets (*Jawa Pos*, 1 September 2004). In many cases, these scandals involved virtually entire assemblies. For instance, by March, 41 of 45 members of the regional assembly in Padang, the capital of West Sumatra, had been charged in a Rp 10.4 billion budget scandal, while a few months later, prosecutors announced that they were questioning 75 members of the Lampung provincial assembly about involvement in a Rp 19.5 billion scandal (*Jakarta Post*, 22 September 2004). The consequent mood of disenchantment with the fruits of *reformasi* hurt all the political forces that had benefited from the *reformasi* process and that had participated in post-Soeharto coalition governments.

Megawati's Indonesian Democratic Party of Struggle (PDI-P) was hardest hit by the popular cynicism. In 1999, it had capitalised on its Sukarnoist heritage and Megawati's image as chief victim of the Soeharto regime to capture the mood for change among the poor. In subsequent years, the PDI-P became better known for the corruption and ineffectiveness of its elected representatives. Moreover, a growing number of people began to see Megawati's aloof style, which had suited her well as silent witness to the repressiveness of the Soeharto regime, as imperiousness. The prominence of her husband, Taufik Kiemas, whose business activities and power-broker role brought to mind the nepotism of the Soeharto family (even if on a much smaller scale), only made things worse. The PDI-P registered the sharpest decline of any of the major parties. Its vote fell by almost half, from 33.7 per cent in 1999 to 18.5 per cent in 2004, dropping most precipitously in urban areas (in Jakarta from 39 per cent to 14 per cent, in Bandung from 39 per cent to 15 per cent).

In fact, however, support declined for *all* five major vote-winners of 1999 (Table 2.1). All had participated, albeit in varying degrees, in the grand coali-

Table 2.2   Results of the 2004 presidential elections (per cent of votes)

Candidates	Round 1	Round 2
Susilo Bambang Yudhoyono (Demokrat) and Jusuf Kalla (Golkar)	34	61
Megawati (PDI-P) and Hasyim Muzadi (NU)	26	39
Wiranto (Golkar) and S. Wahid (PKB)	22	
Hamzah Haz (PPP) and Agum Gumelar	3	
Amien Rais and Siswono Yudohusodo	15	

Source: Komisi Pemilihan Umum (General Elections Commission).

tion governments of the recent period, and all were thus tainted by association with the government. Even Golkar, which a year earlier was confident it would be able to capitalise on growing nostalgia for the Soeharto years, was unable to improve its vote. In the legislative polls, Golkar still failed to impress urban voters and the population of Java. It won only about 9 per cent of the vote in Jakarta, and only 53 per cent of its votes came from Java, although approximately 62 per cent of total votes came from there. Presumably this resulted in part from the fact that many voters associated Golkar with the worst excesses of the New Order period.

Partly as a result of the generalised mood of disillusionment, the political loyalties of the population as expressed in the legislative elections were even more fragmented than in 1999. In the earlier post-Soeharto election, the five largest parties won a combined total of almost 87 per cent of the vote. Now, seven parties share about 80 per cent. Apart from the decline in support for the original big five, two new 'major' parties have arrived on the scene (though both won under 10 per cent of the vote) and there was a proliferation of small parties winning 1–2 per cent of the vote, some of which were formed from splits from the larger parties.

Fragmentation, however, was tempered by readiness to build coalitions. Proponents of direct presidential election had argued that the new system would avoid the 'money politics' and deal-making that went on in the People's Consultative Assembly (MPR) in 1999 and 2001 when Abdurrahman Wahid and Megawati were elected (Crouch 2003: 17). Then, party power-brokers engaged in complex negotiations and vast vote-buying behind closed doors. However, direct presidential elections simply shifted the bargaining process to a new arena. Between the parliamentary polls on 5 April and the finalisation of presidential tickets in early May, there was frenetic horse-trading. Party leaders shuttled between rival camps, and the press was filled with speculation about who would team with whom. Candidates perceived as speaking for large constituencies, especially the traditionalist Islamic organisation NU, were wooed with particular assiduity.

As with the previous system, political principle or ideology had little place in these negotiations. Almost every possible combination of presidential and vice-presidential candidates was considered seriously by party power-brokers. In part, this was because political leaders were looking for combinations with broad appeal. Hence Megawati, as a secular–nationalist candidate, made it clear that she wanted a running mate with credentials as a devout Muslim, while military–civilian combinations were also viewed favourably. But it was also due to more pragmatic considerations, with the press full of open discussion about promises being made about cabinet positions and power-sharing.

The most ambitious coalition attempt was the Koalisi Kebangsaan (Nationhood Coalition), formed in August in the approach to the second-round presidential vote. Because Golkar's candidate, Wiranto, had already been knocked out of contention, it was now possible for the Golkar leader, Akbar Tanjung, to build the alliance with PDI-P that many believed he had always desired. Certainly, a partnership between PDI-P and Golkar was at the core of this coalition, although the United Development Party (PPP) and some smaller parties also participated. Akbar Tanjung exuded confidence that this combination of better-established parties would be victorious. In the *Straits Times* of 20 August 2004, he was reported as saying:

> The combined machinery and network of the parties will give Ibu Mega a big advantage in the election. Bambang does not have a chance if we pool all our resources together.

As it turned out, such confidence misjudged the mood of the electorate and its desire to punish precisely those political forces that possessed the strongest networks, had dominated government, and were best resourced.

THE BENEFICIARIES: PKS AND SBY

Two political forces were the primary beneficiaries of the mood of dissatisfaction. Both tried to depict themselves as outsiders and distance themselves from the government. The first, the Prosperous Justice Party (PKS), was indeed an innovative presence in Indonesian politics. Of the seven major parties in the 2004 election, it was arguably the only one whose origins were entirely separate from the old Soeharto regime. The other six either were vehicles for former

Soeharto-era officials – Golkar and the Democrat Party (PD) – or were formed from socio-political forces that had survived under Soeharto by adapting to his regime's rules. PKS, by contrast, emerged from a mostly semi-underground, even counter-cultural, movement in the Soeharto years. This was the 'Tarbiyah' (Arabic for 'education') movement, consisting of small study circles of campus-based Muslim activists who took their main inspiration from the writings of Hasan Al-Banna, the founder of Egypt's Muslim Brotherhood (Fealy 2001; Furkon 2004). The Tarbiyah activists derived some sustenance from regime-sponsored Islamisation programs on campuses (for example, funding for Lembaga Dakwah Kampus, the Campus Proselytisation Institute), but the movement's aims were transformative and far-reaching. Adherents aimed to gradually Islamise state and society, beginning with individuals and moving through the family and society to the political system.

In the 2004 election, however, the party's publicity material did not empha-sise Islamic appeals. Rather, it stressed members' professional skills and social concern. Like kindred Islamist political movements in the Middle East, PKS combines political campaigning with welfare and good works. Its legislators enjoyed a reputation for simplicity and apparent incorruptibility. Party cam-paign materials highlighted cases where it had exposed corruption scandals in local legislatures. This appeal was obviously attractive to many voters, espe-cially in urban areas. PKS came first in cities like Jakarta (22 per cent), Banda Aceh (32 per cent), Padang (22 per cent) and Bandung (21 per cent).

The second force tapping into the mood for change was SBY himself, and the party that was created to nominate him for the presidency, PD. SBY's per-sonal appeal was interesting. He was a quintessential representative of Indone-sia's New Order political elite. The son of a junior military officer from a small town in East Java, he had married into the upper echelons of the New Order when he became son-in-law to Sarwo Edhie, an army general who had played a key role in the extermination of communists and consolidation of military rule in 1965–66, but who fell out with Soeharto soon afterwards. By the end of the Soeharto era, SBY had achieved high military office, becoming Chief of Staff for Political and Social Affairs. He was one of the more reform-oriented offi-cers of the late Soeharto years, though this did not make him a radical. He became Mines and Energy Minister and then Coordinating Minister for Politi-cal and Security Affairs under President Abdurrahman Wahid, holding the lat-ter post again under Megawati.

SBY was surrounded by people with similar backgrounds. His vice-presidential candidate, Jusuf Kalla, was a big businessman and leading Golkar politician from South Sulawesi who had served as a minister under both Abdur-rahman Wahid and Megawati (Abdurrahman Wahid had sacked him, alleging but never proving corruption). PD and SBY's 'success teams' were full of bureaucrats, Golkar politicians and, especially, military officers from the late and post-Soeharto periods. They included some respected technocrats, but others had hard-line reputations. For example, Djali Jusuf, as military commander in Aceh during 2002–03, had cracked down not only against Free Aceh Movement (GAM) rebels, but also against civilian independence activists. T.B. Silalahi, a prominent retired officer and former minister from the late Soeharto years, was a close business associate of the businessman Tomy Winata, who was notorious for his underworld connections (*Laksamana.Net*, 20 July 2004).

Despite their personal backgrounds and links to the outgoing government, SBY and Jusuf Kalla portrayed themselves as the ticket of renewal and reform. In part, SBY could pull off this sleight of hand because he had always managed to disassociate himself from failing governments in the nick of time:[1] he aligned himself with reform in the dying days of Soeharto's government, maintained a low profile under Habibie, and was sacked by Abdurrahman Wahid when he rejected the latter's decree dissolving the MPR. His final break from the Megawati administration took place immediately after public censure by Taufik Kiemas, who had publicly accused him of being 'childish'. In any event, SBY and Kalla pitched their campaign wholly within the political vocabulary of *reformasi*. Both of them frequently said that the choice facing voters was simply one between 'change' and 'status quo', a clear allusion to the demands of the student protestors of 1998. They promised that their major priorities would be pushing forward the reform process and improving governance in key areas – for example, the elimination of corruption.

Support for SBY also partly reflected an underlying mood of nostalgia for the perceived economic prosperity and political stability of the Soeharto era. SBY did not make such an open appeal to this mood as did the Golkar candidate, General Wiranto, but many of his supporters admired him for his military background and bearing. Many believed that he exuded an air of authority: he was commonly praised for being *tegas*, or 'firm' (though, ironically, former government insiders suggest that SBY is slow to make decisions).

MEDIA, MACHINE AND MONEY POLITICS

For many Indonesian commentators, the most dramatic change of 2004 was that 'personality' (*ketokohan*) had apparently defeated 'political machinery' (*mesin politik*) as the key to political success. SBY lacked a massive political machine, yet defeated the behemoth of the Koalisi Kebangsaan coalition, the embodiment of old-style machine politics. Discussion was often framed in terms of a dichotomy between personality and machinery, because it had long been axiomatic that to succeed politically in Indonesia, politicians needed an effective grassroots political machine that could reach out to the population and mobilise it. This understanding largely dated from the Soeharto period, when

Golkar – essentially the electoral manifestation of the bureaucracy – was the ultimate political machine. But it also had deeper roots in the mass politics of the 1950s and 1960s. Now, the advent of direct presidential elections made possible a new style of politics, where candidates could appeal directly to voters via the media, bypassing party machines.

The 2004 elections thus saw a significant modernisation and professionalisation of politics. A new breed of image consultants, election experts, pundits and pollsters came into their own. The main candidates spent great sums on television advertisements, often designed in consultation with overseas public relations firms. They generated a media barrage of a sort never previously seen. Opinion polls were also very important, with several organisations providing regular scientific surveys of public opinion. These polls themselves played into the political debate, not only recording the surge in popular support for SBY from late 2003, but also contributing to it.

SBY was well adapted to this kind of campaigning. His political machinery was relatively weak. Instead, he tried to project himself as a modern and non-partisan politician, directly appealing to the people via the media. Although his style was rather stiff and he sometimes floundered when it came to relaxed encounters with the public, he nevertheless presented himself in a measured and authoritative way that many in the Indonesian public apparently admired. He performed well in televised debates and other campaign events, always appearing to be in command of policy detail and facts and figures. He tried to distance himself from the culture of deal-making associated with the other parties. For instance, he largely stood aside from the undignified jockeying that led to the creation of other presidential tickets, announcing his own running mate, Jusuf Kalla, relatively early. Afterwards, he said that most seats in his cabinet would go to professionals rather than to representatives of the parties that had backed him in the final round. This appeal was attractive to people disillusioned with parties. His vote was relatively evenly distributed across the country, suggesting it was not primarily dependent on the strength of local organisation.

Megawati had always been different. In the late Soeharto years, her personal image and a sympathetic media had been crucial in her rise to political prominence. But Megawati was also a product of the old system of mass and machine-based party politics. From the start she had been suspicious of direct presidential elections; in 2002 she had questioned whether the people would be 'ready' for such a system by 2004. She had always relied on a sometimes chaotic but always enthusiastic party structure and viewed politics largely through this prism. She was more comfortable delivering rhetoric-laden speeches before crowds of loyal party supporters than discussing policy or economics with journalists. Even so, in the words of one journalist, Megawati soon tried to remake herself as an 'energetic and flamboyant grassroots politician' (*Straits Times*, 14 September 2004). She began to mingle with ordinary people as she criss-crossed the country, often distributing government largesse to needy communities as she did so. She also made a deliberate effort to improve her performance in the televised debates, although most commentators agreed that she failed badly on this score.

However, old-style machine politics were not dead. And, as in the past, machine politics were oiled by money. As in 1999, money politics and fraud were a major concern for many observers in 2004. Many anti-corruption and election watchdogs, to say nothing of losing parties and candidates, alleged that the practice of vote-buying was widespread. However, they mostly pointed to relatively trivial examples as evidence of this, for example, party campaigners giving money or 'door prizes' to participants in campaign events. The same could be said of fraud in the vote-counting process: many people alleged that fraud was widespread, but nobody could prove it was systemic. The few cases of gross abuse that were identified were often bizarre, as if they were exceptions that proved the rule.

The most important arena for money and manipulation was *within* the political parties, where some of the most bitter political contests of 2004 took place. At the end of 2003, parties submitted their lists of candidates for the legislative elections. Around the country, local party branches erupted in furious conflicts as would-be candidates struggled to get winnable positions on party lists. In some places intraparty tensions were between local party activists and national headquarters. More frequently, these were 'horizontal' conflicts between local would-be candidates, each with their own clientele of supporters. In some places, there were angry demonstrations and confrontations between rival mobs.

The underlying dynamic of these conflicts was not difficult to ascertain. For ambitious local businesspeople and other notables, seats in local district and provincial bodies were means to gain access to state funds and, especially, to influence local budgets, tendering and contracts (Hadiz 2003). Indeed, such local seats are arguably more important than their national equivalents, and candidates had a direct financial incentive to invest in contests for them. There were many reports of money changing hands to purchase winnable positions on party lists, and it appears that, for most parties, patronage and money were the key factors in determining candidates' rankings. Most parties also formalised this system by charging their candidates fees to cover campaigning expenses. But the formal payments were themselves a matter of controversy, and were in any case often merely the tip of the iceberg in which under-the-table payments to party power-brokers were made to purchase candidacy. Moreover, candidates usually invested their personal funds heavily in campaigning. They often purchased publicity material themselves or paid for various good works for local communities (for example, providing a cow for slaughter at a festival, or building a small bridge). One candidate for the provincial legislature in Riau estimated he would spend about Rp 50 million on such things (*Kompas*, 20

February 2004). Some reports suggested that PPP and National Awakening Party (PKB) legislators had to pay Rp 200–300 million to party leaders in Jakarta for winnable positions on party lists, alongside payments totalling about Rp 30 million for campaign expenses, official endorsement and commissions to local party leaders (*Media Indonesia*, 12 November 2003). Winning a legislative seat clearly required a major personal investment, with the usual understanding being that most politicians would recoup these expenses once elected.

The logic of this system, however, was that it was more attractive for local power-brokers to invest their funds and energies in the legislative elections. For the presidential election, such people stood to gain little directly. This may have important implications for the future of Indonesian politics, because on 29 September 2004 the DPR passed revisions to Law 22/1999 on regional government, allowing direct popular election of governors, district heads (*bupati*) and mayors. This provision will come into effect in mid-2005. With relatively small constituencies voting for executive positions with authority over local budgets, it may become both feasible and rewarding for local businesspeople and power-brokers to attempt to develop much more systematic methods of vote-buying.

COMMUNAL VOTING: THE RISE OF THE RATIONAL VOTER?

Another topic of public debate was whether the electoral shifts in 2004 suggested that voters were becoming more 'rational' – in other words, whether they were choosing on the basis of individual assessments of the performance of parties and candidates, rather than as part of automatic identification with broader social and cultural identities. People who took this line pointed to several kinds of evidence. First, parties seen as having performed badly while in government were generally punished by voters, whatever their socio-cultural allegiances. Thus, the PDI-P vote declined sharply even in areas like Central Java where the party had traditionally been seen as being strong among nominal Muslims. Second, SBY demonstrated that it was possible to have broad, cross-communal pull. Commentators especially drew attention to the fact that he won the vote in East Java, traditionally the bastion of NU, although his two chief rivals had prominent NU figures as their vice-presidential candidates.

It would be premature to suggest, however, that the party system has suddenly become divorced from cultural and religious identity. The vote for broadly identified Islamic parties, for instance, was similar to that in 1999, at 38.4 per cent of the vote (in 1999 it had been 37.9 per cent). Within this total, about 21 per cent of the overall vote was for parties that might broadly be defined as Islamist, insofar as they formally recognised Islam in their statutes or aimed to implement *shariah* (an increase from 16 per cent in 1999, largely accounted for by the rise of PKS). The combined vote of the two main 'pluralist' Islam-based parties, the National Mandate Party (PAN) and PKB, dipped by a slightly lower figure, from 19.7 per cent in 1999 to 17 per cent in 2004.

While the underlying map of political loyalties did not change dramatically, the logic of electoral competition under a system with a direct presidential poll pushed politicians to make cross-communal alliances. For instance, Amien Rais decided against running as a narrowly defined 'Islamic' candidate, despite the disappointing vote that PAN had secured in the legislative elections. Instead, he tried to broaden his appeal by teaming up with a former Soeharto-era civilian minister, Siswono Yudohusono, who had a Sukarnoist and Golkar background. The same coalitional logic made mainstream 'secular' candidates and parties appeal more assiduously than previously for the *santri* or observant Muslim vote. Indeed, a distinguishing feature of campaigning was the eagerness and frequency with which the presidential candidates strove to present an Islamic public face. Almost every day, the newspapers were full of reports of candidates visiting Islamic boarding schools (*pesantren*), meeting with prominent *ulama*, performing prayers or being endorsed by Islamic groups.

Obvious electoral calculations were behind this. The traditionalist NU constituency, with its millions of followers concentrated in Central and East Java, was an especially important voting bloc, and one that was believed to be especially amenable to influence by its traditional leaders. Megawati and Wiranto wooed it most obviously, both selecting prominent NU figures as running mates. The competition for NU loyalties, however, was greatly complicated by the deep factionalism that divided traditionalists. Despite some commentary that SBY's good result in East Java showed the loosening hold of traditionalist loyalties on NU voters, the real lesson was simply that NU was split. Voting patterns in particular communities largely depended on the alignments of local *ulama* (Asfar 2004).

BEYOND ELECTIONS: THE PROGRESS OF REFORM

A survey of broader political developments shows a dynamic similar to that visible in the elections themselves: formal institutionalisation of democratic politics proceeds apace, but it overlays deeper structural continuity.

Take, for example, the judicial system. One important addition to Indonesia's institutional landscape that began to make its mark in 2004 was the Constitutional Court (Mahkamah Konstitusi). A product of *reformasi*-era constitutional reform, the court is empowered to adjudicate on conflicts between government institutions and on disputed election results, to dissolve political parties, and to advise the DPR on violations of the law by the president. Most importantly, it has the power to determine the constitutionality of laws and declare them invalid. As the body charged with enforcing the constitution, it thus acts as the ultimate arbiter of the rule of law (Wrighter 2005).

One of the court's first decisions, and potentially the most important, was taken in the dying days of 2003. At issue was the scope of the court's authority. The court decided by a six to three majority to set aside a provision in the Constitutional Court law which would have limited its authority to review laws to those passed since the first constitutional amendment in 1999. More controversially, in late July, in the case of an accused Bali bomb conspirator, the court decided by a five to four majority to declare Law 16/2003 invalid. This was the law that had made Indonesia's Law 15/2003 on anti-terrorism retroactive so that it would apply to the 12 October 2002 Bali bombings. The majority of judges acted on the basis of another new constitutional provision that reads in part:

> the right not to be charged on a legal basis that is retroactively enforced is a basic human right that cannot be reduced in any situation whatsoever.

The judges concluded that the Bali bombings did not constitute an 'extraordinary crime' (like genocide or crimes against humanity), in which case retroactivity might have applied. Although government officials insisted that the decision would not affect the fate of the Bali bombers who had already been charged and convicted under the law, it clearly did have an effect on ongoing prosecutions, as revealed in late August when the South Jakarta district court found Idris, alias Jhoni Hendrawan, not guilty for his role in the Bali bomb conspiracy, convicting him only for his involvement in the August 2003 Marriott Hotel bombing (which had taken place after the enactment of the anti-terrorism legislation). The decision gave rise to ferocious debate among legal experts. Some argued that the Bali bombings, and terrorism in general, should be considered an 'extraordinary crime'; others applauded the court for upholding the principle of non-retroactivity and thus protecting human rights.

Despite the presence of this new lighthouse of judicial reform, the legal system remains beset by the problems of corruption and manipulation often noted in the past. Causing particular concern to advocates of press freedom was a decision by the Central Jakarta State Court in September. The court found the editor of *Tempo* magazine, Bambang Harymurti, guilty of criminal libel of a businessman, Tomy Winata. The case centred on a report run by *Tempo* in August 2003 that implied that Winata was behind a blaze in the Tanah Abang district of North Jakarta. Soon after it was published, the *Tempo* office was attacked by goons associated with Winata. They assaulted journalists, including Harymurti himself, in the presence of police officers. Winata, whose interests allegedly include gambling and other rackets, is known to be close to the police. In the authoritarian past, censorship over the press was exercised directly. The *Tempo* case suggests that, although press freedom is still jealously guarded by journalists, it may be threatened by semi-official intimidation and court action.

The military is another area of Indonesian politics where it has been possible to see formal reform overlaying the persistence of long-established patterns of behaviour. The formal de-coupling of the military from the political system was central to Indonesia's democratisation. It was confirmed in 2004 when the military abstained from interfering in the electoral process and when the elections brought an end to military and police representation in legislative bodies. However, it was apparent some years ago that a new *modus vivendi* had been reached in relations between civilian and military leaders. There was no formal agreement, but the price for the military's disengagement from formal politics was several concessions, including impunity for past human rights abuses and a relatively free hand in determining security policy. Hence, party campaigners and presidential candidates carefully avoided making statements that might offend the military, instead generally going out of their way to praise it for its performance in maintaining national stability. At the same time, 2004 witnessed remarkable confidence on the part of several senior generals when it came to speaking publicly on political-cum-security issues. For instance, the head of the National Intelligence Agency (BIN), Hendropriyono, warned in the middle of the year that the government might use 'old measures' against NGOs that sold out the nation (*Jakarta Post*, 28 May 2004). This was an obvious return to the kind of language used to threaten critics under the New Order.[2] The notoriously hard-line Army Chief of Staff, General Ryamisard Ryacudu, was even more outspoken: several times during the year, he repeated his claim that 60,000 foreign intelligence agents were 'roaming around' (*berkeliaran*) on Indonesian soil, intent on causing national disintegration. At one point he added that the main entry point for foreign spies was NGOs, which he described as 'farts' (*Jawa Pos*, 6 January 2004).

Continuing controversy over the military's role was brought into sharp relief by a protracted dispute over the Armed Forces Bill (RUU TNI), which was debated by the DPR in the second half of the year. When this bill was presented to parliament, in a version that had been drafted almost entirely by the military itself, it horrified many NGO activists and liberal intellectuals. Key sections of it read as if *reformasi* had had no impact on military thinking. Especially concerning for critics was the reproduction of formulations that had been used in the Soeharto period to justify far-reaching military intervention in political life (such as recognition of the 'union between TNI and the people' or *kemanunggalan TNI dengan rakyat*). T. Hari Prihatono, the leader of Propatria, a think-tank that specialises in such issues, said that 90 per cent of the bill 'threatened democratisation for the next five years and even beyond' (*Kompas*, 23 July 2004). However, the resulting public furore was apparently enough to prompt legislators to substantially revise the bill and to remove the most controversial passages from it. Some even said they favoured scrapping the military's territorial structure, by which the Indonesian National Army (TNI) maintains a shadow administration paralleling even the lowest level of government. The elucidation of the final law, however, required only that 'forms of organisation that might become an opportunity for practical political interests' should be avoided and that the TNI's structure did not necessarily have to follow that of the government. The law also required the government to take over businesses 'owned and managed by the TNI both directly and indirectly' within five years. In this respect, it went further than previous reform measures, which had mostly left untouched the TNI's ability to control its internal financial and institutional affairs.

POLITICS OF VIOLENCE

A 'settling down' was also visible in the separatist and communal conflicts that marked Indonesia's post-1998 transition. Violent conflicts in places such as Maluku, Papua, Aceh and Poso peaked in 1999–2001. At that time, central state institutions appeared weak and long-established certainties were in flux. Local groups in some areas thus asserted themselves violently in order to renegotiate their 'terms of inclusion' in the state or to break away from the state altogether (Bertrand 2004). With the passing of Indonesia's transitional phase, and the settling into place of a new institutional structure, these conflicts have gradually declined in intensity. This does not necessarily mean that the underlying causes that gave rise to them have been resolved. Rather, it suggests that local actors' calculations of the costs and benefits of violent action have changed. For some, state reconsolidation means that continued violent action is too costly. For others immediate aims have been achieved. In some communal conflicts a state of mutual exhaustion has been reached.

In April 2004, there was a very serious flare-up of violence in Ambon. This began with a protest by a small number of Christians who were commemorating the 54th anniversary of the declaration of the Republic of South Maluku. When the police arrested some participants and marched them through Muslim areas, stone-throwing broke out. Vigilante groups on both sides were primed for violence, and several days of clashes followed, resulting in the loss of about 40 lives. As in the past, there were indications of interservice rivalries between the police and the army. It also seemed that external forces were trying to foment violence; this was especially obvious because many of those killed were shot by apparently well-trained and well-armed snipers (ICG 2004a). In Poso, where violence subsided after the Malino peace agreement in 2002, there were also a few violent incidents, mostly isolated shootings. In both places, however, considerable conflict fatigue has set in. Even in Ambon the violence quickly ran its course.

Aceh was the chief exception. As part of a hardening line on separatism, in May 2003 the government cancelled the peace process hitherto under way with GAM and declared a 'military emergency'. This was replaced by a 'civil emergency' in May 2004, but the pattern and intensity of security operations was unaffected. Throughout 2004, military commanders continued to express great confidence in their approach. Nearly every day, local newspapers were filled with reports of GAM casualties; according to one official count, 1,215 GAM members were killed between 19 November 2003 and 3 September 2004 (*Waspada*, 4 September 2004). The general political atmosphere in the province was repressive. Local military and police leaders lectured the population on the need to be loyal to the state and warned against those who campaigned on issues like 'human rights' and 'democracy' (*Serambi Indonesia*, 27 May 2004). Local politicians and *ulama* no longer dared to criticise the military. Military-linked civilian militias proliferated. Family members of GAM members, and people suspected of sympathising with the movement, were terrorised.

The military offensive has harmed GAM, but it has not achieved a decisive breakthrough. Few important GAM field commanders have been killed or captured; the main exception was Ishak Daud, a leader in East Aceh, whose killing on 8 September was a major symbolic victory for the military. Even so, the military has achieved a 'normalisation' of sorts, especially by restoring security in the main towns. The election was a 'success' in Aceh, with high participation compared to 1999, when only a minority voted, though this was partly because in 2004 officials made it clear that people not participating might be considered GAM sympathisers. The conflict was no longer much reported on television news bulletins. All this does not mean that the Aceh problem is close to being resolved. On the contrary, it is unlikely that military operations will achieve their stated aim of wiping out GAM, let alone reduce Acehnese discontent more generally. In the past, military operations contributed to Acehnese alienation. It is likely they are having the same effect now.[3] However, the Aceh conflict is not now an imminent danger to national integrity. Instead, it has returned to being a low-level, intractable conflict of a sort found in many parts of Southeast Asia. In this sense, we see in Aceh, too, a return to a kind of normalcy.

This normalcy was shattered, however, by the Indian Ocean tsunami on 26 December 2004. It caused massive destruction in Aceh and killed approximately 200,000 people along the coastal fringe, including in the provincial capital of Banda Aceh, about half of which was destroyed. The tremendous loss of life – approximately 10 times as great as that caused by the conflict over the preceding two decades – caused a temporary suspension of politics as usual in Aceh. The government opened the province to international aid agencies and even foreign militaries, which organised a large-scale relief operation in cooperation with the TNI. Both sides in the conflict came under considerable pressure to return to negotiations and, at a meeting with government representatives in Finland in February 2005, GAM announced that it would be willing to accept a negotiated solution based on 'self-government'. Sporadic clashes between the two sides continued, however, and it was not clear what kind of demands would accompany GAM's self-government formula. Despite the disaster and its aftermath, therefore, it appeared that low-level insurgency would continue into the future in Aceh.

A similar dynamic was visible in relation to the terrorism issue. The terrorist threat posed by the Jemaah Islamiyah network continued to dominate international media coverage of Indonesia, especially after a suicide car bomb attack outside the Australian embassy on 9 September killed 11 people. In the past, the terrorism issue did not occupy a prominent position in public debate in Indonesia. There was a degree of both indifference and scepticism in public attitudes, with many Indonesians questioning whether Indonesian Muslim groups were really responsible for the attacks (Jones 2004: 24–25). This first began to shift after the Marriott Hotel bombing in August 2003. It did so even more markedly after the 9 September attack when, again, the victims were ordinary Jakartans. This, plus the fact that the bombing took place on one of Jakarta's busiest thoroughfares and was captured on video cameras, brought home to many members of the public the immediacy of the terrorist threat. There was less public airing of conspiracy theories to explain the bombing than had followed the Bali bombings two years earlier. And Islamic leaders were less defensive about victimisation and stigmatisation of Muslim groups in the pursuit of the bombers. There is now little public scepticism that home-grown Islamist groups are responsible for the bombings, although Jemaah Islamiyah is still rarely mentioned by name. Media attention instead mostly focuses on individual fugitives such as the Malaysian Azahari Husin. Moreover, the police and security forces have made significant inroads into the Jemaah Islamiyah network. All of this does not mean that Jemaah Islamiyah and associated *jihadi* groups do not have the capacity to make further attacks. Key leaders remain at large. Moreover, a bomb blast in Cimanggis in March suggested that splinter groups may be independently developing the capacity to carry out violent attacks (ICG 2004b: 27–28), and there are indications that a Banten-based faction descended from Darul Islam (Abode of Islam), the Islamic rebel group that fought the government in the 1950s, was involved in the Australian embassy bombing. Overall, however, the shift in public mood is likely to further isolate Jemaah Islamiyah, including on the militant Islamist fringe, and weaken its ability to recruit and operate underground.

CONCLUSION

I have argued that 2004 may be viewed as marking a definitive end to the turbulence of Indonesia's political transition. The introduction of the Constitutional Court and of direct presidential elections indicates that most of the major constitutional reforms produced by Indonesia's reform process have now been implemented. The smoothness, even dullness, of the elections indicates that the major political forces have accepted the new political system as legitimate. The violent conflicts that accompanied the peak of the transition period are slowly losing intensity. Moreover, in SBY Indonesia has a president who appears to embody the shift to a post-transitional order. His landslide victory means that he has a mandate of a sort that his immediate predecessors lacked. His personal manner and aura of calm professionalism are also in stark contrast to the erratic and sometimes seemingly indifferent styles of his immediate predecessors.

The shift to a post-transitional phase does not mean, however, that serious problems and challenges do not lie in wait for the new government. For instance, SBY does not command a clear majority in the national legislature and may face difficulties in pursuing his legislative agenda. But the challenges will be of a different order than those involved in the dramatic constitutional reforms and institutional restructuring that preoccupied Indonesia's politicians during the immediate post-Soeharto years. The population will now look to the government to make progress in slowly rooting out money politics, restoring economic confidence, improving the legal system, increasing military profes-sionalism and the like. Yet in each of these arenas, the government will face problems that are deeply entrenched and even systemic. None of these prob-lems are amenable to quick institutional solutions. In dealing with them, even a determined and highly legitimate government would confront powerful vested interests. Given SBY's personal background, his famous indecisiveness and the character of the political forces that surround him, the prospect of a return to the widespread popular alienation that dominated the 2004 elections seems high.

NOTES

*   My thanks to Ken Ward, Marcus Mietzner, Greg Fealy and Budy Resosudarmo for their useful comments.
1   I am grateful to Nezar Patria for suggesting this point.
2   Hendropriyono was commenting amidst a controversy caused when the government, at BIN's instigation, ensured the removal from Indonesia of Sidney Jones, a researcher from the International Crisis Group who was well known for her reports on terrorism and security issues. Following the expulsion, senior security officials engaged in an outpouring of condemnation of NGOs, to an extent not seen since the late Soeharto years. The verbal condemnations did not, however, produce a physical crackdown on NGOs.
3   One possible sign of this was the high vote for Amien Rais (56 per cent) in Aceh in the first round of the presidential election. Although Amien's official policies on Aceh were not markedly different from those of other candidates, he is still remem-bered by many Acehnese as having adopted a sympathetic posture during 1998–99, a time when he was still promoting federalism.

3 THE ECONOMY: HIGH GROWTH REMAINS ELUSIVE

Ross H. McLeod

The economy has performed reasonably well over the last year, as is evident in the most prominent macroeconomic indicators. Much recent commentary has emphasised that this has been achieved at the same time that Indonesia has been undergoing radical political change. In particular, with President Megawati's position under threat, fiscal responsibility could easily have been forgotten, and any number of populist but counterproductive economic policies could have been introduced. Seen from this perspective, macroeconomic performance has indeed been commendable. On the other hand, there has also been a good deal of commentary that is considerably more pessimistic, suggesting that the glass is half empty rather than half full. Observers in this category tend to focus on the things that are not going well, or not as well as they should be, viewed from a more absolutist perspective of economic performance and policy evaluation that abstracts from the political and social context.

GROWTH OF OUTPUT AND PER CAPITA INCOME

Termination of the International Monetary Fund (IMF) program at the end of 2003 has had no noticeable impact on Indonesia's economic performance. For the last two years, output of the economy has been growing at about 4.8 per cent per annum; this compares with an average of 7.5 per cent for the four years just before the crisis (June 1993 to June 1997). Indonesia's recession was so severe that it took about five years for GDP to return to the level it had attained prior to the downturn. By 2004 it was about 10 per cent higher, but in 2003 national income per capita was still more than 4 per cent less than in 1997, as a result of population growth; in this important sense, the economy has yet to return to pre-crisis levels of prosperity. With population growth running at about 1.5 per

Figure 3.1   Consumer and share prices, exchange rate and inflation,
*   2003–04 (June 2003 = 100; per cent per annum)*

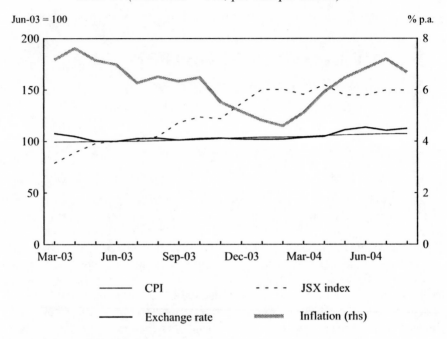

Source: CEIC Asia Database.

cent per annum, per capita incomes are growing by only 3.3 per cent annually
– little better than half the rate of 6 per cent for the four pre-crisis years. At the
pre-crisis rate, average income doubles every 12 years; at the current rate it
takes 22 years. Accelerating economic growth further is therefore crucially
important for poverty reduction.

MONETARY POLICY, INFLATION AND DEPRECIATION

The central bank, Bank Indonesia (BI) managed to bring the inflation rate below
5 per cent per annum in February 2004 (Figure 3.1), down from a peak near 15
per cent recorded early in 2002. Nevertheless, it continues to set rather unambi-
tious targets for inflation – the current target range is 6–7 per cent (BI 2004) –
and so it is no surprise to see a reversal of the declining trend in recent months,
with inflation rising above 7 per cent in July. The rupiah has continued to depreciate, as should be expected as a result of Indonesia's inflation being higher than

Figure 3.2   Monetary policy's non-relationship with GDP (per cent per annum; four-quarter moving averages)

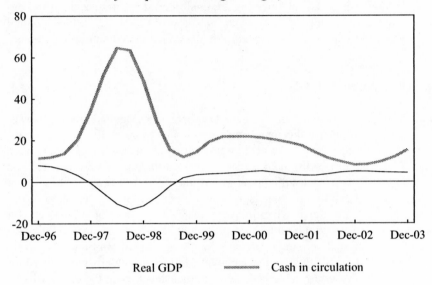

Source: CEIC Asia Database.

its trading partners. Figure 3.1 also shows that asset values (proxied by share prices) have increased far more than consumer prices since March 2003. The Jakarta Stock Exchange (JSX) share price index rose by no less than 91 per cent in the 10 months to January 2004, although it has stagnated since then. Data on net purchases of shares by foreigners show that foreign portfolio investment has been volatile but generally positive throughout this whole period.

BI believes itself capable of significantly influencing the growth rate of the economy through its monetary policy and, despite its legal responsibility to maintain the value of the rupiah, it tends to give higher priority to holding down interest rates in order to boost growth than to holding down inflation. This is somewhat surprising, since there is no clear relationship between monetary policy and output growth (Figure 3.2). The extraordinarily expansionary monetary policy early in 1998 was accompanied by severe decline of the economy into recession; the rapid deceleration of money growth in the second half of 1998 did not prevent the economy from bottoming out and returning to positive growth. Likewise in more recent years, raising money growth significantly to about 20 per cent per annum and maintaining it at this level for about two years (June 1999 – June 2001), and then reducing it to 10 per cent for a year (March 2002 – March 2003), had no discernible impact on the level of economic activity, with GDP growth remaining fairly steady at around 4–5 per cent during this entire period.[1] Output growth remains stubbornly below hopes and expectations, and BI's emphasis on lowering nominal interest rates to accelerate recovery serves only to fuel inflation. Thus, as Kenward (2004: 22–25) has pointed out, recorded inflation usually bears little relationship to BI's inflation targets.[2]

EXTERNAL POSITION

Indonesia's international reserves have also been growing, and this fact is usually listed as another indicator of macroeconomic success. To take a contrary view on this, any country can acquire more international reserves by paying a sufficiently high price for them, so the increase in Indonesia's reserves reflects nothing more than BI's willingness to pay the necessary price in the foreign exchange market – in other words, its willingness to allow the rupiah to depreciate. From another angle, fixation on the size of international reserves is a reflection of muddled thinking about the conduct of macroeconomic policy (to which international economic advisors have contributed, and continue to do so). Having adopted a floating exchange rate, Indonesia actually has no need for a high level of reserves, which now exceed their level when the country had a quasi-fixed exchange rate policy.[3] The purpose of holding reserves is to try to prevent the exchange rate from moving, just as the national food logistics agency, Bulog, tries to stabilise the price of rice by buying into, and selling from, its buffer stock. If stable prices are not the objective, there is no need to hold a buffer stock. Indeed, there is a risk in holding high reserves to facilitate intervention in the foreign exchange market. This is likely to encourage destabilising currency speculation, since there will always be market players willing to back their judgement against that of the central bank as to what exchange rate is sustainable.[4]

THE BUDGET AND NATURAL RESOURCE FISCAL ISSUES

Fiscal policy is another area in which it is possible to see the glass as half empty or half full. The budget has been managed in prudent fashion from a macroeconomic viewpoint, in that the large deficits that emerged in the aftermath of the crisis have become progressively smaller, such that there is no tendency for the size of public sector debt to increase relative to the size of the economy (Marks 2004a).[5] Current budgetary settings calling for deficits of the order of 1 per cent of GDP in 2004 and 2005 are, therefore, broadly sustainable.

On the other hand, the Megawati government effectively abdicated its responsibility for the proper financial management of Indonesia's natural resources, especially oil. Since Indonesia is an oil producer, the government should be enjoying a huge revenue windfall from the current surge in world oil prices. Instead, the policy under Megawati was to hold domestic prices of petroleum products constant, thus causing this valuable resource to be frittered away through a subsidy that encourages wasteful domestic consumption and that has already helped to turn Indonesia into a net oil importer (Marks 2004b: 165–166). The policy is not only inefficient but also regressive, since the biggest subsidies go to the biggest direct and indirect consumers of petroleum fuel products – by and large, the relatively well off. If the new government were to ensure that fuel product prices reflected world prices, it could increase its spending considerably on services such as education and health, which are directly beneficial to the poor. The difficulty of getting acceptance for such a policy from the politically influential middle and wealthy classes should not be underestimated, of course, but the present policy arrangements amount to a significant deviation from fiscal responsibility.

The apparently increasing prevalence of large-scale illegal natural resource exploitation – specifically, logging, fishing and mining – also indicates the failure of the government to manage natural resources properly. Illegal natural resource exploitation is frequently damaging to the environment and, in general, deprives the government of revenue. Successive governments have failed both to ensure that the nation derives maximum net gains from its natural resources (bearing in mind the environmental costs) and to ensure that a reasonable proportion of the revenues they generate flow to the government for the benefit of the general public. This is not to suggest that the rate of natural resource exploitation should be increased: on the contrary, environmental considerations often imply that slower exploitation of resources would be socially optimal. The point is that there appears to be ample scope for significantly increasing the flow of resource rents to the government, even if the output of these sectors is reduced. In relation to forestry, in particular, it should be noted further that the ban on log exports, which attempts to maximise domestic manufacturing of timber, further reduces the potential flow of resource rents to the government. The theoretical upper bound to royalty revenues is the difference between log sales and logging costs, and domestic manufacturers will not be willing or able to pay as much as more efficient manufacturers overseas.

INVESTMENT

Figure 3.3 shows investment relative to its level just prior to the crisis, and relative to GDP. It is evident that all of the positive indications of sound macroeconomic performance already mentioned should not be allowed to lead to complacency. On both measures shown in Figure 3.3, investment has a long

Figure 3.3   Investment, 1997–2004 (June 1997 = 100, per cent)

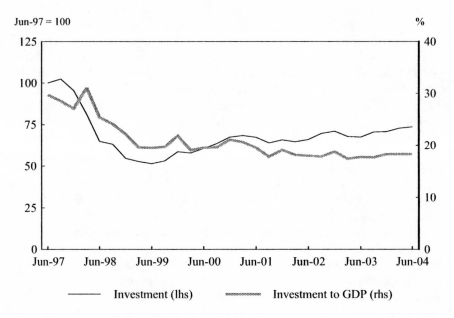

Source: CEIC Asia Database.

way to go before catching up with levels achieved seven years ago. The absolute level of investment is still only three-quarters that of the June quarter in 1997, and as a share of GDP it is now only about 18 per cent, compared with about 30 per cent previously. These figures above all others show that Indonesia has not come close to a full economic recovery. The economy can continue to experience modest growth by virtue of additions to the labour force, modest increases in productivity, expansion of land under cultivation and the like. A return to rapid growth capable of significantly reducing poverty relies crucially, however, on the willingness of the private sector to increase its investment in the capital stock: machinery, plant and equipment, factory and office buildings, and so on. Yet the confidence to undertake such investments clearly is still lacking on the part of both foreign and domestic firms. Moreover, much of the investment that *has* been occurring seems to have been in the form of construction of shopping malls and up-market residential accommodation, suggesting that current economic growth is focused on the rich and the upper middle class, rather than being broadly based.[6] Another indication of the lack of confidence of investors is that the amount of investment activity continues to be less than can be funded by domestic saving, with the surplus being directed offshore;

capital outflows have subsided from the panic levels of 1998, but they still exceed capital inflows.

Explanations for the continuing lack of confidence on the part of investors are not hard to find. The advent of genuine multiparty democracy means that business now faces the possibility of significant but largely unpredictable changes in policy direction as parties and individuals with no track record in government vie for power. The devolution of a wide range of government functions to roughly 400 local governments means that business can no longer content itself with doing what the central government wants but must now deal with the demands of, and hindrances imposed by, provincial and local governments as well. And democratisation has yet to have any noticeable impact on the endemic problem of corruption; indeed, corruption arguably has become even worse with the fragmentation of political power among political parties and among different branches and levels of government.

Dysfunction in government also affects business indirectly, by virtue of the failure of the public sector to provide the hard and soft infrastructure upon which the private sector relies to complement its activities. Hard infrastructure includes such things as transport, telecommunications and electricity distribution networks, and irrigation, drinking water supply, drainage, flood control and waste water disposal systems. All of these have suffered from reduced spending on maintenance and new investment as a consequence of the fiscal difficulties faced by the central and regional governments, and perhaps also from confusion about the division of responsibilities for infrastructure spending among different levels of government following the rush to decentralise (Fitrani, Hofman and Kaiser 2005).[7] Soft infrastructure encompasses the military, the police and the court system, which are collectively responsible for the protection of persons and property. In the last two years, three major bomb attacks by religious fanatics that favour terrorism over the democratic process for furthering their aims provide the most spectacular and horrifying evidence of the problems facing the government. But there are also far more widespread everyday concerns about violence, theft and extortion by thugs and criminals, often in cahoots with the security forces, and about inefficiency and corruption in the legal system that effectively facilitate white-collar theft and extortion.[8]

LABOUR MARKET AND STRUCTURE OF THE ECONOMY

Figure 3.4 shows selected major sectors of the economy, and indicates that Indonesia's economic structure has returned to roughly its pre-crisis state. The share of the manufacturing sector had been rising steadily prior to the crisis, but then fell very rapidly for several months before first recovering and then resuming its upward trajectory. Manufacturing is now by far the largest sector, con-

Figure 3.4   Major sectors' shares of GDP, 1994–2004 (per cent)

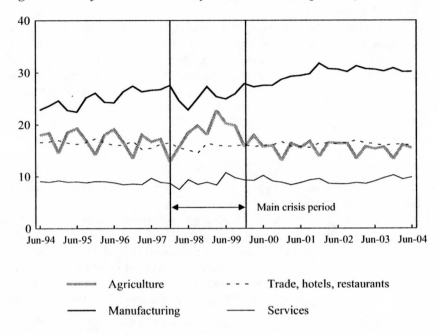

Source: CEIC Asia Database.

tributing about 30 per cent of GDP (measured in current prices). The share of
the agricultural sector, which had expanded considerably during the crisis as it
absorbed labour shed from manufacturing and construction, together with additional workers (mainly female) who felt obliged to enter or re-enter the workforce in order to make ends meet, has declined from about 20 per cent at that
time to about 15 per cent. Shares of the two other relatively large sectors –
trade, hotels and restaurants, and services – have remained fairly constant
throughout the last decade, at about 17 per cent and 9 per cent, respectively.

Given these observations, concern about the possibility of 'de-industrialisation' (Basri 2004) seems somewhat exaggerated. Perhaps more important is
what has been happening to the sectoral composition of the workforce, and its
implications for poverty. Whereas the share of labour employed in agriculture,
forestry and fishing had been declining for decades as the economy provided
more and more higher-productivity, higher-income jobs in the modern, urban
sectors, this trend has been reversed since the crisis began. Thus the agriculture,
forestry and fishing sector accounted for 46 per cent of the workforce in 2003,
up from 41 per cent in 1997. This has been reflected in declines in several other

sectors, including services (down 4.0 per cent), trade, hotels and restaurants (1.3 per cent) and manufacturing (0.9 per cent).

What accounts for the reversal of the previous trend of structural change in the workforce? The issue is complex and cannot be dealt with satisfactorily in a brief discussion. One possibility is that the continuing low level of investment just noted has had a disproportionately strong impact on the modern, urban sectors of the economy, where employment growth had been rapid up until 1997. Related to this is the fact that China has become a very strong competitor in Indonesia's export markets, reducing the incentive to invest in manufacturing sectors that had provided rapidly expanding employment opportunities before the crisis. Another possible explanation is increased government intervention in the labour market during this period. This intervention is often well intentioned, but it is not informed by economic commonsense. Policy-making has been driven by the notion that poverty can be regulated and legislated away, by increasing minimum wage rates, by requiring large severance payments when workers are dismissed and so on. The policy discussion has tended to focus on issues such as workers' 'needs' and arguments about whether employers can afford to pay higher wages – all of which are irrelevant in the face of the law of unintended consequences.

Firms are motivated by profit, so they employ workers only if the extra revenue generated by doing so is greater than the cost thus incurred. Some employees are marginal, in the sense that it makes little difference to profit if they are recruited or not; for these workers, any significant legislated increase in their wage makes it unprofitable to employ them. The unintended consequence is to deprive them of a job, which in turn means that they have to eke out an income in sectors where the minimum wages and other labour market regulations are not effective, such as agriculture or the informal sector. Worse still, by increasing the number of people looking for work in agriculture and the informal sector – where the less-skilled, lower-income workers are to be found – incomes are actually forced *down* in these sectors (Suryahadi et al. 2003; USAID 2004). Figure 3.5 shows that there has indeed been a clear reversal of the pre-crisis trend for formal sector non-agricultural employment to grow much faster than that in agriculture and the informal sector.

The data on real minimum wage changes since the crisis began are consistent with the operation of this kind of mechanism. Figure 3.6 shows average real minimum wages for a large number of provinces during 1997–2004, together with those for a representative selection of these provinces. Real minimum wages[9] had been on the increase prior to the crisis, but fell significantly as a result of the burst of inflation that occurred in 1998. This decline has been more than offset subsequently by large increases in the nominal minima, however. The provincial average real minimum wage is now about 28 per cent higher than it was prior to the crisis.[10] With investment having been so low dur-

Figure 3.5   Trends in labour force structure, 1986–2003 (1986 = 100)

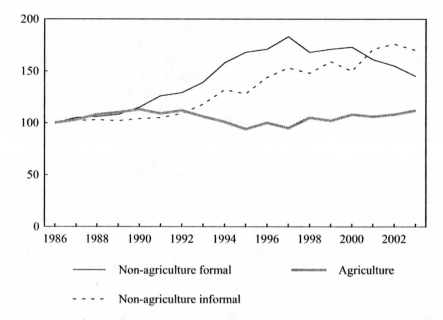

Source: Unpublished data from the Department of Manpower and Transmigration; data processed and kindly supplied by Dr Chris Manning and Dr Kelly Bird.

ing the period – in no small part the consequence of increasingly onerous labour market intervention by governments at all levels – there is no reason to believe that labour productivity has increased to anything like this extent, which suggests that workers are now finding it much more difficult to obtain employment in the modern sectors of the economy where these minima, and other regulations that also increase the cost of employing labour, are observed. The more recent apparent slowdown in real minimum wage increases may well reflect considerable effort on the part of the economics profession to create a greater awareness of the counterproductive impact of such increases on efforts to eradicate poverty (see, for example, the list of references in USAID 2004).

TRADE

Apart from the dramatic rise in the world price of oil, probably the most important external factor affecting the Indonesian economy recently has been the

Figure 3.6   Real minimum wages relative to the 1997 average (selected provinces)

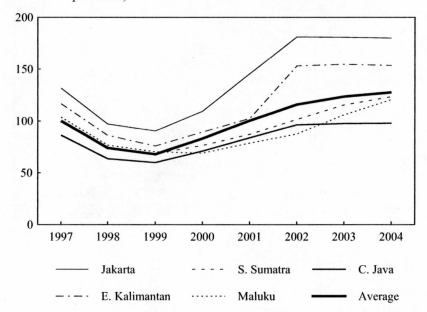

Source: Unpublished data from the Department of Manpower and Transmigration; data processed and kindly supplied by Dr Chris Manning and Dr Kelly Bird.

rapid expansion of China's role in world trade. China has been reaping the benefits of its increasing openness to the global economy in terms of sustained and very rapid growth. At first glance this seems a threat to Indonesia, because the two countries compete with each other in export markets.[11] On the other hand, the growth of China's exports must necessarily be roughly matched by that country's increase in imports: after all, the main purpose of exporting is to be able to import. Thus the rapid growth of the Chinese economy also provides an opportunity for Indonesia to increase its exports to that country.

Over the last year or two, China indeed has become significantly more important to Indonesia, both as an export market and as a supplier of imports. On the export side, there has been a noticeable decline in the share of Indonesian exports going to the United States (from 17.0 per cent in the second half of 2001 to 14.4 per cent during the same period of 2003). No doubt the decline is in part because of increased competition from China, but it has been offset by China taking a rapidly expanding share of exports (from 4.2 per cent to 6.7 per cent during the same period). At the same time, the United States became less

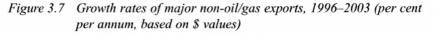

Figure 3.7   Growth rates of major non-oil/gas exports, 1996–2003 (per cent per annum, based on $ values)

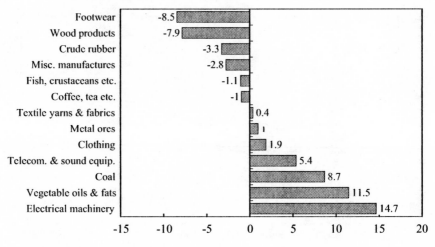

Source: CEIC Asia Database.

important as a supplier of imports (its share falling from 12.5 per cent to 10.5 per cent) as China's share increased (from 6.7 per cent to 10.7 per cent).

Figure 3.7 shows average rates of growth in the US dollar value of major categories of non-oil and gas exports between 1996 and 2003. It implies that the structure of Indonesian exports has been changing quite significantly during this period. Perhaps most striking is the rapid decline of footwear and wood product exports. Footwear exports may have been affected by competition from China in the world market, and also by the increases in minimum wages just mentioned, which make Indonesia less attractive as a source of low-skilled labour (although it should be noted that clothing exports have continued to register positive growth). The decline of wood product exports may reflect increases in illegal logging and a consequent diversion of the supply of logs away from domestic plywood and furniture manufacturers through smuggling. At the same time, however, other categories of exports – including telecommunications and sound recording equipment, coal, vegetable oils and fats, and electrical machinery – have been growing rapidly. Increases in these categories have been more than enough to offset the declines in footwear and wood products, but the impression that there is an ongoing shift away from exports that rely heavily on low-skilled labour to those that are relatively more intensive users of higher skills and natural resources is a matter for concern. Poverty reduction relies crucially on increasing the demand for low-skilled labour.

THE 'END' OF IBRA

The country reached another post-crisis milestone with the winding up of the Indonesian Bank Restructuring Agency (IBRA) in February 2004. IBRA had been set up in January 1998 as a vehicle intended to minimise the government's losses from its guarantee of the liabilities of the domestic banking system at that time. The assets of banks that were closed were shifted to IBRA, as were the most severely compromised (category 5) non-performing loans of the state banks, and of other private banks in which the government acquired majority or sole ownership when it chose to recapitalise rather than liquidate them. IBRA was also the recipient of a vast array of corporate assets handed over to the government by the owners of conglomerates in lieu of cash repayment of liquidity support their banks had received from BI as the crisis deepened. In effect, IBRA was the government's holding company for an enormous collection of bank and corporate assets, and its task was to dispose of these assets and thus to recover as much as possible of the costs the government had incurred by paying out depositors and other creditors of failed banks.

It was always intended that IBRA's existence would be limited to the five years from February 1999,[12] with the possibility of extension if it failed to dispose of all of these assets within this period. The fact that IBRA was wound up on schedule creates the impression that it had completed its work within the allotted time, but in fact this is not the case. It still had assets with a book value of some $8.3 billion when the end came, and these were shifted partly to a new Asset Management Company under the control of the Ministry of Finance and partly to an oversight committee comprising a number of cabinet ministers, along with the responsibility to finish the job (*Financial Times*, 25 February 2004). It was reported that there were still 1,361 unresolved legal cases relating to the residual IBRA portfolio, worth a total of Rp 25 trillion and involving 447 debtors (Guerin 2004a). It remains to be seen if the new mechanisms now in place will be any more successful in maximising recoveries from the remaining assets than IBRA would have been if its life had been extended.

It is difficult to judge whether IBRA can be regarded as a success. Clearly, the amount of cash it has been able to return to the government is only a small proportion (about 25 per cent) of the value of the bonds the government issued to bail out banks' creditors (Table 3.1). From a slightly different perspective, it was able to recover about 28 per cent of the face value of loans it took over from the banks (IBRA 2003: 1). But of course most, if not all, of the assets in IBRA's portfolio were severely compromised at the outset, and there was no realistic expectation that full book value could be recovered. In any case, IBRA's performance suffered greatly from political interference, as could only have been expected given the vast sums involved. Top management of the institution was changed on numerous occasions as presidents came and went and as each president sought to achieve the outcomes desired.

*Table 3.1   IBRA's cumulative fund remittance to the government,
            1999/2000 – end 2003*

Fiscal year	Rp trillion	$ billion[a]
1999/2000	17.1	1.9
2000	20.7	2.3
2001	48.5	5.4
2002	48.5	5.4
2003	28.3	3.1
Total	163.3	18.1
Total bonds issued to bail out bank creditors	644.0	71.6
Net cost of bail-out[b]	480.7	53.5

a   US dollar amounts are converted at Rp 9,000 = $1.

b   The implied recovery rate is 25.4 per cent.

Source: Remittance amounts are from IBRA (2003).

Any evaluation of IBRA should focus not only on what it was able to achieve but also on the more fundamental question of whether providing a government guarantee of bank liabilities – and setting up such an institution to minimise government losses from this guarantee – was the best available response to the unravelling of the banking sector. This response was copied from approaches followed in banking crises in various developed countries, where governments are much less corrupt and the workings of the crucially important legal system far more reliable than in Indonesia. My own view, given the dreadful financial record of Indonesia's state-owned financial institutions over many decades, is that to concentrate such a huge volume of assets within a new state-owned institution was a recipe for disaster. As noted earlier, the ultimate cost of the banking collapse to the government is of the order of $50 billion.[13]

BANKS, THE LAW AND ECONOMIC ACTIVITY

Many commentators argue that the banking sector is holding back recovery: that the continued slump in investment could be overcome if only the banks increased their lending. In fact, bank lending has been increasing quite rapidly. For example, rupiah-denominated bank loans grew at around 28–37 per cent per annum during September 2001 through August 2003, and even though the rate has slowed subsequently, to around 25 per cent per annum in June 2004, it would be dangerous if the banking sector were to accelerate the expansion of its activities again.[14] The risks of lending multiply when it is done too quickly: the feasibility of projects may not be properly analysed; the quality of collateral for loans not adequately assessed; the financial well-being of the intending borrower not sufficiently scrutinised; and loans and collateral not carefully documented. Given the horrendous losses generated in the banking sector just a few years ago, it is astonishing that anyone should now advocate banks throwing caution to the wind.

Moreover, a great deal of the funds for investment normally are provided by the borrower itself, drawing on its retained earnings; banks are understandably reluctant to fund new investments unless the firm undertaking them is also prepared to put a significant amount of its own resources at risk. Even if bank loans were growing slowly, therefore, the most plausible explanation would be that an effective demand for them is lacking; banks, like all other businesses, will expand their activities if the demand exists – and if it appears safe and profitable to do so.

This is not to say that the banking sector is without problems, however. On the contrary. The loss of about $50 billion in the 1997–99 banking collapse (Frécaut 2004) should have provided policy-makers with a strong incentive to analyse exactly what went wrong at that time and, to the extent that this financial catastrophe was a consequence of an unsatisfactory policy environment for the banking sector, to devote maximum effort to redesigning policies as necessary to prevent a recurrence. Indeed, in the government's letters of intent to the IMF there are plentiful references to the need for the central bank to improve its prudential supervision practices (to try to avoid bank failures) and to the need for the authorities to set up a deposit insurance mechanism (to replace the 'temporary' government guarantee and to deal with new banking crises if they cannot be avoided).[15] Perhaps some progress has been made on the first of these, although it is very difficult for the outsider to tell. But the newly enacted law on deposit insurance (Law 24/2004) seems to suggest that in fact very little has been learned about handling or avoiding bank failures. On the contrary, it seems merely to codify the very course of action that proved so disastrous during 1997–99.

There is no room for complacency. If there were a new banking crisis in Indonesia, a deposit insurance agency along the lines now envisaged could well generate losses to the public just as large as those incurred previously. It would proceed in almost exactly the same way the government did when the banks failed in 1998 – that is, providing a government guarantee to banks' creditors, with all the moral hazard problems this implies. The only difference would be that the mechanism would have been set up in advance rather than being an ad

hoc response to bank failures. Moreover, the expectation that prudential supervision will be significantly more effective in preventing bank failures in the
future seems unduly optimistic. As Fane (1998: 291) points out, '599 pages of
new regulations were introduced in February 1991' after the collapse of a
prominent bank, but this did not save the banking sector from collapse during
the 1997–98 crisis. Indeed, there have been two more closures of private banks
in recent months, and both have involved additional (albeit relatively small)
losses to the government (Guerin 2004b).

The major weakness in the banking system is neither the structure of the
industry nor the way that banks are managed or supervised. Rather, it is the
inadequacy of the legal system that is supposed to protect property rights.
Indonesia's legal system is both inefficient and highly corrupt, and the finance
industry – more than any other – is heavily disadvantaged by this. Indeed, this
is the main explanation for the collapse of the banking system in 1998–99:
countless borrowers saw in the unfolding crisis the opportunity to turn their
backs on their debts, and the legal system allowed them to get away with this.
The key concern to any bank is that its loans may not be repaid, and it is essential that it can turn to the legal system to enforce loan contracts, either through
cash repayments or through the seizure of other assets of the borrower. If banks
cannot rely on the legal system, the basis for a sound banking industry simply
does not exist. Exhortations to banks to expand their loan portfolios more
rapidly are quite beside the point. What is required is for the government to
devote a great deal of energy and creativity to providing a legal system on
which banks and other financial institutions, business in general, and individuals, can rely. The strength of entrenched resistance to reform of the legal system has meant that progress in this direction has been very slow, however.

DEMOCRACY AND DECENTRALISATION

Indonesia's transition to democracy involves not only allowing genuine competition between a large number of political parties within the electoral process, but
also devolving many functions previously dominated by the central government
to local governments (districts and municipalities). According to Dr Andi Mal-
larangeng, one of the main architects of decentralisation, the decision to decentralise was taken during the brief reign of President B.J. Habibie, when the latter
was looking for ways to distinguish himself from his predecessor – knowing he
would need to generate popular support quickly if he hoped to extend his term
in office.[16] Very tight control from the centre was of course a crucially important
characteristic of the Soeharto era (Jaya and Dick 2001: 222–223).

The sense that the Habibie interregnum presented at best a brief window of
opportunity to bring dominance by the centre to an end meant that careful plan-

ning and design of what was to be an extraordinarily radical change to the way Indonesia was governed would not be possible. This virtually guaranteed that there would be problems of implementation, but the sponsors of the change felt that this risk was worth taking: if only decentralisation could be enacted, such problems could be dealt with later. Indonesia is now having to face the consequences of this decision.

The issues requiring attention include a need for more careful consideration of an appropriate division of labour between the centre and lower levels of government and among lower levels of government; the failure to link central government funding of local governments to the functions devolved; the resulting propensity of local governments to impose new taxes of their own, including taxes on the movement of goods between districts that tend to fragment the economy (Ray 2003: 261–262); failure to devolve the power to tax land and buildings to local governments; the lack of capacity in many local governments to administer some of the functions devolved; the possibility that local government goals and priorities in relation to some functions might not coincide with those of the central government; and the vulnerability to challenge of the natural resource revenue-sharing arrangements (which heavily favour the regions where the resources are located) in the new Constitutional Court (given that the spirit of Article 33 of the Constitution clearly insists that wealth derived from these resources belongs equally to all Indonesians, regardless of where they live) (McLeod 2000: 33–37).

In short, notwithstanding the obvious merit of the principle of decentralisation, Indonesia's experiment with this still has a long way to run, and a good deal of attention is now being given to revising the relevant legislation. There is a cynical, if well-grounded, fear that this could lead to the whole process being reversed, but this seems highly unlikely. It is to be hoped that revision of the legislation will be driven not solely or primarily by the desire to claw back power in Jakarta, but rather by a consensus that the initial legislation had significant defects that now need to be remedied.

Measuring the overall economic impact of decentralisation is fraught with difficulty, and it is probably too soon even to attempt such a task in any case. Nevertheless, some of the available banking data do throw an interesting light on part of the process. In particular, over the last few years there has been a dramatic shift in the geographical distribution of bank deposits.[17] Figure 3.8 shows the pattern of growth in the value of bank deposits in selected regions, after correcting for inflation. Whereas the growth rates for all regions had been roughly the same for several years before the crisis (all regions doubled their real deposits in the four years to June 1997), the pattern since then has been very different. Despite considerable volatility in the first year of the crisis, deposits were broadly back at pre-crisis levels by September 1998. Since then, however, deposits in Jakarta at first stagnated and then began to decline soon after the

Figure 3.8   Real bank deposits by selected regions, 1992–2004
(June 1997 = 100)[a]

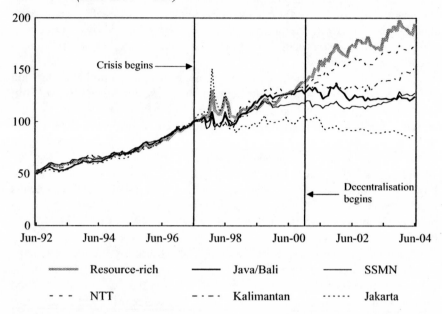

a   See text for regional groupings.

Source: CEIC Asia Database.

advent of the decentralisation era. By contrast, deposits in the other regions resumed their pre-crisis growth trajectories from about September 1998, although the Sumatra/Sulawesi/Maluku/West Nusa Tenggara (SSMN) group's deposits began to stagnate beyond September 1999, as did those in Java/Bali and Kalimantan after decentralisation began at the start of 2001.

On the other hand, aggregate deposits in the four resource-rich provinces (Aceh, Riau, East Kalimantan and Papua) have continued to increase rapidly, growing by 41 per cent from December 2000 through June 2004. Likewise, deposit growth has continued at a rapid pace in the poor province of East Nusa Tenggara (NTT), but this is clearly related to the secession of the neighbouring former province of East Timor. Kalimantan and SSMN have returned to positive growth in the last year, but deposits continue to stagnate or decline in real terms throughout Java/Bali and Jakarta. These observations suggest that decentralisation is having the desired effect of reducing the economic dominance of Jakarta and Java/Bali. Explaining the new pattern more fully will need further research, but one hypothesis worth testing is that accumulation of bank deposits partly reflects the prevalence of corrupt activity in the government and in the legislature of the region in question. In short, the explanation may lie in the decentralisation of corruption. If so, this would provide a salutary reminder that the attainment of better government by 'bringing government closer to the people' cannot be taken for granted.

NOTES

1   Strictly speaking, it is possible that monetary policy does affect Indonesia's GDP growth, and that other factors not taken into account here may have worked in opposing directions, but I have seen no credible evidence to support this proposition.

2   Concern about rapid price increases seems to have been an important determinant of voter intentions in the recent election; by contrast, voters seem quite unconcerned about interest rates. The new government might therefore do well to put more pressure on the central bank to improve its performance in keeping inflation low.

3   The policy for many years before the crisis was to hold the rate of depreciation, rather than the exchange rate itself, roughly constant, at around 4 per cent per annum (McLeod 1997: 33).

4   A famous example is George Soros, who took on the Bank of England in 1992 – and won (Krugman 2000: 121–123).

5   Public sector debt is much smaller now than a few years ago relative to GDP, but this should not be interpreted to mean that the absolute level of debt is falling. There are three main reasons why the ratio has declined. First, the rupiah has recovered much of the ground it lost early in the crisis, such that the rupiah value of the government's foreign debt has become much smaller; second, significant increases in domestic prices have caused nominal GDP to increase commensurately; and third, real GDP has been growing steadily.

6   Ishihara and Marks (2004) report that the share of property investment in total investment rose to about 83 per cent in 2003 compared with 73 per cent prior to the crisis.

7   According to a recent World Bank report, 'public spending on infrastructure has dropped by 80 percent from pre-crisis levels' (World Bank 2004: 4).

8   See, for example, 'Police defend detentions', <http://laksamana.net/>, 27 September 2004.

9   The consumer price index (CPI) is used to deflate nominal minimum wages.

10   With decentralisation, many districts and municipalities are now setting their own minimum wages – at levels even higher than the provinces. Space limitations prevent a full discussion of this here.

11   There is also a threat to Indonesian producers of import substitutes, to the extent that imports from China are cheaper or of better quality. But the gain to Indonesian consumers from this would exceed the losses to its producers.

12   It took a full year for the government to prepare the regulation (Government Regulation 17/1999) that would provide the full legal foundation for IBRA.

13 An alternative proposal for dealing with single or multiple bank failures is set out in McLeod (2004).

14 Dollar-denominated lending grew at an average 8.2 per cent per annum in the two years to June 2004.

15 The original intention was for the guarantee to run for an initial period of just two years from January 1998.

16 As it turned out, the effort was in vain. Habibie had already lost his position to Abdurrahman Wahid by the time decentralisation began to be implemented in January 2001.

17 I thank James Castle for bringing this to my attention.

PART II

Globalisation, Decentralisation and Sustainable Development

4 INDONESIA IN A CHANGING GLOBAL ENVIRONMENT

Warwick J. McKibbin

INTRODUCTION

Indonesia faces a number of important challenges both in the short run and in the longer run. The world economy is currently growing robustly but a number of uncertainties cloud the economic outlook. A strong global economy is being challenged by higher oil prices. The emergence of significant trade imbalances between East Asia and the United States will undoubtedly put pressure on economic and political relations between the major regions of global growth. At the same time as the global economy is providing short-term economic stimulus to Indonesia, there are a number of serious environmental problems that Indonesia needs to face. Key among these are depletion of natural resources, particularly the degradation of forests, and rising greenhouse gas emissions.[1] Global policies to reduce greenhouse gas emissions will directly affect Indonesia, a major fossil fuel producer.

This chapter gives an overview of the current state of the global economy, with a focus on the three most important risks currently facing world growth: the impact of rising oil prices on the global economy, the resolution of trans-Pacific trade imbalances and, related to this, surprisingly low long-term real interest rates throughout the world. The chapter then focuses on two sets of longer-term issues currently facing Indonesia. The first concerns rising energy use, rising greenhouse emissions and the implications for Indonesia of serious global climate change policy. The second concerns the serious depletion of natural resources, particularly forests. I also suggest how we can deal with these two longer-term issues within a single framework that focuses on creating property rights and clear incentives to manage forests and greenhouse gas emissions. This is particularly important for Indonesia, which is the only member of the Organization of the Petroleum Exporting Countries (OPEC) to have ratified

*Figure 4.1   Real GDP growth in selected OECD countries and Asia,
1992–2004 (year-end percentage change)*

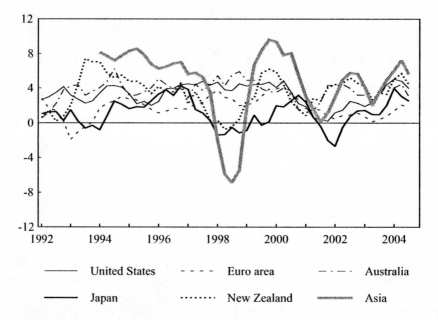

Asia = Hong Kong, Indonesia, South Korea, Malaysia, the Philippines, Singapore, Taiwan and Thailand.

Sources: Australian Bureau of Statistics; CEIC Data Company; Thomson Financial Services and Products.

the Kyoto Protocol to the United Nations Framework Convention on Climate Change.[2]

SHORT-TERM GLOBAL ECONOMIC OUTLOOK

The world economy is growing strongly after several years of slow growth. The latest International Monetary Fund (IMF) *World Economic Outlook* predicts global growth to be 5 per cent in 2004 and 4.3 per cent in 2005 (IMF 2004: 3, Table 1.1). Figure 4.1 shows the composition of this growth in economies of the Organisation for Economic Co-operation and Development (OECD). Strong growth in the United States and Australia, a tentative recovery in Japan and low but rising growth in Europe suggest a sustained economic recovery in OECD economies. More impressive growth continues in Asia, as shown in Figure 4.2. China continues to be a powerhouse despite attempts to cool the economy

Figure 4.2   Industrial production in Asia, 1999–2005 (March quarter 1999 = 100, smoothed)[a]

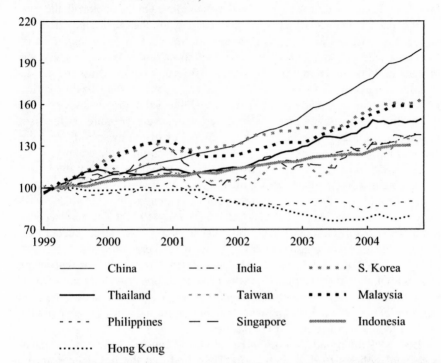

a   Figures for China, India, Indonesia, Malaysia, the Philippines and Taiwan have been seasonally adjusted by the Reserve Bank of Australia.

Source: CEIC Data Company as provided by the Reserve Bank of Australia.

through monetary restrictions and interest rate increases. The contraction of monetary policy will probably be effective but there is unlikely to be a major slowdown in China (see McKibbin and Stoeckel 2004a).

There are more serious threats to global economic growth than policy developments in China. Since early 1999 oil prices have risen sharply, from around $10 per barrel to over $55 per barrel in October 2004. This rise in oil prices is a significant shock to the world economy. The International Energy Agency recently predicted that every $10 per barrel rise in oil prices reduced world GDP by 0.4 per cent (IEA 2004). McKibbin and Stoeckel (2004b) suggest an even higher figure – closer to 0.6 per cent of GDP for every $10 per barrel rise. The current rise in oil prices is not as large in real terms as the oil shocks of the early 1970s, but it is significant and could slow the world economy significantly. In particular, McKibbin and Stoeckel (2004b) find quite different effects on different economies; of Indonesia's trading partners, Japan is likely to be the hardest hit. The effects on Indonesia are likely to be complex. On the one hand, the value of oil exports increases, which generates revenue. On the other hand, growth in key trading partners is likely to slow and the demand for other exports from Indonesia will tend to decline. Moreover, within Indonesia there are severe distortions in domestic energy pricing (discussed further below). In particular, the Indonesian government subsidises domestic energy prices. This has the curious implication that, as world oil prices rise, the dollar value of subsidies provided by the Indonesian government rises, which puts severe pressure on the fiscal position. It is hard to imagine that the current policy of energy subsidies can persist for long without major pressure on the fiscal position of the country.

A second important issue clouds the global outlook. Since the 1997 Asian crisis there has emerged a serious trade imbalance between Asia and the United States. Figure 4.3 shows the current account balances for the Asian newly industrialised countries (NICs) and Indonesia. Since 1998 the current accounts of all Asian crisis economies have shifted sharply towards current account surpluses. This reflects the large capital outflows from these countries. The current account of the NICs went from near balance in 1996 to a surplus of nearly 8 per cent of GDP in 2003. The puzzle is why these trade positions have not reversed given recovery in these countries' economies. Figure 4.3 also shows the gradual deterioration of the US current account deficit from under 2 per cent of GDP in 1995 to nearly 5 per cent of GDP by 2003.[3]

Lee, McKibbin and Park (2004) explore the causes of these trade imbalances and policies to deal with them. They find that the imbalances are not caused by trade policy or exchange rate policy in Asia (in contrast to Dooley, Folkerts-Landau and Garber 2003), but are driven by two other key factors. In order to understand these factors, it is important to realise that the current account is both the difference between exports and imports of countries (adjusted by factor payments) and the difference between national savings and investment. A country with excess national savings relative to investment will experience a current account surplus; a country with low savings relative to investment will experience a current account deficit. The major story behind these current account imbalances is changes in saving and investment balances, not trade policy or exchange rate policy.

One important explanation for the rise in current account surpluses in Asia and the rise in current account deficits in the United States since 2000 is the large increase in US fiscal deficits since 2000. Between the late 1980s and 2001, the US fiscal balance improved dramatically, from negative to positive, peaking at a surplus of 4.4 per cent of GDP in 2000. However, in 2002 the fiscal balance deteriorated significantly due to tax cuts, an increase in spending due to the war on terror, and an economic slowdown. The federal government

Figure 4.3   Current account balance in selected countries, 1995–2004
(per cent of GDP)

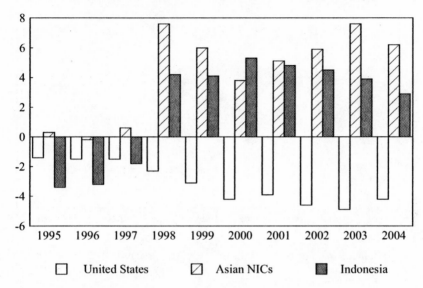

Asian NICs = Hong Kong, Singapore, South Korea and Taiwan.

Source: Lee, McKibbin and Park (2004: Table 1).

budget balance (including the social security surplus) shifted from a surplus of
2.5 per cent of GDP in financial year 2000 to a deficit of more than 4 per cent
of GDP in financial year 2004. This large change in government savings translated into a large fall in national savings and a worsening of the current account
as foreigners increasingly financed US investment.

The second key factor can be seen from Figure 4.4, which shows the ratio
of total investment to GDP in Indonesia, South Korea, Malaysia and Thailand.
Since the 1997 Asian crisis, investment has dropped sharply in all these
economies. For a given savings rate, a sharp drop in investment (both public
infrastructure spending and private investment) should improve the current
account surpluses of these countries. For Indonesia, South Korea, Malaysia and
Thailand, the decline in investment has been 10–20 per cent of GDP. This is
both dramatic and puzzling and explains a significant part of the improvement
in the current surpluses of Asia. It has serious implications not only for trade
imbalances but also for future growth prospects in Asia, since investment is a
critical driver of future productive capacity. In the short run, the United States
is fortunate that, in order to offset its low national savings rate, it can continue
to borrow at very low real interest rates, thanks partly to the collapse in Asian

Figure 4.4   Investment in selected countries, 1995–2003 (per cent of GDP)

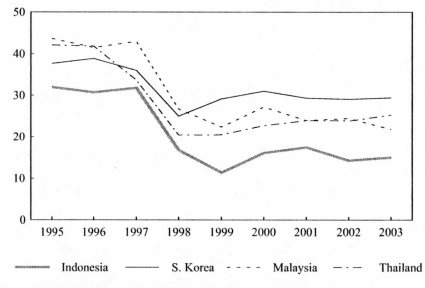

Source: Lee, McKibbin and Park (2004: Table 4).

investment. Low real interest rates may also reflect the extremely low short-term nominal interest rate in the major economies of the United States, Europe and Japan. Monetary authorities in these regions will eventually have to raise nominal policy interest rates. Eventually the large current account imbalances should self-correct through a rise in global real interest rates, a depreciation of the US dollar or both. A gradual adjustment is feasible and should be manageable for countries like Indonesia, but a sharp adjustment in either policy interest rates or long-term real interest rates could cause serious problems for the recovery phase in Indonesia, especially if real interest rates begin to reflect a shortage of global savings.

Thus the global economy looks favourable to Indonesia in the near term, yet there are potential problems such as the global rise in oil prices, the emergence of trade imbalances between Asia and the United States, and an upward movement in world real interest rates.

LONGER-TERM RESOURCE, ENERGY AND CLIMATE ISSUES

Until the 1997 crisis, Indonesia had experienced three decades of sustained economic growth of above 6 per cent per year. As in many countries, this was dri-

*Figure 4.5   Relative trends in energy consumption in Indonesia, 1980–2000
(1980 = 1)*

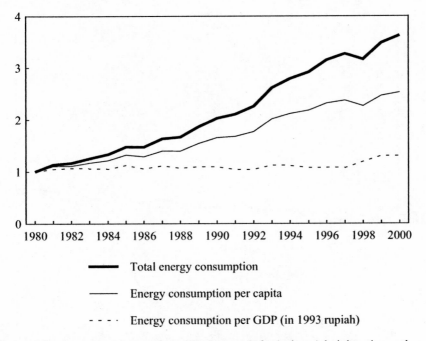

Total energy consumption

Energy consumption per capita

- - - - Energy consumption per GDP (in 1993 rupiah)

Source: Total energy consumption: US Energy Information Administration; others: World Bank (2002), *World Development Indicators*.

ven particularly by access to cheap energy sources. Indonesia is exceptional in that it has large reserves of fossil fuels and is a member of OPEC.[4] Figure 4.5 shows the path of energy use in Indonesia since 1980. In 2000, total energy consumption was more than 3.5 times that of 1980, while per capita energy use was more than 2.5 times that of 1980. Energy use per unit of GDP has remained surprisingly constant during the period, with a slight upward trend since the 1997 crisis. When compared to developed countries, this constancy of energy use per unit of GDP is surprising. In most OECD economies there is a trend decline in energy use per unit of GDP (of approximately 1 per cent per year), reflecting increased energy efficiency as well as a changing economic structure away from energy-intensive manufacturing towards less energy-intensive service industries (McKibbin, Pearce and Stegman 2004). In Indonesia it appears that, over the past few decades, either this gradual increase in energy efficiency has not occurred or there has been a particular pattern of structural change that offsets the effects of energy efficiency. Any lack of energy efficiency is probably

Figure 4.6   Energy consumption in Indonesia by source, 1980–2000 (share of total energy consumption)

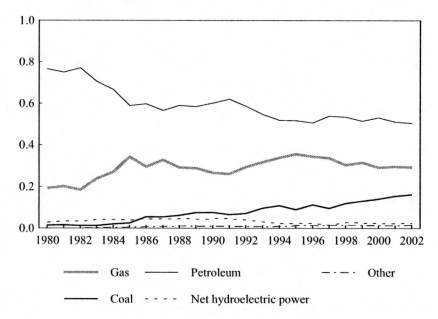

Source: US Energy Information Administration.

due to subsidies of energy prices, which reduce incentives for substitution away from energy use towards labour and capital. As noted above, when combined with the current period of high oil prices, this aspect of Indonesian energy policy may be causing serious structural distortion in the nature of production and creating fiscal problems.

Figure 4.6 shows the composition of energy consumption in Indonesia by energy source as a share of total energy consumption (defined in quadrillion British thermal units). Not surprisingly, oil (petroleum) dominates energy use, followed by gas and then coal. Coal has shown the biggest proportional gain in market share since 1980. The rise in coal use has important implications for greenhouse gas emissions in Indonesia because coal has greater carbon emissions per unit of energy than do oil and gas. Renewable energy sources barely appear on the chart.

The energy trends in Indonesia are problematic. Despite the reliance on fossil fuel energy within Indonesia, one of the positive developments since the early 1980s has been the reduced reliance on fuel exports as a share of total exports – a decrease from 80 per cent in 1982 to just over 20 per cent in 2000.

Figure 4.7   Relative trends in carbon dioxide emissions in Indonesia,
*   1980–2000 (1980 = 1)*

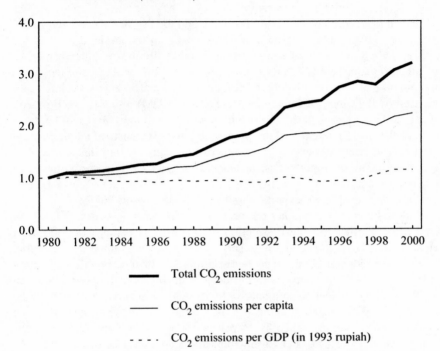

━━━━   Total CO_2 emissions

───── CO_2 emissions per capita

- - - - CO_2 emissions per GDP (in 1993 rupiah)

Source: US Energy Information Administration; World Bank, *World Development Indicators*.

Directly related to energy use are emissions of carbon dioxide, the most important greenhouse gas. As Indonesia has ratified the Kyoto Protocol, its domestic emissions of carbon dioxide will be scrutinised more closely in coming years. I discuss the implications of global climate policy in the next section of this chapter. Figure 4.7 shows that, on a per capita basis and as a share of GDP, the paths of carbon dioxide emissions from fossil fuels look very similar to the paths of energy use (see Figure 4.5). This is not surprising given the almost exclusive reliance on fossil fuels for energy in Indonesia. There was a more than three-fold increase in carbon emissions in Indonesia between 1980 and 2000. The composition of the sources of emissions is somewhat different from the energy use composition shown in Figure 4.6, because each type of fossil fuel produces a different amount of carbon dioxide emissions per unit of energy. Coal emits by far the largest amount of carbon dioxide per unit of energy, followed by oil and then natural gas. By 2001, coal accounted for 18 per

cent of energy consumption but was responsible for 25 per cent of carbon dioxide emissions in Indonesia. Thus since 1980 emissions of carbon dioxide have
risen faster than energy use in Indonesia.

Given ratification of the Kyoto Protocol, and the fact that there is no sign of
a change in the trend of carbon dioxide emissions in Indonesia, it is clear that
changing the future path of emissions will require significant policy responses
if Indonesia is to be a full participant in the Kyoto Protocol system. Optimists
will argue that this can be done by foreign investment in energy technologies
induced by the Clean Development Mechanism (CDM) of the Kyoto Protocol.
It is not clear how much the CDM will cost or how important it will be, but I
believe that the complexity of the process and the high costs of administration
are likely to result in very little new energy investment from this source. For
Indonesia, a more important issue than the impact of domestic policies on
greenhouse emissions may be the economic impact of global policies targeting
one of Indonesia's major exports, fossil fuels. I discuss this below.

Indonesia faces many other resource and environmental issues.[5] Change in
land use – particularly the destruction of forests – is perhaps the one most
closely related to carbon emissions. This is a fundamentally important issue that
needs to be addressed in a much shorter timeframe than carbon dioxide emissions. Figure 4.8 shows the alarming decline in forests in Indonesia between
1990 and 2000 – a decline both relative to the world and in comparison with the
rest of Asia. While plantation area has risen by 38 per cent over the period, the
overall forest cover has fallen by 16 per cent, implying a large decline in natural forest cover. This has environmental implications for ecosystem loss and
soil degradation as well as social implications for native forest users. The burning of the forests has also resulted in emissions of carbon dioxide and black carbon, with important implications for health, agricultural productivity and
localised climate change. Streets (2004), Streets et al. (2003) and others suggest
that direct action to reduce the emissions of black carbon from household
energy use and the burning of forests is an important issue that needs urgent
attention not only in countries like China but also in Indonesia.

RESPONDING TO CLIMATE CHANGE AND OTHER CHALLENGES

For several decades the global community has struggled with the issue of how
to respond effectively to the threat of climate change. In 1992, the United
Nations Earth Summit in Rio de Janeiro produced a landmark treaty on climate
change that undertook to stabilise greenhouse gas concentrations in the atmosphere. By focusing on stabilisation, however, the treaty implicitly adopted the
position that the risks posed by climate change require that emissions be
reduced no matter what the cost. The agreement, signed and ratified by more

Figure 4.8   Change in forest area by type, 1990–2000 (per cent)

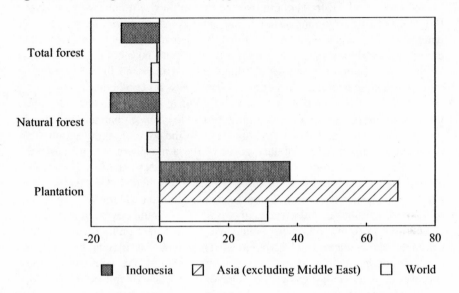

Source: World Resources Institute.

than 186 countries, including the United States, spawned numerous subsequent rounds of climate negotiations aimed at rolling back emissions from industrialised countries to the levels that prevailed in 1990. To date, however, the negotiations have had little effect on greenhouse gas emissions and have not produced a detectable slowing in the rate of emissions growth.[6] The treaty's implementing protocol, the 1997 Kyoto agreement, crawled into life after being heavily diluted at negotiations in Bonn and Marrakech.[7] The survival of the Kyoto Protocol in its current form has been given some impetus by its recent ratification by Russia, yet many problems must be faced before we can see if actions under the protocol are actually reducing emissions. More than a decade of negotiations has produced a policy that is very strict in principle but ineffective in practice.

The problem at the international level is actually worse than it appears from the troubled process of Kyoto ratification. Even when the Kyoto Protocol comes into force (which it had not at the time of writing), it will place restrictions only on industrial economies, and will exclude the world's largest greenhouse emitter, the United States. Developing countries, including Indonesia, have ratified the agreement but have not taken on any responsibilities for reducing emissions except those that emerge from mechanisms such as the CDM and joint implementation. Thus, in a real sense, a majority of future global greenhouse emissions are not bound by the current international agreement. Indeed, both the United States and Australia claim that the reason they will not ratify the Kyoto Protocol is that developing countries are not taking on commitments. The fact that the world's largest emitter, the United States, is not substantially involved in climate policy dilutes global action even further. With no binding commitments by the key developing countries of China, India, Brazil and Indonesia (among others), effective action against climate change is still hypothetical.

Yet developing countries have a valid point in their argument that, while they are prepared to be part of a regime to tackle climate change, they should not be required to bear a disproportionate part of the costs of taking action. Current concentrations of greenhouse gases in the atmosphere are primarily the result of economic activities in the industrial economies since the industrial revolution. Because it is the stock of carbon in the atmosphere that matters for temperature changes, any climate change in the near future will largely be the result of the past activities of industrial economies. Why should developing countries not be able to follow the energy-intensive development paths previously followed by the industrialised economies? This issue has inevitably led to an expectation that the industrialised economies should pay compensation for action taken in developing countries. One of the biggest dilemmas for developing countries is that at some stage they will need to make some form of commitment to curbing greenhouse gas emissions in their own self-interest because, on most estimates, they are the countries likely to incur the greatest damage from climate change (IPCC 2001).

Standing back from the intensity of international negotiations, it is worth clarifying several important facts about the costs and benefits of climate policy, and exploring whether developing countries could take approaches that are not being considered because of the standard refrain that 'Kyoto is the only game in town'. This mindset has already hindered effective action for a decade as countries and industries postpone action until agreements are clarified. The delay in providing clear incentives for moving away from fossil fuel-based systems may ultimately prove to be extremely costly, given the uncertainties of climate change and the kinds of decisions on energy systems being made in regions of the developing world that are growing rapidly, including Indonesia. At some stage Indonesia will probably substitute away from oil into other energy sources, which may include coal rather than more greenhouse-friendly options.

One of the largest sources of anthropogenic greenhouse gas emissions is the burning of fossil fuels. The cheapest way to make the global energy system less reliant on fossil fuels is to remove these emissions from future rather than existing energy systems. It is costly to change existing energy systems because of the huge investments in physical and human capital surrounding them. It is much cheaper to change future investments (which will largely occur in developing countries) before they are undertaken. Technology will ultimately be the source of reductions in emissions, whether through the development of alternative sources of energy or through ways of sequestering carbon released by burning fossil fuels. In terms of carbon intensities, developing countries have a huge opportunity to avoid the pitfalls experienced by industrialised economies in their development process. The key issue is how developing countries can be encouraged to establish energy systems that are less carbon intensive over time. If climate change does emerge as a serious problem, developing countries will ultimately have to move towards a less carbon-intensive future. It is likely to be significantly cheaper to do this over time than to face massive restructuring at some future period and the sorts of problems industrialised economies encounter today.

The current state of global policy on climate change is as follows. The United States, the largest emitter of greenhouse gases, has rejected the Kyoto Protocol and is arguing for policies that directly or indirectly reduce emissions through technological change. The European Union is committed to emission targets, assuming Russia provides a great deal of the reductions required through selling emission permits. On 1 January 2005, the European Union will also implement a Europe-wide emissions trading scheme (though it will exempt key sectors such as aluminium, motor vehicles and chemicals), but the scheme only has caps that effectively bind by the end of 2008. Japan is considering what it can do given that current emissions are 16 per cent above target in an economy recovering from a decade of recession. And developing countries have refused to officially discuss taking on commitments.

Given this background, there are several ways in which Indonesia could begin to address carbon emissions. The most obvious first step would be the removal of energy subsidies. The second step would be to raise the price of energy to reflect the true economic and environmental cost of burning fossil fuels. A third option would be the direct importation of less carbon-intensive technologies provided by the CDM. This outcome is possible but not likely, for the reasons already outlined above. Thus I focus on the first two options in the discussion below.

Economic theory provides guidance on the structure of a possible climate change policy for Indonesia.[8] Since greenhouse gases are emitted by a vast number of highly heterogeneous sources, minimising the cost of abating a given amount of emissions requires that all sources clean up amounts that cause their marginal cost of abatement to be equated. To achieve this, the standard economic policy prescription would be a market-based instrument, such as a tax on emissions or a tradable permit system for emission rights. In the absence of uncertainty, the efficient level of abatement could be achieved under either policy, although the distributional effects of tax and emission trading policies would be very different.

Under uncertainty, however, the situation becomes more complicated. Weitzman (1974) showed that taxes and permits are not equivalent when marginal benefits and costs are uncertain, and that the relative slopes of the two curves determine which policy will be better.[9] Emission permits are better than taxes when marginal benefit schedules are steep and marginal costs are flat: in that situation, it is important to get the quantity of emissions down to the threshold. A permit policy does exactly that. In the opposite situation, when marginal costs are rising sharply and marginal benefits are flat, a tax is a better policy. The potential inefficiency of a permit system under uncertainty is not just a theoretical curiosity: it is intuitively understood by many participants in the climate change debate by the expression of the concern about a policy that 'caps emissions regardless of cost'.

Applying this analysis to climate change shows that, because of the uncertainties surrounding climate change, a tax is likely to be far more efficient than a permit system. All evidence to date suggests that the marginal cost curve for reducing greenhouse gas emissions is very steep, at least for developed countries. Although the models show considerable disagreement as to how expensive it would be to achieve a given reduction in emissions, all models show that costs rise rapidly as emission targets become tighter. At the same time, the nature of climate change indicates that the marginal benefit curve for reducing emissions will be very flat.

Although a tax would be more efficient than a permit system for controlling greenhouse gas emissions, it is a major political liability in that it would induce income transfers from firms to the government, and the amounts would probably be perceived as unreasonably large. In particular, firms would end up paying far more in taxes than they spent on reducing emissions, because a tax is levied on all emissions, not only those that are removed at the margin. As a result, the transfers would dominate the political debate and would give firms a powerful incentive to fight the proposal. The political problem is not just that firms dislike paying taxes; rather, it is that the transfers would be so much larger than the abatement costs that they would completely dominate the political debate.

Given the advantages and disadvantages of the standard economic instruments, is it possible to combine the attractive features of both systems into a single approach? Further, is it possible to develop a system that is common in philosophy across developed and developing economies but in which developing economies do not incur short-run costs to the economy in the form of higher energy prices until they have the capacity to pay?

Any climate change regime should include several goals. First, there is a need to recognise the trade-off between economic efficiency and equity within and between countries. Second, there is a need to recognise that policies should be based on clear property rights over emissions and clear long-run emission targets, but on near certainty in the short-run costs to the economy. Third, a sensible climate policy should create domestic institutions that allow people to self-insure against the uncertainties created by climate change. Fourth, there should be market mechanisms that give clear signals about the current and expected future costs of carbon. Fifth, countries should encourage, as much as possible, the creation of self-interested coalitions that will keep climate change policy from collapsing, rather than focusing on the creation of a system that survives only through the imposition of effective international sanctions.

The McKibbin–Wilcoxen blueprint (McKibbin and Wilcoxen 2002a, 2002b) was created explicitly to deal with these issues. It is a hybrid system that blends the best features of taxes and emission permit trading.[10] It can be applied across developed and developing countries, but it recognises that developing countries should not bear the same economic costs as industrial countries in the short run.

The approach is set out in detail in McKibbin and Wilcoxen (2002a), but it will be briefly outlined here. The basic idea is that governments in each country impose a requirement that energy producers have an annual emission permit to produce energy each year, based on the carbon content of that energy. The government would create a fixed quantity of perpetual permits that allow a unit of emission every year for 100 years. These would be traded in a market with a flexible price. The government would also be able to create additional annual permits in any year at a guaranteed price. Permits that satisfy the annual constraint for energy production could be either a perpetual permit or an annual permit provided by the government at a fixed price. The price of emissions in any year would never be higher than the fixed price set by the government, and the amount of emissions in any year would be whatever the market delivers. Thus we have a long-term target in terms of emissions but an annual target in terms of the maximum cost of carbon to industry. In a developing country like Indonesia, the annual price would initially be zero if we allowed an allocation of perpetual permits well in excess of current emissions. However, the price of perpetual permits would reflect the expectation that Indonesia would eventually reach the emission levels that caused the carbon emission constraint to be binding. Thus the perpetual permit market with positive prices would provide a financial incentive for Indonesia to begin to change its carbon emissions over time, even though a carbon permit would initially have zero annual cost to industry.

The attractiveness of this blueprint for creating institutions that aid economic development in developing countries should not be underestimated. The ability of investors in energy systems to effectively hedge their investment over a long period should prove very attractive for the development of energy systems in developing countries. The timeframe of the assets whose creation we propose (by committing to a global climate regime) is currently unparalleled.

Indonesia could use the new asset as a way of attracting foreign investment and enhancing the development process by creating what is effectively a futures market in energy. This is far more likely to induce foreign investment than the CDM or similar mechanisms that face very high administrative costs. Critics might argue that Indonesia would be unable to create the sorts of institutions such a scheme would require. This may be a problem in the near term, but it would be easier for Indonesia to create property rights and institutions within the country in accordance with its characteristics as a developing country than to impose within it the sorts of institutions and property rights that would be required under the Kyoto Protocol if Indonesia were to sell carbon rights into a global market. The difficulty in implementing the Kyoto Protocol outside the existing small group of industrialised countries with similar institutional structures arises exactly because of the difficulty of achieving the required global synchronisation of property rights in a form that acknowledges the problems experienced in developing countries in the area of property rights.

Indonesia could adapt the system proposed above to include a mechanism for creating credits to maintain and enhance its forests. Introducing property rights into forest management and providing a direct market incentive for managing forests is likely to be the only credible way to reduce the startling decline in forest cover in Indonesia.[11] By combining both carbon emissions and forestry directly in a system with clear property rights, Indonesia could make substantial progress in solving some of its longer-term environmental issues while at the same time creating institutions to assist in economic development and, in particular, encourage foreign direct investment.

SUMMARY AND CONCLUSION

This chapter summarises the outlook for the global economy and raises several important potential problems facing Indonesia as well as other countries in the Asia–Pacific – high oil prices, an adjustment to trans-Pacific trade imbalances and a return of world real interest rates to more reasonable levels. It also highlights several important environmental issues facing Indonesia which have both local and global implications.

The chapter outlines a domestic response that Indonesia could work towards to address the issues of forest degradation, carbon emissions and black carbon emission reductions within a single framework. It argues that Indonesia could implement policies such as the McKibbin–Wilcoxen blueprint as part of a broader strategy of actions to both price future carbon emissions and encourage more sustainable economic development. Such a policy should be an attractive option for Indonesia because it encourages the development of institutions to manage risk, as well as demonstrating a clear commitment to effective action against future carbon emissions. If the policy was successful in both stimulating foreign investment in energy development and reducing the rising trend of greenhouse emissions through market-based incentives based on the clear establishment of property rights, the demonstration effect across the developing world would be powerful. It would certainly invalidate arguments by countries like the United States and Australia that they should not be required to take action on carbon emissions because developing countries have not made binding commitments. That alone would probably reduce greenhouse gas emissions significantly in future decades.

The alternative strategy for Indonesia is to wait for a resolution of the stalemate over an effective Kyoto Protocol, and to wait for large sums of financial assistance to accompany the transfer of energy technology from the industrial economies though some other Kyoto-like endeavour. This will be a very long wait if past experience is any guide. But delaying action ignores the fact that Indonesians are already making decisions on long-term energy investments, with very few incentives for them to move away from reliance on the country's abundant, low-cost fossil fuels. If the creation of a framework for committing to action on climate policies is delayed, the Indonesian economy could suffer unnecessary structural shocks caused by an eventual need to adapt to the realities of a world with serious climate problems. Indonesia could implement the McKibbin–Wilcoxen blueprint unilaterally without an international agreement, although it could make the policy consistent with Kyoto-style systems if necessary. The approach has many advantages, including a great deal of flexibility for adaptation as the world learns more about the threats and challenges of climate change.

NOTES

*   The author thanks Alison Stegman for excellent research assistance and Budy Resosudarmo, Mark Thirlwell and an anonymous referee for comments. The views expressed in the paper are those of the author and should not be interpreted as reflecting the views of the institutions with which the author is affiliated, including the trustees, officers or other staff of the Lowy Institute or the Brookings Institution.
1   See WRI (2004) for an overview.
2   Further details on the Kyoto Protocol can be found later in this chapter.
3   By the second quarter of 2004 this figure was closer to 5.7 per cent of GDP.
4   For an overview of Indonesia's energy profile, see Resosudarmo and Tanujaya (2002).
5   See Resosudarmo, Subiman and Rahayu (2000) for a discussion of marine resource depletion in Indonesia.
6   See McKibbin and Wilcoxen (2002a) for a summary of the negotiations and a critique of the approach.

7   Earlier estimates of the cost of Kyoto can be found in Weyant (1999). Direct com-
     parisons of the versions of the protocol from the third and seventh conferences of
     the parties can be found in Bohringer (2001), Buchner, Carraro and Cersosimo
     (2001), Kemfert (2001), Löschel and Zhang (2002) and McKibbin and Wilcoxen
     (2004).
8   See McKibbin and Wilcoxen (2002a) for a survey and Pezzey (2003) for a compar-
     ison of taxes and permits.
9   See also Pizer (1997) for a more recent discussion of the issue.
10   The intellectual idea actually dates back to Roberts and Spence (1976) for general
     environmental policy and McKibbin and Wilcoxen (1997) for climate change pol-
     icy.
11   See Chomitz and Griffiths (1996) for a discussion of the causes of deforestation in
     Indonesia.

5 INTERNATIONAL TRADE AND THE NATURAL RESOURCE 'CURSE' IN SOUTHEAST ASIA: DOES CHINA'S GROWTH THREATEN REGIONAL DEVELOPMENT?

Ian Coxhead

INTRODUCTION

The 'natural resource curse' is one of the more colourful phrases to be coined about a major subject in development economics, alongside the ill-fated 'East Asian miracle'. The 'curse' is that of slow growth due to a failure to sustain efficient factor use, especially in industrial sectors where the potential for productivity gain is highest. According to Sachs and Warner (2001: 828):

> there is virtually no overlap between the set of countries with large natural resource endowments – and the set of countries that have high levels of GDP ... resource intensity tends to correlate with slow economic growth.

Predictions derived from these apparent empirical regularities raise two puzzles for students of Southeast Asian economic development. First, are resource-abundant Southeast Asian economies that have experienced sustained high rates of economic growth different in some way from the group of countries from whose data the Sachs–Warner statement is derived? Second, is there anything in current market and policy trends that might predispose Southeast Asia's resource-abundant economies to lower growth in the future?

Two concurrent phenomena challenge the continued economic success of Southeast Asia's resource-rich economies. First, the growth and structural transformation of China, along with its increasing integration in world markets through actions such as accession to the World Trade Organization (WTO), abolition of the Multi-fibre Arrangement (MFA) garment export quotas, and reduced trade barriers with Japan, East Asia and ASEAN, is expected to have significant effects on the structure of Southeast Asian production and trade.

Recent World Bank estimates indicate that China's increasing size and involvement in global and regional trade will cause Southeast Asia's resource-abundant economies to become more intensive in resource-based exports, and less so in low-end, labour-intensive manufacturing such as garments. These trends will increase exploitation rates of natural resources directly, through product market changes, and indirectly, by driving down the price of low-skilled labour.

The second phenomenon is decentralisation of control over natural resource stocks and their disposal in the countries of Southeast Asia. Decentralisation, while it has many positive attributes, has a distinctly mixed record where management of 'national' wealth (forests, fisheries, water resources) is concerned. A theme of this chapter is that if decentralisation undermines the management and protection of natural resource stocks, the China trade effect could lead to a lower-welfare outcome.

The chapter begins with a discussion of the 'curse' and a review of related evidence. I then consider briefly the relevant data from resource-rich Southeast Asian countries. This analysis leads to the question 'What effect will China's expansion and increasing integration with world markets have on the structure of Southeast Asian production and trade?' Subsequently, I explore possible ways in which the hypothesised structural changes might interact with a new policy and institutional setting in decentralising Southeast Asian resource-rich economies. I conclude with some more speculative thoughts on possible future growth paths, welfare results and environmental outcomes for Southeast Asia.

THE 'CURSE' OF NATURAL RESOURCE ABUNDANCE

What is the curse?

Resource abundance, it is argued, contributes to low growth rates and thus to divergence in per capita incomes between resource-rich and resource-poor economies. For example, Sachs and Warner (2001) show a negative relationship between GDP growth rates and natural resource wealth for a large sample of countries.

More than one explanation can be offered for this. First, the 'Dutch disease' effects of natural resource exports inhibit growth in manufacturing, a sector whose growth is commonly believed to confer positive productivity externalities, giving rise to increasing returns at the sectoral level. Slower growth of manufacturing, due to competition for labour and capital from resource sectors and secondary growth in non-traded sectors, reduces the gains available from manufacturing growth.[1]

Second, it has been argued that exploitation of natural resource wealth reduces the return to human capital, and thus diminishes incentives for educational attainment (Gylfason 2001). Resource-rich countries therefore encounter a form of low-level equilibrium trap when attempting to climb product variety or quality ladders in manufacturing, where human capital inputs are increasingly intensively employed.

Third, a variety of political economy arguments present some form of the case that resource wealth promotes the ascendance of the 'predatory state' over the 'developmental state', either by actively encouraging the former through corruption related to resource rents, or by undermining the latter when revenue flows associated with resource extraction reduce the efficiency of policy and administration (Auty 2001). This set of arguments has been made with particular force in case studies of Latin American and sub-Saharan Africa (Acemoglu, Johnson and Robinson 2002, 2004).

Fourth, lower growth has also been attributed to the destabilising consequences of Dutch disease, which causes relative shrinkage in non-resource tradable sector output. The greater relative prominence of non-tradable sectors in GDP due to the spending effects of a boom increases aggregate vulnerability to terms-of-trade shocks or global market volatility, since the burden of adjustment, rather than being distributed between a combination of intersectoral resource movements and expenditure effects, falls on expenditure effects alone, creating real exchange rate instability (Hausmann and Rigobon 2002).

Despite the intuitive appeal of these arguments, the natural resource curse hypothesis has also attracted considerable critical attention. A number of arguments can be made to the effect that what may appear to be slow growth caused by natural resource wealth is instead the product of other phenomena not directly related to resource exploitation. In particular, it is important that the slow growth observed by Sachs and Warner and others in a sample of developing economies is not consistent over time; rather, growth rates in many resource-abundant economies were very high in the 1960s and 1970s, but decelerated in the 1980s. The structural stability of regression results in which growth rates (the endogenous variables) are averaged over fairly long periods is questionable. Slower growth rates in the 1980s, in particular, were not unique to resource-abundant economies, and could instead have been the products of debt overhang or other post-oil shock imbalances and incomplete adjustment (Manzano and Rigobon 2001), in addition to the effects of the global commodity price collapses of the early 1980s.

Other criticisms have focused on the econometric strategies from which empirical conclusions about the existence of the curse have been derived. One such argument distinguishes between measures of resource *abundance* and resource *dependence*. Sachs and Warner and others mainly use dependence measures (for example, trade intensities), but these are vulnerable to claims of endogeneity, especially when the effects of policies affecting exchange rates or the growth of other tradables sectors are taken into account.

Another question concerns the definition of abundance (or dependence) and the stability of the group of countries defined as resource abundant or resource dependent. This debate is analogous to that over 'openness', in which a country might be classed as 'open' by one set of measures but not by another (Rodriguez and Rodrik 1999). In contrast to the approach taken in the trade and growth literature, Sachs and Warner (1995, 2001) do not offer a firm criterion for resource 'abundance' or 'dependence'; however, their conclusions beg the question of how much resource wealth is 'too much'.

Finally, it is of interest to note that, in the empirical growth literature, there are very few instances of regression models *not* focused specifically on the resource curse hypothesis in which resource abundance emerges as a significant factor affecting long-run growth rates (for a survey, see Li and Coxhead 2004).

A reasonable conclusion to draw from this review is that, while there are strong theoretical grounds to suspect a broad correspondence between natural resource wealth and low rates of economic growth, the causal link, if it exists at all, is neither direct nor simple. Rather, the negative association requires one or more distortions, market failures or perhaps institutional failures. It may be that each resource-abundant country experiences its own resource wealth–growth relationship, based on unique institutional and economic characteristics, but that all such experiences lead to similar outcomes.[2]

How Southeast Asia averted the curse

All of the above symptoms of the 'curse' can be seen in some form in each resource-abundant Southeast Asian country. Paradoxically, however, the region's resource-rich economies have in fact grown very rapidly by world standards. Therefore, if the curse does apply to developing countries in general, the economies of this region have undergone (or are undergoing) some other development experience unique to them (and perhaps to a very few other economies, such as Botswana) that more than compensates for its effects. The most obvious explanation is the post-Plaza Accord boom in Japanese and East Asian foreign direct investment (FDI) in the region, a trend whose intensity kick-started labour-intensive industrialisation and ensured the inclusion of Thailand, Malaysia and Indonesia in the World Bank's group of eight East Asian 'miracle' economies, alongside the much richer Northeast Asian industrial economies and Singapore. Not only did these three economies grow very rapidly and in sustained fashion over more than a decade after 1986, they also underwent structural changes that dramatically reduced their relative reliance on natural resources. By the early 1990s, all of Southeast Asia's market economies exported far more manufactures by value than agricultural and natural resource products. For these economies, then, we may hypothesise that the rapid expansion of labour-intensive manufacturing employment in the mid to late 1980s, caused by heavy inflows of foreign investment, forestalled the onset of the resource curse by inducing rapid structural change.

For virtually all other resource-abundant developing economies, the 1980s were a 'lost decade' in which export price crashes, high and rising debt service costs and net capital outflows led to sustained low or negative rates of GDP growth. Southeast Asia's resource-rich economies, except the Philippines, experienced very mild recessions or slowdowns in 1985, followed by a decade of historically rapid expansion. Since the late 1990s, however, the region has seen a significant change in international conditions, with declining FDI inflows, increased demand for natural resource exports and intensified competition in global markets for labour-intensive manufactures – all three trends driven in large part by the emergence of China in the global economy. Given these trends, could Southeast Asia still succumb to the resource curse?

Barring wars and catastrophic policy reversals, a *necessary* condition for the emergence of China as a threat to the continued growth of the semi-industrialised, resource-abundant Southeast Asian economies is that their comparative advantage shifts dramatically back in the direction of natural resources. Such a shift clearly is not a *sufficient* condition, however; it will hurt growth only if it interacts with market failures or other distortions. Distortions make it possible, in principle, for specialisation in resource exports to lead to overrapid depletion of resource stocks, as well as slower growth of manufacturing output and jobs, reduced human capital investments, and the loss of productivity spillovers associated with manufacturing industry growth. In the next two sections I first explore the shift in comparative advantage, then examine some ways in which such a shift might interact with known market and institutional failures to produce a 'new' resource curse outcome.

SOUTHEAST ASIAN RESPONSES TO CHINESE GROWTH

Intra-East Asia[3] trade volumes have expanded enormously since the 1980s. At 15 per cent per year in 1985–2001, trade growth within East Asia far exceeded that for any other region. (For the North American Free Trade Area, the corresponding figure is 9.1 per cent.) East Asia–China trade is an increasingly important component of intraregional trade, rising from less than 1 per cent of the total in 1975 to 7 per cent in 2001 (Ng and Yeats 2003). China, with 43 per cent of regional GDP in 2001, accounts for 30 per cent of the region's exports (Ng and Yeats 2003: 9). China's growth, sustained at a rate of about 7 per cent per year for many years, is a major driver of increased regional trade. At the same time, the Chinese economy has also become far more trade-dependent since the late 1980s, a shift caused by many factors, not least of which are the country's accession to the WTO and the liberalisation of trade with regional neighbours, including ASEAN countries.

In the 1990s, ASEAN's share in China's total imports rose from 6 per cent to 9 per cent, a 390 per cent increase in value terms (Ianchovichina and Walmsley 2003: 4). ASEAN economies saw big increases in the share of their regional trade going to China, and the value of their exports to China rose much faster than total exports (Table 5.1, and see Ng and Yeats 2003: Table 6.1). This pattern of growth is expected to continue for at least the next decade, albeit not necessarily at the same rate.

Competition in global markets

In manufacturing industries, China's expansion is expected to have mixed effects. Implementation of the Agreement on Textiles and Clothing (ATC) – which establishes the process for an orderly dismantling of the MFA – will be highly influential. By eliminating the MFA's national quotas on apparel exports to the United States and the European Union, the ATC will remove a serious distortion that has worked against the lowest-cost producers, notably China.[4]

At the same time, ASEAN–China competition has intensified in third-country markets – mainly, but by no means exclusively, in labour-intensive, low-tech products. China's WTO accession, which increased its market access and reduced the cost of imported intermediates for its manufacturers, undermined the international competitiveness of key Southeast Asian manufacturing sectors (Ianchovichina and Walmsley 2003; Ianchovichina and Martin 2004). Furthermore, if new FDI flows match the shifting pattern of production, then China's lead in these sectors can be expected to widen further in the longer run.

How important are these trends? The answer depends, in part, on the extent to which China and Southeast Asian countries compete or complement one another in trade. One measure of this, the extent of overlap in export product categories, reveals a high overlap between China's exports and those of Indonesia, and rising overlap between China and exports from other Southeast Asian economies except the Philippines (Table 5.2). The degree of overlap has been increasing as the Chinese manufacturing sector expands (increasing the number of product lines exported) and becomes more capital-intensive (Kwan 2002; Weiss and Gao 2002).[5]

Measures of revealed comparative advantage (RCA) (Balassa 1965) provide more detailed indications of multilateral trade intensity. The RCA ratio measures the intensity of a country's exports of a good relative to the intensity of world exports of that good.[6] By convention, values of RCA_{jkt} of more than 1 are inferred to mean that country j has comparative advantage in production of good k in year t and values of less than 1 are inferred to mean a comparative disadvantage.[7] Table 5.3 reports RCA measures computed from the most recent data for major product categories in China and several Southeast Asian countries; values greater than 1 are shown in bold. China shows low RCA values for

Table 5.1   Southeast Asian countries' trade with China (per cent) and ranking of China among their trading partners, 1990–2003

Country	1990	1995	2000	2001	2002	2003
Malaysia						
Exports	2.10	2.56	3.09	4.33	5.63	10.78
Rank	*10*	*9*	*9*	*6*	*5*	*3*
Imports	1.92	2.20	3.94	5.19	7.74	6.82
Rank	*7*	*7*	*5*	*4*	*4*	*4*
Indonesia						
Exports	3.25	3.83	4.46	3.91	5.08	7.43
Rank	*5*	*5*	*5*	*5*	*5*	*4*
Imports	2.97	3.68	6.03	5.95	7.76	11.72
Rank	*7*	*8*	*5*	*5*	*4*	*2*
Philippines						
Exports	0.75	1.20	1.74	2.47	3.85	12.00
Rank	*10*	*10*	*10*	*10*	*8*	*3*
Imports	1.40	2.34	2.28	2.95	3.54	6.99
Rank	*9*	*8*	*9*	*7*	*7*	*4*
Thailand						
Exports	1.16	2.87	4.07	4.40	5.16	7.09
Rank	*10*	*6*	*6*	*5*	*5*	*4*
Imports	3.31	2.84	5.45	5.98	7.61	8.00
Rank	*6*	*7*	*4*	*3*	*3*	*3*
Vietnam						
Exports	0.31	6.44	10.61	9.44	6.45	6.40
Rank	*6*	*3*	*2*	*2*	*4*	*4*
Imports	0.16	3.94	8.96	9.91	11.82	14.06
Rank	*8*	*6*	*4*	*4*	*2*	*1*

Source: Asian Development Bank, *Key Indicators*, <http://www.adb.org/Statistics/>, accessed August 2004.

*Table 5.2   Southeast Asian competition with China in the US market,
1990–2000 (per cent overlap in export product categories)*[a]

Country	1990	1995	2000
Singapore	14.8	19.2	35.8
Indonesia	85.3	85.5	82.8
Malaysia	37.1	38.9	48.7
Philippines	46.3	47.8	46.1
Thailand	42.2	56.3	65.4

a   Aggregated using value weights.

Source: Kwan (2002: Table 2).

most agricultural sectors (product categories 00–23; 41–43) and natural resource sectors (24–32), and very high values for all kinds of assembly (71–81, notably electrical equipment, electronics, computers and components, and office equipment), for furniture (82) and for garments, footwear and accessories (83–85). In Southeast Asia, Indonesia, Thailand and Vietnam have the greatest range of high RCA values in agriculture and resource sectors. These economies, like China, show evidence of comparative advantage in labour-intensive industries such as furniture, garments, footwear, bags and accessories, electrical appliances and electronics.

Trends in bilateral comparative advantage

The RCA measures compare country export intensities using global data. Rising bilateral trade shares between ASEAN countries and China motivate a comparison of bilateral comparative advantage, as a means of evaluating the likely effects of China's growth on Southeast Asian trade patterns. These comparisons can be made by subtracting the China RCA value from that of each Southeast Asian country, and are shown for Indonesia and Vietnam in Figures 5.1 and 5.2.[8] The bilateral data display a very clear pattern in which these countries have a relative advantage in agricultural and natural resource industries as well as in a few processing sectors that involve the intensive use of natural resource or agricultural inputs; China dominates in heavy industry and most light assembly operations. The extent to which Southeast Asian economies, particularly Indonesia and Vietnam, are, or are becoming, complementary with China is revealed also by correlation coefficients of the RCA measures (Table 5.4). Negative values of this measure indicate a tendency for countries to specialise in exports of products other than those in which China is specialised; positive numbers indicate greater overlap. The trends in the table suggest that Malaysia is complementary with China and that Thailand's overlap is diminishing; Vietnam has high overlap and Indonesia shows a trend from weak complementarity to more overlap.

On current trade trends, Southeast Asian countries can expect to become major suppliers of natural resource products to the Chinese market, importing a wide range of manufactures in return; with continued growth of the China market, these patterns will become increasingly dominant in overall Southeast Asian trade.

The drivers of shifts in the structure of Southeast Asian production and trade are potentially large and operate both directly and indirectly. Direct effects on exporters of many manufactures will be measured through negative terms-of-trade shifts, though these will be offset in some industries by cheaper imported intermediates. Indirect effects will be felt through adjustments in the markets for labour and other factors, and possibly also through shifts in the sectoral composition and national distribution of FDI flows. A very large fraction of the Southeast Asian manufacturing labour force is employed in garments, textiles and other labour-intensive, low-tech industries identified as being under threat from Chinese competition. In Indonesia, textile and apparel production accounts for 20 per cent of non-oil exports by value and for 25 per cent of employment in large and medium-sized manufacturing industries (James, Ray and Minor 2003). In Vietnam, garments are 14 per cent of exports by value and the industry employs more than 24 per cent of a manufacturing labour force of 4.6 million workers; in Cambodia, garments account for 80 per cent of exports and 80 per cent of the manufacturing labour force (UNIDO 2004).[9] Loss of these sources of export revenue, and the lower wages (or reduced wage growth) that this will cause, will tend to reduce labour costs in natural resource industries, contributing indirectly to increased profitability over and above the direct effects from growth in Chinese demand for natural resource products.[10] Another indirect driver will be FDI flows; the evidence is ambiguous, but one likely trend is for a reduction in FDI in Southeast Asian industries where competition with China is intense, perhaps offset somewhat by increased FDI in medium-tech or high-tech sectors (Ng and Yeats 2003; Krumm and Kharas 2003).

Another important area in which China's growth, trade expansion and huge FDI inflows all combine to affect Southeast Asian trade is forest products. China's imports of forest products – logs, lumber, pulp and paper, plywood, veneer, woodchips and other products – have more than doubled since 1997 (Sun, Katsigris and White 2004). Flows increased when China imposed a ban on domestic logging in 2001. Much of the new demand has been met by increased imports from Russia, but Indonesia, Malaysia and Thailand continue to supply a large proportion of total imports. Moreover, the rapid industrialisa-

Table 5.3   RCA values for China and Southeast Asia (2000–03 average)

Name	Code[a]	CHN	IDN	MYS	PHL[b]	THA	VNM[c]
Live animals	00	0.78	0.39	0.72	0.06	0.23	0.18
Meat & meat preparations	01	0.58	0.06	0.04	0.01	**1.77**	0.29
Dairy products & bird eggs	02	0.06	0.27	0.23	0.19	0.27	**1.85**
Fish, crustaceans, etc.	03	**1.83**	**3.47**	0.51	**1.44**	**7.59**	**13.60**
Cereals & cereal preparations	04	0.70	0.16	0.20	0.12	**3.12**	**5.54**
Vegetables & fruit	05	**1.14**	0.46	0.20	**1.62**	**1.67**	**2.78**
Sugars, sugar preparations	06	0.43	0.43	0.44	0.75	**4.78**	**1.08**
Coffee, tea, cocoa, spices	07	0.46	**4.28**	0.84	0.09	0.26	**10.41**
Animal feed	08	0.34	0.49	0.36	0.27	**1.29**	0.06
Miscellaneous edible products	09	0.68	0.83	0.98	0.52	**1.64**	**1.72**
Beverages	11	0.27	0.04	0.23	0.08	0.26	0.10
Tobacco & tobacco manufactures	12	0.40	**1.26**	0.70	0.32	0.32	0.44
Hides, skins & fur skins, raw	21	0.03	0.03	0.05	0.01	0.03	0.45
Oil-seeds & oleaginous fruits	22	0.59	0.09	0.04	0.02	0.05	**1.32**
Crude rubber	23	0.14	**10.92**	**4.41**	0.29	**15.08**	**7.12**
Cork & wood	24	0.28	**1.25**	**2.58**	0.13	0.47	0.54
Pulp & waste paper	25	0.01	**3.47**	0.00	0.28	0.55	0.00
Textile fibres (not yarn or fabric)	26	0.95	0.78	0.27	0.17	**1.23**	0.15
Crude fertilisers & minerals nes	27	**1.66**	0.78	0.19	0.22	**1.81**	0.35
Metalliferous ores & metal scrap	28	0.07	**4.25**	0.11	0.84	0.23	0.37
Crude animal & vegetable materials nes	29	**1.34**	0.58	0.16	0.82	0.69	**1.49**
Coal, coke and briquettes	32	**2.84**	**7.26**	0.00	0.00	0.00	**1.93**
Petroleum & petroleum products	33	0.24	**1.98**	0.96	0.15	0.42	**3.42**
Gas, natural and manufactured	34	0.06	**8.68**	**3.14**	0.09	0.26	0.00
Electric current	35	**1.17**	0.00	0.02	n.a.	n.a.	0.07
Animal oils and fats	41	0.09	0.08	0.02	0.02	0.07	0.07
Vegetable fats & oils, refined	42	0.11	**13.02**	**13.44**	**4.51**	0.42	**1.28**
Animal or vegetable fats & oils, processed	43	0.07	**3.38**	**15.22**	0.78	0.88	0.08
Organic chemicals	51	0.54	0.83	0.65	0.05	0.53	0.10
Inorganic chemicals	52	**1.62**	0.57	0.23	0.19	0.24	0.07
Dyeing & tanning materials	53	0.73	0.34	0.38	0.08	0.29	0.07
Medicinal & pharmaceutical products	54	0.30	0.07	0.04	0.03	0.08	0.02
Essential oils & resinoids	55	0.25	0.72	0.36	0.15	0.71	0.45
Fertilisers (other than group 272)	56	0.56	**1.10**	0.62	0.52	0.12	0.13
Plastics in primary forms	57	0.17	0.62	0.70	0.07	**1.78**	0.04
Plastics in non-primary forms	58	0.27	0.57	0.49	0.20	0.58	0.17
Chemical materials & products nes	59	0.53	0.30	0.57	0.13	0.61	0.26
Leather, leather manufactures nes	61	**1.34**	0.44	0.11	0.04	**1.73**	0.33
Rubber manufactures nes	62	0.74	0.96	0.52	0.27	**1.54**	0.31

Table 5.3 (continued)

Name	Code[a]	CHN	IDN	MYS	PHL[b]	THA	VNM[c]
Cork & wood manufactures excluding furniture	63	**1.22**	**8.83**	**3.11**	0.81	**1.08**	**1.21**
Paper & paperboard	64	0.31	**2.10**	0.22	0.15	0.53	0.25
Textile yarn, fabrics & articles nes	65	**2.51**	**2.11**	0.45	0.31	**1.12**	0.92
Non-metallic mineral manufactures nes	66	0.91	0.63	0.36	0.26	**1.19**	0.60
Iron & steel	67	0.55	0.34	0.37	0.02	0.52	0.13
Non-ferrous metals	68	0.71	0.98	0.47	0.52	0.29	0.09
Manufactures of metals nes	69	**1.67**	0.41	0.44	0.19	0.76	0.26
Power-generating machinery	71	0.40	0.28	0.29	0.08	0.64	0.15
Machinery specialised for particular industries	72	0.31	0.10	0.27	0.18	0.18	0.19
Metalworking machinery	73	0.37	0.04	0.23	0.13	0.25	0.06
Industrial machinery & equipment nes	74	0.71	0.19	0.36	0.15	0.88	0.06
Office & data-processing machines	75	**2.00**	0.72	**3.52**	**3.72**	**2.19**	0.55
Telecom. apparatus & equipment	76	**1.98**	**1.19**	**2.57**	0.70	**1.23**	0.14
Electrical machinery & appliances nes	77	**1.05**	0.46	**2.76**	**5.12**	**1.60**	0.32
Road vehicles	78	0.26	0.10	0.05	0.22	0.45	0.09
Other transport equipment	79	0.30	0.07	0.12	0.13	0.19	0.04
Prefabricated buildings; sanitary, plumbing, heating & lighting fixtures & fittings nes	81	**2.45**	0.37	0.22	0.36	0.64	0.18
Furniture & parts thereof	82	**1.88**	**2.44**	**1.51**	0.93	**1.28**	**1.69**
Travel goods, handbags & similar	83	**5.12**	0.87	0.06	**2.48**	**2.00**	**4.33**
Articles of apparel & clothing	84	**4.12**	**2.28**	0.68	**2.15**	**1.61**	**3.88**
Footwear	85	**4.59**	**3.02**	0.13	0.24	**1.51**	**13.42**
Professional & scientific instruments	87	0.55	0.06	0.62	0.20	0.25	0.07
Photographic apparatus & watches	88	**1.25**	0.29	0.79	0.99	**1.05**	0.21
Misc. manufactured articles nes	89	**2.10**	0.55	0.58	0.42	**1.06**	0.54
Special transactions & commodities	93	0.09	0.01	0.42	0.01	**1.09**	0.83
Coin (other than gold coin)	96	0.78	0.01	0.07	0.12	0.27	0.01
Gold, non-monetary	97	0.00	**1.67**	0.36	0.80	0.51	0.06

RCA = revealed comparative advantage; CHN = China; IDN = Indonesia; MYS = Malaysia; PHL = Philippines; THA = Thailand; VNM = Vietnam; nes = not elsewhere specified; n.a. = not available; bold type indicates RCA value > 1.

a   Standard International Trade Classification (SITC) 3 product categories.

b   2000–02 only.

c   2000–01 only.

Source: United Nations Comtrade data.

Figure 5.1   RCA differences, Indonesia minus China[a]

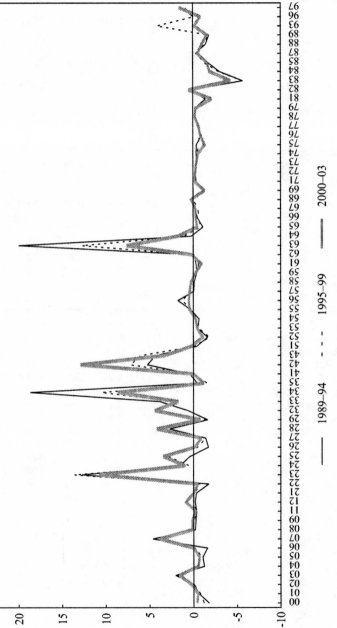

——— 1989–94   - - - 1995–99   ——— 2000–03

a   See Table 5.3 for an explanation of the commodity codes shown on the horizontal axis.

Source: Author's computations from Comtrade data.

Figure 5.2 RCA differences, Vietnam minus China[a]

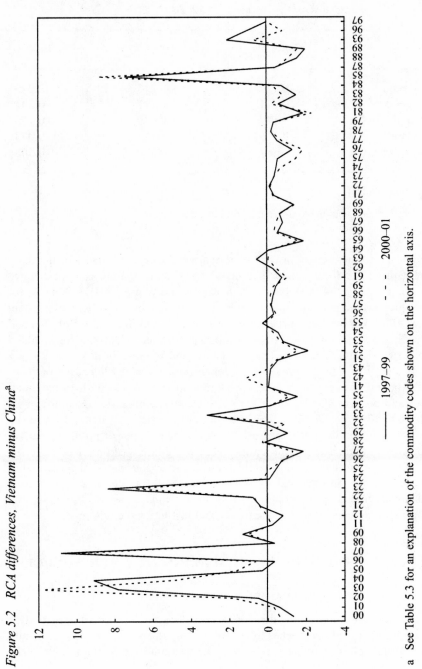

a   See Table 5.3 for an explanation of the commodity codes shown on the horizontal axis.

Source: Author's computations from Comtrade data.

*Table 5.4   Correlation coefficients of RCA measures between China and
Southeast Asian economies, 1989–2003*

Country	1989–94	1995–99	2000–03
Indonesia	–0.036	–0.015	0.010
Malaysia	–0.141	–0.127	–0.144
Philippines	0.147	0.049	0.173
Thailand	0.311	0.125	0.078
Vietnam	n.a.	0.379	0.408

n.a. = not available.

Source: Author's computations from Comtrade data.

tion of the Chinese economy has seen relative declines in imports of the more highly processed forest products in favour of logs and lumber, as domestic processing capacity has expanded (Sun, Katsigris and White 2004). Indonesia, for example, has increased its forest product exports to China by about 60 per cent since 1997, but the largest increases by far have been in the form of logs and lumber; plywood, once the major export, has declined. Malaysia and Thailand have had similar experiences (Sun, Katsigris and White 2004).

In summary, China's growth and globalisation are likely to cause Southeast Asian countries to experience negative terms-of-trade shocks for their manufactures and positive shocks for primary products. The countries most obviously affected will be Indonesia and Vietnam. Domestic adjustment to China's growth, if it occurs, will increase Southeast Asia's output of products that are intensive in their use of *both* natural resources and low-skilled labour. In the short to medium run, this shift could stimulate aggregate economic growth; but the longer-run growth and welfare effects will be contingent on more unknowns, including the continued growth of China, other world market and policy trends,[11] and the domestic policy and institutional environment.

DECENTRALISATION AND THE MANAGEMENT OF RESOURCES

Local government mandates and motives

Conventional wisdom in the development community has turned decisively in favour of devolved approaches to economic growth and even to environmental and natural resource management (see, for example, World Bank 2000). The devolution trend has been welcomed in principle by many development specialists, especially as it coincides with and is reinforced by a general trend towards democratisation at the subnational level.

There are, however, clear problems with decentralised management. Paramount among these is that local administrations are far more motivated to raise revenues and create jobs than to protect the environment, especially when the benefits to the environment may be exported beyond local boundaries and planning horizons to communities downstream, elsewhere or as yet unborn.

Several other problems are also frequently observed. Incomplete democratisation of local governments is a critical constraint on the effectiveness of local management: where local administrations are not accountable to their constituents, devolving authority may merely result in accelerated degradation. Capacity constraints bedevil the efforts of even the best and most sincere local administrations; most are simply too small to cover the fixed costs of specialists in resource management, legislative design, enforcement and other critical areas. Moreover, the question of optimal policy 'control areas' for local administrations whose resource management activities affect production of transboundary externalities (downstream, nationally and, in the cases of biodiversity and atmospheric carbon releases, globally) has yet to be seriously confronted (Rola and Coxhead 2005). The cards are thus stacked against effective local management of natural resources.

Lastly, ill-conceived administrative rules on decentralisation undermine capacity for policy or action at all levels of government. In most countries, decentralisation includes a shift of personnel away from central government offices, and the power of local branches of central government environmental agencies is frequently subordinated to that of local jurisdictions. If local administrations are weak, however, or compromised by conflicting goals and/or corrupt practices, the result of this shift is that control is exerted neither at the centre nor at the local level.

Legal and institutional frameworks

The period of decentralisation has seen central governments commit to giving local governments and communities more power over environmental and natural resource management. However, the legal basis for such actions is only weakly established, and the practical issues of implementation are far from being worked out (Rola and Coxhead 2005).

Indonesia, unfortunately, exemplifies the range of ways in which decentralisation can undermine effective resource management. Under the New Order regime, forest management policies and processes were codified, for the most part, in the 1967 Basic Forestry Law (Law 5/1967). It established a legal and institutional framework for state-supported commercial forest exploitation. The

central government was paramount; in particular, tensions between commer-
cial/industrial rights and rights of communities over forest use were resolved by
'categorically excluding' the latter and denying legitimacy to *adat* (traditional)
law (Colfer and Resosudarmo 2002: 215). Laws passed in 1999 amended the
Basic Forestry Law; laws passed in 2000 devolved substantive powers to local
government. However, these initiatives, which marked the country's first genuine attempt at decentralised forest management, are unclear on state versus
local powers and responsibilities. They were, moreover, enacted in a transitional moment during which regional and village elites, freed from the strictures
of centralised New Order governance, began themselves to initiate a de facto
decentralisation of local development policy. Colfer and Resosudarmo (2002:
24) note that, lacking either a strong (though arbitrary) central state or a clear
set of rules for decentralised forest management:

> policy implementation has depended to a great degree on personalities and place.
> The lack of certainty in the law, combined with the lack of a legal structure linking
> the forest resource to its users, has created a free-for-all in which forest management
> has become the responsibility of no-one.

Virtually the only certainty is that Indonesian timber removal rates, at about 80
million cubic metres per year, exceed even Jakarta's own 'sustainability criterion' by a factor of more than three (Colfer and Resosudarmo 2002: 216).

Fiscal policies

Other design faults in Southeast Asian decentralisations have helped to create
conditions under which local governments are likely to tolerate high rates of
resource depletion. In general, local governments have very limited capacity for
revenue raising through taxation, charges or user fees. In Indonesia, the general
purpose equalisation transfer (DAU) to subnational governments applies a formula for 'fiscal capacity' that counts only a fraction of natural resource revenues. There is, in other words, a reduced fiscal penalty for resource-rich
subnational administrations that choose to increase resource extraction rates.
Lewis (2001: 333) notes that:

> [t]his is a significant windfall gain for those local governments that receive large
> amounts of shared revenues from natural resources.

Brodjonegoro and Martinez-Vazquez (2002) also discuss this point. Under Law
25/1999 on fiscal decentralisation, Indonesia's regions retain 15 per cent of oil
revenues, 30 per cent of gas revenues and 80 per cent of revenues from other
forms of natural resources (Hill 2002: 26).

National government expenditures on the environment in Indonesia are low
by regional standards. During the crisis of 1997–98, they were shown to be

especially vulnerable to cuts, falling relative to both GDP and the national budget (Vincent et al. 2002). If these data are indicative of the central government's commitment to environmental protection, local administrations bent on raising revenues through environmentally damaging (or resource-depleting) means need not worry unduly that Jakarta will call them to task.[12]

Vietnam's recent experience is similar. In 2003 its major exports by value were dominated by textiles and garments (18 per cent), but all the other major categories were resource products: marine products (11 per cent) and rice, coffee, wood products and rubber (11 per cent). China is a key trading partner (Table 5.1). Decentralisation in Vietnam is stimulating a race for resources similar to that in Indonesia, with inadequate legal sanctions for violators of laws on land, forest and water use. As in Indonesia, an increase in Vietnam's comparative advantage in natural resource products relative to its enormous neighbour and trading partner will lead to increased demand for land, forest conversion and related resource-depleting trends. In this setting, local administrations – even those with significant pro-environment constituencies – will be hard-pressed to enforce limitations on resource depletion or pollution.[13]

Localisation, globalisation and the resource curse

The shifts in the Southeast Asian economic structure caused by China's expansion and increasing global integration are potentially huge, and seem systematically to involve expansion of natural resource-intensive industries and contraction of many labour-intensive assembly sectors. As was pointed out earlier, however, these changes can only *reduce* growth or economic welfare in the way predicted by the resource curse hypothesis if they encounter distortions that inhibit an optimal policy response. In Southeast Asia, there is a high probability that such a distortion will be encountered in the form of incomplete controls over exploitation of natural resource stocks. Moreover, recent steps towards decentralisation appear greatly to have reduced the probability that resource stocks will be managed in a socially optimal manner in the future. With resource management powers poorly defined and imperfectly or corruptly exercised, the economies of the region are coming to resemble ever more closely the hypothetical economy in Brander and Taylor (1997), in which an economy having comparative advantage in an open-access natural resource reduces its own welfare by entering into trade. In the absence of effective controls on resource depletion, and with no guarantee of future control over resource rents, such an economy experiences a race by all actors to liquidate natural resource wealth in the short term; in the longer term, therefore, it grows more slowly or not at all. China's expansion could well fuel such a sequence of events in Southeast Asia. If it does, the real problem will lie not in China's voracious import demand, but in the failings of Southeast Asian domestic policies and institutions.

CONCLUSIONS

Southeast Asian countries' past experience contradicts the resource curse hypothesis. But will continuing globalisation render the region's most resource-abundant economies vulnerable to a new variant? In particular, will China's growth deliver slower growth to the economies that escaped the crisis of the 1980s?

The trade and investment effects of China's expansion are predicted to have slightly negative overall effects on the region, moderating the generally positive predicted effects of global trade liberalisation and growth. Countries like Vietnam and Indonesia, whose industry sectors are less diversified, will suffer relatively more than those like Malaysia, especially given the latter's strength in high-tech sectors. The all-important apparel, footwear and related industries are especially vulnerable, and their decline may have economy-wide consequences through labour market adjustments. Growth in demand for natural resource products, accompanied by declining or stagnant real wages, will stimulate output in extractive industries such as forestry and mining, in rubber, palm oil and other industrial crops, in specialised horticultural crops (tropical fruit, coffee) and in fisheries. The growth of these sectors' output will reflect shifts in Southeast Asia's comparative advantage associated with the China effect.

The long-term consequences of this possible reorientation of Southeast Asian economies will be slight if there are legal and economic institutions to account for the true opportunity costs of the new mix of activities. However, to the extent that additional demand for timber, fisheries and agricultural land is unrestrained by legal safeguards or externality-correcting economic instruments, higher commodity demands and lower labour costs may spark an acceleration in resource-extracting activities, including the conversion of forests to industrial agriculture. In some areas of the region, these changes – being difficult, if not impossible, to reverse – could spell long-term reductions in earnings power and increased vulnerability to environmental disasters. I have argued in this chapter that the likelihood of such outcomes is higher where incomplete decentralisation has devolved powers over resource use without commensurate responsibilities.

Some caveats should of course be borne in mind. Continued rapid growth in the Chinese economy will eventually begin to drive wages up, a trend that will reduce the competitiveness of China's most labour-intensive sectors in global markets. Revaluation of the yuan, fixed for a decade relative to the US dollar, would have an analogous effect, with the most import-intensive Chinese industries and those mainly serving the domestic market gaining relative to others – both trends that will undercut labour-intensive, high valued-added industries such as garments and furniture. In Southeast Asia, niche market producers of specialised product lines will undoubtedly survive and thrive, even in an era of general decline of the industries to which they belong. Finally, economies with greater complementarity or diminishing overlap, such as Malaysia and Thailand, will stand to gain from freer trade with a rapidly growing Chinese economy, and the growth of specialised sectors such as computer components and other high-end electronics should offset some of the more harmful effects described in this chapter. (These prospects are not especially strong in the most resource-abundant economies, however, especially Indonesia and Vietnam.) Each of these possibilities merits careful attention and more detailed research.

Turning to policy implications, it remains to be seen whether the possible changes identified in this chapter will merit the term 'curse'. First, these changes will take place in a context of overall (predicted) gains from globalisation, from which the China effect could shave perhaps 25 per cent (Ianchovichina and Walmsley 2003; Strutt and Anderson 2000). Sustained economic growth, as is well known, simultaneously raises demands for the conservation of resources and creates the capacity to implement such demands – mechanisms captured in the idea of an environmental Kuznets curve. Second, the resource curse depends on market or institutional failures, including the effects of weak institutions of governance. Where such institutions are strong, property rights (including those of consumers of pollution) are generally better protected, thereby inhibiting race-to-the-bottom resource exploitation strategies. On this score, the uplands of Vietnam and the other Indo-Chinese countries, and the Outer Islands of Indonesia – areas in Asia where the restraining hand of central government is weakest – appear to be the most vulnerable. Other countries and regions display more heterogeneous experiences, some of which may be relevant to more vulnerable areas. How the interactions of decentralisation and global market trends affect natural resource management in these areas will be a critical factor determining the future of their forests, soils and other natural resource stocks and, ultimately, the welfare of their human populations.

NOTES

*   I am indebted to conference participants for helpful comments, and to Muqun Li and Aksarapak Wongcharoen for excellent research assistance.

1   These negative trends, it is stressed, are independent of endogenous terms-of-trade explanations for low growth in resource-abundant countries, as posited by the Prebisch–Singer hypothesis (Prebisch 1959).

2   This may be analogous to the biological concept of convergent evolution, in which (for example) birds and bees both have wings not because they have a common ancestor, but because they have adapted to their environment in similar ways. More formally, observation of a negative relationship between resource wealth and growth does not imply that all the data points are generated by a common under-

lying process. A test of this would involve searching for significant differences and dividing the data accordingly, as has been done for the empirical growth literature (Durlauf and Johnson 1995; Brock and Durlauf 2001).

3   Defined to include ASEAN.

4   To see this, it is necessary only to compare China's market share in the US and EU markets with that in the non-quota constrained Japanese market (James, Ray and Minor 2003).

5   Some of the increasing similarity in structure of manufacturing production is reflected not in competition in third markets but in intraregional, interindustry trade (Athukorala 2003), though these potential gains are countered by apparent diversion of FDI from ASEAN to China.

6   For country j, good k and time period t, the RCA is defined as

$$RCA_{jkt} = \frac{X_{kt}^{j} / X_{Kt}^{j}}{X_{kt}^{W} / X_{Kt}^{W}}$$

where K denotes the sum of all exports from country j or the world respectively.

7   Of course, these *ex post* measures are subject to distortion from several sources, most obviously trade policies. The calculations presented below ignore these sources of inaccuracy.

8   Similar computations for other countries (excluded here to save space) are available from the author on request.

9   Simulations using the Global Trade Analysis Project (GTAP) global trade model indicate that the cumulative effects of China's WTO accession over the 2001–10 period will be negative for real GDP growth in developing Southeast Asian countries, though with mixed sectoral and country stories. The two big winners are natural resource sectors and high-tech industries. The clear losers are apparel, textiles, and some industries of medium capital intensity such as automobiles; apparel exports are predicted to fall by 20–25 per cent, depending on the country (Ianchovichina and Walmsley 2003). Vietnam, heavily dependent on apparel and with few complementary manufacturing sectors, is predicted to experience the greatest loss, of about 0.4 per cent of GDP. For Indonesia, an economy-wide analysis of the effects of China's WTO accession predicted marginally slower growth of GDP as a whole, but faster growth in forestry, minerals and agriculture and in some secondary industries using these as inputs. This analysis also predicted a spectacularly large decline (23.4 per cent) in the textiles, clothing and leather sectors (Strutt and Anderson 2000).

10   The extent to which labour is mobile from urban manufacturing sector jobs to agriculture is of course an empirical question. Labour market adjustments during the recent Asian economic crisis provide helpful pointers: in Indonesia, an official labour market data survey in August 1998 found that among workers leaving jobs in manufacturing and construction the previous year, 39 per cent shifted to agriculture (Manning 2000: 126), contributing to a net gain of 4.7 million farm jobs, a 13.3 per cent year-on-year increase (Hugo 2000).

11   Within many US producer groups, growing concern about the expansion of China trade is motivating calls for additional restrictions. See, for example, 'Textile quotas to end soon', *New York Times*, 2 November 2004.

12   For excellent recent analyses of decentralisation and forest management in Indonesia, see Colfer and Resosudarmo (2002). Papers in this volume also provide insightful coverage of the complex issue of the distribution of resource management powers between central and local agencies in the Indonesian context.

13   According to the *New York Times* ('Rivers Run Black', 12 September 2004), this has been documented among local governments within China itself: '[T]he countryside, home to two-thirds of China's population, is increasingly becoming a dumping ground. Local officials, desperate to generate jobs and tax revenues, protect factories that have polluted for years. Refineries and smelters forced out of cities have moved to rural areas'. See also *Financial Times*, 27 July 2004.

6 UNFINISHED EDIFICE OR PANDORA'S BOX? DECENTRALISATION AND RESOURCE MANAGEMENT IN INDONESIA

James J. Fox, Dedi Supriadi Adhuri and Ida Aju Pradnja Resosudarmo

INTRODUCTION

The prologue to the first Law on Local Government (Law 22/1999)[1] resoundingly announces its intention to (1) underscore the principles of democracy, social participation, equity and justice and (2) give emphasis to local potentialities and diversity. The prologue to the companion Law on Fiscal Balancing between the Central Government and Regional Governments (Law 25/1999)[2] is equally forthright in its intention to (1) provide the opportunity to increase democracy and local capacities, (2) enhance social prosperity and create a civil society free of corruption, collusion and nepotism and (3) increase social participation, openness and responsibility. These laws by their stated objectives and identifiable phrasing stand out as key components of a period of intensive legislative reform initiated by President B.J. Habibie.

The effect of these critically important laws on decentralisation, and more particularly on the subsequent management of natural resources, cannot be disentangled from a whole range of related laws and decrees that have carried forward the process of reform since the fall of President Soeharto's New Order. Contrary to their proclaimed rhetoric, however, these laws have not led to the establishment of more effective means for the management of local resources, or to greater openness and responsibility in the use of such resources. In giving the widest possible authority to hundreds of regional governments, they have created a diversity of systems of management and mismanagement with no mechanism for supporting one or discouraging the other.

Law 22/1999, in several places, emphasises the importance of 'initiatives' (*prakarsa sendiri*) in shaping the vision and future actions of local authorities.

Such 'initiatives' have indeed occurred, producing a diversity of procedures for exploiting local resources to increase revenues, and safeguarding valuable sources of revenue from exploitation by others. Many of these initiatives have been based on exaggerated expectations of immediate gain or on apprehensions of a significant loss of revenue. Some have been carried out in a spirit of reform that has not always remained within the bounds of the law itself. This in turn has produced a wave of challenges to jurisdiction and authority that have been difficult to resolve.

This chapter is chiefly concerned with the effects on the management of natural resources of the various laws on decentralisation. The chapter looks at different sectors – fisheries, forestry and mining – in an effort to highlight some of the key consequences of the implementation of these laws in each of these sectors, particularly at the local level, while at the same time endeavouring to identify commonalities.

FISHERIES AND MARINE RESOURCES: RIGHTS TO TERRITORY

Article 3 of Law 22/1999 allocates to provinces authority over the sea for a distance of 12 nautical miles from the shoreline. Within this jurisdiction, Article 10 allocates to each local region – either district (*kabupaten*) or municipality (*kota*) – the authority 'to explore, exploit, conserve and manage' the resources of the sea for four nautical miles from its shoreline. Each of these local entities has responsibility for the administration of its area of sea and for laws and regulations that govern its use.[3] In effect, the law established new boundaries for all provinces and for all coastal districts and municipalities. At the time of the passage of this law and its implementation, none of these boundaries – some quite irregular given the exigencies of coastlines – were clearly demarcated, although they needed to be for the sake of enforcement of local jurisdictions.

The official elucidation (*penjelasan*) of Article 10 introduces a problematic qualification to the rights of local authorities over marine resources within their jurisdictions by exempting 'traditional fishing' from local exclusion zones (*khusus untuk penangkap ikan secara tradisional tidak dibatasi wilayah laut*). 'Traditional fishing' in the Indonesian context is not well defined. It is certainly not defined by historical or heritage considerations pertaining to a particular area; it is defined, rather, by the methods used in fishing, such as the use of boats of less than five gross tonnes (GT) or with motors of less than 15 horsepower. All coastal regions are therefore open to exploitation by simple methods, and small-scale fishers from any area can assert rights in any other area by claiming to use traditional methods. Instead of offering clarification, this qualification undermines the capacity of local fishers to sustain their particular marine resources. Thus without (as yet) clearly defined sea boundaries, and with rights within these boundaries ambiguously defined, the law has so far promoted dispute and conflict.

In 2000, President Abdurrahman Wahid issued a presidential decree (PP 177/2000) establishing a Ministry of Marine Affairs and Fisheries whereas formerly fisheries had formed part of the Ministry of Agriculture. The new ministry was given far wider functions than had previously been given to fisheries within the Ministry of Agriculture. Chief among these were the responsibility to guide and monitor the implementation of local autonomy within the 12 nautical mile provincial marine jurisdiction zones and to resolve disputes between provinces in claims over marine and fishery resources.[4] The new ministry was also given responsibility to establish national policy on the conservation, exploitation and management of marine resources and to authorise and regulate commercial activities beyond the 12 nautical mile provincial limits and in Indonesia's exclusive economic zone.

One of the first decrees of the new ministry, Decree 41/2000, set out guidelines for sustainable community-based small island management. This decree appears to give state recognition to customary law in the resource management of small islands. It also gives authority to either province or district to conduct planning, zoning and assessment of local resources, and impetus for the local population to engage in surveillance activities. In the following year, another decree (Decree 58/2001) called for the establishment of a surveillance system (*siswasmas*) empowering local institutions and populations to carry out active surveillance. At the time, both the autonomy legislation and the various ministerial decrees were at variance with the statutes of the prevailing Fisheries Law (Law 9/1985).[5]

Conflict within local community fisheries

Given the ambiguity over 'traditional' fishing rights, the entitlement of both provinces and districts to issue licences for exploitation of resources, and the call for local involvement in surveillance, it is no surprise that a host of conflicts have arisen over local marine resources.

Since 2000, such conflicts have occurred in North Sumatra, Bengkulu, Lampung, Pontianak, on both the north and south coasts of Java and in Madura. These conflicts were over either fishing ground violations – the intrusion of fishers from one area into the area of another fisher group – or the use of inappropriate (generally advanced) technology by one group of fishers in an area claimed by another group. All such cases involved recourse to the politics of exclusion based on claims to regional rights to resources.

Fishing ground violations have occurred at every level, from village and subdistrict to district and province. Thus, for example, in Pontianak eight mini-trawl vessels from the village of Sampit in the subdistrict of North Matan Hilir were burnt by fishers from the village of Sukabaru in the subdistrict of South Matan Hilir because their owners refused to pay a fine of Rp 3 million demanded of them for fishing in Sukabaru waters. In this case, the dispute was between villages in different subdistricts of the same district.

Disputes among Javanese fishers have been particularly prominent.[6] In one case, in November 2000, a boat belonging to fishers from Central Java was burnt by local Masalembo fishers in East Java. Earlier that year, Masalembo fishers had burnt six boats from Pati and Tegal in Central Java, taking their crews prisoner for fishing by lamplight in their fishing grounds. The reverse of this case – in which fishers from Brebes and Tegal in Central Java took Madurese fishers from East Java captive for fishing in their waters – can also be cited. Fishers from Pangandaran in West Java captured and held hostage eight fishers from Cilacap in Central Java over fishing ground violations and the use of a particular kind of net technology.[7]

An interesting local case that appears to have been resolved by agreement occurred in March 2002 when local fishers from the subdistrict of Ujung Pangakah in Gresik, East Java, who claimed 'traditional fishing rights', confiscated 16 mini-trawl boats owned by fishers from the subdistricts of Paceng in Gresik and Panciran in Lamongan, East Java. The conflict was settled by restricting the operation of mini-trawl vessels to waters of 30 fathoms or more in depth and by acknowledging local fishers' rights of surveillance, arrest and destruction of boats that violated this restriction.

Another case of interest involved a dispute between two groups of fishers from the subdistrict of Sungai Liat in Bangka Induk, one group using bag seine nets (*payang*) and the other using purse seine nets (*gaek*).[8] The dispute between the two groups was of long standing but reached its climax in 2004 when the catches by the purse seine fishers outstripped those of the bag seine fishers, thus dominating the market and seriously jeopardising the incomes of their rivals. On the verge of a violent confrontation, the leaders of the two groups met and drew up an accord that divided their fishing grounds into separate zones for each, as well as a shared zone and a zone closed to fishing for both. They defined sanctions for violations of these fishing zones and appointed arbiters to make judgements and apply the sanctions as required. In effect they established their own community-based management system, invoking the autonomy legislation, in particular Law 22/1999, as the legal basis for their actions.[9]

Yet another case of an attempt to establish local management of marine resources in line with directives on regional autonomy is that of West Lombok. Members of the Coral Reef Management and Rehabilitation Program (Coremap) were able to assist in the development of a set of regulations (*awig-awig*) to protect the reefs around three islands (Gili Air, Gili Meno and Gili Trawang) that form a marine natural tourism park. These *awig-awig* prohibit destructive fishing methods; levy fines and sanctions including the confiscation of fishing gear; establish seasonal closure for certain fishing activities; and even define a system of marine zoning that includes a conservation zone within these coastal waters.[10] All of these regulations were accepted as early as 2001, but when they were put into practice, fishers felt that their fishing grounds had become too confined to maintain their livelihoods. In voicing their objections they came into conflict with the management of the marine park. Although the Ministry of Marine Affairs and Fisheries might appear to be the appropriate authority to oversee this marine park, the park is actually under the jurisdiction of the Ministry of Forestry. As a result, the park with its reefs and fishing grounds continues to be a source of contention between the central government and the devolved regional management (Satria, Matsuda and Sano 2004).

The future of marine resources

The escalation of disputes over local fishing grounds is by no means simply the result of ambiguous jurisdiction and the reform impetus of the new autonomy legislation. The disputes reflect growing pressures on diminishing resources. For decades, the image of Indonesia's bountiful seas has been widely promulgated. Ever-rising fish capture and marine production statistics have been accompanied by assurances that these figures represent only a portion of a larger potential. Now new efforts at stock assessment have begun to take a more realistic and sombre view of the existing fishing potential.

Technical reports for the last three years (2001–03) from the Center for Research on Fish Capture of the Ministry of Marine Affairs and Fisheries have provided detailed assessments of stock capacities throughout Indonesian waters. These reports have revised earlier estimates of stocks. A key conclusion of one of these reports is that 65 per cent of all fish (including shrimp) resources in Indonesian waters have now been fully exploited (MMAF 2001a). The possibilities for overexploitation are evident in many regional fisheries.

The stock assessment report for 2001, prepared in cooperation with the Indonesian Institute of Sciences (LIPI) Research and Development Centre for Oceanography, lists nine regional fisheries where there is no opportunity for expansion but instead where there is a need to establish management strategies to set limits on fishing activities. The areas identified in this report include the Java Sea and the Malaka Strait, where resources are under the greatest strain and disputes have been particularly acute. These nine partially or fully exploited fisheries are shown in Table 6.1.

For all of the regional fisheries identified as overexploited, the Center for Research on Fish Capture has called for implementation of 'rational management' that would impose a limit on fishing intensity and levels of catch. This would require a limitation on fishing licences for foreign and domestic vessels as well as an effective means of controlling illegal fishing. While some steps

Table 6.1   Regional fisheries and species overexploitation

Regional fishery	Overexploited species
Java Sea	All fish resources
Malaka Strait	All fish resources
Makassar and Flores Sea	Demersal fish species and shrimp
South China Sea	Shrimp species
Banda Sea	Small demersal fish species and shrimp
Seram Sea and Tomini Bay	Shrimp species
Sulawesi Sea and Pacific Ocean	Large pelagic species and shrimp
Arafura Sea	Large pelagic species, demersal species and shrimp
Indian Ocean	Demersal species and shrimp

Source: MMAF (2001a).

have been taken to improve licensing management, the task of enforcement remains formidable.

Parliament passed a new Fisheries Law (Law 31/2004) in the final days of the Megawati presidency. With an emphasis on conservation and appropriate management, the new law gives the Minister of Marine Affairs and Fisheries the right to exercise authority in local ports through a *syahbandar* (harbour master) who is responsible for ensuring compliance with fishing regulations. The law also creates the possibility of more vigorous patrolling of Indonesian territorial waters but leaves this issue to be worked out through further implementing regulations. More significantly, it establishes regional 'fisheries' courts in Jakarta, Medan, Pontianak, Bitung and Tual and sets out court processes for dealing with fisheries violations, with potentially heavy fines for those found guilty. In the tug-of-war between local and national interests, it remains to be seen whether local courts will effectively enforce regulations to satisfy national objectives.

FORESTRY

The transfer of authority over the management of forest resources has been a contentious process driven for the most part by the existence of two laws, both with the same legal status but contradictory to each other. Local governments have endeavoured to make decisions based on the regional autonomy law (Law 22/1999), which transferred authority for forestry to their jurisdiction, whereas the central government has relied on the revised forestry law (Law 41/1999), which gives control of forestry to the Ministry of Forestry.

The Indonesian experience in the decentralisation of forestry has to date revolved around one important issue: the control of the resource among levels of governments. All three levels of governments – national, provincial and district – have claimed control of forestry resources. At issue are disputes over (1) the allocation of forest extraction rights or logging permits and (2) the redistribution of forest revenues from the centre to local governments.[11]

Allocation of logging permits

Beginning in 1999–2000, district governments issued hundreds of small-scale logging licences to local communities.[12] This was made possible by the enactment of a government regulation in January 1999 (PP 6/1999) and was further strengthened by a ministerial decree in May 1999 (SK Menhut 310/1999). The spirit of the distribution of these small-scale logging licences was ostensibly to empower local communities.

Once given the authority to issue small-scale logging licences, district governments were quick to recognise the opportunity to raise revenues. This spurred a proliferation of small-scale logging licences, particularly in East and West Kalimantan and in Papua. Basically these licences applied to areas of 100 hectares, had a short duration, usually of up to one year, and were granted to community groups.[13] Communities formed groups, usually cooperatives, that could legally operate as a business entity. These entities then applied to the district governments for logging permits. In practice, however, because of their limited capital, technical skills and marketing channels, communities had to find business partners to conduct logging activities on their behalf. These partners carried out the felling, transportation and marketing of logs as well as administrative activities. Communities obtained a fee that was dependent on their negotiating skills and position *vis-à-vis* their business partners.

Local governments would generally apply a single fee (*sumbangan pihak ketiga*, literally, a 'third party contribution') for these licences and a forestry levy (*retribusi*) based on the volume of timber extracted.[14] The national government also gained financially from these permits. Depending on the type of permit, these operations also required Forestry Royalty (PSDH) and Reforestation Fund (Dana Reboisasi or DR) payments to the central government, a portion of which was to be redistributed to the regions.

Although communities benefited directly from small-scale logging activities in terms of short-term cash, these opportunities also gave rise to conflicts among communities, mainly revolving around local rights to the piece of land associated with the logging permit. Conflicts also arose between members of the cooperatives and village heads over matters of management. Members were often suspicious that they would receive less than their entitlements, since only managers or village heads dealt with the business partners. Conflicts between licence holders and their business partners were also reported, where business partners were suspected of having insufficiently compensated the community. Another area of conflict was overlapping licence allocations, where a small-scale, locally licensed operator would log in an area claimed by a large-scale, centrally licensed logging company.

Small-scale logging operations also posed problems for forest management because the regulations for small-scale operators contained no provisions for replanting or systematic felling, unlike the regulations for centrally licensed logging companies.[15] Because of the short duration of these permits, there were no incentives for the permit holders or their business partners to follow measures supporting sustainable forest management.

In April 2000, realising the consequences of what was occurring, the Ministry of Forestry delayed the implementation of the critical decree (SK Menhut 310/1999) and then in November 2000 issued a decree that redirected the authority to issue logging permits to provinces and districts (SK Menhut 05.1/2000). However, in February 2002 the Ministry of Forestry issued yet another decree (SK Menhut 541/2002) cancelling its November decree. Faced with this series of decisions, most districts continued to issue licences.[16]

In June 2002, the implementing regulation (PP 34/2002) for Law 41/1999 on forestry was passed, superseding an earlier regulation (PP 6/1999). It affirmed that the authority to allocate logging licences rested with the central government. Based on this regulation, the Ministry of Forestry has the sole authority to issue permits for the utilisation of wood products on the recommendation of the lower levels of government. Many observers see this regulation as affirming a trend toward recentralisation in forestry.

Districts have responded differently to the new national policies. Some have apparently continued to grant licences even after the enactment of PP 34/2002. The district of Sintang in West Kalimantan is reported to have continued to issue small-scale licences in 2003. Between 2000 and 2003 the district head (*bupati*) issued 602 small-scale logging permits (IHPHH), although only about half are active (Universitas Tanjungpura and Yayasan Konservasi Borneo 2004). In 2001, the district of Bulungan in East Kalimantan granted 618 small-scale logging permits covering an area of 62,940 hectares; in 2002 the district extended or revised 222 permits covering 23,250 hectares; and in 2003 it issued 189 permits covering 18,234 hectares (Lembaga Pionir Bulungan 2003).

The centre has continued to pressure local governments to comply with national regulations, through ministerial letters or circulars, governor's letters or circulars, and investigations by district attorneys and the Inspectorate General of the Ministry of Forestry and the Ministry of Home Affairs. Pressure from the centre, either directly or through the provincial governments, in the end has forced some districts to adjust their policies.[17]

Redistribution of forest revenues

The other contentious issue in the implementation of decentralisation has been the redistribution of forest revenues to the regions as required by Law 25/1999 on fiscal balancing. The central government collects three major taxes and fees from the forestry sector: PSDH, a volume-based royalty on each cubic metre of timber harvested; DR, a volume-based fee on each cubic metre harvested, collected to support reforestation and forest rehabilitation activities; and forest concession licence fee (IHPH), a one-time area-based fee paid to obtain a logging licence. Of the three, PSDH and DR payments are the most significant; DR is roughly two times the amount of the PSDH. Forestry companies are required to make these payments directly to the central government's accounts in Jakarta.

Law 25/1999 provides the legal basis for fiscal decentralisation by specifying the major components of regional revenue sources and establishing a new system of central government fiscal transfers. It specifies four sources of funds for regional governments to finance decentralisation: (a) regionally generated revenue (PAD); (b) balancing funds (*dana perimbangan*); (c) regional borrowing (*pinjaman daerah*); and (d) other legal sources of income. The balancing funds comprise an appropriate share of natural resource revenue, personal income tax and property tax; general allocation funds (DAU); and specific allocation funds (DAK). One specific category of DAK relevant to forestry is the DAK–Reforestation Fund or DAK–DR, specifically used for forest and land rehabilitation (*rehabilitasi hutan dan lahan*). Of the balancing funds, the arrangement for sharing forestry revenues with forest-rich regions, and the redistribution of DAK–DR to regions, are of particular interest.

Table 6.2 indicates just how much forest-rich regions stand to benefit from their forest revenues compared to the New Order period. To provide some examples, in 2003 PSDH redistributed to the district of Bulungan was Rp 21 billion (about $2 million), while the district of West Kutai received Rp 35 billion (about $4 million).

From the point of view of local governments, however, the process of redistribution has been neither smooth nor transparent. Complaints centre on the timing of redistribution and the amount redistributed. Districts in general complain that their share of PSDH and DR is distributed well into the budget year. As PSDH and DR are recorded in the district budget, this complicates districts' budget estimates and budget realisation, and consequently affects the implementation of local development activities.

Table 6.2 Forestry revenue-sharing scheme (per cent of revenue collected)[a]

Source	Pre-autonomy			Post-autonomy			
	CG	PG	LG	CG	PG	RPLG	OLGP
Forest concession licence fee (IHPH)	30	70		20	16	64	
Forestry royalty (PSDH)	55	30	15	20	16	32	32
Reforestation fund (DR)	100			60		40	

a CG = central government; PG = provincial governments; LG = local governments; RPLG = resource-producing local governments; OLGP = local governments in a province other than RPLG.

Source: Resosudarmo (2004b).

The Ministry of Finance specifies PSDH and DR allocations based on the figures provided by the Ministry of Forestry. The latter first has to reconcile its data with the data from the regions. This reconciliation is one of the major reasons for the tardiness of the redistribution. The Ministry of Forestry has made an effort to improve its mechanisms for recording PSDH and DR receipts through a 15-digit computerised system, but only 40 per cent of payments currently follow the new system.[18]

The process of allocation of PSDH and DR has not been transparent. Although local governments do have data on the amount of PSDH and DR paid by companies operating in their jurisdictions, they have little say in how much is redistributed to them. As a result, some districts have instructed logging companies to pay their PSDH and DR obligations to district governments directly, or to retain them rather than submitting them to the central government.

The Ministry of Forestry has warned these local governments to comply with national regulations. More recently the ministry, through its Inspectorate General, has worked closely with the relevant authorities in the Ministry of Home Affairs, the district attorney's office and the regions to carry out investigations of 'troublesome' districts. As a result, payments have started to flow into central government accounts.

The DR is a particularly large issue, in terms of both the quantity of the allocation and its use. According to Law 25/1999 and PP 104/2000, the portion of the DR that is supposed to be redistributed to producing regions (*daerah peng-*

hasil) as part of the natural resource revenue-sharing scheme (DAK–DR) is 40 per cent.[19] Existing legislation, however, does not specify what is meant by a 'producing region'. This has given rise to different interpretations. Some districts interpret a 'producing region' to mean a 'producing district'. Law 22/ 1999, on the other hand, defines regions as provinces, districts and municipalities. In reality, in the allocation of DAK–DR, the 40 per cent is allocated to the producing province. The province then allocates this to all districts and municipalities within the province (that is, not only producing districts) according to criteria specified in the guidelines prepared by the Ministry of Forestry, Ministry of Finance, Ministry of Home Affairs and National Development Planning Agency (Bappenas). This means that the producing district may end up getting less than 40 per cent, a result that has caused unhappiness among some districts.

Reforestation activities and improved forest management under decentralisation

When carried out appropriately, reforestation could provide a means to partly address Indonesia's problem of forest degradation and deforestation. Unfortunately, reforestation activities, particularly those funded through the DAK–DR, have not been optimal. For instance, the appropriateness of the utilisation of the DAK–DR funds has not been unquestioned. Although legislation and central government guidelines specify that the use of the funds is restricted to forest and land rehabilitation activities, there have been reports of local governments using these funds for other purposes.

There have also been reports of irregularities associated with reforestation and rehabilitation activities, including planting done only on paper and the embezzlement of funds. Project leaders (*pimpinan proyek* or *pimpro*) responsible for the 2001 DAK–DR projects in West Kutai and Bulungan districts are both being investigated by the district attorney.

The future of the forests

The height of Indonesia's financial crisis in 1997–98 also saw the occurrence of one of the worst El Niño episodes of the century. The forest fires that devastated Indonesia at that time and the reforms that followed the fall of President Soeharto, including the passage of the new Forestry Law, should have opened the way for an improvement in forest management (Fox and Applegate 2000). Instead, by all estimates, the problems of deforestation in Indonesia have accelerated. Plantation clearing has continued, fires have become a regular annual occurrence, and illegal logging has outstripped the already excessive and unsustainable levels of legal logging. A booming Chinese economy has provided an insatiable demand from China for forest products. As a result, it is estimated that the rate of forest clearance has doubled from one million hectares to two million hectares per annum during the period of reform. Seen from this perspective, the push for local autonomy in the management of the forests has not contributed to better management and, in the face of a rapidly diminishing resource, the time available for improving the management of Indonesia's forests is limited. Again, as with fisheries, local and national interests are involved in a struggle over the control of diminishing resources.

MINING[20]

The mining sector presents another perspective on how the implementation of the autonomy laws has affected the utilisation of natural resources in Indonesia. Most of the same issues of ambiguity over jurisdiction and levels of authority in the marine or forestry sector apply with equal force to the mining sector. One difference affecting these sectors is found in Article 6 of Law 25/1999 on fiscal balancing. Whereas Article 6 states that 80 per cent of marine revenues are to be distributed equally (*secara merata*) among all districts and municipalities, in the case of mining Article 6 distributes 80 per cent of both land rent (*iuran tetap*) and royalties (*iuran eksplorasi/eksploitasi*) by a formula that allocates 16 per cent of the revenues to the province and 64 per cent to districts and municipalities. The article specifies, however, that half of the revenues intended for districts and municipalities should be allocated to producing areas (*daerah penghasil*) and the remaining half to other districts and municipalities in the same province. This differentiation among regional units – without clear guidelines on how to distinguish among them – has contributed to a growing welter of disputes over the flow of revenues from the centre. The Ministry of Finance determines the allocation of funds to each province; each province then becomes the distributor to its districts.[21] In this process, provinces can claim not to have received their rightful share from the central government, and districts within provinces can also claim that their appropriations were inappropriate, inadequate or nonexistent.

Under existing legislation, this long chain of revenue transfers extends to the district level where the elected head of the district is charged with the management of funds. Subdistricts and villages – the areas most immediately affected by mining operations – are the least likely to benefit from any lucrative resource extraction. The 'feeder chain' on revenues is too long and too large to permit substantial benefits to accrue to its lowest level. Hence local exasperation with the effects of mining often spills over into disruption and disputes.[22]

Mining operations, especially large ones, require major capital expenditures in their initial phase and are most disruptive when these operations are begun.

The initial need for labour often attracts large numbers of construction workers from outside the local area and this influx can swamp the presence of local residents. In addition, many sites attract illegal miners – both local and non-local – whose presence adds to overall disruption from mining.

Prior to 1999, the mining industry was regulated by individual contracts of work (CoWs) established directly by negotiation between the central government and the company. These arrangements rarely provided explicit contractual benefits to regions. Some companies did offer assistance to the local area affected by their operations, usually as a gesture of goodwill rather than as part of their contractual obligations. Localities certainly had reasons for claiming to be overlooked and ignored in the mining process.

The implementation of the autonomy laws gave impetus to each region to raise its own PAD revenues. In the pursuit of PAD in regions where mining operations are dominant, local governments have issued a variety of taxes and levies on mining companies. These financial imposts, in addition to those specified in individual CoWs, are regarded as an increasing and arbitrary burden on companies to make up for real or apparent financial imbalances among regions and between provinces and the central government. Law 11/1967 on Mining, which dates from the beginning of the New Order, was incompatible with new autonomy legislation. The mining companies responded by calling for one of two possible options: either that regional administrations become parties to the next generation of CoWs and that the companies' taxation regimes be negotiated within the terms of individual contracts or, alternatively, that CoWs remain as bilateral contracts but contain offset provisions for the taxes and royalties demanded by the regions. The response has been Law 22/2001 on mining, which has reaffirmed the right of the central government to award mining contracts and set the terms of these agreements, including the way in which profits, royalties and fees are determined and distributed.

Whereas, in the case of marine and forestry resources, exploitation appears to have increased in the course of decentralisation, the reverse seems to have been the case for the mining sector. According to PricewaterhouseCoopers, more than 150 exploration projects in Indonesia have been suspended or withdrawn or are currently inactive (Boulan-Smit 2002: 58). The present uncertainties have militated against long-term, large-scale investment.

CONCLUSIONS

It is possible to recognise various commonalities across resource sectors in the implementation of regional autonomy. Some of these have been noted more generally: (1) widely varying preparedness for the implementation of autonomy in the regions; (2) a general perception among regions of a reluctant commitment by the central government to autonomy; (3) complications in the bureaucratic restructuring necessary for decentralisation; (4) the lack of a clear allocation of functions within regional administrations, between local administrations, and between them and the central authorities; and (5) a rampant pursuit of local revenues at the expense of efficient and effective governance.[23] In the case of all the resource sectors, the most prominent contested issues have concerned (1) the extent of regional authority (*kewenangan*) and its precise jurisdiction and (2) the formulae and mechanisms to effect the transfer and allocation of central funding. The lack of clarity and of mutual agreement on these issues has prompted actions on the part of local populations and administrators to forge their own solutions – some of which have been challenged both regionally and nationally. The infusion of funds to the regions does not seem to have lessened misappropriation or mismanagement; it appears only to have 'decentralised' it.

Whereas there is general agreement that more time will be needed to improve local management procedures, there is a hope – across all sectors – that further legislation will lessen ambiguities and enhance efficiencies. At the moment, there is a great deal of draft legislation that could impact on resource management. This includes draft legislation on coastal management and small islands as well as further expected legislation for the mining and forestry sectors. At a higher level, a draft natural resources law was issued for public consultation in April 2004. This legislation is intended to replace the Basic Agrarian Law of 1960 and, in its place, provide an umbrella law for both land and natural resource management.

Of significance for the process of decentralisation is the new regional autonomy law, Law 32/2004, which was enacted just before Megawati stepped down. It is too early to say how effective this new law will be. More than any further new law, what is needed is a harmonisation of existing laws, regulations and decrees. At present, the plethora of legislation is itself a major obstacle to efficient regional management. Decentralisation is as yet an unfinished edifice. Whether, having granted wide-ranging autonomy, the government will now find it possible to re-regulate its operation remains to be seen.

Finally and perhaps most importantly, it is by no means certain that better laws with greater harmonisation of legislation along with improved demarcation of jurisdictions will result in more efficient management of Indonesia's natural resources. Decentralisation is essentially a political process involving competition among competing vested interests. At stake is the control of critical resources. The struggle to control these resources is, it would seem on present evidence, unlikely to promote exemplary management (Hadiz 2004).

NOTES

1   Undang-Undang 22/1999 tentang Pemerintah Daerah.

2   Undang-Undang 25/1999 tentang Perimbangan Keuangan antara Pemerintah Pusat dan Daerah.

3   Previously all coastal areas had been the responsibility of the central government. Based on a decree of the Ministry of Agriculture (607/1976), commercial fishing in coastal areas was supposed to be regulated according to the boundaries set in terms of four zones. In Zone I (shoreline to 3 nautical miles) vessels of 5 GT or 10 horse-power or less were permitted; in Zone II (3–7 nautical miles) vessels of 25 GT or 50 horsepower or less were permitted; in Zone III (7–12 nautical miles) vessels of 100 GT or 200 horsepower were permitted; in Zone IV (12–200 nautical miles) pair trawling was permitted. Without effective means of enforcement these regulations cannot be said to have been rigorously enforced. A subsequent government regula-tion (54/2002) delegated authority to provincial governors to issue fishing enterprise certificates (*ijin usaha perikanan*), licences for fish catching (*surat pengangkapan ikan*) and licences for fishing vessels (*surat ijin kapal pengangkapan ikan*) to nation-ally owned and operated vessels of 10–30 GT or 90 horsepower or less operating within their areas of jurisdiction; and gave heads of regional governments the author-ity to issue similar certificates and licences for vessels of 10 GT or 30 horsepower or less. These same heads were given authority to develop freshwater, brackish water and mariculture resources within their jurisdictions provided no foreign workers or capital were involved in these activities. All licensing of foreign vessels and enter-prises remained the prerogative of the Ministry of Agriculture.

4   One of the first tasks of the new ministry was to involve itself in the mapping of local boundaries between different regions, a task that continues to the present.

5   Undang-Undang Perikanan 9/1985.

6   It is probably the case that the disputes that occur among Javanese fishers are more likely to be reported in the national press than comparable disputes among fishers in isolated areas of the Outer Islands.

7   It is often the use of trawl technology that has provoked local anger. There have been substantial protests by fishers in North Sumatra against local government attempts to license commercial trawling operations. Similarly, in Bengkulu, fishers claiming traditional rights have resisted the intrusion of other fishers from North Sumatra and South Sulawesi using either trawl or purse seine nets, rejecting the offer by outside fishers of a share in the catch. For more discussion of these and other cases, see Adhuri (2003).

8   The bag seine fishers operated their nets in the early hours of morning, whereas the purse seine fishers used powerful lamps to operate their nets throughout the night.

9   The local protocol agreed to by the fishers of Sungai Liat has all the features of a community-based management system (Ruddle 1999; Jentoft 1989). Where the government is also involved, this is usually referred to as a 'collaborative' manage-ment system (Pomeroy and Berkes 1997). Such systems are seen as improvements on, or as corrections to, heavily centralised government management regimes. See Ballard and Platteau (1996) and Jentoft, McCay and Wilson (1998); for a discussion of the Indonesian situation, see Bailey and Zerner (1992).

10   The four *awig-awig* systems established for the coastal villages of West Lombok
     are: (1) Awig-Awig Gili Indah for Kecamatan Pemenang; (2) Awig-Awig Kelompok
     Nelayan Pantura for Kecamatan Kayangan; (3) Awig-Awig Sari Laut for Keca-
     matan Bayan; and (4) Awig-Awig Lembaga Masyarakat Nelayan Lombok Utara for
     the Kecamatan of Tanjung, Pemenang, Kayangan and Bayan (Satria, Matsuda and
     Sano 2004: 9–11).
11   One other relevant issue has been the tug-of-war among levels of governments with
     respect to the spatial planning of forest areas.
12   For discussion and documentation of this process, see for instance Barr et al. (2001)
     and Resosudarmo (2004a).
13   Although these licences carried different names, they had similar characteristics. In
     Kalimantan they were known as *ijin hak pemungutan hasil hutan* (IHPHH), *ijin
     pemungutan hasil hutan kayu* (IPHHK), *ijin pemungutan dan pemanfaatan kayu*
     (IPPK) and *ijin pemanfaatan kayu* (IPK), while in Papua they were labeled as *ijin
     hak pemungutan hasil hutan masyarakat adat* (IHPHHMA).
14   Some analysts, suggested, however, that there were significant informal costs asso-
     ciated with the entire process, from the issuance of permits (McCarthy 2001a;
     Alqadrie et al. 2001) to the transportation of logs.
15   Many of the centrally licensed logging companies were also known not to follow
     the replanting scheme required by the central government, but at least efforts were
     made to apply this requirement.
16   Their arguments were strengthened by the fact that the legal status of ministerial
     decrees is not explicitly defined within the Indonesian legal hierarchy, whereas the
     status of the district regulations, which provided the legal basis for the licensing of
     district logging permits, is explicitly defined. The order of Indonesia's legal hierar-
     chy is as follows: (1) the Constitution; (2) Decrees of the People's Consultative
     Assembly; (3) Laws; (4) Government Regulations in Lieu of Law; (5) Government
     Regulations; and (6) Regional Regulations.
17   For example, in February 2004 the *bupati* of Bulungan sent a letter to the East Kali-
     mantan governor confirming that all original, extended or revised permits had
     expired by December 2003. This letter was apparently written in response to pres-
     sure from higher levels of government, articulated through a letter from the East
     Kalimantan governor, to halt the issuance, revision or extension of small-scale log-
     ging permits issued by the district. The *bupati* of West Kutai acted sooner than his
     Bulungan counterpart in formally complying with the centre's policy. West Kutai
     halted the issuance of small-scale licences at the end of 2001. Whatever has for-
     mally been stated, however, in practice at least some small-scale logging activities
     continue. In the case of West Kutai, although all permits should have expired by
     December 2002, in March 2004 the district forestry office continued to provide
     administrative services, such as the required timber transportation documents, for
     logs associated with district-licensed logging activities.
18   Interview with a high-ranking Ministry of Forestry official, 1 July 2004.
19   The remainder is managed by the Ministry of Forestry. This is now mainly used to
     finance the National Movement of Forest and Land Rehabilitation (Gerakan
     Nasional Rehabilitasi Hutan dan Lahan). It is also ultimately distributed to regions,
     but mostly to non-producing regions.

20   'Mining' here refers to ores such as gold, nickel, copper and tin. Coal, oil and gas
      are covered by separate legislation.
21   Government Regulations 104, 105 and 106 issued by the Ministry of Finance in
      November 2000 provide the formulae and procedures for the sharing of revenue.
      Regulation 104 sets out the detailed formula for the sharing of revenue from the
      exploitation of natural resources but also the formula for calculating the amount of
      the DAU to each province and district. Regulation 105 sets out the procedures for
      regional governments to prepare their annual revenue and expenditure budgets
      (APBD). Regulation 106 establishes the guidelines for management and account-
      ability of decentralised activities.
22   It is particularly on matters of environmental management and protection that vil-
      lages and subdistricts are most significantly affected but unable to have their griev-
      ances heard: hence a frustration over real or apparent lack of financial benefits.
23   See Usman (2003) for a discussion of these and other aspects of the implementation
      of regional autonomy.

7   DOES INDONESIA HAVE THE BALANCE RIGHT IN NATURAL RESOURCE REVENUE-SHARING?

Armida S. Alisjahbana

INTRODUCTION

Decentralisation has changed the fiscal relationship between the centre and the regions, a relationship in which natural resource revenue-sharing plays a significant role. Resource-rich regions are now receiving a fairer share of the revenue generated by their natural resources, fulfilling a longstanding demand of those regions.

However, three years after decentralisation, there are concerns about how the present arrangements for sharing natural resource revenue are affecting interregional fiscal disparity. I approach this question by comparing fiscal disparity across regions before and after decentralisation, taking into account all sources of regional revenue, not just natural resource revenue. A related issue is how the present arrangements are affecting regional development in the resource-producing and non-producing regions. Although it is too early to reach firm conclusions at this stage, some differences in regional expenditure patterns are emerging between the two types of regions. A final issue is whether the current share of natural resource revenue given to the producing regions is fair and appropriate. I consider whether a greater share would be warranted given the existing fiscal relationship between the centre and the regions and the varying fiscal conditions of the regions.

In addressing the above issues, I try to shed light on whether Indonesia has the balance right in its approach to natural resource revenue-sharing, and identify the issues that warrant immediate attention. The discussion is preceded by an examination of how decentralisation has changed the role of natural resource revenue in central and regional budgets.

THE SITUATION BEFORE DECENTRALISATION

Natural resource revenue and the central budget

Natural resources, especially oil and gas, have played a crucial, albeit declining, fiscal role in Indonesia since the 1970s. Oil and gas revenue is derived from corporate income taxes (tax revenue) and revenue generated by profit-sharing agreements between the central government and the oil companies (non-tax revenue). In the central budget it is supplemented by income from other sources (non-oil/gas tax and non-tax revenue).

Oil revenue grew steeply during the oil booms of the 1970s to reach a peak of more than 70 per cent of central budget domestic revenue in the early 1980s (Figure 7.1). The importance of oil for the budget is determined by several factors: the level of oil production, growth in oil prices and growth in the non-oil sector. In the early 1980s central budget dependence on the oil sector began to decline as real oil prices fell and the non-oil sector started to grow. Non-oil tax revenue began to make an increasing contribution to the budget as a result of both the tax reform of 1983 and the restructuring of the Indonesian economy away from the oil sector.[1] The share of the oil sector in central budget revenue reached its lowest point of around 20 per cent in the mid-1990s. The impact of the economic crisis in combination with higher oil prices and a depreciated rupiah led to a temporary increase in the sector's share of domestic revenue to about 20–30 per cent for several years after the crisis.

The proceeds from oil were not earmarked for specific purposes, but rather accrued to the central budget as general revenue. It is fair to say, however, that central budget allocations during the mid-1970s through to the mid-1980s were financed largely from oil revenue when its share of domestic revenue was at its height.

Natural resource revenue and regional budgets

Before decentralisation was implemented in 2001, regional governments received most of their resources from the central government through central transfers. There were two types of central transfers: autonomous regional subsidies under the SDO scheme, comprising about 75 per cent of transfers; and special grants under the Presidential Instruction (Inpres) scheme, comprising about 25 per cent of transfers (Alisjahbana 1998). The SDO covered most of the regions' routine and recurrent expenditures.[2] Regional development spending was funded by Inpres block grants and Inpres specific purpose grants. Regions had some say in the use of the former, but the latter were tied to the financing of specific programs and projects in areas such as reforestation, education and health, and were therefore not subject to local control (Silver, Azis and Schroeder 2001).

*Figure 7.1   Oil and gas revenue as a share of domestic revenue,
1969/70–2003 (per cent)*

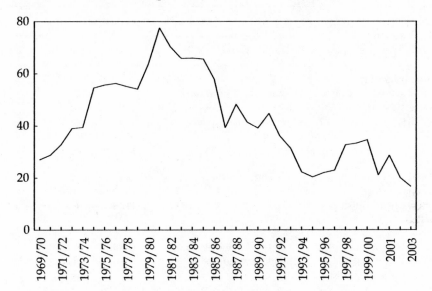

Source: Ministry of Finance, central government budget (APBN) (various years).

In addition to central transfers, the regions received funding from the central budget (APBN) through the deconcentrated offices of the central government. Again there were two types of funding: the DIK for routine expenditures and the DIP for development spending. DIK funding covered the routine expenditures of central government vertical units in the regions, that is, of *kanwil* at the provincial level and of *kandep* at the district level. DIP funding was used to pay for central government development projects located in the regions. Both types of funding were allocated directly by the centre through its vertical units in the regions and thus did not form part of the regional budget.

Shared revenue before decentralisation was limited mainly to non-tax revenue. Of all the taxes levied by the central government, only the land and building tax (PBB) was shared between the centre and the regions. The regions received 80 per cent of the revenue generated by this tax, with 64 per cent going to the districts and 16 per cent to the provinces. Other shared revenue consisted mainly of mining land rents, exploration and exploitation contributions (royalties), forest product royalties and forest concession rights (Table 7.1). About 64–70 per cent of these shared revenues went to the district/municipality (*kabupaten/kota*) level of government with the remainder going to provinces and the central government.

Table 7.1   *Natural resource revenue-sharing arrangements before and after decentralisation*

Revenue classification	Revenue-sharing mechanism	
	Old	New
Forestry sector		
Forest product royalty (Iuran Hasil Hutan or IHH)[a]	Generally, 45% is allocated to both provincial and local governments and 55% to the centre	• Centre = 20% • Province = 16% • Producing district = 32% • Other districts in the relevant province = 32%
Forest concession licence fee (Iuran Hak Pengusahaan Hutan or IHPH)[b]	• Centre = 30% • Local = 70%	• Centre = 20% • Province =16% • Producing district = 64%
Reforestation fund (Dana Reboisasi) (included in the DAK)	Unclear (included in non-budget revenue)	• Centre = 60% • Producing district = 40%
Mining sector		
Land rent (Iuran Tetap)[c]	Under PP 32/1969 Section 62: • Centre = 30% • Local = 70% Under PP 79/1992: • Centre = 20% • Province (Dati I) = 16% • District (Dati II) = 64%	• Centre = 20% • Province = 16% • Producing district = 64%
Exploration and exploitation contribution (Iuran Eksplorasi dan Iuran Eksploitasi) (royalty)[d]	Under PP 32/1969 Section 62: • Centre = 30% • Local = 70% Under PP 79/1992: • Centre = 20% • Province (Dati I) = 16% • District (Dati II) = 64%	• Centre = 20% • Province = 16% • Producing district = 32% • Other districts in the relevant province = 32%
Fisheries sector		
Fisheries operations tax (Pungutan Pengusahaan Perikanan or PPP)[e]	Unclear	• Centre = 20% • Local = 80% (divided evenly among all districts)

Table 7.1 (continued)

Revenue classification	Revenue-sharing mechanism	
	Old	New
Fisheries output tax (Pungutan Hasil Perikanan or PHP)[f]	Unclear	• Centre = 20% • Local = 80% (divided evenly among all districts)
Oil and natural gas sector		
State revenue from oil after tax has been deducted	Not shared	• Centre = 85% • Relevant province = 3% • Producing district = 6% • Other districts in the relevant province = 6%
State revenue from natural gas after tax has been deducted	Not shared	• Central = 70% • Relevant province = 6% • Producing district = 12% • Other districts in the relevant province = 12%

a   This is now called the Forest Royalty (PSDH). The PSDH rate ranges from Rp 5,000 to Rp 100,000 per cubic metre; from Rp 2,000 to Rp 700,000 per tonne; or from Rp 10,000 to Rp 35,000 per piece, depending on the product type and the region.

b   The IHPH rate ranges from Rp 2,600 to Rp 50,000 per acre for a set time (usually 20 years), depending on IHPH status, region and the group of forestry resources.

c   The rate is based on the stage of activity for a domestic investor (*kuasa pertambangan*) and the stage of activity for a foreign investor (*perusahaan kontrak karya*). The former are charged a fixed fee of Rp 50–1,500 per acre; the latter are charged a fixed fee of $0.025–3 per acre.

d   The royalty rate ranges from 2 to 7 per cent of gross contractor income depending on the kind and quality of the mined product.

e   The rate is based on ship size in deadweight tonnes (DWT). The PPP rates are $500 for ships of less than 50 DWT; $1,000 for ships of 50–100 DWT; and $250 per 50 DWT for ships weighing more than 100 DWT.

f   The rate is based on the type of fish and is levied only on exports. It currently stands at 1–2 per cent of exports by value.

Source: Bappenas, NRM and LPEM-FEUI (2000a).

Because of the limited availability of shared revenue and own-source revenue before decentralisation, their role as a source of regional budget revenue, and hence regional spending, was also limited. On average, shared revenue and own-source revenue comprised less than 10 per cent of regional budgets. As mentioned earlier, the important and substantial revenues from oil and gas resources accrued solely to the centre, and the regions received these back only in the form of earmarked transfers over which they had little control.[3]

The reliance of the regions on earmarked central transfers created discontent in resource-rich regions, which wanted a fairer share of the revenue generated by their own natural resources. Although the resource-rich provinces tended to have higher GDP per capita than other provinces, since the mid-1970s their gross regional domestic product (GRDP) per capita had been growing at a slower rate than national GDP per capita (Thee Kian Wie 2000).[4] Both issues – that is, earmarked central transfers and the relatively poor economic performance of resource-rich regions – contributed to tension between the centre and the regions. This would later explode in calls for greater autonomy and a fairer share of natural resource revenue for the regions after the fall of Soeharto. The end of the Soeharto regime and the beginning of the *reformasi* era was seen as an opportunity to address regional discontent, including that of the resource-rich regions, by allowing greater participation of the regions in managing their own economies.

THE SITUATION AFTER DECENTRALISATION

The enactment of Law 25/1999 on Fiscal Balancing between the Central Government and Regional Governments has fundamentally altered the fiscal relationship between the central government and the regions. The law greatly increased regional governments' share of government resources. These are now distributed through general block grants (DAU), shared revenue and a small number of specific purpose grants (DAK). Other sources of regional financing are own-source revenue and local borrowing.[5] Thus, in the new system central transfers to the regions remain the dominant means of financing, but earmarking is largely gone (World Bank 2003).[6]

The new system of intergovernmental fiscal relations relies heavily on DAU general allocation funds. Based on 2003 data for consolidated regional government revenue, central transfers comprise about 92 per cent of total regional revenue, the bulk of it (68 per cent) from the DAU. Own-source revenue comprises about 7 per cent and shared revenue another 23 per cent of total regional revenue. Clearly, the importance of shared revenue has increased greatly since decentralisation. The inclusion of personal income tax and oil and gas revenue as sources of shared revenue is one of the most significant changes. The inclusion of the latter in particular has gone a long way to appease the dissatisfaction of resource-rich regions over the unfair deal they felt they were receiving from the central government in relation to their natural resource revenue.

Table 7.1 describes the formulae for the allocation of natural resource revenue between the centre and the regions before and after decentralisation. Under the new system, 85 per cent of oil revenues and 70 per cent of gas revenues go to the central government with the remainder going to provinces and districts. The distribution of forestry and mining sector revenue has changed substantially: a higher percentage is now given to the producing district and other districts in the same province, with the central government and the province in which the producing district is located receiving only a minor share.

The formulae include some element of equalisation. In the case of oil and gas revenues, mining royalties and forest resource rents, although the producing district receives the largest share of the revenue generated, the province and other districts in the same province also receive a share. However, mining and forestry land rents are not shared with non-producing districts. Revenue from fisheries is also equalising: the central government takes 20 per cent with the remaining 80 per cent being distributed equally among all local governments.[7]

Special autonomy laws for Nanggroe Aceh Darussalam (Aceh) and Papua treat natural resource revenue from oil and gas in a special manner: both regions receive 70 per cent of the revenue earned from their oil and gas resources while the centre receives the remaining 30 per cent. These two provinces were accorded preferential treatment to help resolve the longstanding conflict in these regions, which has its roots in part in the unfair sharing of natural resource revenue. Another reason given was to accelerate the development of education, health and infrastructure in these provinces, which had lagged behind that in other regions.

I look next at how the new revenue-sharing arrangement for natural resources has changed the fiscal capacity of regions. It can be expected that the fiscal capacity of resource-rich regions will have improved since 2001, and that the role of natural resource revenue in financing development will have become much more important.

INTERREGIONAL FISCAL CAPACITY AND EQUITY

Since decentralisation, the fiscal resources of the regions have included own-source revenue (PAD) and revenue from the central government's balancing fund (*dana perimbangan*). The latter consists mostly of shared revenue and DAU grants. It comes as no surprise to find that the additional revenue given to regions with abundant natural resources has given rise to large differences in fiscal capacity across regions (Figure 7.2). Regions rich in oil and gas have seen

*Figure 7.2   Average fiscal capacity per capita of oil/gas and non-oil/gas-
producing districts before and after decentralisation
(Rp thousand, constant 1996 prices)*

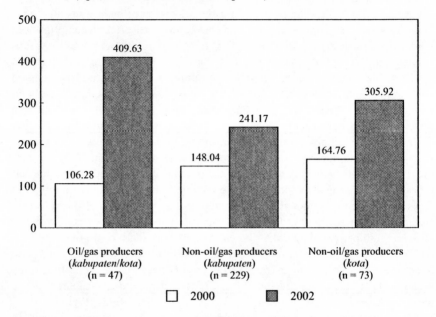

Source: Sistem Informasi Keuangan Daerah (SIKD), Ministry of Finance.

their fiscal capacity per capita jump almost four-fold, putting them well ahead
of non-oil/gas-producing *kabupaten* and *kota*. The variation in fiscal capacity
per capita across oil and gas-rich *kabupaten/kota* is even more astounding (Figure 7.3). These differences among resource-producing regions are explained by
the amount of natural resources they produce; districts with more resources,
such as Siak and Bengkalis, would naturally receive more revenue than other,
less well-endowed, regions.

The reasons for the wide variation in fiscal capacity can be disentangled by
looking at the sources of regional revenue (Table 7.2). Before decentralisation,
own-source revenue per capita across *kabupaten/kota* was highly unequal, as
indicated by the various inequality indicators of regional revenue (coefficient of
variation, standard deviation of log and Gini coefficient). Tax and non-tax revenue-sharing had a small equalising effect, but as very little revenue-sharing
took place at the time, its effect on variations in interregional fiscal capacity
was minimal. On the whole central government transfers were also equalising.
SDO transfers were more equalising than development transfers because they
are used to fund routine expenditures.

Figure 7.3   *Fiscal capacity per capita of selected oil/gas-producing districts before and after decentralisation (Rp thousand, constant 1996 prices)[a]*

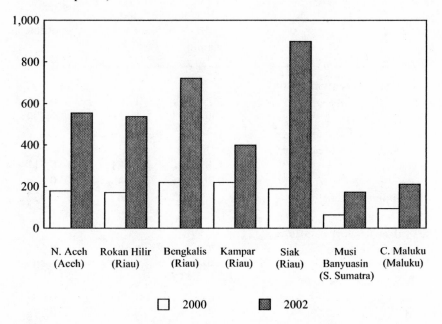

a   The districts shown in the graph were selected because they are the largest oil and gas-producing regions for which data were available for both years. The province in which the district is located is given in parentheses.

Source: Sistem Informasi Keuangan Daerah (SIKD), Ministry of Finance.

Although it is true that natural resource revenue-sharing has led to large inequalities in fiscal capacity per capita across regions since 2001, its effect has been mitigated by equalising DAU grants (Table 7.2). The formulation of the DAU takes shared revenue from natural resources into account in the computation of regions' fiscal capacity.[8] Regions with greater fiscal capacity and a smaller fiscal gap will therefore tend to receive smaller DAU allocations than other regions.[9]

On balance, the existing arrangements for natural resource revenue-sharing complemented by the general block grant mechanism appear to be achieving the purpose of returning some revenue to producing regions while at the same time mitigating disparity in regional revenue per capita across the regions. This may not be a perfect solution, but it is workable for the time being.

*Table 7.2   Variation in revenue per capita of districts by source of revenue,
            fiscal years 2000 and 2002*

Source of revenue	Coefficient of variation	Standard deviation of log	Gini coefficient
2000 (before decentralisation)			
Own-source revenue	2.491	1.762	0.566
+ Shared tax revenue	1.401	1.688	0.490
+ Shared non-tax revenue (including natural resource revenue)	1.362	1.721	0.511
+ SDO	0.768	1.643	0.376
+ Development grant	0.930	1.663	0.427
2002 (after decentralisation)			
Own-source revenue	0.728	0.600	0.352
+ Shared tax revenue	0.911	0.690	0.409
+ Shared natural resource revenue	2.387	1.086	0.694
+ DAU	0.882	0.625	0.374

SDO = Autonomous Region Subsidy; DAU = General Allocation Fund.

Source: Sistem Informasi Keuangan Daerah (SIKD), Ministry of Finance.

IMPLICATIONS FOR REGIONAL DEVELOPMENT

Patterns of regional expenditure after decentralisation

While it is difficult to disentangle the patterns of regional expenditure before
and after decentralisation related solely to natural resource revenues, a picture
is gradually beginning to emerge. Expenditures have jumped drastically in all
regions since decentralisation. This was to be expected given that about 30 per
cent of the central budget is now decentralised compared with 15 per cent previously. A common characteristic among regions is their larger budget allocations to routine (recurrent) expenditures than to development expenditures.

There is a distinct difference, however, between oil/gas-producing regions
and non-oil/gas-producing regions with respect to the share of the budget allo-

Figure 7.4   Routine and development expenditures of oil/gas and non-oil/gas-producing cities and districts before and after decentralisation (per cent)

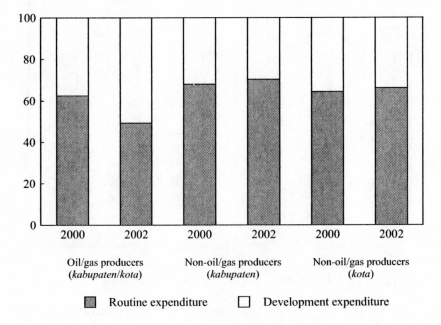

Source: Sistem Informasi Keuangan Daerah (SIKD), Ministry of Finance.

cated to routine and development expenditures since decentralisation (Figure 7.4). Both the amount and the share of the budget allocated to development spending has increased in the former regions but has remained largely unchanged or has even fallen in the latter regions. On average resource-rich regions now spend almost half of their budgets on development programs. Whether one looks at actual amounts or at development expenditures as a percentage of the total budget, it is clear that oil and gas-producing regions are spending more on development than their non-producing counterparts.

Nevertheless, this observation should be interpreted with care. It should be noted that some routine expenditure items, in particular personnel expenditures, include budget allocations for service delivery. For example, salary payments to school teachers and medical workers are clearly a cost of providing services to local people. While it is not necessarily bad for regions to spend more on routine expenditures for service delivery, it certainly reduces funding for development purposes.

*Figure 7.5   Development expenditures of oil/gas and non-oil/gas-producing
             districts before and after decentralisation (per cent)*

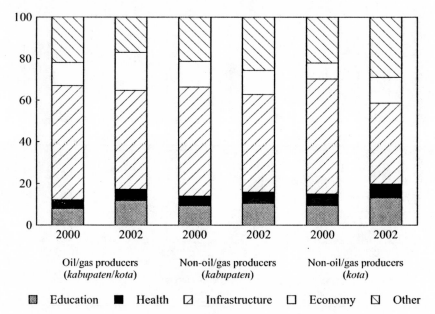

Source: Sistem Informasi Keuangan Daerah (SIKD), Ministry of Finance.

The way that resource-rich and resource-poor regions are choosing to allocate their development budgets across sectors also differs (Figure 7.5).[10] In all regions both the amount and the share of the budget allocated to education and health have increased, while allocations for infrastructure have decreased. However, oil/gas-producing regions are allocating more to the economic sector and less to 'other' sectors than non-oil/gas-producing regions, both in percentage terms and in actual amounts.

What do these budgetary patterns imply for regional development? While it is difficult to derive any direct implications for regional economic performance per se, it is fair to draw the following conclusions. First, all regions are allocating more of their budgets to education and health and less to infrastructure. Second, oil and gas-producing regions are spending more on development, which has the potential to stimulate the local economy directly, whereas non-producing regions are spending more on providing and maintaining basic services. In other words, oil and gas-producing regions appear to be attempting to diversify their economies towards the non-oil and gas sector, the results of which will only be seen over the medium to longer term.

Do regions need more transfers from natural resource revenue?

After three years of decentralisation, Indonesia is still attempting to resolve problems concerning the transparency, amount and method of disbursement of shared natural resource revenue.[11] Some resource-rich provinces, most notably Riau and East Kalimantan, are continuing to demand a larger share of oil and gas revenues than is currently allowed by law. Their demands have been prompted by the special treatment accorded Aceh and Papua under their special autonomy laws. In addition, oil and gas-*processing* regions (as opposed to *producing* regions) are claiming a share of the country's oil and gas revenues. So far, however, the government has rejected their demands on the grounds that it would be difficult to disentangle the sources of the oil and gas being processed in various regions – some could easily come from other regions or even be imported (*Kompas*, 20 September 2004).

For the time being, the central government has appeased the resource-rich regions by agreeing to raise their share of resource revenue slightly; a revision of Law 25/1999 increases their share of oil revenue from 15 per cent to 15.5 per cent effective five years from now. Although this temporarily resolves the issue, the regions' demands for a higher share of natural resource revenue raise two more basic questions: is the present system for natural resource revenue-sharing appropriate, and do regions really need more transfers from natural resource revenue?

With regard to the first question, the current arrangement for natural resource revenue-sharing does appear to be fair and should be sufficient at least for the medium term. The system gives a substantial share to the producing regions and makes special allowance for some regions. The share retained by the central government can be expected to benefit the less well-off, resource-poor regions. The system therefore maintains a careful balance between treating natural resource revenue as a resource for the population of Indonesia as a whole and treating it as a form of compensation for resource-producing regions.

On the second question, there is no convincing evidence that the regions need more transfers, including those from natural resource revenues. From nil prior to decentralisation, the average local government budget surplus grew to about 10 per cent of total expenditure in 2001 (Lewis and Chakeri 2004; Usui and Alisjahbana 2003). The post-decentralisation surplus has resulted in a large stock of local government reserves. By 2002, total local government reserves had grown to 16 per cent of total expenditures. This trend has been driven by an underestimation of revenues and, to a lesser extent, by an overestimation of expenditures.

On balance, there is no obvious reason to support a higher level of natural resource revenue transfers in the immediate future given the adequacy of the existing formula for natural resource revenue-sharing and the present fiscal conditions of the regions. However, there is one more issue that warrants special consideration, namely how the proceeds of non-renewable natural resources such as oil, gas and minerals should best be used.

Intergenerational equity issues and non-renewable resources

Intergenerational equity is an important aspect of the use of revenue from natural resources (World Bank 2003; Bahl and Tumennason 2002). The question is whether the revenue from natural resources, especially non-renewable resources, should be shared with future generations. This issue is critical for regions such as Riau, Aceh, East Kalimantan and Papua where most of Indonesia's oil, gas and other minerals are concentrated. They may be receiving substantial additional revenues from non-renewable resources at present, but these will last only until the resources are exhausted.

There are two alternative ways of dealing with the issue of intergenerational sharing of non-renewable natural resource revenue. First, the experience of Alaska, Norway and Chile suggests that setting up a heritage fund would be one option. Part of the revenue from natural resources would be placed in an investment fund, the proceeds of which would be set aside for future generations.[12] The second and more common option would be to use most of the revenue for investment in infrastructure and education, the benefits of which would extend to future generations.

Which of these two options is more feasible for Indonesia's regions? As Alaska, Norway and Chile have learned, the key to successful establishment of a heritage fund is fiscal discipline. Moreover, designing the specific financial architecture for such a fund would be challenging.[13] The second option therefore appears more reasonable for Indonesia, at least in the short term. This option is already being followed in the cases of Papua and Aceh, whose special autonomy laws specifically earmark a certain percentage of natural resource revenue for investment in education.

CONCLUDING REMARKS

Decentralisation and the changes wrought by natural resource revenue-sharing have undoubtedly increased the fiscal capacity of resource-producing regions, potentially widening fiscal disparity across regions. Fiscal disparity is not the central issue, however, as block grants distributed through the DAU mitigate the actual extent of fiscal disparity. The issue, rather, is the implications of natural resource revenue-sharing for regional development, and whether the current arrangement is sufficient in light of continuing demand from resource-rich regions for a greater share of natural resource revenue.

While it is interesting to note the different expenditure patterns emerging between resource-producing regions and non-producing regions, the implications of these patterns for development in the respective regions are still unclear. It is, for example, too early to say whether resource-rich regions will experience better regional economic performance because they are spending more on development and focusing more on the economic sectors. Nevertheless, there can be no doubt that these regions, especially those that rely heavily on non-renewable resources, are taking the correct course of action. The windfall revenues they are receiving at present will disappear once their resources have been fully exploited. It is therefore a prudent strategy for them to try to reorient their economies towards the development of non-resource-based sectors.

Although there is not much of a case for more natural resource revenue to be transferred to producing regions, there is some justification for setting aside funds from non-renewable resources for investment in projects that would benefit present and future generations. This funding would be in addition to existing transfers of natural resource revenue to the resource-abundant regions. Regions such as Aceh and Papua are already implementing this idea by earmarking a certain proportion of their natural resource revenue for investment in education. A similar requirement would be justified in the case of other resource-abundant regions. One possible solution would be to create a new type of central transfer that the resource-rich regions could use only for specific types of investment spending based on an assessment of their particular long-term development needs. The funds would ideally be spent on education, health and infrastructure provision.

NOTES

1   The share of primary sector (agriculture and mining) value-added declined from the 1970s until the economic crisis of 1997, while that of the manufacturing and service sectors increased.

2   The chief component of routine expenditure is civil servant salaries, mainly for teachers.

3   In the late 1990s the Inpres program was replaced by a Regional Development Fund (Dana Pembangunan Daerah) consisting mainly of block grants. Despite this change, the regions continued to have little leeway in how central transfers were used because most (75 per cent) were still in the form of SDO subsidies (Alisjahbana 1998).

4   Two other factors also explain the persistence of regional disparities. First, Java and Bali have benefited disproportionately from Indonesia's rapid industrialisation and the expansion of modern service sectors. Second, provinces outside Java have suffered under onerous regulations and restrictive practices prevalent in the agricultural sector.

5   Law 34/2000 on Regional Taxes and Regional Levies complements Law 25/1999
     by giving local governments greater leeway in setting their own taxes.
6   DAK grants are still allocated but play only a minor role in overall regional budgets
     because of the relatively small amounts involved.
7   Note, however, that the share of natural resource revenue that regions receive is
     counted in the calculation of their fiscal capacity and consequently reduces their
     DAU allocations. The complexity of the natural resource revenue-sharing mecha-
     nism may well make it redundant (World Bank 2003).
8   The DAU formula is based on the fiscal gap, that is, the difference between a
     region's fiscal needs and its fiscal capacity. For a complete discussion of DAU
     formulation, see Ministry of Finance (2002). A thorough discussion of the DAU for-
     mula and its evolution since 2001 is also given at <www.djpkpd.or.id>.
9   The generally equalising nature of DAU grants is, however, often undermined by
     political compromises made during the actual process of allocation (World Bank
     2003).
10   The sectors are grouped as follows: education, health, infrastructure (water, trans-
     portation, dwellings and residences, regional development), economy (industry,
     mining and energy, agriculture, trade, tourism) and 'other' (labour; environment;
     science and technology; politics; information; law, security and public order;
     demography and social welfare; religious affairs; and civil service and administra-
     tion).
11   The delays in disbursing shared natural resource revenue are of great concern to the
     regions because they affect the implementation of their budgets.
12   The fund could be set up by the central government or by an independent commis-
     sion. In either case, the central government would have to put money into the fund
     (Bahl and Tumennason 2002).
13   For small recipients the funding could be tied up as a specific grant from the cen-
     tre, but for large recipients it would have to be part of a larger development strat-
     egy (Bahl 2002).

8 DEVELOPMENT PERFORMANCE AND FUTURE SCENARIOS IN THE CONTEXT OF SUSTAINABLE UTILISATION OF NATURAL RESOURCES

Iwan J. Azis and Emil Salim

INTRODUCTION

Sustainable development requires the integration of economic, social and environmental dimensions, also known as the 'ESE triangle' (WCED 1987; Azis and Roland-Holst 1999). Sustainability may be thought of as strong or weak. Weak sustainability requires that aggregate resources do not decline over time; strong sustainability requires that individual resources do not decline over time. In this chapter, we review the Indonesian development experience in the context of sustainable development and describe some future scenarios that would be more consistent with the goal of a balance between the economic, social and environmental dimensions of development. We focus on the interconnection between sustainable development and utilisation of natural resources.

It is generally agreed that sustainable development requires the prioritisation of resource investment rather than resource depletion. This is relatively obvious for renewable resources, but we argue that it is not reflected in Indonesia's policy record. In the case of non-renewable resources, the government apparently felt that depletion was inevitable and that therefore mining resources should simply be used as needed to support public expenditure. We develop scenarios of alternative rates of resource depletion, analyse the consequences of each and derive some policy implications.

ASSESSING PAST PERFORMANCE

'Plant a stick into Indonesian soil and it will grow into a tree' is the usual perception of Indonesia's rich base of natural resources. Situated on the equator, surrounded by two major oceans and consisting of more than 17,000 islands, Indonesia ranks near the top of the list for global flora and fauna diversity. In species richness, it ranks first for parrots, butterflies, tropical insects and herbs, second for mammals (behind Brazil) and oceanic fisheries, fourth for primates, fifth for birds generally, and sixth for amphibians. It also has a wide variety of highly valued tropical forests and is rich in mineral resources (Resosudarmo and Subiman 2003).

For many years Indonesia's natural resources were largely untouched due to the political turmoil that swept the country following independence in 1945. Economic development was difficult as a result. However, in the late 1960s Indonesia began a steady, long-term development program based on conventional economic factors rather than social or environmental factors. Such an approach was not unusual at the time: development was considered to be a function of the exploitation of natural resources with the assistance of labour, capital, skill and technology. In Indonesia's case, the approach was straightforward. First, the government would get its finances in order by slashing the budget deficit, controlling inflation, striving for a realistic exchange rate and obtaining financial stability as the first condition for growth. Second, the government would rehabilitate roads, harbours, airstrips, telecommunications, electricity and other economic infrastructure to lay the groundwork for sensible development. Third, the government would focus on meeting basic needs. For example, there would be self-sufficiency in the main staple foods, and primary education and basic health services such as *puskesmas* (community health centres) would be provided through the allocation of public funds directly to villages, bypassing the unnecessary bureaucracy involved in activities such as the presidential Inpres projects. The oil boom in the 1970s provided an impetus for these projects to be implemented on a broader scale (Azis 1990; Thorbecke 1992).

During these early years, as well as ensuring that Indonesia had a predictable and conducive economic environment, the government considered it important to obtain foreign exchange inflows through exports, foreign direct investment and aid.[1] In the initial stages, Indonesia's rich natural resources provided the main attraction for foreign capital. Old plantation managers came back from Europe to explore the possibilities for further investment. Other potential investors focused on the mineral sector. The first large foreign investments were in copper in West Papua, with investment in nickel and aluminium following. In the 1970s, oil became the main attraction. Through contracts of work (CoWs), foreign investors and the state oil company Pertamina made arrangements to develop Indonesia's oil and gas resources, which soon provided most of the country's foreign exchange earnings.[2]

The direct social effects of mining exploration are often negative, especially for local communities. The infamous case of the Freeport McMoRan Copper & Gold operation in Papua clearly points to the fundamental linkages between the natural resource, environmental and social aspects of development (Walton 2004).[3] Theoretically, indirect social effects through government spending (funded by captured rent) could have been favourable in this case, but in practice the damaging effects of the mining often exceeded the benefits, especially for indigenous people.

Local and indigenous communities complained that their activities in and around the mining area were unjustly disrupted or banned as soon as a foreign company appeared, depriving them of their main sources of income with little or no compensation. Furthermore, damaging environmental impacts from the operation of large mining companies often adversely affected the livelihoods of many local people. For example, fish in the rivers died due to pollution from the mine site, and there was less clean water for cleaning and drinking or for livestock. This was one reason why the World Bank initiated the Extractive Industries Review, chaired by Emil Salim. The recommendations he presented to the World Bank in December 2003 included a proposal to enforce a condition that any decisions on mining projects must be communicated to the indigenous people directly affected by them, in order to ensure that indigenous people have all the information they need to negotiate a fair deal. The goal is to 'elevate the position of the poor and vulnerable to strike a better balance with that of the strong and privileged' (Salim 2004).

On the macroeconomic side, a reliance on primary activities has the potential for countries to experience the adverse effects of the 'Dutch disease'.[4] To some extent, Indonesia experienced a Dutch disease effect when the price of oil surged during the 1970s. However, the impact was softened by two factors. First, the government provided heavy subsidies to the agricultural, rural and infrastructure sectors, so there was an increase in the production of many agriculture-related products (Gelb 1988). Second, there were increased government deposits in the central bank account because the government had saved some of the windfall revenues from the second oil boom. This helped to prevent non-tradable prices from soaring.

The forestry sector was another important earner of foreign exchange for Indonesia. In 1967, the government introduced a system of forest concessions under which firms or individuals were given the right to exploit forests through a system of 'selective cutting' that was intended to provide sufficient time for trees to rejuvenate. Unfortunately, the distribution system for the concessions was far from transparent. Most people who gained concessions were members of the 'inner circle', the power elite (Barr 1998). Foreign investors were not allowed to move into the forestry sector.

The state had control over most forest areas; other stakeholders had only limited control over the land on which their livelihoods depended. Although about 12 million people lived in and around forests, local communities were frequently not consulted prior to the selection of concession sites. Even when negotiations were conducted, the local communities were often at a disadvantage because property rights were not well defined and laws were not well enforced. For example, even though concession-holders had no rights over settlement areas within the concession sites, they sometimes acted as though they did. In the post-Soeharto period, the effect may have worked in the opposite direction: some communities have reclaimed land or forest on which firms or individuals hold concessions, or have claimed forest on which there are multiple claims (Rhee 2000). Public expenditure could have enhanced the social development of local communities, but its effect was limited by the lower-than-potential rents captured by the government.

In the past, forests were considered purely as a source of revenue; they were not valued as a source of biological diversity, medicinal plants or food. In most cases the legitimate forest concession-holders contracted their concessions to businesspeople with capital. Logs attracted high export prices, so the forestry sector contributed significantly to Indonesia's foreign exchange earnings. It was also a stepping-stone for the growth of big conglomerates (Barr 1998).

In 1981–85, the government banned the export of logs. This stimulated the growth of plywood, craft and paper factories, so increasing the value-added and income received per unit of timber. However, the policy was not without controversy, particularly because of its perceived effects on employment. Azis (1992) has shown that the ban was detrimental to employment in the short run, but positive in the medium run. In 1980–85, demand for an additional 392,000 jobs induced by the increase in 'processed wood' exports failed to offset the loss of 463,000 jobs due to the decline in 'logging and sawmilling' exports. However, by taking into account the direct and indirect employment effects of the changes in exports during the period, the loss of 2,500 jobs from the decline in 'logging and sawmilling' exports was overwhelmingly exceeded by the 1.7 million new jobs from the increase in 'wood products' exports.[5]

Unfortunately, the ban on logging exports failed to reduce the amount of logging, because there was a rapid expansion of domestic and foreign demand for wood products. The government recognised the need to intensify reforestation activities and imposed compulsory fees for this purpose. However, the large amount of funds it accumulated through this means was more likely to be used to write off the debts of the national airplane factory (Christanty and Atje 2004) or build new offices for the Ministry of Forestry than for reforestation.

Meanwhile, the rate of deforestation has steadily increased – from approximately 1.6 million hectares per annum in 1985–97 to 3.8 million hectares per annum in 1997–2000 (Holmes 2000; Purnama 2003). It is estimated that around 65 per cent of Indonesia's wood supply has come from illegal logging. Total forest area is currently estimated at around 109 million hectares. If deforestation continues at the current rate of 3.8 million hectares per year, the total forest area will drop to approximately 50 million hectares by 2024. This sharp reduction will have serious environmental implications, especially for the hydrology cycle, with negative effects on the groundwater table and water run-off. Indonesia's rich biological diversity will disappear with the forests. In particular, the rapid conversion of forest in Sumatra, Kalimantan and Papua threatens the well-being of several types of endangered primates.[6]

The food sector has also been important. In the 1970s, Indonesia was the world's largest importer of rice. However, the International Rice Research Institute (IRRI) developed a 'miracle rice' variety that provided the opportunity for Indonesia to aim for self-sufficiency in rice production. As Indonesians' main staple food, rice was considered to be a strategic commodity whose price and availability in the market strongly affected the domestic inflation rate. Its price also affected the poverty line: any increase in the rice price would result in more people being below the poverty line and was thus likely to increase the incidence of poverty. The Indonesian government was therefore determined that the country would become self-sufficient in rice once and for all.

However, the growth of 'miracle rice' required dams, irrigation networks, chemical fertilisers, pesticides and other agrochemicals. Moreover, it required harvesting methods and systems that were different from those used for traditional strains. For example, on 'miracle rice' plantations, male labour replaced the female labour of traditional plantations. Indonesia did achieve self-sufficiency in rice production, but only at an environmental cost from chemical-intensive food production. At the time, government officials were not aware of the potential environmental costs, but later experience has indicated that it takes more than 10 years for the soil to recover from the application of artificial chemicals. Agrochemicals have also affected biological resource diversity and polluted the country's rivers. The experience of Rachel Carson in *Silent Spring* (1962) suddenly became vivid. In addition, many of Indonesia's own domestic strains of rice were lost as a result of their replacement by 'miracle rice'.

Indonesia moved forward rapidly on the economic front in the 1970s, 1980s and 1990s, as revealed by the fact that it changed from a low-income country to a middle-income country. However, the environmental dimension of development was not considered, mainly because of the early focus on development priorities described above. Initially the government did not consider the impact of development on the environment. The business-as-usual conventional economic development model adopted by Indonesia raised the level of economic goods and services, but was far from environmentally and socially sustainable. Figure 8.1 indicates the current status of development in Indonesia. The ESE triangle forms the base of the triangular pyramid; the apex represents the maximum possible level of each parameter – economic, social and environmental. The shaded area represents Indonesia's current approach to development, with the greatest emphasis on economic parameters and the least emphasis on social and environmental parameters.

*Figure 8.1   The ESE triangle: Indonesia's economic, social and
            environmental development performance*

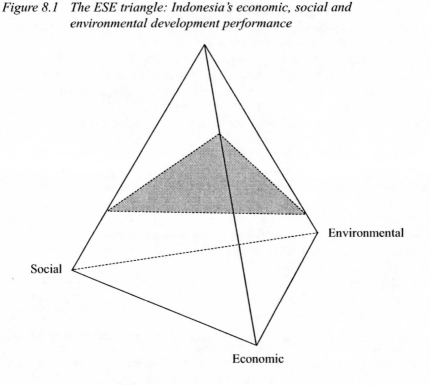

In 1972 Indonesia participated in the United Nations Conference on the Human Environment, in Stockholm, Sweden. The conference took place in an international setting where fresh aid was difficult to obtain from the developed countries. The 'Group of 77', consisting of developing country representatives in the United Nations, campaigned for a 'new international economic order' based on an unconditional aid target for developed countries of 0.7 per cent of GDP. But the focus of discussion soon shifted to the 'conditionality of aid', with developing countries viewing the issue of the environment as a disguised method by which developed countries could impose new conditions on developing countries. Developing countries asked why environmental issues had not been raised when pollution first became an issue for developed countries, why developed countries preached messages about actions they had not themselves implemented, and why developing countries were now being asked to bear the burden of environmental cost.

Nonetheless, the conference prompted the Indonesian government to explore how environmental considerations could be applied in the country's five-year development plans (Repelita). Progress was slow for a number of reasons, but particularly because of the lack of good governance – a lack that continued to allow such practices as illegal logging. Sustainable development cannot be achieved without good governance, but good governance requires a participatory democracy in which civil society is actively involved in consultation, deliberation and joint decision-making with government and the business community. This kind of participatory democracy was lacking in Indonesia for more than three decades. During the 30 years of President Soeharto's regime, new generations emerged with new demands. People wanted more democratic freedoms rather than continued authoritarian rule; more decentralisation rather than rigid centralisation; a more transparent, rules-based economy rather than a closed, crony-based economy; more democracy with a participatory approach rather than iron-fisted rule with a top-down approach; and good governance rather than poor governance based on corruption, collusion and nepotism.

Indonesia has now entered a new era of democracy and decentralisation. This change is leading to a more balanced economic, social and environmental development model in which civil society, the business community and 'clean' government are able to play a greater role. The main question now is what Indonesia must do to achieve a balance in its economic, social and environmental development.

FUTURE SCENARIOS IN THE CONTEXT OF SUSTAINABLE DEVELOPMENT

In this section, we outline several alternative development scenarios for Indonesia and describe some policies that can be expected to achieve a better balance in the ESE triangle and lead the country towards a path of sustainable development. The scenarios are developed to provide a better understanding of the numerous linkages between the resource-based sectors and the rest of the economy. These insights may help policy-makers anticipate the positive and negative effects – both direct and indirect – of their decisions, leading to policies that promote greater real economic diversification and that both broaden and strengthen the sustainable basis for development.

In generating future scenarios under different assumptions for the rate of resource depletion in Indonesia, we employ a dynamic computable general equilibrium (CGE) model.[7] We focus on three critical areas of economic activity: food; mining; and primary non-food products (mainly forestry and fisheries). In each of these areas, the country faces substantial challenges if it is to reconcile past and current resource use with sustainable growth objectives.

Our scenarios are based on two main premises. The first is that the primary sector will continue to be an important component of GDP in the foreseeable future, ensuring that the sustainability of resource-intensive activities will remain an essential issue for policy-makers. The second is that the critical link between resource depletion/degradation and sustainable growth works through changes in the productivity of different sectors.

Indonesia's abundant natural resources may soon be exhausted if there is no concerted effort to stop irresponsible exploitation. In the food sector, the present patterns of land and agrochemical use are reducing long-term soil productivity and crop resilience. In the mining sector, the country faces declining total reserves and volatile price trajectories. And in the non-food primary production sector, both forestry and fishery resources are seriously threatened by over-exploitation. In each of these sectors, the extent to which resource depletion will prevent sustainable economic development will generally depend on the relative size of the sector and its linkages to the rest of the economy.

We generate five scenarios of resource depletion towards 2020, using a dynamic CGE model. The different scenarios reflect differences in productivity change in the food, mining and primary non-food sectors. We analyse the consequences of each scenario by comparing the simulation results with those generated under a baseline scenario. Figure 8.2 shows trends for real GDP under the six scenarios we now outline.

Baseline scenario. In this scenario we assume that GDP will grow at 5 per cent per annum between 2000 and 2020. Total factor productivity (TFP) in the food, mining and primary non-food sectors is assumed to be constant at the 2000 level. This scenario represents the situation where government, civil society and business stabilise resource utilisation in each sector at 2000 levels. However, we must remember that Indonesia will not achieve sustainable development in these circumstances.

Scenario 1 (worst-case scenario). In this scenario, we assume that there is an increase in resource utilisation in the food, primary non-food and mining sectors throughout the 2000–20 period, with TFP in the three sectors declining at an annual rate of 1.5, 2.0 and 2.5 per cent respectively. The scenario is intended to depict the opportunity cost of government failure to recognise sustainability as a generalised policy objective over the next 20 years. The results demonstrate the devastating consequences of doing nothing to improve the sustainability of resource use.

Scenario 2. This scenario assumes that in the food and primary non-food sectors the pattern of resource utilisation remains the same as in 2000 but that unsustainable mining activities continue and the productivity of the mining sector declines by 2.5 per cent annually. This could be an underestimate of declining productivity, but we take into account the fact that technological advances may lead to greater productivity in some subsectors.

Scenario 3. In this scenario, we assume that in the mining and primary non-food sectors the pattern of resource utilisation remains the same as in 2000, with TFP also remaining the same as in 2000, but that the government intro-

Figure 8.2   Trends in real GDP, 2000–20 (2000 = 1)

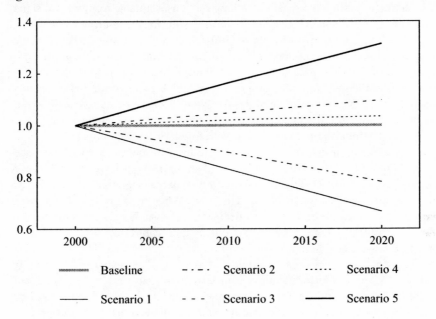

duces an environmentally friendly agricultural policy that leads to better productivity in the food sector, whose TFP rises monotonically by 1.5 per cent per annum over the reference period. This is similar to a scenario developed by Resosudarmo (2001).

Scenario 4. In this scenario, we assume that in the food and mining sectors the pattern of resource utilisation is maintained at 2000 levels but that government policy fosters a more integrated development of biological resources by promoting investment, improving productivity in sustainable forest products, developing coastal fisheries, and undertaking other innovative activities designed to promote and use Indonesia's tropical habitats in a sustainable manner. This scenario describes the situation where there is a focus on high value-added subsectors, for example by shifting to innovative, biodiversity-intensive products in the forestry sector and by investing in more sustainable fishery activities such as aquaculture. Under such a policy, the productivity of the primary non-food sector could rise by 2 per cent annually.

Scenario 5 (best-case scenario). In this scenario, we assume that Indonesia makes a special effort to prevent the unsustainable utilisation of resources. In such circumstances, there is an increase in TFP for all resource-based sectors between 2000 and 2020, of 1.5 per cent for the food sector, 2.0 per cent for the primary non-food sector and 2.5 per cent for the mining sector.

The results of the modelling of trends in real GDP shown in Figure 8.2 provide some interesting insights. In the long run, unsustainable resource utilisation (scenarios 1 and 2 and the baseline scenario) results in slower growth than would occur with better patterns of resource utilisation such as those depicted in scenarios 3, 4 and 5. The adverse effects of resource depletion are significant in every sector, but their precise nature varies according to demand responses. For example, in the mining sector progressively higher extraction costs undermine profits and output to a relatively greater extent because of more elastic export demands than in the food and primary non-food sectors, which have large sales shares in the domestic market and are therefore less severely affected.

As expected, unsustainable resource use in all resource-based sectors (scenario 1) results in the lowest GDP (more than 30 per cent lower than the baseline GDP in 2020). Different scenarios of resource depletion show different impacts mainly because of changes in TFP. When a sector's TFP increases because resources are better used or decreases because there is a deterioration in the pattern of resource utilisation, there is a significant effect on the long-term trend of value-added in that sector.

The dramatic shortfalls in GDP that occur under scenario 2 are to be expected given the historical significance of Indonesia's oil sector. The result highlights the importance of another aspect of sustainable development policy: the need for economic diversification and the development of non-primary resources. Continued growth that is leveraged on external markets will require continuing diversification and the continuing development of non-primary resources such as human capital.

From Figure 8.2, we can also see (scenarios 3, 4 and 5) an asymmetry in the impact of resource depletion and resource improvement in the mining sector. Although, as mentioned above, resource depletion in this sector would drag GDP down more than resource depletion in the food and primary non-food sectors,[8] this is not the case under the productivity improvement scenarios, because GDP will increase more when productivity improvement occurs in the food and primary non-food sectors. In the short and medium run, the mining sector might stay on target because of the important foreign exchange its activities earn. However, the sector generally acts as an enclave, with minimal linkages to the rest of the economy, so a forward-looking government should not give it prominence in policy development.

Sustainable utilisation of resources in Indonesia's food production would generate higher GDP, and so would the sustainable utilisation of resources in the primary non-food sector. The assumed annual percentage improvement of productivity in the food sector is lower than in the primary non-food sector (1.5 per cent versus 2 per cent), but the resulting GDP is higher under the improved food productivity scenario.

Figure 8.3   Trends in the price index, 2000–20 (2000 = 1)

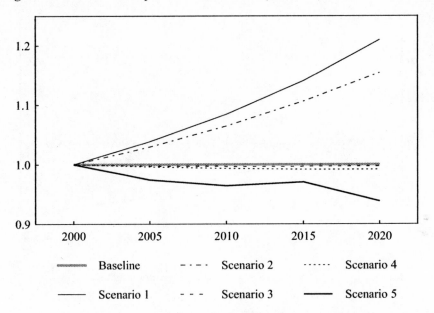

Under the most ideal scenario (scenario 5), GDP would be approximately 30 per cent higher than for the baseline scenario. This is the case despite the fact that in scenario 5 we use a rather conservative estimate of productivity improvements in resource-based activities. Scenario 5 shows how Indonesia's enormous biological potential can be realised through innovative approaches to resource development and use, including the use of new technologies.

Environmentally sustainable production also has a favourable effect on inflation, as shown in Figure 8.3. Under scenarios 3 and 4, the inflation rate is lower – albeit slightly – than under the baseline scenario. The impact is stronger – about 6–7 per cent lower inflation – when more sustainable production is assumed for all resource-based sectors (scenario 5).

Figure 8.4 shows trends in the current account deficit under different scenarios. Unsustainable resource utilisation (scenarios 1 and 2 and the baseline scenario) has a heavy impact on trade, with a direct reduction in export capacity and thereby a decrease in import purchasing power. In the food and primary non-food sectors, resource depletion and productivity growth have a smaller effect on the current account than in the mining sector because the latter is more export-oriented. Thus, unsustainable mining could have a more devastating long-term effect on the country's balance of payments than other unsustainable

Figure 8.4   Trends in the current account deficit, 2000–20 (2000 = 1)

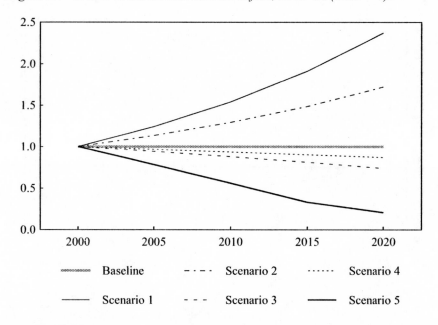

activities (scenario 2). Scenarios 3 and 4 capture the extent of untapped export potential in the country's food and primary non-food sectors, including biotechnology-intensive and sustainable high-value forest and fishery products. However, technology requirements for these products are also high, so imports will increase and the relative size of the current account deficit is likely to be lower than in the baseline scenario.

Nonetheless, when production in all resource-based sectors is unsustainable, the current account deficit can be as much as 130 per cent of that under the baseline scenario (Figure 8.4, scenario 1). On the other hand, with continued productivity improvement in all resource-based sectors, the current account deficit could be 70 per cent lower than in the baseline scenario (Figure 8.4, scenario 5). It is clear that the economy's capacity to earn foreign exchange would be undermined by unsustainable resource use.

Producing and exporting higher value-added and processed resource products not only raises dynamic efficiency and provides more foreign exchange, but also reduces the rate of resource depletion and offers other environmental benefits. In the case of forest products, for example, higher value-added production improves the dynamic efficiency of milling activities and thus stimulates exports; at the same time it limits the rate of deforestation, with benefits for biodiversity conservation, water catchment management, erosion control,

Figure 8.5   Trends in the Gini index, 2000–20 (2000 = 1)

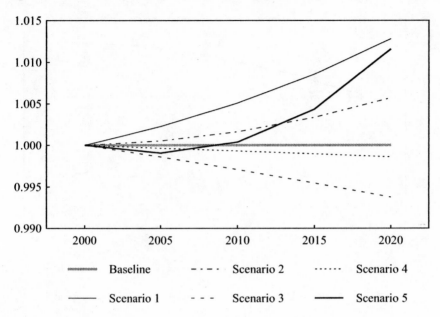

flood control and wildlife habitat management (Goodland and Daly 1996). Unfortunately, the promotion of such a policy is not without challenges, especially from the world trading system. For example, developed countries may impose high import duties on processed products and low import duties on raw materials. It is a fact of life in the global world that developing countries seem doomed to be suppliers of raw materials, with all the implied pollution and depletion of non-renewable resources, while developed countries enjoy higher value-added, higher employment and higher income. In this way, the widening gap between the developed and developing countries is perpetuated.[9]

Salim (1993) discusses the link between the environment and the distribution of income. Our simulations indicate that sustainable production has a positive social impact. To better understand the linkages between distribution and development policies, we revisit the six scenarios described above and look at their distributional consequences. Figure 8.5 shows trends in the Gini index as an indication of income equality. In the food, mining and primary non-food sectors, resource depletion (scenarios 1 and 2 and the baseline scenario) worsens the income inequality index. Under scenarios 3 and 4, income is more equally distributed as indicated by the Gini index. However, the ideal scenario (scenario 5) does not produce the most favourable distribution of income; rather, from 2010 the index is even higher than that under the baseline scenario. The main reason

Figure 8.6   Trends in employment, 2000–20 (2000 = 1)

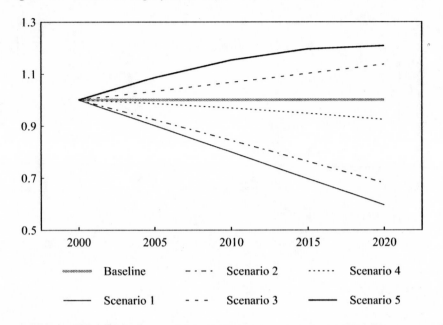

is a change in the circumstances of high-income households, which receive the most revenue from the mining sector.

Figure 8.6 shows employment trends under the different scenarios. Like the GDP trends discussed above, they are generally positive for all sectors. However, there is a difference between food and primary non-food sectors. In the latter, improved productivity is likely to be accompanied by a greater use of technology and a reduced requirement for labour-intensive activities. Thus, in the primary non-food sector a more sustainable use of resources will create fewer new jobs than under the baseline scenario. By contrast, more sustainable food production is likely to be accompanied by an increase in employment. Figure 8.6 shows that, when combined with more sustainable mining operations, productivity improvements in the food and primary non-food sectors create some 12 per cent higher employment than under the baseline scenario.

Figure 8.7 depicts trends in the poverty line under the six different scenarios of resource depletion; Figure 8.8 shows the resulting incomes of the poor. From Figure 8.7 it is clear that the sustainable utilisation of resources (scenarios 3, 4 and 5) is likely to result in a poverty line that is roughly 16 per cent lower that that in the baseline scenario. Figure 8.8 confirms that the sustainable use of resources results in higher incomes for the poor than the other scenarios.

Figure 8.7   Trends in the poverty line, 2000–20 (2000 = 1)

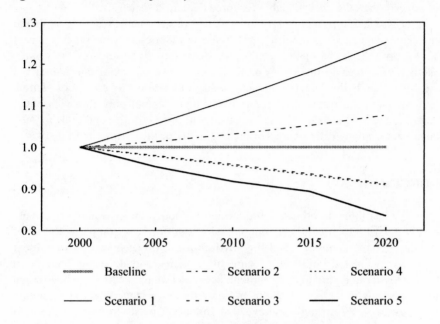

Figure 8.8   Trends in incomes of the poor, 2000–20 (2000 = 1)

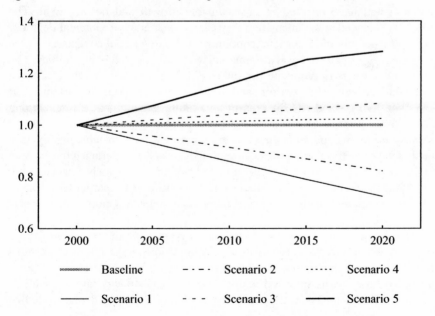

In other words, the sustainable use of resources will result in a lower incidence of poverty than the unsustainable resource depletion scenarios.[10]

Our simulation results clearly indicate that unsustainable resource depletion can have substantial long-term costs. Even if Indonesia maintains 5 per cent annual growth (the baseline scenario), the benefits will be undermined significantly if resources decline in any or all of the three sectors being considered. On the other hand, the benefits of sustainable utilisation are enormous. Direct investment in the resource sector is likely to result not only in a substantial growth dividend but also in better social conditions. Thus the conditions for sustainable development as defined at the beginning of this chapter are satisfied.

CONCLUSIONS

Over the last three decades, the Indonesian economy has grown at a relatively steady rate of more than 6 per cent annually, a performance on par with that of the East Asian economies. But the environmental dimension of development has been neglected, and many economic policies and decisions have been adopted without regard to environmental considerations. There have been some improvements in the social sector, but they too have lagged behind economic achievements. We strongly believe that Indonesia needs to balance the economic, social and environmental components of the development triangle. Increased resource depletion and degradation have been at odds with economic progress and have resulted in unsustainable growth and development. The 1997–98 financial crisis intensified the risks of greater environmental degradation and a deterioration in social conditions, including social conflicts.

Indonesia is confronted with remarkable challenges and opportunities. The main challenge is to reconcile the interests of a diverse electorate in a more democratic system while crafting and implementing an economic program that can raise living standards for present and future generations. By developing alternative scenarios of resource depletion using a dynamic CGE model, we identify programs and strategies that are consistent with sustainable development. One of the principal lessons of our analysis is the importance of systemic linkages and indirect effects. The sum total of these routinely exceeds (and sometimes can contradict) the direct effects that motivate particular policies. However, indirect effects are quite difficult to anticipate with intuition or partial analysis.

Our simulations reveal that, if Indonesia is to make the transition from a low-income primary exporter to a mature and diversified economy, it must reduce resource exploitation, invest in resources and increase long-term productivity. Productivity improvement will be a critical strategy for the country's future development. The simulations presented in this chapter demonstrate that such a strategy would greatly improve not only economic objectives but also social conditions and environmental efficiency. In this way, Indonesia will have a more balanced ESE triangle. Planning and implementing such a strategy will be daunting and is likely to involve many trade-offs, but there is no realistic alternative if the country is to achieve sustainable development.

NOTES

1   At the time Indonesia was suffering under huge foreign debt. This situation was satisfactorily settled using a formula developed by Dr Abs, a famous German banker, and approved by the Inter-Governmental Group on Indonesia, an aid consortium that became the Consultative Group on Indonesia in the 1990s.

2   Under the CoW, Pertamina gained monopoly control over oil at the point of exploitation. It also collected oil taxes on behalf of the state and took care of the needs of foreign contractors. Later on Pertamina moved to implement production-sharing contracts to increase its control over oil operations (see Chapter 11 by Seda in this book). With a relatively weak government fiscal administration, Pertamina quickly became a major political and economic power centre that obsessively advocated high-technology industrial development.

3   The negative impact of the Freeport mining operation was particularly felt by the indigenous people, the Amungme and the Kamoro in the Timika area. This is to be contrasted with the United Nations Draft Declaration on the Rights of Indigenous Peoples (Article 30) which recognises indigenous peoples' right to

> determine and develop priorities and strategies for the development or use of their lands, territories and other resources, including the right to require that States obtain their free and informed consent prior to the approval of any project affecting their lands, territories and other resources, particularly in connection with the development, utilisation or exploitation of mineral, water or other resources. Pursuant to agreements with the indigenous peoples concerned, just and fair compensation shall be provided for any such activities and measures taken to mitigate adverse environmental, economic, social, cultural or spiritual impact.

A smaller-scale example is Aurora Gold's PT Indo Muro Kencana mine in Central Kalimantan, an Australian goldmine that has often been embroiled in conflict with the indigenous Dayak community.

4   Named for the paradoxically adverse effects experienced in the Netherlands after the discovery of North Sea gas, the Dutch disease refers to the rise in currency values, fall in manufactured exports and increase in imports that may accompany the discovery and exploitation of a natural resource.

5   It is widely recognised that economic activities that add value to natural resources also provide diverse occupational opportunities, relatively high-wage jobs and a stable economy that is relatively unsusceptible to boom–bust cycles; such activities are consistent with a balanced ESE triangle.

6   An official at the Office of the State Minister of the Environment recently warned that in the last decade Indonesia has lost one species a day and that 70 per cent of

the original habitat of those species has been destroyed. Unless urgent action is taken, these losses in biodiversity will continue at the same rate in the future.

7   A CGE model, in general, is a mathematical system of equations that represents the behaviour of all agents (consumers and producers) and the market-clearing conditions of goods and services in an economy. The model we use is fairly comprehensive, linking the real sector and resource block, trade block, financial block and distributional poverty module. It is updated from Azis and Roland-Holst (1999) and Azis (2000, 2002).

8   This is not just because of the assumed larger percentage decline in mining productivity. Results of several trials using different percentage figures do not change the general conclusion.

9   The tragedy of today's global economy is that the World Bank, the International Monetary Fund (IMF) and the World Trade Organization (WTO) cannot make substantial changes, since such changes would not meet the interests of developed countries. In each institution, a board of executive directors makes decisions on the basis of 'one dollar, one vote'; the boards consist mainly of representatives from rich developed countries that contribute large sums to increase the size of their vote.

10 The importance of the linkage between resource depletion and poverty has been widely documented. EIR (2003) provides one good elaboration of the link.

PART III

Sectoral Challenges

9 OLIGARCHY IN THE TIMBER MARKETS OF INDONESIA: FROM APKINDO TO IBRA TO THE FUTURE OF THE FORESTS

Paul K. Gellert

The relationship between political and economic power, timber markets and the sustainability of the forests in Indonesia, after decades of relative certainty, has been in a period of change and uncertainty since 1998. This chapter reviews the domestic and international political and economic alliances that supported oligarchic power in the timber sector during the New Order period (Robison and Hadiz 2004). Oligarchy in the timber sector was part of a more general phenomenon in the Indonesian political economy – of concentrated benefits from economic growth (Winters 1996). However, the social and environmental costs of such growth have been dispersed. In the case of timber, these costs have been concentrated in the resource-rich regions of extraction in Sumatra, Kalimantan and, increasingly, eastern Indonesia.

The *reformasi* period since 1998 and the specific International Monetary Fund (IMF) conditionalities that dismantled the marketing power of the Indonesian Plywood Producers' Association (Apkindo) have altered longstanding relations in the timber sector. Globalisation of markets and changes in regional markets, notably the emergence of China as a key importer, further challenge the old forces. Signs of the enduring power of the old oligarchy have also emerged, however. They include the re-implementation of the log export ban, the formation of a new industry organisation, the Wood Industry Revitalisation Agency (BRIK), and the lack of resolve within the Indonesian Bank Restructuring Agency (IBRA) to use its authority over financially troubled industries to reduce excess industrial capacity in the timber sector. The persistence of the old oligarchic powers, in conjunction and competition with decentralised state forces (including the military) and market forces, both legal and illegal, poses an increasing threat to the sustainability of Indonesia's timber resources.

THEORETICAL FRAMEWORK: OLIGARCHY AND RESOURCE EXTRACTION

The Indonesian case presents a fascinating framework within which to examine the emergence, persistence, effects and reorganisation of oligarchy.[1] Out of the carnage of 1965–66 and the rise to power of Lieutenant General Soeharto, a system of rule known as the New Order emerged and persisted through an extensive system of political patronage. However, this system was more than patronage; it was transformed into 'a capitalist oligarchy that fused public authority and private interest, epitomised in the rise of such families as the Soehartos' (Robison and Hadiz 2004: 43). As Robison and Hadiz argue, the fragmented amalgam of families, as well as private charitable foundations known as *yayasan* and largely ethnic Chinese business groups, forged a 'politico-bureaucratic oligarchy' that flourished in the 1980s and 1990s, benefiting from global and regional flows of capital (Winters 1996; Bernard and Ravenhill 1995).

Moreover, although the World Bank and others touted Indonesia as a model of developmental success worthy of inclusion among the East Asian manufacturing 'miracle' economies (World Bank 1993; Hill 2000), natural resource industries such as oil, gas, mining and forestry have played a significant role as the material basis of the oligarchy's power and wealth. It is important to note that these natural resource extractive industries – including ostensibly renewable resources such as timber – have their own particular dynamics, based on the physical properties of the raw materials and the geography and topography of extraction, processing and transport (Boyd, Prudham and Schurman 2001; Bunker 1992, 2003; Barham, Bunker and O'Hearn 1994). In forestry, for example, the spatial dispersion of commercial timber species and the dynamics of depletion shape the capacities of both state and private actors within the oligarchy, as well as the social and environmental effects of their extractive activities (Gellert 1998a).

The Soeharto presidency collapsed in 1998 amid protests against the corruption, collusion and nepotism (KKN) of the oligarchy. It was followed by a democratisation of the national political system culminating (thus far) in the direct election of President Susilo Bambang Yudhoyono. This period of reform and transition offers an important opportunity to examine whether the oligarchy will continue to hold in a time of global (neo)liberalisation and democratisation, and if so, how. Predominant theories of political–economic transition argue that military–bureaucratic elites will give way to the political rise of economic elites. However, Robison and Rosser (2000: 173) observe that

> the decay of entrenched regimes simply opens the door to new contests between contending social and political interests to define the rules that govern markets. They

may be replaced by systems dominated by oligarchies or nationalist regimes, or by an era of disintegration in which gangsters and robber barons flourish.

All these seem possible within Indonesia's timber sector. What seems less certain is whether any countervailing social forces are emerging (or will emerge) that can alter the oligarchy's hold on power and challenge its use thus far 'to cement the position of the elite itself, *not* in the pursuit of some more broadly based conception of the national interest' (Beeson and Robison 2000: 13).

THE NEW ORDER, FORESTRY AND THE BUILDING OF OLIGARCHY

Forestry was one of the founding pillars of Soeharto's New Order, along with oil, gas and mining. Upon ascension to power, Soeharto introduced Law 5/1967 on forestry and Law 1/1967 on foreign investment, effectively opening the forests to logging and foreign investment. Exports of logs boomed in the 1970s, followed by booms in plywood exports in the 1980s and 1990s, and pulp and paper exports in more recent years. Forest products were Indonesia's most important non-oil and gas exports from the 1970s until the 1990s, when they came under challenge from textiles (Hill 2000). At its peak in 1989, the forest product sector accounted for almost 15 per cent of total exports and 30 per cent of industrial exports (Simangunsong 2004: Table 1, based on *Economic Indicators* published by the Central Statistics Agency, BPS).

Taking advantage of this resource wealth, the Soeharto regime began to build an oligarchy through the highly centralised allocation of hundreds of large-scale 20-year forest concessions (HPHs). Some of the early HPHs went to foreign firms such as Weyerhaueser and Georgia Pacific. Mostly, however, Soeharto used the allocation process to disperse patronage and benefits, especially to the military, both through foundations (*yayasan*) that were officially not for profit and directly to individual generals as a kind of retirement package (Robison 1986; Crouch 1988; Winters 1996; Ross 2001). By the 1990s, up to 585 HPHs had been allocated. They covered some 60 million hectares of Indonesia's 144 million-hectare forest estate in Sumatra, Kalimantan and, later, eastern Indonesia. All were made without the prior knowledge of the millions of Indonesians living in and around the concession areas (Barber, Johnson and Hafild 1994; Brown 1999).

The power of the oligarchy was strengthened during the New Order period through two unusual steps, both taken to bolster downstream processing of timber. First, Indonesia announced and followed through on a log export ban, phased in from 1982 to 1985. It was surprisingly effective both in comparison to the Philippines and in comparison to the current period of illegal logging and

Figure 9.1   Export value of forest products, 1990–2002 ($ billion)

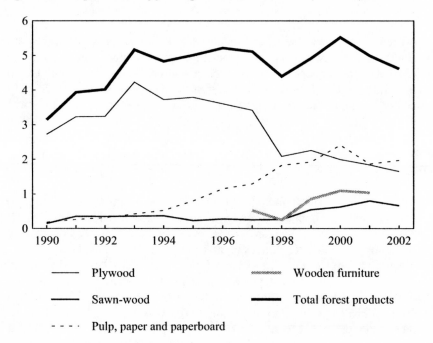

- Plywood
- Sawn-wood
- Pulp, paper and paperboard
- Wooden furniture
- Total forest products

Source: Wooden furniture: Asmindo data in Simangunsong (2004); all others: FAOSTAT database.

smuggling in Indonesia. The ban was accompanied by subsidies and regulations aimed at the construction of a national plywood industry. They included a ban on manual logging (*banjir kap*) in the early 1970s in favour of large, mechanised logging operations and also a vertical integration requirement for processing mills to have HPHs to supply them. The industry grew from 21 plywood mills in 1979 to 101 in 1985 (FAO–GOI 1990), and became a $3–4 billion export industry in the early 1990s (Figure 9.1).

Amid nationalist pressure to build processing facilities, the direct ownership and operation of logging operations by foreign firms declined. As well, the Indonesian military was pushed out, or forced into joint ventures with well-connected firms (Ross 1996; Robison and Hadiz 2004: 74).[2] These firms included leading Chinese-Indonesian conglomerates owned by Soeharto cronies such as M. (Bob) Hasan, Prajogo Pangestu and Eka Tjipta Widjaja as well as firms owned by or connected via directorships to the Soeharto family (Brown 1999; Ross 2001).

Despite this seeming privatisation of the timber industry, the military remained involved in the sector due to extraordinary financial incentives. For example, the military continued to provide security to logging operations, as a result of which it became involved in innumerable conflicts (Jarvie et al. 2003). More importantly, the military relied on logging and other off-budget sources for about two-thirds of its budget, a situation of 'auto-financing' that persisted in 2004 (Ascher 1998; Jarvie et al. 2003). As a result, the military remains a part of the oligarchy steering the Indonesian economy rather than being a force in regulating legal operations and controlling illegal ones.

The second unusual step was to penetrate Japanese and other (at the time) non-traditional markets. This step was taken using the organisational and institutional strength of Apkindo. Under Bob Hasan's leadership, and based on his longstanding personal relationship with President Soeharto (Barr 1998), culminating in Hasan's appointment in 1998 as Soeharto's first Chinese-Indonesian cabinet member, Apkindo was allowed to control plywood exports. Its regional marketing boards held authority over 'standard prices', quantities and export destinations. Apkindo also collected numerous fees from its members and required them to use Hasan's shipping and insurance companies. The power of the oligarchy served to limit the industry's numbers and maintain a degree of concentration in the sector (Brown 1999).

Importantly, the domestic oligarchy of politico-business families and the military relied on a transnational alliance to gain market share in Japan. To break the domination of Japan's trading houses (*sogo shosha*) over plywood imports, Hasan formed an alliance with a smaller trading house, Kanmatsu Trading Company, to create Nippindo (Gellert 2003).[3] Nippindo became the sole importing partner for Apkindo's controlled exports at a time when Japan obtained nearly all its imports from Indonesia. The fees that Nippindo was able to charge clearly benefited Hasan and his Japanese partner (Barr 1998); over time the market access at favourable prices benefited the oligarchy more broadly.

The dominance of the Indonesian and transnational oligarchy in the global tropical plywood industry both contributed to and benefited from high prices in the 1990s. Market reports from the International Tropical Timber Organization (ITTO) acknowledged Indonesia as the price-setter in tropical plywood, both through its domination of the sector and through the institutional relations described above. Manoal Sobral Filho, Executive Director of the ITTO, notes that on the eve of the Asian financial crisis the price of 2.3 mm 'thin' plywood reached $700 per cubic metre (Rutten and Tan 2004: Foreword). This figure seems a bit high, but definitely the price was well over $400 (Adams and Johnson 1998) whereas before Apkindo existed it was below $200.

Not surprisingly, given the power of the oligarchy, the economic benefits of the sector were not widely distributed in Indonesia, and perhaps not even widely distributed within the timber sector. In the nationalised oil and gas sector, 85 per cent of the economic rent was appropriated in production-sharing agreements, but in timber only roughly 15 per cent was appropriated (Ahmad 1992; Ascher 1998). Moreover, the largest amount of rent was collected through the Reforestation Fund (Dana Reboisasi), which was controversially (mis)used for B.J. Habibie's IPTN plane factory and to subsidise the expansion of pulp plantations, among other uses. According to an Ernst & Young audit, $670 million of the $2.5 billion collected between 1993/94 and 1997/98 was lost to disbursements unrelated to reforestation (Barr 2001: 81–82). Well before the 1997–98 crisis, supporters of policy reform increasingly came to recognise that reform was impossible without fundamental change in the political economy (Barber, Johnson and Hafild 1994).

However, the sustained power of the oligarchy from the forest industry was also beginning to be undermined by commodity-specific dynamics of depletion that were already in motion by the 1990s. As easily accessible forests were depleted, HPH holders logged more species and smaller-diameter trees further into the forests, as well as illegally re-logging areas in a practice known as *cuci mangkok* (washing the bowl) (Gellert 1998a; Barr 2002). New HPHs opened further east, in Maluku and Papua. Plywood mills slowly shifted the major source of raw material from the Indonesian Selective Cutting and Replanting System (TPTI) to clear-cutting of forest areas under IPK timber utilisation permits.

IPK permits were made available from the late 1980s due to the push to establish timber plantations (Barr 2002; WALHI 1995). Ironically, dominant fast-growing plantation species such as albizia and eucalyptus are less suited for plywood mills than for the pulp and paper sector, which grew by 700 per cent from the 1980s to the end of the 1990s, with more than $12 billion of investment despite doubts about the real extent of plantation establishment (Barr 2001). The deforestation and more permanent transformation of the landscape associated with clear-cutting created growing social unrest and conflict in the regions concerned.[4] Not surprisingly, such conflicts were a significant part of the clamour to overturn the system of KKN that underpinned the oligarchy (LATIN 1998; Colfer and Resosudarmo 2002).

CHALLENGES TO THE OLIGARCHY: THE IMF, OVERCAPACITY, MARKET STRUCTURE AND DECENTRALISATION

In the last six years, Indonesia's timber oligarchy has faced tremendous challenges, including the short-term conjuncture of the Asian crisis and structural adjustment; long-term trends in the structure of Asian timber markets; domestic overcapacity; and decentralisation policies. The challenges are thus economic, socio-political and part of the dynamics of extractive economies.

The Asian crisis and IMF structural adjustment: Dismantling oligarchy?

The Asian crisis led to significant falls in the price and export volume of Indonesian forest products because of economic decline in Japan and other markets. The plywood export price, which had been relatively stable at around $450 per cubic metre in the mid-1990s, dropped precipitously to $250 in May 1998 (ITTO 1999: 169). In 2004, Indonesian and Malaysian plywood prices reached only 80 per cent of their 1997 levels while Meranti log prices reached 90 per cent (ITTO MIS 2004).

Of more immediate effect on the power of the oligarchy was the IMF's structural adjustment program within Indonesia (Sunderlin 2002). The IMF's second letter of intent of January 1998 included specific items to dismantle the power of the oligarchy – not only in timber but also in other sectors, such as rice and automobiles. To be sure, the IMF framed its intentions not in terms of dismantling oligarchy but rather in terms of freeing the market from 'monopolies' and improving efficiency and rationality in wood product markets. The two most important conditionalities related to timber called for an end to the log export ban and an end to the marketing power of Apkindo.[5] In addition, the Reforestation Fund was moved on-budget and thus away from Department of Forestry to Department of Finance control with legislative oversight.

Further pressure from international donors and NGOs led to inclusion of forestry in Consultative Group on Indonesia (CGI) discussions for the first couple of years after the crisis. However, in later meetings, achieving (or failing to achieve) the points of agreement in the forestry agenda has not been a condition for continued disbursements and rescheduling of Paris Group loans. In any case, both key IMF conditionalities have been dismantled, at least in part (see below).

Overcapacity and market shifts

The Indonesian wood products industry faces broader challenges in maintaining the market power that was constructed by – and for – the oligarchy during the New Order period. These challenges, which began to be apparent during the 1997–98 crisis, are both domestic and international. To the extent that the sector declines, of course, there is less wealth available to support the oligarchy's continued power.

Domestically, there is a crisis of overcapacity in the timber sector. The 'structural timber deficit' between industrial capacity and legal and sustainable supply had reached 40 million cubic metres by 1997 (Barr 2001) and currently stands at 60–75 million cubic metres (Tacconi, Obidzinski and Agung 2004).[6] Calculating round-wood equivalents from Food and Agriculture Organization production and trade data, Tacconi, Obidzinski and Agung (2004: 5) found that the supply of about 60 million cubic metres[7] included almost 50 million cubic metres of illegally harvested wood.

At the same time, the structure of the wood products sector has shifted from plywood towards pulp and paper. Figure 9.1 shows that plywood exports peaked in the early 1990s at about $4 billion (from a volume of 10.1 million cubic metres). According to ITTO data, production of plywood declined from 8.2 million cubic metres in 2000 to 6.6 million cubic metres in 2002, of which 5.5 million was exported (ITTO 2004: Tables 1-1-d and 2-4). In the last couple of years, the combined exports of pulp, paper and paperboard have exceeded the value of plywood.

Debate continues about whether sustainable forest management is possible under current conditions (Barr 2002). However, it seems clear that the sector is relying on an unsustainable supply to keep it going in the short term. Overlogging continues due to the rapid expansion of pulp and paper and the issuing of IPK clear-cutting permits to feed mixed tropical hardwood to the mills. Barr (2000: 9) estimates that 92 million cubic metres of mixed tropical hardwood was cut from an 835,000-hectare area between 1988 and 1999. As a consequence, in the late 1990s deforestation rates increased to perhaps 1.7–2.0 million hectares per year (Holmes 2000; FWI–GFW 2002). In more recent years, due to the severely degraded condition of the forests, the Ministry of Forestry, as part of a 'soft landing' policy for the industry, reduced the annual allowable cut of legal harvest to 6.9 million cubic metres in 2002 and 5.7 million cubic metres in 2004. Were law enforcement to prevail, the future would be grim for much of the timber industry. Already, a number of plywood factories have closed, with thousands of workers laid off in 2004 and more lay-offs forecast in 2005.[8]

However, with processing and illegal logging continuing at high levels, the prospect is not for a soft landing but for a hard landing in the medium term. This prospect is heightened as Asian producers' global market share has declined in the face of competition from Latin America in plywood and Africa in logs and sawn-wood (Rytkönen 2003: xi). Tropical timber products are also losing market share to temperate products, particularly in plywood and other panel products (Ruttan and Tan 2004). Such pressures would be particularly threatening to the Indonesian oligarchy if it were not for perennially 'insensitive' markets such as Japan and China.

The regional importance of China

Chinese markets are the biggest 'new kid on the block' in Asian and global markets (ITTO 2004; Sun, Katsigris and White 2004) and pose additional challenges for Indonesia's timber oligarchy. In astounding fashion, between 1997 and 2003 (preliminary data), the total volume of Chinese forest product imports grew from 40 million cubic metres to over 106 million cubic metres in round-wood equivalents (Sun, Katsigris and White 2004: Figure 1). Pulp and paper accounts for over 60 per cent of China's forest product imports. With a domestic ban placed on logging in southwest China following the floods of 1998, China has also become the world's leading importer of industrial round-wood (that is, logs), with imports in 2002 of over 24 million cubic metres. An additional 7.7 million cubic metres in round-wood equivalents was imported as sawn-wood. By value, China's total forest product imports have moved from seventh to second in the world (Sun, Katsigris and White 2004: 2).

Within this import boom are several other trends that have implications for Indonesia's timber sector. Since 1997, log imports have shifted from almost 80 per cent hardwood, which is mostly tropical in origin, to 65 per cent softwood, especially larch from Russia. Legal log imports from Indonesia jumped to over 1 million cubic metres before Indonesia again banned the export of logs in October 2001, while discrepancies between sawn-wood imports reported in China and Indonesia's reported exports led to Indonesia banning the export of sawn timber in September 2004. While Indonesia's total forest product exports to China have continued to increase, their share of the country's total imports has declined from almost 20 per cent in 1997 to less than 10 per cent in 2002 (Sun, Katsigris and White 2004: 17). Plywood exports have also declined, although Indonesian ply still accounts for 70 per cent of Chinese imports.

China has moved quickly into downstream processing and export of wood products. In 1997 higher-value products such as plywood and other panels were almost half of imports, but four years later logs and sawn-wood represented 80 per cent of imports (Sun, Katsigris and White 2004: 7). Between 2001 and 2002, Chinese tropical plywood exports more than doubled, to 437,000 cubic metres, and they increased another 19 per cent in 2003 to 520,000 cubic metres, almost the level of Brazil, the third largest exporter after Indonesia and Malaysia (ITTO 2004: vi). China's exports of secondary processed wood products have also surged; in 2002 they reached a value of more than $7.2 billion, making China the world's largest exporter, even surpassing Italy (ITTO 2004: viii). Much of this growth is in wooden furniture exports to the United States, Japan and elsewhere. In 2004 the United States made an anti-dumping ruling against bedroom furniture, though this was based on state subsidies for factories, not the illegal procurement of raw logs from Southeast Asia.

There remain many questions about China's continued growth and how the country's timber sector has managed to move so quickly into downstream processing. For Indonesia's producers (and forests), the problem is that there is increased Chinese demand for raw logs and sawn-wood – both legal and, increasingly, illegal – while demand for processed products such as plywood is declining. There is also growing demand for pulp, putting further pressure on natural and plantation forests in Indonesia (and elsewhere).

Meanwhile, in Japan, demand is flat or declining, albeit still exceeding 4 million cubic metres of plywood in 2003. Indonesian wooden furniture exports exceeded $1 billion in 2000 and 2001 (Association of Furniture and Handcraft Industry (Asmindo) data in Simangunsong 2004). Furniture is one potential area of growth but Indonesian manufacturers must compete with Chinese and other producers for investment and market share. Finally, as investment and trade are liberalised within ASEAN and between Southeast Asia and China, one will need to be increasingly careful about the interpretation of 'national' production and trade figures; for example, designations such as 'Chinese', 'Indonesian' or 'Russian' may disguise transnational ownership and joint venture investment patterns.[9]

Decentralisation[10]

The last area of challenge for the timber oligarchy is decentralisation. Given the top-down allocation of HPHs and the trampling on people's rights to land and livelihood that marked the New Order, decentralisation was met with enthusiasm when it began under Law 22/1999 during President Habibie's term in office. The decentralisation agenda was also lent intellectual support by researchers and activists who believed that locally managed forest areas could be more sustainable and just, although democratic decentralisation has proven difficult to achieve (Ribot 2002; Dermawan and Resosudarmo 2002).

During the Habibie and Wahid presidencies, district-level governments were given authority to allocate timber utilisation permits (IUPHHK) for 20 years on areas up to 50,000 hectares and timber extraction permits (IPHHK) for one year on smaller areas of up to 100 hectares. The result was a boom in permit allocation, including the issuing of permits inside the borders of existing HPHs, the issuing of permits over areas larger than 100 hectares (either in one permit or in groups of permits) and de facto legalisation of illegal logging (see, for example, Barr et al. 2002; McCarthy 2002). Given this legitimation of flows of otherwise illegal timber, the attitude of the industry towards decentralisation is not a foregone conclusion. As one industry association official remarked, '*Asal jelas, kita tidak peduli*' ('As long as it's clear, we don't care [whether authority is decentralised or centralised]').[11] The problem, from the industry's point of view, is that the small concessions are unreliable sources of supply and concession holders may prefer to sell their logs (now illegally) over the border.

During President Megawati's term in office, the Department of Forestry tried to 're-centralise' authority over the forests.[12] In 2002, the government issued a new regulation, PP 34/2002, cancelling district and provincial rights to grant licences.[13] However, the regulation was promulgated without consultation with significant stakeholders and is reportedly unpopular with regional governments, communities, NGOs and even the timber firms, who worry that the central government might prove stricter than the regional levels of govern-ment.[14] PP 34/2002 revokes district authority over logging (except for personal needs and public facilities) while still giving the provinces and districts signif-icant responsibilities for forest management (including the supervision of log-ging operations), for environmental services and for non-timber forest product extraction. It delegates licensing authority for wood industries with an annual capacity of over 6,000 cubic metres to the Ministry of Forestry, and licensing authority for smaller industries to the governor (rather than the district head or *bupati*). It also gives the provincial government authority to approve the annual cutting plans known as *rencana kerja tahunan* (RKTs).

The struggle between the centre, the provinces and the districts is far from over. Numerous districts continue to issue small-scale logging permits and levy local fees, while the collection of central fees is minimal and perfunctory. In October 2004, the attorney-general brought a corruption charge against the *bupati* of Berau, East Kalimantan, for embezzlement (*penyelewengan*) of Rp 88 billion ($9.4 million); the charge resulted from the *bupati*'s decision to relieve companies of tax obligations to the central government.[15] Earlier in 2004, the governors of the four Kalimantan provinces united in their rejection of the Min-istry of Forestry's unilateral reduction in their annual allowable cutting quota by 17 per cent. Both NGOs and the industry association umbrella organisation, the Indonesian Forestry Society (MPI), were critical of their action as threaten-ing the future sustainability of forestry production. Forestry Minister Muham-mad Prakosa admitted that 'The governors may be able to get away with this, but we have the authority to revoke the operating licences of forestry firms or to ban the exports of their products'.[16]

INDONESIA'S TIMBER OLIGARCHY RESPONDS: IBRA AND BRIK

As Indonesia faces these short-term and long-term economic and political chal-lenges, the question arises as to whether the (national) timber oligarchy can sur-vive, and if so, how. Robison and Hadiz (2004: 60) have put it this way:

> To what extent can we consider these disparate and fragmented figures and groups an oligarchy in the longer term, able to reproduce themselves across generations, to survive the departure from office of their founder and to survive even the collapse of the regime?

In addition to regime collapse, in a natural resource sector like timber, the oli-garchy is faced with the problem of depletion dynamics and the pressing ques-tion of whether the industry will be able to survive and compete in the region and globally. Thus far, the answer seems to be that, despite such competitive pressures, the power of the oligarchy is intact. It has responded to the threats it faces in several ways.

Refinancing oligarchy through IBRA

First, the ailing oligarchy has come out of the crisis and associated financial troubles with a new financial breath of air. IBRA was established in 1999 in the aftermath of the fiscal crisis and IMF structural adjustment to re-establish Indonesia's flailing banking sector. Approximately $2.5 billion (Rp 22 trillion) in corporate debts associated with Indonesia's forestry conglomerates came under IBRA auspices (Barr et al. 2002). At the CGI meeting in February 2000, the government of Indonesia agreed to close some of these heavily indebted forestry companies and wood industries. Yet there have been few closures, and this has led to a debt recapitalisation that has the potential to further degrade Indonesia's forests. Rather than collect the debts, IBRA opted to write off most of them (Simangunsong and Setiono 2004). Barr and Setiono (2003a, 2003b) argue that financial institutions failed to carry out due diligence in making loans and investments based on ill-founded assumptions about the adequacy of the efforts to establish forest plantations to supply the timber sector (Barr 2000). Instead, investment decisions implicitly relied on the continued power of the oligarchy to obtain access to raw materials from the natural forests – by force if necessary. In effect, the largely foreign investors either did not know of the risks or were confident about the capacity of the Soeharto regime to crush dissent and establish sufficient plantations.

The most striking case is Bank Mandiri, now Indonesia's largest lending institution. The outcome of debt write-offs from Mandiri is that 'a capital subsidy of $1 billion or more' has gone to the same forestry-based conglomerates that prospered during the New Order (Barr and Setiono 2003b: 14). Over 300 international financial institutions are also said to be involved in the financing of Indonesia's pulp and paper expansion without due diligence on the risks of illegal logging, unsustainable raw material supplies and social conflict (Matthew and van Gelder 2001). Whether or not current calls for legal reform and bankruptcy laws could serve the interests of the powerless at the same time as they challenge the interests of the oligarchy remains to be seen.

Re-empowering oligarchy under BRIK

In addition to financially re-empowering the oligarchy through IBRA, there has been a political re-empowerment. In December 2002, the Ministry of Forestry and the Ministry of Trade and Industry officially created a new industry organisation, BRIK. The stated aim was to prevent Indonesian companies from purchasing illegal logs and thereby alleviate industry problems by assuring consumers in Europe and North America that they were not buying products obtained from illegal or unsustainable sources. BRIK has been given the responsibility to conduct an audit of domestic firms to ascertain the amount of logs used by each. All firms exporting forestry-related products are required to hold a new licence – *eksportir terdaftar produk industri kehutanan* – to export wood products. BRIK's role is to collect the mill reports on wood consumption (*laporan mutasi kayu*) and the transportation documents for the logs (SKSHH). Under this system, in 2003, BRIK reported issuing export licences to 3,900 companies for 4.7 million cubic metres of exports valued at roughly $1.85 billion.[17]

In theory, BRIK can check whether companies, individually or collectively, are producing more than their legal supply and whether each recipient company's supply is accompanied by the requisite transportation documents. However, BRIK's system relies wholly on the legality of the raw materials; in practice, there is a severe forgery problem with SKSHH documents in the extractive regions (DTE 2004). In short, critical analysts (DTE 2004; Kato 2005) worry that in creating a self-certification system BRIK prefers to focus on legality over sustainability, because legality is ambiguous and easy to manipulate in Indonesia. In addition, a recent study confirms there has been little change in the practices of the (legal) HPHs supplying the mills: only 11 per cent of forest concessions and plantations were deemed to have good (that is, non-corrupt) performance; most not only had unpaid forestry taxes but had not implemented planning or reforestation activities (Warta FKKM 2004).[18]

(Dis)unity within the oligarchy

There are some signs of disunity in the oligarchy. In the early reform years, the industry umbrella organisation, MPI, was countered by a shadow organisation, MPI-Reformasi. Its leader was a former head of MPI, Agus Miftach, who accused the association of collecting $10 billion in fees from its members.[19] During that period, Bob Hasan was convicted of corruption in using government funds in connection with a contract to provide aerial photographs of the forests to the Ministry of Forestry. He was sentenced to jail for six years, although he was released early in 2004 for good behaviour.

Also in early 2004, a public split formed in the leadership of APHI, the Indonesian Association of Forest Concessionaires. An extraordinary national meeting, opened by the Minister of Industry and Trade, was held in March to elect new leaders, but the old leadership promised to regroup under Apkindo and MPI.[20] New reports charge that during Adi Warsita's term as head of APHI from 1998 to 2003, Akbar Tanjung – Speaker of the People's Representative Council (DPR) and head of Golkar, Indonesia's second largest party – corruptly used Rp 268 billion (about $30 million) of APHI funds to cover Golkar's needs (*Gatra*, 13 November 2004: 24–34).

The Department of Forestry's role in the oligarchy is somewhat ambiguous at present. With the Department of Industry and Trade, it has done much to support the large industrial players that traditionally form the core of the oligarchy. After the log export tariff was reduced to 20 per cent in 1999 and 15 per cent in 2000,[21] the log export ban was reinstated in October 2001 by joint decree of the Minister of Forestry and the Minister of Industry and Trade.[22] The same two ministries introduced a ban on rough sawn-wood exports in September 2004; the underlying rationale was that such a ban would support efforts to reduce illegal logging.[23] While this may be true, the bans also support continued secure access to raw materials for existing capacity in the plywood and pulp and paper industries.

On the other hand, Minister Prakosa declared a 'soft landing' policy for the industry by reducing logging quotas in the regions. He revoked the timber plantation licences of companies engaged in illegal or unsustainable practices, although a successful legal challenge was made in the courts (Murniati and Djamaludin 2004).[24] In an effort to root out corruption in his department, he reassigned a number of top-echelon bureaucrats and also signed a memorandum of understanding with Indonesian Corruption Watch and Greenomics Indonesia in June 2004 to monitor internal affairs. It is too early to tell what the new Minister of Forestry, M.S. Kaban, will do. In his first days in the job, he voiced support for forest industry revitalisation and growth modelled on the heyday of Bob Hasan; mentioned plans not to pursue a strong government regulation in lieu of legislation (*perpu*) on illegal logging proposed by Minister Prakosa; and yet also forwarded a list of the financial backers (*cukong*) of illegal loggers to the attorney-general's office for prosecution. Of 25 illegal sawmills operating near Bukit Tigapuluh National Park in Sumatra, 13 were found to be backed by the armed forces (Indonesia–UK Tropical Forest Management Programme 1999, cited in EIA–Telapak 2002a). It remains to be seen whether the new government will pursue such police and military 'backing' for large-scale illegal logging.

CONCLUSION

The politico-bureaucratic oligarchy that benefited from and also drove the expansion of a wood panel industry and then a pulp and paper industry in Indonesia is in the midst of reconstituting itself. It faces many challenges, not least of which is the depletion of the raw materials that formed the foundation of its economic wealth over the last several decades. There is little evidence of sufficient investment in plantations to relieve the pressure on the remaining forests; were such investments to begin in earnest now, they would take six or more years to become productive.

In the meantime, who will challenge the power of the oligarchy? Civil society remains relatively weak. Some NGOs continue to call for a total moratorium on logging to allow time and space for the restructuring of the industry that seems inevitable given current difficulties in obtaining raw materials. But their pleas have been ignored while the oligarchy puts seemingly eternal faith in the natural resource wealth of Indonesia. Labour, too, is weak, especially in a sector that is laying people off and expanding in capital-intensive products like pulp and paper. Moreover, in this race to the finish, indigenous groups find it difficult to withstand the pressure to take short-term payments for logging.

Without a broader-based social and/or political movement, the challenges do not represent threats to the power of the oligarchy as a whole. The transnational character of the oligarchy in timber does seem to have eroded in a period of regional and global competition. If anything, the regional challenges seem the most pressing on the interests of the oligarchy, although most provincial and district leaders favour greater extraction associated with financial flows to elites. However, the refinancing of the firms through IBRA in the face of international financial pressure demonstrates that 'the assumed link between structural shocks and reform of the economic regime has not been realised' (Robison and Hadiz 2004: 264). Most of the actions taken by the oligarchy's key players in government and industry have been 'rearguard' measures to shore up a threatened industry and the oligarchy's power for as long as the forests will sustain them.

NOTES

1   In sociology, the inevitability of oligarchy was debated by Robert Michels ('Who says organisation says oligarchy') and Max Weber, who believed the iron cage of capitalist bureaucracy could be challenged by charismatic leaders or democratic practices. While their concern was with the oligarchic tendencies of political parties, the tension between concentrated leadership and democratic governance is relevant to the future of the timber industry.

2   But see Brown (1999), who found that in 1998 the 'armed forces/army' was the sixth largest holder of HPHs, albeit not officially acknowledged.

3   Hasan established similar exclusive marketing companies for other markets, including Singapore (Fendi Wood), Hong Kong (Celandine Co. Ltd), South Korea (Indo Kor Panels Co. Ltd), the Middle East (PT Fendi Indah in Jakarta), Europe (Kiani UK) and the United States (Chesapeake Hardwoods).

4   See Jarvie et al. (2003); Human Rights Watch (2003); Fried (2003); and 'Conflicts between locals and timber companies to grow', *Jakarta Post*, 9 March 2000.

5   In addition, the IMF called for an opening of investment in palm oil, a particularly controversial move given the association of land clearing for palm oil plantations with the forest fires of the 1997–98 El Niño event, and conflict and deforestation more generally (Gellert 1998b).

6   See also Brown (1999) and World Bank (2001).

7   It is worth noting that about one-third of plywood and two-thirds of sawn-wood
    production are consumed domestically.
8   'Buruh industri kayu mendekati tutup buku', *Kompas*, 14 September 2004: 31; 'Pil-
    ihan sulit buruh kayu di kaltim', *Kompas*, 14 September 2004: 31.
9   For example, the large pulp and paper producers are Asia-wide conglomerates (Barr
    2000) and much of the Chinese furniture expansion is in joint ventures with US,
    Taiwanese and other firms (ITTO 2004: viii).
10 This section on decentralisation relies on a series of case studies conducted by the
    Center for International Forestry Research (available at <www.cgiar.cifor.org>), as
    well as conversations with Bambang Setiono, who shared a draft paper on the topic.
11 This comment was made at a workshop called 'Can decentralisation work for
    forests and the poor?' at the National Forest Poli~y Seminar organised by the Cen-
    ter for International Forestry Research (CIFOR), the Australian Centre for Interna-
    tional Agricultural Research (ACIAR) and the UK Department for International
    Development (DFID) (Bogor, 1 September 2004).
12 According to several attendees at the workshop described in the previous note, I
    was not the only one for *resentralisasi* was a new term.
13 Peraturan Pemerintah tentang Tata Hutan dan Penyusunan Rencana Pengelolaan
    Hutan, Pemanfaatan Hutan dan Punggunaan Kawasan Hutan (Government Regula-
    tion on Forest Arrangements and Planning of Forest Management, Forest Use and
    Forest Estate Use).
14 Interview with environmental activist, Jakarta, 17 September 2004. NGOs have
    brought the decree to the Supreme Court for judicial review.
15 'Regent a graft suspect', *Jakarta Post*, 21 October 2004: 5.
16 'Plantation plan overshadows regreening', 10 January 2004, <www.laksamana.
    net>, accessed 7 September 2004; see also 'Akselerasi HTI demi industri kayu',
    Kompas, 8 September 2004: 14. One of the reviewers of this paper noted that the
    larger issue was the switch to pre-payment of Dana Reboisasi taxes and Forest Roy-
    alty (PSDH) on timber operations – that is, before the beginning of the RKT –
    although this may be deemed a government–industry conflict rather than a centre–
    region one.
17 'Indonesia: Ailing timber industry pays high cost of revival: Indonesia's timber
    industry has been in the doldrums since the beginning of 2003', *Jakarta Post*, 30
    December 2003.
18 Greenomics and Indonesian Corruption Watch have been leading an effort to pub-
    licly expose the recalcitrant taxpayers (see press releases at <www.greenomics.
    org>).
19 See 'Bob memang bandit hutan', *SiaR*, 28 October 1998, available at <http://www.
    hamline.edu/apakabar/basisdata/1998/10/28/0006.html>.
20 'Perselisihan APHI memuncak', *Tempo Interaktif*, 14 April 2004.
21 The reductions were made by decree of the Ministry of Finance, respectively SK
    Menteri Keuangan 107/1999 and SK 567/1999 effective in 2000. The original struc-
    tural adjustment called for a reduction to 10 per cent by 2000 but this was never
    realised. Thanks to Ahmad Dermawan for tracking down this information.
22 Kepetusan Bersama Menteri Kehutanan RI Nomor: 1132/Kpts-II/2001 dan Menteri
    Perindustrian dan Perdagangan RI Nomor: 292/MPP/Kep/10/2001.

23 The ban on sawn-wood exports came through Joint Decision (SKB) 350/Menhut-VI/2004 and 598/MPP/Kep/9/2004 (Surat Keputusan Bersama Larangan Ekspor Bantalan Rel Kereta Api Dari Kayu dan Kayu Gergajian) signed on 24 September 2004.

24 After appeals to higher levels, the case was settled out of court, according to a senior ministerial official.

10 IF ONLY FISH COULD VOTE: THE ENDURING CHALLENGES OF COASTAL AND MARINE RESOURCES MANAGEMENT IN POST-*REFORMASI* INDONESIA

Ian M. Dutton

INTRODUCTION

Indonesia is undergoing an unprecedented and transformative period of change. From the perspective of coastal and marine resources management in Indonesia, two very notable changes are already in effect: the introduction of laws relating to regional autonomy and the establishment of a Ministry of Marine Affairs and Fisheries. The former changed the regulatory framework for management by creating a wide range of decentralised authority. The latter elevated coastal and marine management to a new level and enables fisheries-related marine issues to be considered in an integrated manner for the first time in the history of Indonesia (Dahuri 2001). In combination, the innovations have set the stage for improved coastal and marine resources management.

The Food and Agriculture Organization has estimated that Indonesia has 6.7 million marine and freshwater fishers and dependants in 7,000 coastal villages (FAO 2000). From this perspective, the management changes outlined above have occurred against a backdrop of increased conflict and contrasting fortunes. The conflict is due to increased competition between local and outside fishers for fish stocks. It is symptomatic of the lack of effective regulatory systems to control access to fisheries stocks, and of the lack of strategic guidance to balance fisheries development with other marine resource uses such as coastal reclamation and settlement, oil and gas extraction, tourism and conservation. The contrasting fortunes reflect the influence of global markets in recent years: factors such as rapid growth in demand for fisheries products, loss of supply from other sources in Asia, new technologies and currency fluctuations have created extraordinary opportunities for entrepreneurs and other 'middlemen'.

Many commercial fishing companies and key individuals within communities dependent on marine fisheries have benefited greatly from the associated increased export value of fish products since 1998. Annual estimated receipts from reported fisheries exports exceed $2 billion.[1] However, these benefits primarily accrue to a fisheries 'elite' and are often derived at the expense of other community members and Indonesian society at large, particularly if one examines closely the distribution of all costs and benefits. As a consequence of the overexploitation of stocks and other development pressures, there are now many fishing communities who live in abject poverty and who have little prospect of sustainable livelihoods (Yowono 1998).

From the perspective of fish and the ecosystems they depend upon, things are getting worse, not better. More and more fishers are legally and illegally catching more fish with both legal and destructive technologies. Few of the many regulations that seek to prevent illegal exploitation and pollution are being enforced. Vast areas of key habitat are being destroyed by inappropriate forms of coastal and marine development. Less than 7 per cent of Indonesia's coral reefs are in excellent condition (Hopley and Suharsono 2000). In short, a marine eco-catastrophe is happening, but there is inadequate public knowledge about these trends. Equally importantly, there is no political urgency in dealing with what the trends mean for fish resources and the millions who depend on fisheries for livelihood and subsistence.

Recent advances in coastal and marine resource management involving millions of dollars of investment in capacity-building, poverty alleviation, fisheries development and similar projects have so far done relatively little to ensure that the enormous benefits that may be derived from healthy fish stocks and marine ecosystems will be sustained. That situation must change, and it must change quickly, in order to protect Indonesia's economic, social and environmental well-being and long-term security.

A comprehensive, integrated and sustainable approach to coastal and marine resource development and management is urgently needed as part of the post-*reformasi* process. In devising solutions, much can be learned from the integrated coastal management efforts tested in recent years under programs conducted by, among others, the US Agency for International Development (USAID) and Indonesia's National Development Planning Agency, Bappenas (the Coastal Resources Management Project Program: see Knight and Tighe 2003); the Center for Coastal and Marine Resources Studies at Bogor Agricultural University; and the Marine and Fisheries Research Agency and the Ministry of Marine Affairs and Fisheries.

IMPORTANCE OF INDONESIA'S COASTAL AND MARINE RESOURCES

Indonesia occupies a strategic position at the intersection of the Pacific and Indian oceans. The archipelago contains the world's largest remaining mangrove forests and Indonesia has the largest area of coral reefs of any country (Hopley and Suharsono 2000). Indonesia's waters are among the most productive of all tropical seas. They are the epicentre of global marine biodiversity and provide globally significant corridors for migratory species (Rais et al. 1998; Kahn 2003).

Coastal and marine industries such as oil and gas production, transportation, fisheries and tourism account for 26 per cent of GDP and employ more than 15 per cent of Indonesia's workforce. Some 140 million Indonesians live within 60 kilometres of the coast, many within the large coastal cities that occupy a predominant position in the national economy (Dahuri and Dutton 2000). The following discussion focuses primarily on fisheries-related marine industries, partly because of their particular social and economic significance and partly because there is only limited reliable information on non-fisheries components of the marine sector.

Marine fisheries

Indonesia's fisheries produced an estimated 4.5 million tonnes of fish in 1997 (FAO 2000). Marine fisheries comprised the majority of total fish production (3.7 million tonnes). The major types of fisheries were (in order) purse seine, lift net, trammel net and pole and line tuna fisheries. Some 94 per cent of this estimated production was reported to be captured by small-scale fishers. However, the overall catch was significantly underreported, so that figure is misleading. The total fishing fleet was estimated to comprise 402,000 vessels and had grown from only 334,000 vessels in 1988. Of these boats, 57 per cent were non-powered; of the remainder, 55 per cent used outboard engines.

The vessel limits reinforce the importance of near-shore fisheries and clearly define the focal area for much of the potential fishing effort by local fishers. However, as the Commission for the Conservation of Southern Bluefin Tuna notes (CCSBT 2003), it is also critical to take a multilevel perspective on catches in order to develop appropriate management regimes; near-shore fisheries are just one component of that larger system.

There has been a sharp increase in subsistence and export fisheries in most areas as a result of the *krismon* (economic crisis). This is due to both the high value of capture fisheries and the increased costs of alternative protein sources. It is evidenced by the increased range of many larger fleets, particularly those emanating from South Sulawesi, where there is a large, highly skilled and wide-ranging fishing fleet. It is also evidenced by the increased numbers of people engaged in fishing on at least a part-time basis. For example, in highly populated coastal areas such as Jakarta, Surabaya, Semarang, Makassar, Manado and Lampung there has been a significant increase in part-time fishing coinciding with a rise in local unemployment.

Aquaculture production

Aquaculture is an increasingly important component of Indonesia's fisheries. Fish culture occupied about 560,000 hectares in 1998, with some 60 per cent of this in estuarine or former mangrove areas and the remainder under paddy field aquaculture and freshwater ponds (PCI 2001). Brackish water production yielded some 370,000 tonnes of fish and shrimp (55 per cent of total aquaculture production), with shrimp production worth some $1.24 billion in 2000. The majority of production is directed to the Japanese market.

The most commonly cultured fish species are the ubiquitous milkfish (73 per cent), tilapia (12 per cent) and mullet (6 per cent). There is increasing interest in new finfish species, particularly grouper and sea bass (barramundi). Production of these species is limited to government research facilities at this time, but the Nature Conservancy is making a significant investment in their mariculture to provide an alternative to live fish exploitation near Komodo National Park.[2] Aquaculture is also a large employer. Some 2.05 million fish farmers were employed in 1998, with the majority (65 per cent) in Java.

Food security

Around 46 per cent of Indonesia's fish production is consumed fresh, partly because of the nature of demand and production (largely artisan fisheries with little post-catch processing capacity) and partly because of the historically limited export orientation of most producers. Some 30 per cent is dried, salted or smoked for local or provincial consumption. Fish availability is important to the daily survival of many residents of coastal communities, particularly in drier areas where alternative agricultural production is limited.

Perhaps the most important single measure of the importance of fisheries resources to the health, welfare and food security of Indonesians is the FAO (1997) assessment of sources of animal protein supply. Some 53 per cent of Indonesia's total animal protein supply comes from fish – well above the reported global average of 16.5 per cent and much greater than for developed nations such as the United States (6.8 per cent) and Australia (6.5 per cent).

Moreover, this single measure does not fully indicate the significance of coastal resources for certain areas and during periods of scarcity such as economic recession, or in areas where there are limited alternative agricultural options. For example, in fish-producing areas such as North Sulawesi, consumption averages 50 kilograms per person per year, more than 2.5 times the national average.

The importance of multiple sources of household income (for example, from agriculture, commerce and fisheries) has been well documented in several recent studies of coastal communities (for example, Tulungen, Kusoy and Crawford 1998; Crawford et al. 1999). Access to coastal resources became even more important to rural and urban households following the Asian economic crisis because people needed to substitute locally available produce for expensive imported foodstuffs (Dutton and Bengen 2001). There is clearly a need for more comprehensive research on poverty, conflict and fisheries, but evidence from long-term studies of fishing communities in Java suggests that the sustainability of coastal fisheries is a key factor in community cohesion, peace and prosperity (Yowono 1998).

THREATS TO COASTAL RESOURCES AND DEVELOPMENT

Threats to coastal and marine resources and their dependent communities can be divided into two main categories: natural and anthropogenic. The effects of the former are not widely recognised in the design of many coastal and marine development projects but are critical in shaping ecosystem functioning and the context for management.

Natural threats include storms, volcanoes (including underwater eruptions), earthquakes, tsunamis, crown-of-thorns starfish outbreaks and other biological perturbations, and floods. Dutton, Bengen and Tulungen (2001) note that these key processes have a range of impacts on coastal communities and act synergistically with human-induced change to affect the resilience and response of ecosystems. They greatly influence habitat development and fisheries functioning. As one example, coastal flooding may destroy fish larvae, resulting in less recruitment, which in turn reduces the potential yield from selected fisheries in particular seasons or even in subsequent seasons. Few management schemes currently factor such impacts into the management framework. Indeed, the concept of managing to protect the functional integrity and resilience of marine ecosystems is a relatively new concept globally (Salm, Smith and Llewellyn 2001).

Anthropogenic threats are much better described. There are 10 main types of threat. The first is destructive fishing practices. These have become more prevalent during the last decade as demand for live reef fish has increased and alternative supplies from the Philippines and other countries have dwindled. Pet-Soede, Cesar and Pet (1999) note that it is extremely difficult to dissuade those engaged in practices such as bombing and poisoning to desist, particularly when their competitors will step into the void they leave and undertake such activities, and where the regulators lack the will to enforce regulations. Cesar et al. (1997) calculated the economic losses to Indonesia from all sources of reef degradation and overfishing at some $410,000/km^2 per year, assuming a 10 per cent discount rate. The total loss for all coral reefs (including fisheries) over the next 25 years was estimated at a staggering $30 billion.

The second type of threat is overfishing, including illegal, unregulated and unreported fishing. Such activities are a huge threat to the proper management of Indonesian fisheries; Box 10.1 describes in more detail some problems related to offshore fishing.[3] Establishing the true state of Indonesia's fish stocks is a difficult task, although there is clear evidence of reduced catch per unit effort (CPUE) in western and central Indonesia. CPUE is a measure of resource availability, so this suggests a decline in fisheries stocks. PCI (2001) noted that the maximum sustainable yield for Indonesian fisheries was exceeded more than a decade ago but that there is still excess fishing capacity in the country; they proposed an immediate moratorium on new licences. In one of the few detailed studies at the local level, Pet-Soede et al. (2001) showed that overfishing in the Spermonde Archipelago area of South Sulawesi has caused a long-term change in fishery composition and structure.

The third threat is climate change. In the last two decades, large-scale bleaching events have increased in intensity, frequency, and local and geographic distribution (Wilkinson 2000). In 1998, the worst year on record, complete loss of live coral occurred in some parts of the world. The effects in Indonesia were variable, with generally more extensive bleaching occurring in central and western reef systems, although eastern reefs were also affected.

The fourth threat is increased and concentrated run-off and sediment. Large-scale agricultural development (especially irrigation schemes), forest-clearing, mining[4] and infrastructure development typically pay little attention to erosion control and in most areas have more than doubled already high sediment loads in coastal waters (Hopley 1999).

The fifth threat is sewage and other land-based pollutants. With no appreciable sewage treatment capacity in any large coastal cities and with largely unregulated industrial waste disposal, pollution loads in near-shore waters are very high. A Ministry of Environment study of the Jakarta Bay watershed estimated that some 370 kilograms of mercury enters the bay every hour (MOSE 1996). Edinger and Risk (2000) rate land-based pollution as the most important threat to Indonesian reef ecosystems and note that on reefs exposed to such threats, coral species diversity was consistently reduced by 40–60 per cent.

The sixth threat is oil pollution and shipping. Indonesia is one of the world's largest offshore oil and gas producers, so there is a potential for significant oil pollution from land and ship sources. People are increasingly paying attention to the effects of spills on fisheries. For example, the owners of the tanker *MT*

BOX 10.1 OFFSHORE FISHING

Indonesia's marine capture fisheries are of two kinds. The first is inshore fishing by domestic subsistence and artisanal fishers using small boats and gear; the second is offshore fishing by larger vessels (over 30 gross tonnes and often foreign-owned), licensed to operate only beyond 12 nautical miles from the coast reserved for small craft (that is, between the islands and out to the 200 nautical mile limit of Indonesia's exclusive economic zone). Recent decentralisation policies transferred jurisdiction over inshore bands (within 4 and 12 nautical miles from shore) to the *kabupaten* and province respectively. The central government retains jurisdiction over all catch boats over 30 gross tonnes. The size of vessels and the nationality, wealth and political influence of their owners differ between inshore and offshore fishers and present different challenges to fisheries management.

Indonesia's waters are fertile, but all accessible marketable species are now everywhere overfished. Butcher (2004) has documented the changes in domestic and international demand and prices and in the design and size of vessels, fish-finding gear, catch gear and fish-preservation technologies that have depleted both demersal and pelagic species. The process began in the inshore west. As catches and fish sizes fell for each type of gear, fishing fleets changed gear and target species and moved progressively east and into ever deeper and further offshore waters. Moreover, fleets from other Asian nations began to fish in Indonesian waters in colonial times; from the 1970s, foreign boats increased as their fishing capacity depleted stocks in their own waters.

By 2000 there were about 1,500 fish and shrimp trawlers operating in Indonesian waters, plus pelagic purse seine and pole and line vessels and their mother ships and reefers (international frozen cargo carriers). Only about 700 trawlers were licensed. Nearly all of the trawlers are built, repaired and owned by companies in Thailand, Taiwan, South Korea, China, the Philippines and Japan. Since the early 1980s, trawlers have been licensed to operate only east of longitude 130°E (that is, east of the Tanimbar Islands). However, many operated outside the permitted zone, through collusion with navy or local officials. Most of these foreign-owned catch vessels were reflagged as 'Indonesian' by registering them as owned in joint venture or chartered in the name of a local company that in fact provided only the vessel and fishing licences and, in some cases, port services. The Indonesian company received a fee to arrange papers for the vessel and crew; to arrange supplies of fuel at the domestic price that was much lower than the world price; to arrange supplies of water and food; and to deal with officials. It had no ownership

King Fisher, which hit a reef near Cilacap in April 2000, were required to pay local fishers Rp 18 billion (roughly $2.1 million) in compensation, though this was lower than the Rp 80 billion originally demanded (Dutton, Bengen and Tulungen 2001).

The seventh threat is mining and quarrying of sand and coral. Road and house foundations in many coastal villages were historically constructed from in the vessel, gear or catch and had no share in the profit or loss. Inkopal, the navy's cooperative, held many of these 'joint venture' licences.

From 1998 to 2001, I carried out research on trawling in eastern Indonesia. I observed that in port each foreign trawler weighed and made a true tally of the weight of each of over 100 fish or other species, as it transferred plastic bags of frozen fish to a reefer. The trawler and reefer faxed those lists to their vessel owners abroad to allow settlement of accounts between their companies. No Indonesian official was aboard to check the tally. The catch vessel did not give a copy of that true record to any Indonesian company or authority. Instead, the system allowed the Indonesian counterpart company to invent and give to the relevant authorities a short list of around eight species that understated both the tonnes of fish transferred and the price per tonne of 'mixed frozen fish'. My observations indicated that foreign trawlers revealed only about 30 per cent of true weighed catch. That practice allowed the foreign fishing companies to avoid local and national taxes. It has made it difficult for Indonesia to document the extent and pace of depletion of marine stocks before such stocks collapse.

Only the state can manage offshore fisheries. Since 2000 the Ministry of Marine Affairs and Fisheries has been trying to implement reforms. Among other things, it has tried to computerise the system of licensing vessels; to set and raise licence fees according to the catching capacity of each size of vessel and its gear as well as to the proper resource rent; to restrict the number of vessels licensed to fish with each type of gear in relation to the 'calculated sustainable catch' in each of the nine Indonesian marine areas; to detect and prosecute vessels fishing without a valid licence; and to collect more reliable data on fish catches and exports by industrial-scale vessels. In September 2004, the legislature passed a new fisheries law. Previous laws have been written in ways that made them difficult to interpret and implement. It has been difficult to coordinate and fund the several ministries and national plus local government agencies to enforce the laws.

Even when laws and reforms for fisheries management are good, it is difficult to implement them in a huge area of water and in the face of resistance by domestic and foreign fishing companies with political protection. We have not seen significant results from the steps taken so far. Meanwhile, unlicensed fishing vessels and underreported fish catches remain a rampant problem.

Dr Brian Fegan
Freelance development consultant
Sydney

coral rock and shells. This practice is now regulated, but coral remains an important source of construction material in many areas, and coral and sand mining continue to destroy fish habitats, particularly in the Riau archipelago of Sumatra.

The eighth threat is tourism and associated infrastructure development. Tourism is often promoted as a positive force for development in Indonesia, but it also has a range of negative ecological and social effects. While most direct effects are relatively localised (for example, habitat destruction in resort areas), their cumulative impact has prompted specific management efforts (for example, a program to establish anchor buoys to minimise coral damage from visiting boats, which are the main form of Komodo tourist accommodation). Of more concern is the larger-scale impacts of coastal engineering works such as the Denpasar (Bali) airport runway. The runway was extended over a fringing reef and has caused substantial loss of coral and erosion of adjacent reefs and beaches. It has made traditional fishing more difficult for local communities, and has prompted yet another costly beach restoration program, which may well have to be repeated regularly to protect Bali's tourism assets (Dutton and Saenger 1990).

The ninth threat is coastal urbanisation. Indonesia's largest cities are located on the coast. Apart from the pollution load generated by these centres, there are increasing direct impacts and other types of conflict generated by land reclamation and infrastructure projects designed to service urban expansion. In Lampung, Manado, Makassar and Denpasar, these developments are now under increasing scrutiny; however, as yet there are no strict policies to prevent building in sensitive habitats or areas of traditional importance.

Finally, there is the threat of mangrove and seagrass destruction. Most of the original mangrove forests of Java and Sulawesi have been lost; and in other islands conversion is continuing at unprecedented rates, mainly to enable shrimp pond construction. Between 1982 and 1999, some 1.6 million hectares of mangrove were cleared (Bengen and Dutton 2004). Seagrass losses have not been estimated, but some key fish-breeding areas (for example, the Bone Gulf) have been degraded by illegal trawling and sedimentation.

THE EVOLUTION OF COASTAL AND MARINE RESOURCES MANAGEMENT

Pre-*reformasi*

There are several distinct eras of coastal and marine development policy in modern Indonesia. Under the first 25-year development plan (PJP I, 1969–93) and related five-year development plans (Repelita), national planning policy placed considerable emphasis on terrestrial development, particularly in Java and Sumatra (Sloan and Sughandy 1994; MOSE 1996). The first marine protected area (Pulau Seribu) was formally gazetted only in 1982; it was not until the late 1980s that strategic attention was given to management on broader scales (Alder, Sloan and Utolseya 1994; Sloan and Sughandy 1994; Purwaka 1995).

In the first Repelita of PJP II (1993–98), four goals for coastal and marine resources development were established (Dahuri, Sitepu and Dutton 1999). The first was to provide support for expanded coastal and marine enterprises throughout Indonesia, especially in eastern regions. The second was to provide support for offshore industries, especially oil and gas production. The third was to strengthen national sovereignty and jurisdiction by mapping continental shelves and the exclusive economic zone. The fourth was to establish a coastal and marine geographic information network.

In order to attain these goals, the government set up a marine unit within Bappenas and established national strategies. It also undertook a series of projects intended to build knowledge of coastal and marine resources and institutional capacity for their management. The Marine Sciences Education Project, which was funded by the Asian Development Bank (ADB), established the first national curricula for marine science in six universities. The Marine Resources Evaluation and Planning (MREP) Project was implemented in 10 provinces between 1993 and 1998. The Coral Reef Rehabilitation and Management Program (Coremap), a multilateral aid project, began operations in 1998 after a lengthy design process and is being implemented in phases between 1998 and 2013 (GEF 1998). NGOs such as the World Wide Fund for Nature, the Nature Conservancy, the Asian Wetlands Bureau/Wetlands International, Telapak/ Jaring Pela and Conservation International have set up marine conservation programs. There are various bilateral aid programs, including Proyek Pesisir, Mitra Pesisir and the Coastal Resources Management Project, which are supported by USAID; the Norwegian Seawatch project; and the Canadian Collaborative Environmental Project. Finally, there are collaborative research and education programs such as the Netherlands–Indonesian Buginesia and Teluk Banten programs; the Joint Indonesian–German Marine Ecosystems and Resources Program; the ASEAN Living Coastal Resources Program supported by the Australian Agency for International Development (AusAID); and UNESCO's Man and the Biosphere Programme.

Sofa (1998) evaluated coastal management and related projects between 1987 and 1998. She estimated that some $400 million was spent on coastal and marine resource management projects (excluding fisheries) during that period. She also noted that relatively few of these initiatives continued when direct funding via central government agencies ceased and that very few had a direct impact on the quality of life of coastal communities or the quality of marine ecosystems.

Under the *wawasan nusantara* (archipelagic outlook) concept that Indonesia successfully championed in the formulation of the United Nations Convention on the Law of the Sea, decision-makers argued that all marine areas are deemed to be part of the national estate and thus indivisible for management purposes. That interpretation resulted in unclear responsibility for regulating access to marine resources, for resolving conflicts between uses and for ensuring that marine resources are managed on a sustainable basis. No one agency was specifically responsible for coordinating different sectors or different levels of government.

In Indonesia, some 22 statutes and hundreds of regulations and ministerial decrees relate to coastal resources (Patlis, Knight et al. 2003a). The consequences of this multiplicity of rules have been increasingly unclear (and often overlapping) jurisdictions and a lack of coordination of policies. A classic example is an experience in the Lembeh Strait of North Sulawesi in 1996–97 when a foreign fisheries company installed a vast system of trap nets that became known as the 'Walls of Death'.[5] Because the company was based in Jakarta and was therefore subject to central government regulations, it took more than a year for local objections to take effect and for the 'walls' to be dismantled.

That example is indicative of how provinces and local governments face a common and seemingly insurmountable hurdle – how to obtain a formal voice in decision-making about marine and coastal development at the local level. There has been a clear need to decentralise decision-making, to enable local governments and communities to protect their interests and to prevent inappropriate central interventions. Through the mid-1990s, there were various efforts to stimulate increased local governance efforts in some provinces (Hunt, Dutton and Duff 1998; Crawford et al. 1998). However, for the most part it was 'business as usual' because most capacity-building projects came into being through the central government, so local government depended on central agencies to define their agendas.

Post-*reformasi* reforms

In May 1999, with the passage of what has proven to be a controversial law on regional autonomy, a large part of that hurdle was removed. Law 22/1999 specifically made provision for provincial governments to exercise authority over the territorial seas (up to 12 nautical miles[6]) and for district/city administrations to have authority for the first third of that area (up to a maximum of four nautical miles). Law 22/1999 was supported by a related law on financial and revenue-sharing authority, Law 25/1999.

A further fillip for the marine sector occurred in October 1999, when the then newly elected president, Abdurrahman Wahid, established a ministry specifically concerned with the identification and development of marine and coastal resources, particularly fisheries. He appointed a veteran and respected former minister, Sarwono Kusumaatmadja, to lead the ministry. This historic decision marked a true watershed in marine resource management and symbolised an increased level of political recognition of the significance of Indonesia's seas.

Implications for fisheries and coastal management

The new minister identified improved fisheries and coastal management as two key priorities (Kusumaatmadja 2000a). He ordered a comprehensive review of fisheries development policy, which resulted in proposals for a series of sweeping reforms for fisheries management (PCI 2001). The reforms stimulated the ministry to restructure and improve fisheries management in concert with marine and coastal resources management at large. For example, as outlined by the Ministry of Marine Affairs and Fisheries, initial reforms redirected fisheries development policy towards two key objectives: fishery resource utilisation to increase the welfare and prosperity of the Indonesian people; and conservation of resources for sustainable optimal utilisation (MMAF 2002a).

Many of the issues that were once outside the responsibility of the former Directorate-General of Fisheries are now central to the mission of the ministry, and there has been a significant investment in improved systems to support fisheries management decision-making. There has also been a strong and deliberate emphasis on the establishment of improved policy frameworks for small-island development and integrated coastal management. In 2002, the ministry promulgated the first ever national guidelines for coastal management – a legacy of the MREP Project (Hunt, Dutton and Duff 1998; MMAF 2002b). These drew together principles for coastal development that help guide provincial and local governments as well as NGOs and regional government associations such as the Association of Indonesian Districts/District Heads (Apkasi).

Since 2000, the ministry has been engaged in the development of a draft national coastal management act. This reform has long been proposed (see Rais et al. 1998) and has involved an exemplary process of global learning and public engagement in legal drafting (Patlis et al. 2003). Several districts have now enacted regulations relating to integrated coastal management. Minahasa in Northern Sulawesi was among the first, and its community-based coastal management by-law (*perda*), enacted in June 2001, is the most comprehensive. Since then two other *perda* have been enacted, in the districts of Bengkayang in West Kalimantan and Gresik in East Java. An estimated further 40 districts are presently developing *perda* to manage coastal resources.

Despite these advances, many challenges remain. There is a lingering overestimation of, and undue emphasis on, maximum sustainable yield as a fisheries management tool. There is ineffective surveillance and regulation of offshore fisheries and of illegal long-lining and trawl-fishing. There is little understanding of regulations at the provincial and local levels and little capacity for implementation. There are inadequate data for making management decisions at all scales. And there is an ongoing lack of interdepartmental coordination of marine conservation and resource management projects; for example, marine protected areas are primarily under the jurisdiction of the Forestry Department and are not managed to achieve fisheries objectives.

Global assistance

In recent years, there has been a marked change in the nature of foreign aid for marine resource management (Dutton, Bengen and Tulungen 2001). However, there remains a strong legacy of misdiagnosis and misapplication of technologically based fixes to complex social and ecological problems. Some of the larger coastal and marine projects in recent years have involved complex processes of consultation and progressive phasing based on results. But the financing practices of lending agencies and most donors are seemingly at odds with true learning and adaptive management. Few donor agencies seem prepared to invest with enough flexibility and long-term commitment to ensure lasting outcomes. Recent experience with the few projects that have applied a learning approach has shown that the diverse nature of Indonesia's maritime cultures also requires locally adapted or derived models, and not transplanted clones (see, for example, Parks et al. 2001; Schuttenberg 2001; Crawford et al. 2003).

TOWARDS SUSTAINABLE MANAGEMENT

Considerations for sustainability

The costs of unsustainable marine resource exploitation are borne by all Indonesians. The 'Reefs at Risk' study (Burke, Selig and Spalding 2002) shows this clearly. Over a 20-year period, fishing sustainably can generate as much as $63,000/km^2 more than overfishing on healthy reefs (Cesar 1996). That is the difference between the $39,000 that an individual would gain from fishing unsustainably and the $102,000 that society could expect from sustainable fishing. Issues of equity and social justice thus underpin much of the current debate on sustainability. The principal argument as to why we should be concerned about sustainability relates to providing opportunities for future generations (Rais et al. 1998). Sustainability requires the equal promotion of social, economic and environmental (or ecological) goals within the development process. It is difficult to achieve such balance, particularly when there are trade-offs between the goals under different systems of social organisation. Recent national development has traditionally favoured economic interests above social and ecological interests, even when there are traditional rules that seek to achieve sustainable use of a resource (Thorburn 1998).

Fisheries management epitomises the trade-offs. Even when fishers know that stocks are overexploited, they do little to regulate their level of exploitation spontaneously (Walters and Maguire 1996). The global nature of demand reinforces such behaviour. The continuing high prices for sharkfin throughout Asia and the current substitution of products from manta rays is a perverse example of this.

Requirements for sustainability

Sustainability need not be at odds with economic development, but if coastal and marine resource use in Indonesia is to be sustainable, the country will need to meet several requirements.

First, there is a need for better knowledge of the marine ecosystems. Dutton and Hotta (1995) argue that, in order to put the pattern of development on a more sustainable footing, there has to be a willingness to invest in understanding how the system works. Despite a remarkable legacy of marine science dating back to the 17th century (Rumphius 1705) and the compilation of a comprehensive state of knowledge about Indonesia's marine resources up to the mid-1990s (Tomascik et al. 1997), we know disturbingly little about Indonesia's marine systems either generally (for example, the distribution and abundance of species) or in more detail (for example, the location of breeding areas of key species or the relationship between species harvest and recruitment). Over the past decade, there has been a rapid improvement in our knowledge of some systems (for example, coral reefs); however, we continue to exploit in ignorance, as revealed by the discovery of a coelacanth in North Sulawesi waters in 1998 (Erdmann 1999). There is an urgent need for a repeat of the broad-scale marine ecosystem surveys undertaken in the 1980s and for more targeted studies of the status of key species such as commercially significant fish, whales, dugongs, turtles, trepang and clams. The surveys should also establish protocols for the ongoing monitoring of system and species health in ways that are the most cost effective (that is, not reliant on foreign assistance) and that are meaningful to local decision-makers, communities and industries.

Second, there is a need to 'build the constituency'. The first national survey of public attitudes towards marine resources revealed that Indonesians are poorly informed about the geography of Indonesia's vast marine resources and about their social and economic significance (Dutton et al. 2001c). Significant gaps in basic knowledge and understanding limit the ability of individuals to manage coastal and marine resources effectively. More significantly, Indonesians are very concerned about the state of the nation's seas and their ability to sustain the many values these provide. Clearly there is an emerging constituency for the functions of the new Ministry of Marine Affairs and Fisheries. Pollution of the sea is ranked as the sixth most pressing national problem. The survey indicated that individuals are willing to engage more actively with local government and other bodies to manage coastal and marine resources more effectively, but that they need education, guidance and trust. Efforts such as SeKarang,[7] the national coral reef education campaign, have shown how influential social marketing campaigns can be (Storey 2000). But they need to be complemented by more fundamental advances in education at all levels and by more mechanisms that enable communities to engage actively in decision-making about the resources they depend on.

Third, there is a need to learn how to manage. Over the past 15 years, various long-term investments in conservation and development projects have tested a wide variety of models. Notable among these are the projects supported by the USAID–Bappenas Natural Resources Management Program. The project began in the early 1990s with the development of a zoning plan for the newly created Bunaken National Park, and has produced one of the first effective 'user pays' systems for marine parks in Southeast Asia. A more diverse set of integrated coastal management models was created under Proyek Pesisir[8] (Knight and Tighe 2003), in four provinces and at the national level. The results of these projects confirmed the project hypothesis that

> meaningful participation in planning, implementation and decision-making by all key stakeholders at the local level can and will lead to more sustainable and equitable use of coastal resources.

However, the project also demonstrated the importance of tailoring interventions to local situations, working simultaneously at national and local levels, taking the time to build capacity for management at all levels, and staying engaged for an adequate period of time to enable learning and adaptation (Crawford et al. 2003).

Fourth, there is a need to build resilient networks of marine protected areas (MPAs). There are some 27 formally gazetted MPAs covering an area of 4.5 million hectares, or less than 1 per cent of Indonesia's exclusive economic zone. This is well short of the target of 10 million hectares by the end of 2000 set by the government in 1990 (Alder, Sloan and Utolseya 1994). Most MPAs are inadequately funded and act as 'paper parks'. There is inadequate or no enforcement of regulations, including the regulation of user access. Very few MPAs are designed or managed to ensure connectivity between elements or resilience in the face of climate change. However, results from the relatively few long-term projects implemented to date both in large MPAs such as Komodo and in small MPAs such as those under the jurisdiction of Blongko, Bentenan-Tumbak and Talise villages in North Sulawesi have shown them to be effective in protecting hard coral and fish when no-take regulations have been appropriately enforced (Moreau 2001).

Global experience with MPAs has shown that ultimately perhaps 30 per cent of Indonesia's seas may need to be set aside as no-fishing areas if marine biodiversity and productivity are to be maintained (Roberts et al. 2001; Halpern and Warner 2002). A National Committee on Indonesia's Marine Conservation has been formed to enhance integrated and sustainable management of Indonesia's living marine resources. The committee has been asked to develop technical recommendations for further processing into policy advice over the next two years. The proposed recommendations will relate to the development of functional and effective MPA networks; sustainable fisheries management; and effective species and genetic conservation.

To be fully effective, the national MPA plan will have to be nested within a national sea-use zoning system similar to the terrestrial zoning systems that are widely used throughout Indonesia (Hunt, Dutton and Duff 1998). Initial efforts to develop such a system have failed, largely because they were overdesigned and too complex to implement. If such a system is not developed soon, individual provinces and even local governments may institute their own systems, creating a series of uncoordinated and inappropriate plans.

Fifth, there is a need for better-targeted development assistance. Historically, fisheries resource management assistance and marine resource management assistance have been at cross-purposes, with little coordination by either donors or aid recipients. Institutional structures have made such coordination difficult, and typically donors have had to deal with different partners to achieve their various objectives. The ministry needs to present a more strategic perspective on opportunities for marine resource development. There are many possible projects that would greatly enhance the value-added of current fisheries (for example, better post-harvesting techniques) and others that would enable mariculture to transform livelihoods in areas of high poverty. Similarly, donors need to apply greater consideration of sustainability criteria to investment projects and look for ways to protect the resilience of marine systems. Independently verifiable project outcome-tracking systems should be applied to assess the social, economic and ecological impacts at various stages. These results should in turn be used to adapt project design and inform future investments.

CONCLUSION

Marine and coastal systems provide vast economic, social and environmental benefits to Indonesia and form the basis for key industries that have the potential to yield even greater value to society on a long-term basis if managed sustainably. Unfortunately, due to a legacy of past mismanagement, ineffective governance and a lack of proper regulatory control, the potential of these vast resources to meet the needs of current and future generations is quickly and irretrievably being eroded. This is largely because the current modes of development emphasise short-term gain to individual actors over the long-term interests of Indonesian society. Clearly our current approaches to marine resource development and management are failing to take account of the wider social equity and ecological dimensions of sustainability.

Indonesia has extraordinary global significance as a repository of global marine biodiversity, as a habitat and transit territory for migratory species of global concern and as a country that depends greatly on marine resources for economic and food security. It would be very short-sighted of the global community to fail to assist Indonesia to carry forward the ambitious program of marine and coastal management that has gained pace in the post-*reformasi* period.

Without well-coordinated and carefully targeted long-term development assistance for sustainable management of Indonesia's seas, the long-term prognosis for both Indonesia's marine resources and the millions who depend on them is bleak. The consequences of system failure will exacerbate the poverty of coastal communities, contribute to conflict between communities and between fishers and other marine resource users, and threaten the viability and peace of coastal villages. It will lead to increased rates of exploitation of globally significant protected species and create incentives for fishers to roam into other sovereign jurisdictions to obtain target species. A proactive program to assist Indonesia's governments and communities to ensure sustainable marine resource use is seemingly a strategic investment that would be a win–win for Indonesia and development partners.

NOTES

* I would like to acknowledge inputs to this chapter from colleagues who, over the past decade, worked with me at the Marine Science Education Project, the Marine Resources Evaluation Project, Proyek Pesisir, Mitra Pesisir, the Centre for Coastal and Marine Studies at the Bogor Agricultural Institute and the Nature Conservancy. I particularly thank Richard Kenchington, Craig Leisher, Jason Patlis, Jos Pet, Budy Resosudarmo and two anonymous reviewers for their comments on an earlier draft. The views expressed in this paper are those of the author and do not reflect any institutional affiliation, past or present.

1 This is roughly the same as the estimated losses from illegal, unreported and under-reported fishing activity in Indonesian waters (R. Dahuri, former Minister of Marine Affairs and Fisheries, Jakarta, personal communication).

2 See <www.komodonationalpark.org>.

3 See also Fegan (2003) and Charoenpo (2003) for important cases of illegal fishing conducted by foreign-owned trawlers.

4 See the controversy regarding submarine tailings disposal in North Sulawesi waters at <http://www.minesandcommunities.org/Action/press342.html>.

5 See <http://darwin.bio.uci.edu/~sustain/bio65/indonesia/indon97k.html>.

6 One nautical mile equals 1.9 kilometres.

7 *Selamatkan terumbu karang sekarang* = 'Save our coral reefs now'.

8 Coastal Resources Management Project, implemented under the USAID–Bappenas Natural Resource Management Program for 1996–2003.

11   PETROLEUM PARADOX: THE POLITICS OF OIL AND GAS

Francisia S.S.E. Seda

It is often assumed that an abundance of natural resources such as oil and gas will increase the potential for success of the development process in developing countries. However, the experience of Indonesia over the past five decades does not support such an assumption – indeed, many would argue that the reverse has occurred (Karl 1997; Ross 1999; Sangkoyo 2003). Hence the main questions posed in this chapter are as follows. First, why is Indonesia still a poor country despite its abundance of natural resources? Second, what has happened to the revenues generated from oil and gas – in particular, to what extent have they been used for development? And third, why have the majority of Indonesians not been able to enjoy a trickle-down effect from the revenues generated by Indonesia's vast oil and gas reserves?

In answering the above questions, this chapter describes the politics of oil and gas extraction in Indonesia, as well as the politics of development strategy. Attention is focused on the state oil company, Pertamina, as the main institution responsible for the oil and gas industry, as well as on former President Soeharto, his cronies and the military, who were the dominant players in Indonesian politics during the New Order period.

PERTAMINA, THE STATE OIL COMPANY

Established in 1968, Pertamina is Indonesia's only state oil company. As the major player in the Indonesian oil and gas industry, it is expected to channel the revenues from oil and gas to the government (Aden 1992; David 1995). In reviewing why this has not occurred smoothly and efficiently, the most important thing to keep in mind is the nature of the powers controlling the management of Pertamina.

During the period of political transition during which power shifted from President Sukarno to President Soeharto (1966–67), a struggle took place between two opposing groups for control of Permina, the larger of the two state oil companies existing at the time.[1] There were those in the government, such as Bratanata, the Minister of Mines, who wished to regularise Permina's operations and make it accountable to the ministry. On the opposing side were people like Ibnu Sutowo, the president director of Permina, who for obvious reasons wanted to retain Permina's autonomy *vis-à-vis* the government. In 1967 the conflict came to a head when Bratanata challenged Sutowo's authority over the allocation of drilling concessions, the process of tendering and the investment of Permina funds (Bartlett et al. 1972; Robison 1986).[2]

President Soeharto, supported by the military, took Sutowo's side, making the president director directly responsible to him. Sutowo's grasp on the state's oil and gas operations tightened even further in 1968 when Pertamin and Permina were merged and he was appointed president director of the merged entity, now called Pertamina. Pertamina was given sole authority for domestic distribution of oil and gas and the allocation of drilling concessions. Soeharto closed Pertamina's operations to public scrutiny, leaving it immune to public accountability. No annual balance sheets were published and parliament (the DPR) was not given the opportunity to discuss Pertamina's finances publicly (David 1995).

Soeharto's and the military's interests in Pertamina were clear. As Robison (1986: 234) has noted:

> Pertamina constituted the channel through which the bulk of the state's revenue flowed, as well as the largest and most concentrated source of contracts for construction and supply. Pertamina therefore was the strategic focus of economic power and the crucial source of revenue. The autonomy and hegemony of the military was closely dependent upon its ability to maintain its control over this terminal and to prevent its absorption by any regularised state apparatus.

Pertamina became the key element in the appropriation of the state apparatus by Soeharto and the military, the resulting exclusion of civilians and political parties from power, and the increasingly authoritarian and arbitrary nature of military rule.

During the early 1970s, Pertamina's revenue increased significantly. The company became involved in several mega projects, with corruption rampant in its tendering and contract activities (Robison 1986; Sangkoyo 2003). Corruption in Pertamina quickly became a major public concern. In 1970 Prime Minister Wilopo attempted to deal with the problem by enacting a specific law, Law 8/1971, that would change Pertamina's structure. Under this law, Pertamina was placed under the supervision of a board of commissioners consisting of five government ministers. The intention was to curtail the influence of Sutowo, and of Soeharto, over the running of the company. But in practice this attempt proved futile because none of the ministers who were on the board felt able to reject the demands of either of these powerful men (Ramses Hutapea, personal interview, Jakarta, 14 December 2000).

By 1972 Sutowo had transformed Pertamina into a huge conglomerate involved in many industries, many of them unrelated to the oil and gas industry, and many funded through international short-term loans (Robison 1986; David 1995). In response to this situation, another attempt was made to control Pertamina by establishing a stronger board of commissioners, and all loans negotiated by Pertamina were required to be approved by the central bank (Bank Indonesia) and the National Development Planning Agency (Bappenas). In 1973, the Financial Auditing Board was authorised to examine the budgets of state-owned companies (Robison 1986).

None of these efforts were successful in reducing Pertamina's autonomy because the state mining company was legally responsible only to the president. Soeharto clearly was not going to change a situation from which he, Sutowo and the military were deriving so much benefit. Pertamina had also become the vehicle for the personal enrichment of many other Indonesians, including government officials and those who exercised political control over them (Robison 1986).

In 1975, to the surprise of the general public, Pertamina went bankrupt. It scarcely seemed possible that less than two years after the 1973 oil boom, an oil company could go bankrupt, but overexpansion, corruption and falling oil prices had left Pertamina without the means to repay a $40 million short-term loan due to a consortium of foreign banks. This amount was actually less than 3 per cent of Pertamina's total short-term debt overhang of approximately $1.5 billion, and other lenders threatened to exercise their contractual rights under cross-default procedures to call in their loans to Pertamina as well. In all, Pertamina had accumulated some $10 billion in debt, equivalent to 30 per cent of Indonesia's GDP at the time (McCawley 1978).

The situation demonstrated that mismanagement and corruption at Pertamina had gotten out of hand, shaking the credibility of the Soeharto regime in the eyes of foreign investors whose investments were critical to the New Order's development strategy. The president therefore had little choice but to allow the economic technocrats in his cabinet to take control of Pertamina; to guarantee Pertamina's debt using public funds; and to sideline Sutowo. By renegotiating loans and selling many of Pertamina's non-mining assets, the technocrats were able to keep Pertamina afloat.

In the 1980s Pertamina's performance improved significantly due to an increase in liquefied natural gas (LNG) production.[3] By 1991/92, gross revenues from LNG exports were running at approximately $4 billion annually, comprising 14 per cent of Indonesia's export earnings. Indonesia was the world's leading exporter of LNG with nearly 40 per cent of world trade (Barnes

1995). However, Pertamina remained responsible only to the president; corruption was still rampant; and significant amounts of revenue continued to be siphoned off to fund the regime in power. As a result, Pertamina's contribution to government revenues was less than optimal. One could argue that this situation persists to the present day.

THE PRODUCTION-SHARING CONTRACT

Until 1966 mining concessions for foreign companies were governed by the contract of work (CoW). In 1966, Sutowo developed a new type of drilling concession contract: the production-sharing contract (PSC). In that year, the first PSC was implemented with the signing of an agreement with the Independent Indonesian American Petroleum Company (IIAPCO), a group of independent oil operators from the United States. In January 1967, IIAPCO began carrying out its PSC as a contractor (Machmud 2000). Since then all new and renewed drilling concession contracts have been in the form of a PSC.

The PSC had several noteworthy features and characteristics. First, it contained a management clause that forced contractors to consult regularly with Pertamina and seek its approval on certain basic operational matters. The effect of this clause was that the foreign oil companies had to operate in a more transparent manner, thus establishing a learning process for Pertamina officials with regard to operational matters and inducing technology transfer. Second, the PSC was expected to put an end to the constant disputes over posted prices as the basis for tax calculation that were occurring under the CoW-based concession system. The PSC called for a more conciliatory relationship between the government and the foreign oil companies because, after cost recovery, production would be split. Also, a clause on the valuation of crude oil made it possible for all parties to agree on one mechanism for determining valuations, to be revised annually. Third, the PSC fulfilled national aspirations for greater state autonomy as inscribed in Article 33 of the Constitution of 1945. Finally, the PSC ensured that contractors dealt with only one entity of the Indonesian government, namely Pertamina (Machmud 2000).

In practice, under a PSC, the foreign company provides the technology, organisation and all of the risk capital required to find and develop an oil or gas field. If hydrocarbons are found, Indonesia and the foreign contractor, after taking into account the cost of production, divide production between them. The original shares were 65 per cent for Pertamina and 35 per cent for the contractor, but Pertamina's share has since increased and the contractor's share correspondingly decreased.

Critics of the PSC did exist. First, the PSC actually resulted in a lower net income per barrel for the state than the CoW. For example, in 1973 companies operating under PSCs paid on average only 36 per cent of their net production income per barrel in taxes, compared with an average of 50.5 per cent for companies under CoWs (Arief 1977). The major reason for this disparity was that the foreign oil companies operating under PSCs raised their recoverable costs by including both depreciation charges and rental expenses as components of such costs. They were able to get away with this questionable practice because Pertamina did not carry out effective management and control of the foreign companies within the context of the PSC (Arief 1977). Second, because Pertamina has largely been ineffective in carrying out its control function, it is questionable whether the PSCs have accelerated the transfer of technology as originally intended.

Nevertheless, what was crucial for Sutowo, Soeharto and the military was that the PSC was a way to gain greater state autonomy for the oil and gas industry. This was one target that was achieved. Thus the New Order regime was able to 'fully' extract the revenue from the oil and gas industry for its own political objectives, at the expense of less revenue for the government and, in the end, for the people of Indonesia.

DEVELOPMENT STRATEGY AND THE OIL AND GAS INDUSTRY

Nationalists versus technocrats

To understand how the government spent the income from the oil and gas industry requires an understanding of Indonesian development strategy during the Soeharto era. It is important to note that during the 1970s and 1980s, Indonesia's annual income from oil and gas was more than 60 per cent – in many years even reaching 70 per cent – of total government revenue. Throughout the 1990s and even now, the share of oil and gas in total government revenue has always been more than 30 per cent (Hill 2000).

Throughout the New Order era two groups, the economic technocrats, mostly in Bappenas and the Ministry of Finance, and the bureaucrat nationalists, mostly in the Ministry of Trade and Industry and the State Ministry of Research and Technology, competed to set the direction of Indonesia's development strategy. The technocrats, led by Professor Widjojo Nitisastro, mostly consisted of economists from the Faculty of Economics at the University of Indonesia. They advocated deregulation of markets and the privatisation of state assets as the best way to achieve high economic growth. They believed that less state control and greater reliance on the market mechanism would improve the efficiency and productivity of all sectors of the economy, putting the country on an export-oriented growth path. They argued in favour of downsizing the public sector, leaving government to concentrate on helping private business exploit Indonesia's comparative advantage, particularly its large sup-

ply of labour. The government could best achieve this by investing in infrastructure such as roads and ports, as well as in education and health (Woo,
Glassburner and Nasution 1994). Over time it has become apparent that these
kinds of investments, some made possible by revenue from the oil and gas
industry, have contributed significantly to the development of the country and
the welfare of the people (Hill 2000).

The nationalists, mostly consisting of engineers, wanted to use state
resources to shape domestic markets. They hoped this would encourage faster
technological progress and shift Indonesian industry towards production of
higher value-added products. To achieve this, the nationalists argued that the
government should implement import substitution policies and put more
resources into high-tech state enterprises. The nationalists felt uncomfortable
with the free market policies advocated by the technocrats in part because they
believed they would unfairly advantage the ethnic Chinese Indonesians who
already dominated the private sector, and multinational corporations. Sutowo
was among the early nationalists. Towards the end of the New Order period,
Professor (later President) B.J. Habibie was considered the leader of this group
(Woo, Glassburner and Nasution 1994).

The direction Soeharto chose in steering the country's development strategy
depended on the strength of the national economy at the time. In periods of economic boom the nationalist industrial strategy won out; during periods of economic stagnation, a more open and export-oriented industrialisation strategy
was preferred. From the early 1970s until the mid-1980s, Pertamina's wealth
played a central role in allowing Soeharto to embark on an industrial strategy
based on economic nationalism; during this period a significant amount of the
company's revenue was spent on the investments of various state enterprises,
some of them very large and expensive projects. As Robison (1986: 72) has
emphasised:

> Early efforts at this were pioneered by Sutowo, who used Pertamina as a source of
> finance for industrial ventures in steel, petrochemicals, and shipping which were
> outside the plans of the more market-oriented National Economic Planning Board
> (Bappenas).

Development strategies under Soeharto

The first decade of the New Order regime, particularly the 1970s, coincided
with the rapid exploitation and export of raw materials such as timber, minerals and, particularly, oil. The oil boom years were a period of rapid expansion
in import-substituting manufacturing. The government imposed high tariffs on
imports and invested heavily in high-tech industries. It provided generous subsidies to state enterprises for their raw material and energy inputs. Despite
Sutowo's dismissal after the 1975 Pertamina scandal, the program of state-

financed industrial projects actually increased. The nationalists' primary goal was to create an integrated national industrial entity with interrelated forward and backward linkages (Robison 1986).

Between 1982 and 1986 world oil prices fell dramatically, with the worst decline experienced between January 1986 ($25/barrel) and August 1986 ($10/barrel). Indonesia's income from oil and gas exports dropped significantly, inducing an economic crisis (Prawiro 1998). Despite absorbing significant amounts of government funding over many years, the state enterprises fostered by the nationalists were still unable to generate significant revenues for the government, let alone export earnings. Clearly major structural adjustment was called for. As stated by the chief economic minister at the time, Finance Minister Radius Prawiro (1998: 221):

> In one stroke, Indonesia faced the worst economic crisis since the New Order came to power in the mid-1960s. There were only two possible routes to restore the economy: oil prices would have to rise again and quickly or the economy would have to be rapidly and drastically restructured away from its heavy dependence on oil.

Soeharto had no choice but to undertake an economic structural adjustment program. The restructuring of the economy began with a program of trade, financial and investment liberalisation to encourage labour-intensive, non-oil manufacturing exports and decrease the country's reliance on foreign exchange earnings from oil. To ease the fiscal pressure on the state, the government cancelled or postponed many of its large industrial and infrastructural projects, eliminated subsidies and tried to increase domestic revenue by implementing tax reform. However, the government managed to maintain its level of spending on infrastructure, education and health. Although the oil crisis forced Soeharto to abandon the nationalist development strategy, the regime's commitment to a nationalist ideology as well as vested interests formed major constraints to the wholesale adoption of the alternative development strategy proposed by the technocrats. Nevertheless, reforms were instituted and did lead to an improvement in the economy. Exports of labour-intensive products such as garments and footwear increased significantly. By the end of the 1990s, total non-oil and gas exports were much higher than oil and gas exports. Government earnings from value-added taxes in the non-oil/gas sector increased significantly, exceeding government revenue from the oil and gas sector (Hill 2000). Poverty incidence also fell significantly during this period.

By the beginning of the 1990s the Indonesian economy had recovered from the oil shock crisis, but the battle between the technocrats and the nationalists continued. The technocrats in Bappenas and the Ministry of Finance continued to argue for a reduced role for state enterprises, leaving government to focus on providing the environment for the rapid development of private business. The nationalists in the Ministry of Trade and Industry and the State Ministry of

Research and Technology, on the other hand, wanted more state resources to be invested in state enterprises producing high-tech products such as ships and planes.

Nevertheless the two camps were not always in conflict. The nationalists were not necessarily against economic deregulation, but wanted to confine it to sectors considered ready for world competition; their chief concern was to avoid domination of the Indonesian economy by multinational companies (Borsuk 1999). It was the nationalists, for example, who developed the Batam free trade zone, often held up as a successful case of development, and they also supported the proposal for an ASEAN free trade zone. Hence, the development strategy pursued in the 1990s can be seen as a combination of the views of the technocrats and the nationalists.

It was the continuing influence of the nationalists that ensured continued government support for large state enterprises well into the 1990s. Only a few of these have performed well, and none has become a major exporter.[4] Thus the development of large state enterprises during the 1990s created only costs for the government, with no compensating revenues of any significance. One could argue that the government money spent on these large state enterprises – a sizeable chunk of it from the oil and gas industry – was wasted or at least used inefficiently.

Another problem was that privatisation and economic liberalisation were not accompanied by the necessary steps to reform the legal system and democratise the political system. Such policies may have had positive effects in terms of inducing high economic growth and reducing poverty, but they only strengthened crony capitalism and the conglomerates. Although most macroeconomic variables signalled a healthy economy in the years leading up to the financial crisis, corruption and favouritism in the industrial and financial sectors meant that the economy was not as solid as it seemed. When the financial crisis struck in 1997, the Indonesian economy collapsed. Indonesia became the worst affected of all the countries hit by the crisis during this period, and found it hardest to recover (Kuncoro and Resosudarmo 2004).

ENDEMIC CORRUPTION IN THE NEW ORDER ERA

Why was corruption so endemic throughout the New Order era? One answer lies in the pervasive patrimonialism of the Soeharto regime. Patrimonialism is a pattern of politics in which the ruler's power derives primarily from his capacity to win and retain the loyalty of key sections of the political elite by satisfying their aspirations, especially their material interests, through the distribution of perquisites such as fiefs and benefices. Politics takes the form of competition within the elite among rival factions and cliques who are concerned principally with gaining influence with the ruler, and with the distribution of spoils. The maintenance and durability of patrimonialism depends heavily on the masses remaining politically quiescent, and on the containment of rivalries within the elite so that they do not threaten its basic unity of interest (Crouch 1988).

The oil boom of 1973 vastly increased the regime's revenues, giving Soeharto an unprecedented ability to patronise his supporters and threaten or deny his opponents and critics. This allowed him to quickly strengthen his hold over the state and transform the bureaucracy into an instrument of presidential power. Not only was the bureaucracy expected to provide a growing number of development services, it also performed security functions and carried out policies of co-optation and control designed to prevent potentially countervailing institutions of civil society from developing. The bureaucracy both implemented and supervised its own development projects, resulting in an unusual concentration of power and making it the dominant institution in society. No other group was in a position to challenge the regime.

Soeharto gave key government personnel the opportunity to hold monopolies over information and the authority to grant licences and permits in certain economic areas. This allowed them to extract substantial financial resources from private parties, in return for kickbacks for themselves and the regime. Following Soeharto's example, these key personnel would in turn distribute the less valuable information and the authority to grant some licences and permits to the personnel under their supervision who were important to the success of their bureaucratic programs. The distribution of exclusive information and authorities continued right down the line through the government bureaucracy, so that even officials at the lowest levels of government could extract financial resources by 'selling' information and permits to private parties. Corruption and cronyism thus became the main mechanism to gain wealth for those loyal to their patrons and, at the top level, to Soeharto. This system of patron–client relationships was the key to keeping Soeharto in power for more than 30 years (Kuncoro and Resosudarmo 2004).

In the early 1990s, Soeharto's closest cronies included Chinese business people such as Liem Siu Liong and Bob Hasan, in addition to his own children. Soeharto assisted his children to obtain monopolies over the import and distribution of major commodities. They were successful in obtaining tenders for several large government projects, financed by low-interest loans from state banks that were often afraid to ask for repayment (Schwarz 2000). With cronyism rife even within the president's own family, the development of an effective program to combat corruption in Indonesia was unthinkable.

During the late 1980s and early 1990s, the area in which the cronies wreaked the most economic damage was the banking sector. Soeharto's cronies depended heavily on the vast pool of deposits collected by state-owned banks to pay for their projects. State bank involvement was also crucial given that some of the projects were of such dubious quality that private lenders would have shunned them. The state-owned banks were in most cases willing to fund these projects firstly because they were instructed to do so by Soeharto or his associates, and secondly because some of their high-ranking officers were receiving kickbacks from Soeharto cronies. In many cases the projects were funded by a consortium of foreign banks and Indonesian state banks. The foreign banks were prepared to overlook the questionable prospects of repayment as long as a state bank was also a lender to the project, thereby giving the underlying project a de facto government guarantee (Schwarz 2000). This practice of 'command loans' from state banks, often with the participation of foreign banks, was perhaps the most profound factor in weakening the banking system in the country (King 2000).

The financial crisis of 1997 caused the majority of the banks, both state and private, to collapse. With the economy deteriorating quickly, by mid-1998 the economic crisis had turned into a political crisis that forced Soeharto to step down. The fall of Soeharto created a tremendous opportunity for big bang political change. Indonesian politics moved rapidly from being authoritarian to being much more democratic, and Indonesia was able to conduct two relatively democratic elections, in 1999 and 2004. In 2004 the people of Indonesia were able to elect their president directly for the first time. The government system switched in just three years from being very centralistic to being relatively very decentralised.

Many thought that the fall of Soeharto, rapid political change and decentralisation would destroy patrimonialism and reduce the level of corruption in the country. Soeharto-style patrimonialism may have broken down, but there is no sign that the level of corruption has fallen. Rather, there seems to have been an increase in fragmentation of the national economy, an increase in corruption and an increase in the misuse of local authority since the fall of Soeharto. During the New Order, the nature of corruption was very centralised – a 'one-stop shop'. Now, however, it is rife throughout the country, with central and local government officials, the military/police and legislative members at both the national and local level all demanding bribes (Kuncoro and Resosudarmo 2004).

Corruption seems embedded in Indonesian society. Petty corruption in the government as well as in society at large therefore seems very likely to continue for a long period of time (King 2000).

CONCLUSIONS AND CHALLENGES FOR THE FUTURE

This chapter has described the politics of power controlling Pertamina and the drilling concession system developed by Sutowo, as well as the development strategies pursued during the New Order era. The main conclusions of the chapter are as follows. First, Pertamina's decision to move from a CoW system to a PSC system, at least in the initial period, reduced the income received from foreign oil companies because Pertamina was unable to carry out adequate supervision of the foreign firms' operations. Another consequence of this supervisory failure was that technological transfer, the main goal of the system, was not effectively realised. Nevertheless, the PSC system did enable Pertamina to gain full control over the exploitation of oil and gas, and thus – because Pertamina was an autonomous agency – over the income acruing to Indonesia from oil and gas.

Second, although Pertamina's income increased significantly during the oil boom of the 1970s, much of this revenue was frittered away on unprofitable mega projects, some not even related to the oil and gas industry. Even though Pertamina reduced its involvement in mega projects outside the oil and gas industry during the 1980s and 1990s, corruption was still rife throughout the company. Thus much of the revenue Pertamina earned during this period continued to be wasted. One of the main reasons Pertamina could get away with such behaviour was that it was a fully autonomous body responsible only to the president. No other agency could monitor or control Pertamina's business activities.

Third, corruption in Pertamina and elsewhere in Indonesia was the essential mechanism in the pyramid of patron–client relationships that allowed Soeharto to retain his hold on power. Corruption became so embedded in all sections of society that even after the fall of Soeharto it continued to flourish.

Fourth, Pertamina's oil and gas revenues had only a limited effect on the welfare of the Indonesian people for two major reasons. First, some of the revenues disappeared on corrupt government tenders and projects. Second, the government invested heavily in state-owned enterprises that were never likely to turn a profit. The share of oil and gas revenues spent on infrastructure, education and health did contribute positively and significantly to the welfare of the general population, especially after the economic liberalisation program of the 1980s and the promotion of labour-intensive, export-oriented industries. The poverty level was much lower in the mid-1990s than it had been at the beginning of the 1970s. However, income per capita did not increase to the extent that it could have, and Indonesia is still considered one of the world's poorer countries.

The end of the Soeharto era has brought continuing political change and the opportunity to restructure Pertamina to eliminate the losses due to corruption and mismanagement. Currently parliament, government agencies and NGOs are drafting a new law on the oil and gas industry. The first issue under consideration is whether to replace all PSCs with CoWs. However, although it is true that Pertamina's revenue fell following the move to a PSC system in the 1970s, changing back to a CoW system does not guarantee that Pertamina's revenue will increase.

The second issue under consideration is how to restructure the management of Pertamina. The goal is clearly to make this state-owned company more transparent and more accountable to the public. It has been suggested that Pertamina's monopoly over oil and gas should be dismantled, to curb its influence over the Indonesian oil and gas industry. Pertamina could be broken up into several agencies, some managing its upstream oil and gas businesses and others managing its downstream businesses (Fatchurrochman 2000). But it would be hard to gain general acceptance for this suggestion because many Indonesians still believe that Pertamina should be both an agent of development carrying out large development projects and a profit-oriented company.

The third issue is how to provide a mechanism to investigate and prevent corruption, cronyism and collusion within Pertamina. The upcoming new law clearly has very ambitious goals in this area, but given the entrenched corruption, cronyism and collusion in Indonesian society, whether it will be able to achieve these goals remains to be seen.

NOTES

1   At the beginning of the 1960s there were three state oil companies: Permina headed by Sutowo, Pertamin and Permigan. In 1966 Permigan was dissolved into Permina. The remaining two companies merged to become Pertamina in 1968.

2   Bratanata and Ibnu Sutowa also came into conflict over two other matters. First, Bratanata preferred the existing system of contracts of work (CoWs) to govern Indonesia's relations with foreign oil companies whereas Sutowo preferred the system of production-sharing contracts (PSCs) he had developed himself (Bartlett et al. 1972). Second, Bratanata favoured the coexistence of two or more state oil companies whereas Sutowo wanted only one integrated company. The PSC is discussed in more detail in the next section.

3   On 24 October 1971 Mobil Oil discovered natural gas at Arun in Aceh. In November of the same year Huffco made another giant discovery of natural gas at Badak in Bontang, East Kalimantan. The first sales agreement for Indonesia's LNG was signed between Pertamina representing the Indonesian government and a Japanese utility and steel company in December 1973. President Soeharto officially opened the first LNG production facility at Bontang in August 1977. One week later the first Indonesian LNG cargo was on its way to Japan (Pertamina 1985; Baharuddin 1997).

4   Two prominent examples of successful state enterprises are PT Indosat and PT Telkom. However, both telecommunications companies rely on domestic consumers for most of their income.

PART IV

Illegal Extractions and Conflicts

12   ILLEGAL LOGGING IN INDONESIA: MYTH AND REALITY

Krystof Obidzinski

INTRODUCTION

Illegal logging has emerged as a critical issue in debate on Indonesia's forest policy and as a key environmental concern. People have long known that Indonesia's forestry sector has been affected by organisational and operational irregularities for much of its history.[1] However, the fall of Soeharto's New Order regime in 1998 enabled these problems to be discussed more openly.[2]

Criticism of illegal logging in Indonesia initially spanned a range of cross-cutting sectoral issues. They included abuses associated with large-scale concession-based logging; industrial overcapacity; clear-cutting for plantation estates; problems resulting from the activities of cartel-like timber extraction and trade associations; and small-scale community-based timber extraction.[3] However, there has been a gradual shift in the government and general public perception of what is wrong with Indonesia's forests.

In this chapter, I use the generally accepted definition of illegal logging as any activity associated with timber extraction or processing that contravenes existing forestry regulations – for example, overcutting, cutting outside authorised blocks, underreporting of production, manipulation of documents or bribery (Contreras-Hermosilla 2001; ITTO 2001; FWI–GFW 2002). While the government, the media and NGOs generally agree with this definition of the term 'illegal logging', they tend to single out small and medium-sized logging operations based on district-level permits and cross-border smuggling and identify them as the essence of the illegal logging problem in Indonesia.[4] Such perceptions seriously affect the outcome of measures currently in effect to oppose illegal logging. In particular, law enforcement agencies assume that small and medium-sized logging operations are the main perpetrators of illegal logging and target them without looking at the issue more broadly.

In this chapter, I examine three key assumptions of the 'official' view of illegal logging in Indonesia. The first is that illegal logging is a recent phenomenon due largely to the post-1998 breakdown of law and order. The second is that illegal logging is an outcome of a conspiracy between small and medium-sized logging enterprises with links abroad (particularly Malaysia and China). The third is that illegal logging is a major cause of rising deforestation. I argue that one reason people place the blame for illegal logging mainly with small and medium-sized logging operations and cross-border timber-smuggling operations is that the timber establishment and government forestry authorities in Indonesia want to maintain control over forest (timber) resources. I also discuss measures that could be used to improve the illegal logging situation.

HISTORICAL OVERVIEW

The perception that illegal logging is a recent phenomenon due largely to the post-1998 breakdown of law and order, and that small and medium-sized logging operations are primarily to blame, is not borne out by a historical review of logging activities. Rather, illegalities in Indonesia's forestry sector go far back in time and have been associated with operations throughout the sector, not just relatively small operations.

Late colonial period

Until the early 1930s, the native states/sultanates (particularly those outside Java), in what was then called the Netherlands Indies, were free to engage in logging ventures of any kind because forests were the exclusive economic and political domain of the sultans (Post 1993). At that time, exploitation was primarily through the *opkoop*, or buying-up, of timber from local teams of loggers (*bevolkingskap*). At the top of the trade network were large-scale traders and firms that had secured profit-sharing agreements with the sultans (Het Bosch 1935a). The Chinese and Malay middlemen implemented the logging contracts by hiring local loggers to cut timber and deliver it to agreed locations (Dijk 1938).

In 1934, the Dutch colonial government, dissatisfied with the perceived economic inefficiency, social abuses and financial irregularities associated with the *opkoop* timber exploitation system, curtailed the sultans' authority over forest resources by requiring all prospective logging ventures to acquire official concessions (Potter 1988). By the end of the year, nearly 800,000 hectares of concessions were registered with district (*afdelingen*) forestry authorities. However, more than 90 per cent of those concessions were less than 10,000 hectares in size, and were being operated by small-scale timber enterprises seeking to minimise operational costs by subcontracting. Subcontractors, in turn, relied on the well-tested practice of hiring local logging teams for the felling and delivery of timber (Het Bosch 1935a, 1935b).

As a result, the practice of timber exploitation through *opkoop* continued despite government regulations to the contrary. Logging activities of this kind were technically illegal but were tolerated because they helped to maintain the appearance of native states' authority and prestige in areas that were under indirect rule. Economically, the native Indonesian ruling classes generated substantial income from timber, while the Dutch colonial government enjoyed considerable tax revenues as well.

Illegal timber exploitation occurred not only in small-scale operations but also in large-scale operations. A widely publicised example was that of the Japanese logging company NRKK (Nanyo Ringyo Kabushiki Kaisha) in East Borneo (Linblad 1988; Post 1993). In the early 1930s, the company conducted large-scale logging in the Bulungan area, employing more than 1,000 'coolies'. It was found to be operating without proper documentation and its activities are thought to have resulted in vast volumes of ironwood leaving Bulungan for Japan without any customs formalities. This and several similar cases prompted the Dutch authorities to tighten timber exploitation regulations.

Sukarno's 'Old Order'

In 1945, the Japanese left Indonesia and the Dutch returned. The economies of East Borneo and other Outer Islands were in a shambles. There was a black market and people smuggled various products, including timber, for subsistence needs. In order to have a semblance of control over timber extraction in the context of slow economic recovery, the Dutch re-legalised logging through the *opkoop* schemes that had officially been outlawed since 1934 (Dienst van het Boswezen 1949).

Between 1949 and 1967, the Sukarno years following independence, timber emerged as an economically and politically significant commodity in Indonesia's Outer Islands. Timber concessions became an important item on the list of rewards for political cooperation. Initially, such rewards were extended to the ruling elites and other locally influential individuals in exchange for their alliance with emergent political parties (Rocamora 1970). Subsequently, politically motivated rewards were used to pacify disgruntled military personnel in revolt-prone regions as well as to remunerate Indonesia's civil government and armed forces in the regions (Mackie 1962).

In such circumstances, there was a sharp rise in the value of small concessions as an economic and political asset (Nadjamuddin 1960; Sarjono 1961; Trihadi 1964). In the early 1960s, the system received a defining boost from the cooperative agreement between Indonesia and Japan that led to the formation of the Kalimantan Forestry Development Corporation (KFDC).

The aim was to open five forestry units in East Kalimantan and, by the end of the decade, achieve a massive production output of 800,000 cubic metres per year (Patter and Visser 1979: 24). However, by the time the scheme was cancelled in 1970, the annual production of the forestry units was only half the intended amount. The KFDC operation suffered from cost overruns and chronic production deficits throughout. Despite projections that between 1960 and 1968 the scheme would generate $52 million in profits for Indonesia, it resulted in losses of more than $10 million (Pauker 1961: 123; Manning 1971: 36).

In the eyes of Japanese shareholders and managers, KFDC was essentially a failure. But it was a boon for local timber businessmen in East Kalimantan. Small-scale timber operators not only found it profitable to work their logging teams for KFDC, but also found it easy and more profitable to deliver logs to the coast and sell them independently. The Japanese offered to pay their Indonesian partners international market prices for their teams' timber, but in reality these prices were substantially lower than those the Indonesians could obtain elsewhere, because of deductions linked to Indonesia's credit obligations. The end result was that a sizeable portion of production was steadily diverted and sold elsewhere.

Eventually, increasing numbers of small-scale loggers did not even bother to obtain official permits for their logging operations. In 1963, the government authorities in East Kalimantan issued an official warning in the form of a provincial regulation that required all parties except the state-owned forestry firm Perhutani to register, to acquire official logging areas (*kappersil*[5]) and to confine their activities to licensed areas (Monografi Kaltim 1968: 16). In 1964, illegal logging was mentioned for the first time when the East Kalimantan Forestry Bureau identified the elimination of *penebangan liar*, illegal logging, among the most urgent issues to be addressed (Monografi Kaltim 1968: 16, 1970: 65).

Soeharto's New Order

Sukarno was ousted in 1965 and replaced by Soeharto. The new president's first priority was to stimulate economic growth as a way out of grinding poverty. The first step towards this objective was promulgation of liberal domestic and foreign investment laws in 1967 and 1968.

The results of the strategy were quickly visible across a range of sectors, particularly those based on natural resources such as forestry and mining. In the forestry sector, the regulatory changes stimulated a period of logging frenzy known as *banjir kap*, flood-logging (Manning 1971; Slamet 1971; Daroesman 1979; Peluso 1983). Stimulated by expanding consumer markets for tropical timber in Japan, South Korea and Taiwan, logging operations experienced tremendous growth as people obtained *kappersil* and extracted timber using chainsaws or other simple logging methods. Immediately after the implementation of the 1967 investment laws, the total area covered by *kappersil* in East Kalimantan increased to almost 600,000 hectares (Monografi Kaltim 1968: 16). In the same year, the first large logging concessions (HPHs) were granted to domestic and foreign companies.

In 1968, small-scale logging permits already covered nearly 800,000 hectares (Monografi Kaltim 1969: 41). In 1969, the *kappersil* area increased to just over 1.2 million hectares and the number of foreign and domestic companies possessing HPH concessions, or in the process of applying for them, increased to 27, for a total of 5.5 million hectares (Monografi Kaltim 1969: 68–75). At the same time, illegal timber extraction and shipping intensified, attracting more public attention in the province and drawing timid admonitions from forestry officials (Monografi Kaltim 1969: 68; see also Soepardi 1972).

In 1971, *banjir kap* logging was banned in favour of HPH concessions. East Kalimantan entered another timber rush period, but this time it was based on large-scale, mechanised logging operations.[6] The statistics for this period are impressive. According to Daroesman (1979: 47):

> Some 15 million ha of concessions, virtually the entire area of East Kalimantan's productive forests, were granted in the period 1967–76, the great majority of them during 1970–73.

The volume of timber exports increased dramatically, from 300,000 cubic metres in 1968, when the first mechanised operations began, to nearly 10 million cubic metres in the peak year of 1979. In 1979, exports were estimated to have generated over $1 billion in government income.

This spectacular growth of HPH concessions occurred for two reasons. First, profits from logging were extraordinary. For 1972, according to Koehler (1972: 108):

> the gross profit of the big concessionaries [was] estimated to be in the range of 30 to 40 per cent and in some cases even considerably more ...

Such profitability was made possible by very liberal regulation of the logging industry, as companies enjoyed very low taxation that allowed them to capture most of the value of the resource. In addition, there was widespread underreporting of production as well as tax evasion.[7] Some estimates suggest that during this period the Indonesian government officially captured no more than 20 per cent of the actual value of the timber that had been extracted (Ruzicka 1979).

The logging concession boom was also fuelled by the Indonesian government's very limited supervision of the burgeoning forestry sector. In theory, concessionaires were required to follow numerous regulations, including the preparation of 1-year, 5-year and 20-year management plans showing how selective felling and reforestation would be carried out. In addition, companies were not allowed to subcontract their work and by the seventh year of operation they were expected to process up to 40 per cent of their log output locally (Daroesman 1979: 48). By 1980, hardly any HPH companies complied with these rules (Sacerdoti 1979; Jenkins 1980).

In 1983, the government imposed a log export ban as a means to tie the extractive HPH sector to plans for a timber-processing industry (Awanohara 1982). This led to the emergence of timber conglomerates in Indonesia, for example, the Kalimanis Group, the Barito Pacific Group, Kayu Lapis Indonesia, Djajanti and Alas Kusuma. Eventually, all operated large plywood plants and held millions of hectares of forest concessions.

The combination of the banning of log exports and the low timber royalties and reforestation fees provided a powerful incentive for the uncontrolled expansion of plywood production capacity (Dauvergne 1994; Brown 1999; Firman 1999). Indonesia's plywood exports increased from 1.25 million cubic metres in 1982 to 8.96 million cubic metres in 1991 (Barr 1999: 193). Through subsidisation and unchecked expansion of production, plywood producers were able to generate as much raw material (logs) as they needed, manipulating the effective forest management regulations or ignoring them altogether. For example, Schwarz (1990) estimated that in the late 1980s plywood-linked HPH concessionaires not only routinely overharvested their forest concessions, but also illegally extracted at least 2 million cubic metres of timber each year from protected forest areas.

The imbalance between the production capacity of woodworking industries and the officially sanctioned log harvest (supply) was exacerbated by the parallel growth of the sawn timber sector. In the 1990s, this sector became completely uncontrollable with the rapid expansion of the pulp and paper sector (Barr 2000). By the end of the decade, the log supply deficit reached tens of millions of cubic metres per year, pushing illegal logging to ever higher levels.

Post-Soeharto period

In May 1998, under domestic and international pressure, Soeharto stepped down, ushering in the process of democratisation in Indonesia (*reformasi*). The political and regulatory changes arising from *reformasi* (such as decentralisation and regional autonomy) created conditions that contributed to the acceleration of illegal logging in the country and also brought the issue to the fore in forest policy debates.[8] The new decentralisation laws and the decline in law and order were other important factors leading to the boom in illegal logging.

After the fall of Soeharto, the Indonesian government was forced to show an intent to reform the forest sector. First, the Ministry of Forestry and Plantations issued instructions that communities residing in or near forest areas could be actively involved in forest exploitation through cooperatives, work groups and village associations.[9] Subsequently, the central government implemented legislation that devolved elements of authority to manage forests from the central government to the provincial and district authorities.[10] This legislation gave district heads (*bupati*) the authority to issue permits for small forest concessions in the form of small-scale forest harvesting concession rights (HPHH) and timber extraction and utilisation permits (IPPK).[11] Within weeks of putting these policies into effect, the offices of the *bupati* in the province of East Kalimantan were flooded with applications for HPHH and IPPK permits. By 2001, these concessions already covered hundreds of thousands of hectares of forest in East Kalimantan and other provinces.

Laws 22 and 25 on decentralisation and fiscal balancing between the central and regional governments (particularly district governments) were passed in 1999 and implemented in 2001. They strengthened the devolution of some rights over the utilisation of natural resources to districts and provinces.

Decentralisation and regional autonomy were thought to be the cure for the centralistic unfairness and repression of the New Order, but these new political processes soon proved to be the source of a plethora of problems. Decentralisation and regional autonomy were based on vague and poorly drafted laws, so the door was wide open to varying, interest-based interpretations. The districts (and to a lesser extent the provinces) soon began to draft their own rules governing natural resources in order to maximise income from those resources. The new political framework rendered *bupati* so powerful that all government and private sector actors in the districts tended to heed the *bupati*'s will first, and only subsequently think of the central government. This led to a general breakdown of law and order, as flouting the national laws often became the sign or proof of the commitment of district or provincial policy-makers to decentralisation. For example, for a long time the districts opposed Jakarta's demands for the withdrawal of local regulations supporting HPHH and IPPK logging permits.

The rise of small logging permits became the preferred means of timber production for a range of small, medium and large forestry companies. HPH concessionaires participated very actively in the HPHH/IPPK logging boom as reduced red tape, low operational costs and minimal tax and forest management (reforestation) responsibilities provided short-term relief from debt problems, concession encroachment and legal uncertainty. Throughout the boom, all players carried out the now familiar abuses of cutting outside the authorised block, overcutting, underinvoicing, falsifying shipment documents or outright smuggling (Obidzinski and Palmer 2002).

Clearly, illegal logging has had a long history in Indonesia. Logging activities in breach of effective government regulations have been an inseparable part of forestry operations ever since timber became at first marketable and subsequently a valuable commodity on international markets. There is a historical continuity in what is currently termed illegal logging – exploitation of timber that contravenes existing regulations – although its scope is much wider than most people think. Illegal logging is not only a problem associated with small logging permits and smuggling; it is associated with essentially all timber extraction and processing in Indonesia.

FOREIGN INVOLVEMENT

As log exports grew and small and medium-sized enterprises in the forestry sector gained a higher profile, the logging and woodworking establishment in Indonesia – the Indonesian Association of Forest Concessionaires (APHI) and the Indonesian Plywood Producers' Association (Apkindo) – with support from the Ministry of Forestry, launched a campaign against small concessions and the export of logs.[12] The campaign alleged that logging activities based on district permits and the smuggling of timber abroad were anchored to rogue Indonesian businessmen and their foreign (largely Malaysian) sponsors.[13] The Indonesian and Malaysian perpetrators of illegal logging were labelled *cukong*. These were the mainly ethnic Chinese entrepreneurs who provided the financial support for logging operations.[14]

The campaign sought to focus the attention of the mass media (its primary target) on catchy issues such as the vast volumes of timber smuggled out of Indonesia; the key perpetrators (Malaysia and China); their Indonesian accomplices (*cukong* and their regional networks); the loss of tax revenues ($1–$5 billion annually); the shortage of raw material for the mills; and employment implications.[15] The underlying message was that illegal logging was caused by small and medium-sized logging operators, not by large-scale HPH operations: if only the export of logs was stopped and timber-smuggling eliminated, the illegal logging problem in Indonesia would disappear.

The fact is, however, that APHI and Apkindo member companies are no strangers to cutting outside authorised blocks, overcutting, underinvoicing, falsifying shipment documents and smuggling. Obidzinski and Andrianto (2004) have recently shown that in East Kalimantan, for instance, nearly all timber operators holding large-scale HPH permits and IPK clear-cutting permits in the districts of Berau and East Kutai commit such violations *en masse*. In both districts, only about half the large-scale log production is properly reported and taxed.

In 2001, the total timber harvest in Indonesia was 60 million cubic metres, of which 50 million cubic metres was estimated to have been harvested illegally (Tacconi, Obidzinski and Agung 2004). The volume of timber smuggled out of Indonesia is estimated at 10 million cubic metres per year.[16] This is a cumulative figure for all kinds of logging, with small-scale logging being responsible for only a portion. Small-scale operations also supply logs to the domestic market, but research indicates that they are not the dominant force (Budiarto 2003; Obidzinski and Andrianto 2004). Yet the media have been remarkably successful in portraying small-scale logging operators as villains and HPH concessionaires and associated plywood producers as victims.[17]

DEFORESTATION

Because small and medium-sized logging enterprises holding district-level permits and small-scale freelance village loggers are being identified as the root of the illegal logging problem in Indonesia, they are also being identified as the cause of deforestation in the country.[18] Deforestation is an issue of growing concern in Indonesia. There is little agreement over past and present rates of deforestation, mainly because of differences in the definition of what constitutes forest, but there is little doubt that over the past few decades the pace of deforestation has accelerated (Barber and Talbott 2003; Tacconi and Kurniawan 2004). In 2003 and 2004, Indonesia Forest Watch, the Indonesian Forum for Environment and the Ministry of Forestry estimated that the rate of deforestation was approximately 4 million hectares per year.

Could such a large area have been deforested solely by the activities of small-scale logging operators and timber smugglers? Selective logging operations in Indonesia extract between 10 and 20 cubic metres of timber per hectare, and most large and small-scale timber-harvesting activities in Indonesia adhere to this standard (Dinas Kehutanan Kalimantan Timur 2000; BPS 2002). On this basis, the smuggling of 10 million cubic metres of logs could affect between 0.5 and 1 million hectares of forest annually. If small-scale loggers are responsible for illegally extracting the remaining 40 million cubic metres annually for domestic consumption, then they are indeed the cause of forest degradation and deforestation in Indonesia. However, facts on the ground and the views of forestry sector insiders do not support such a one-sided scenario (Budiarto 2003; Obidzinski and Andrianto 2004).

There is little doubt that deforestation involves forces considerably larger than log smugglers and small or medium-sized logging enterprises in the districts. HPH operations, plywood industry cartels, industrial timber plantations and other plantation estates (especially oil palm plantations) are almost certainly in large part responsible for destroying millions of hectares of Indonesia's forests. This fact is scarcely mentioned in the Indonesian mass media and is rarely discussed in forestry and research forums. The perception that smuggling and small concession logging equals illegal logging equals deforestation is firmly established.

CONCLUSIONS

The Indonesian timber establishment's drive to influence the illegal logging discourse seems to be motivated by the desire to ride out the current political upheaval in Indonesia, minimise losses and hold on to the vestiges of what was formerly unlimited power over forest resources.

The logging and plywood corporate associations in Indonesia indeed have a lot at stake, particularly the opportunity to continue the highly profitable (rent-generating) integrated forestry operations (Broad 1995; Barr 1999; Brown 1999, 2001). In the 1980s and for most of the 1990s, Indonesia and Malaysia together supplied more than 90 per cent of the world's tropical plywood exports, with roughly one-third of production going to Japan. Indonesia currently has 110 operating plywood mills, with a capacity of 11.3 million cubic metres per year. However, the country's plywood production fell from 11.6 million cubic metres in 1993 to 7.0 million cubic metres in 2003.[19] Predictably, this is blamed on illegal logging and log-smuggling by *cukong* networks to Malaysia and China; there is little mention of the decrease in large-diameter logs due to more than 30 years of intensive timber exploitation.[20]

The decline in the production and export of Indonesian plywood as a result of stiffening competition, particularly from China, is also blamed on illegal logging and log-smuggling by *cukong* networks (Palmer and Obidzinski 2002). The Indonesian plywood establishment maintains that in the international timber markets it is losing ground to Chinese plywood producers because the latter are able sell their products at artificially low prices due to cheap, illegal raw material (logs) flowing from Indonesia. This is a self-serving argument bearing little semblance to reality. Currently, China imports nearly 100 million cubic metres of wood products a year. The majority of its log imports come from the Russian far east; whatever volumes of Indonesian timber are smuggled into the country have very little effect on the overall economic outlook of China's plywood sector. Of far greater importance are factors such as cheap labour, strong investment and technological advances that give China's plywood producers an advantage over Indonesian competitors (Palmer and Obidzinski 2002).

The Indonesian plywood producers grouped under Apkindo are well aware of what really allows the Chinese to outcompete other plywood makers in the region.[21] Although it is a slow process, they are restructuring production operations, targeting niche markets and retooling factories to increase efficiency. The cornerstone of their success is maintaining access to undervalued logs on closed domestic timber markets. Subsidies have been the foundation of their success for nearly 25 years.

It is politically expedient for some people to portray illegal logging as a practice financed by neighbouring countries such as Malaysia and China that have a high demand for timber but limited supplies of it.[22] Shifting the blame onto timber-hungry neighbours achieves a number of objectives. It diverts unwanted attention from difficult issues such as the long history of forest mismanagement, the complexity of industrial restructuring and the reduction of overcapacity, with associated adverse impacts on employment and social stability. When Indonesian policy-makers blame foreigners for illegal logging, they usually couch their comments in nationalistic rhetoric, allowing them to score easy political points at home.

There are five main ways in which Indonesia could control illegal logging.

Law enforcement. There is a lot of emphasis on law enforcement (*penegakan hukum*) because of pressure from the media, government forestry agencies, NGOs and research institutions. On its own, law enforcement is unlikely to produce results because the benefits from illegal forestry activities far outweigh the risks. Law enforcement operations tend to focus on smuggling, but their ability to reach into the managerial ranks of timber-smuggling networks is extremely limited.

Bilateral agreements. Indonesia has signed bilateral agreements with timber-importing countries such as China, Japan and South Korea to eliminate trade in illegally harvested timber. However, the agreements have remained dormant.

Restructuring of Indonesia's woodworking industries. It is critical to maintain the spotlight on the difficult, yet critical, issue of restructuring the enormous overcapacity of Indonesia's woodworking industries, which drives the insatiable demand for logs. It is also important to ensure that the revitalisation of the forestry sector currently promoted by the Ministry of Forestry will result in a reduction of capacity, not just the retooling of the factories.

Anti Money Laundering Law. The Anti Money Laundering Law passed in late 2003 has the potential to address large-scale illegal logging activities by freezing the financial assets of parties identified as perpetrators of illegal logging and limiting financial services to them. However, this law has yet to be implemented.

Eco-sensitive market links. Some people have tried to establish eco-sensitive market links between Indonesian timber suppliers and major timber-consuming countries in the Asia Pacific, particularly China and Japan. The scheme would require certification and verification of legality. However, it faces a major obstacle in that demand for certified and/or legally verified timber products in China and Japan continues to be very limited.

At present the interpretation of these measures tends to be driven by economic and political interests that do not want the logging and woodworking establishment to be seen as being associated with illegal logging. The measures are unlikely to have a meaningful impact until this situation changes. There is a need to couple them with a nationwide drive to galvanise civil society groups to scrutinise and pressure forestry officials, police and other relevant government agencies to push for greater transparency and accountability in the forestry sector, to increase the political cost of illegal forest activities and thus to reduce the incentives for illegal logging.

NOTES

1   See Barr (1998, 2001); Broad (1995); Brown (1999, 2001); Dauvergne (1994, 1997); Ross (2001).
2   See Contreras-Hermosilla (2001); EIA–Telapak (1999, 2000, 2002b); FWI–GFW (2002); ITTO (2001); Petebang (2000a, 2000b).
3   See, for example, Muhtadi (1999); 'Pengusaha HPH sengsarakan rakyat', *Banjarmasin Post*, 1 March 1999; and 'HPH rusak hutan Aceh Selatan', *Kompas*, 29 April 1999.
4   See, for example, 'Ironi perbatasan Serawak-Kalbar (3) HPH bupati, marak illegal logging', *Detikom*, 12 June 2003; 'Lima km hutan Indonesia dijarah cukong Malaysia', *Gatra*, 17 October 2003; 'Kayu Malaysia itu "Made in Indonesia"', *Kompas*, 28 October 2003; 'Tolak HPHH tutup', *Pontianak Post*, 4 June 2003; 'Ilegal logging libatkan mafia internasional dan oknum pejabat', *Pontianak Post*, 19 June 2003; 'Singapura dan Malaysia penampung kayu seludupan terbesar', *Tempo Interaktif*, 12 September 2003.
5   *Kappersil* is the term used for a small logging concession. PP 1/1957 provided for three types of *kappersil* logging permits: for areas of 10,000 hectares, awarded by governors; for 5,000 hectares, awarded by district heads; and for 100 hectares, awarded by subdistrict officials.
6   See Raharjo (1972); Miraza (1973); Roeder (1973a,1973b); Goldstone (1974).
7   Interviews between 1999 and 2000 with HPH staff posted in East Kalimantan during the 1970s and 1980s.
8   See Casson (2001a); Khan (2001); McCarthy (2000, 2002); Obidzinski, Suramenggala and Levang (2001); Casson and Obidzinski (2002).
9   PP 62/1998 and SK Menhutbun 677/1998.
10 PP 6/1999, SK Menhutbun 310/Kpts-II/1999 and SK Menhutbun 317/Kpts-II/1999.
11 An IPPK permit covers 100 hectares; an HPHH permit usually covers a much larger area.
12 See 'Plywood group wants ban on log exports', *Jakarta Post*, 20 February 2001.
13 See 'Pencuri kayu geser patok batas RI-Malaysia', *Kompas*, 23 May 2000; 'Perdagangan kayu bulat banyak diselewengkan', *Kompas*, 15 August 2002; 'Hutan di utara kaltim terancam. IPK dikeluarkan, pengusaha tawau banyak masuk', *Suara Kaltim*, 19 February 2001; 'Bupati rama Asia diadukan ke kejati. Dituduh terbitkan isin HPHH dengan imbalan Rp 50 Juta', *Suara Kaltim*, 27 February 2001; 'Polda tangkap WNA di Malinau. Diduga support dana bagi pengusaha lokal', *Suara Kaltim*, 28 February 2001.
14 See 'Kerjasama polri-dephut tak berdaya menhadapi cukong kayu', *Kompas*, 28 June 2002; 'Cukong kayu asal Malaysia menjadi raja', *Kompas*, 24 August 2004.
15 See 'Indonesia losing $3.7 billion annually from illegal logging', *Asia Pulse*, 18

June 2003; 'Kerugian akibat "illegal logging" Rp 46 triliun', *Media Indonesia*, 18 June 2003.

16 See 'Pencuri kayu geser patok batas RI-Malaysia', *Kompas*, 23 May 2000; 'Perdagangan kayu bulat banyak diselewengkan', *Kompas*, 15 August 2002; 'Kerjasama polri-dephut tak berdaya menhadapi cukong kayu', *Kompas*, 28 June 2002; 'Cukong kayu asal Malaysia menjadi raja', *Kompas*, 24 August 2004.

17 See 'Ironi perbatasan Serawak-Kalbar (3) HPH Bupati, Marak Illegal Logging', *Detikom*, 12 June 2003; 'Lima km hutan Indonesia dijarah cukong Malaysia', *Gatra*, 17 October 2003; 'Kayu Malaysia itu "Made in Indonesia"', *Kompas*, 28 October 2003; 'Tolak HPHH tutup', *Pontianak Post*, 4 June 2003; 'Ilegal logging libatkan mafia internasional dan oknum pejabat', *Pontianak Post*, 19 June 2003; 'Singapura dan Malaysia penampung kayu seludupan terbesar', *Tempo Interaktif*, 12 September 2003.

18 See 'Laju kerusakan hutan di Indonesia tiap tahun dua juta hektar', *Analisa*, 13 September 2003; 'Kerusakan hutan di Indonesia, terparah di planet bumi', *Gatra*, 7 November 2003; '43 juta hektare hutan rusak: Akibat maraknya aksi penebangan liar', *Pikiran Rakyat*, 22 September 2003.

19 The plywood production figures quoted range from 4.5 million cubic metres to 7 million cubic metres depending on whether the source is the Ministry of Forestry, the Central Bureau of Statistics, the Ministry of Trade and Industry or Customs.

20 See 'Plywood group wants ban on log exports', *Jakarta Post*, 20 February 2001; 'Kayu Indonesia lebih murah di LN', *Bali Post*, 30 May 2003.

21 Interviews with APHI and Apkindo functionaries in East Kalimantan, 2003–04.

22 See 'World demand increases illegal logging', *Jakarta Post*, 9 September 2003; 'EU urged to reject KL wood products', *Jakarta Post*, 15 October 2003; 'Indonesia calls on Malaysia to deal with illegal logging issue', *Asia Pulse*, 15 October 2003.

13 ILLEGAL COALMINING IN WEST SUMATRA: ACCESS AND ACTORS IN THE POST-SOEHARTO ERA

Erwiza Erman

Since the economic crisis of 1997 and the arrival of the post-Soeharto reform era, illegal mining has spun out of control. It not only is causing great harm to the environment and resulting in enormous losses of state revenue, but also has given rise to conflicts between local people and newcomers, between illegal miners and mining companies, and among local elites. My intention in choosing the coalmining business in the city of Sawahlunto and the district of Sawahlunto-Sijunjung, both in West Sumatra, as the subject of this case study is to analyse the causes and development of illegal coalmining as well as local bureaucrats' reactions to the development of this business.

ILLEGAL COALMINING IN WEST SUMATRA

Illegal mining is not a new phenomenon in Indonesia. Long before independence and afterwards, local people in the Bangka and Belitung islands carried out illegal tin mining and illegal trade in tin (Vous 1990; Andaya 1993; Erman 2004). Under the New Order regime, the first officially recognised case of illegal mining involved the Lusang Gold Mining Company, which was illegally extracting gold in Lebong Tandai in the province of Bengkulu in the early 1980s (Aspinall 2001). Today's illegal mining activities have spread to coal, tin, diamonds and even mixed minerals. Illegal mining mainly takes place on the periphery of legal mining operations in West Sumatra, West Java, Kalimantan and North Sulawesi, although in all 16 provinces are affected (*Jakarta Post*, 29 October 2001).

The term 'illegal mining' (*penambangan liar*) was used during the New Order period to refer to mining activities, typically small-scale operations using traditional equipment, undertaken without a licence from the government. In the post-Soeharto era, two new terms related to illegal mining are officially used: *penambangan tanpa ijin* or *peti* (mining without a licence) and *tambang rakyat* or *rakyat penambang* (people's mines). The latter term refers to small-scale mining activity carried out by local people using traditional equipment on their own land, but without a government licence (Aspinall 2001). However, much of the present illegal mining activity is not covered by these terms. For example, some large, legal mining companies are carrying out illegal practices such as mining outside their concession areas. Others are operating without a licence. Some small-scale miners have a government licence, but not from the proper government agency. And some small-scale mining activity is carried out by 'outsiders', people from outside the region, using both traditional and modern equipment. For the purposes of this chapter, it is probably safe to refer to illegal mining as any mining activity that contravenes any existing mining regulation.

It is difficult to determine the exact extent of illegal mining in Indonesia. A very rough estimation would tell us that there are approximately 68,000 illegal miners throughout Indonesia, far more than there were at the end of the New Order period. The numbers have soared, first, because illegal mining has absorbed many of the workers laid off during the 1997–98 economic crisis. Second, illegal mining became an increasingly attractive source of income for locals as the rupiah depreciated in the years after the crisis, because mining commodities were paid for in US dollars (*Kompas*, 6 March 2001). And third, many financial backers (*cukong*) saw illegal mining as a high-return business, and hence were willing to provide the financial support necessary for illegal mining activities.

The illegal coalmines examined in this chapter are located in the vicinity of the city of Sawahlunto and the district of Sawahlunto-Sijunjung in West Sumatra. Two large coalmining companies operate in the area: PT Tambang Batubara Unit Produksi Ombilin (PTBA-UPO), a state-owned company set up in 1892, and PT Allied Indo Coal (PT AIC), a joint venture company. In addition, many illegal miners have been mining coal in the area without a permit since the crisis.[1] In mid-1998, it was estimated that there were approximately 1,115 illegal miners with an average daily production of 1,930 tonnes. The number of illegal miners had increased to about 2,600 by 2000.[2]

Using both basic traditional equipment and modern equipment such as excavators, bulldozers and trucks, the illegal miners operate in the concession areas of PTBA-UPO and PT AIC as well as in surrounding areas where mining is prohibited, such as Langkok. Their system of operation typically neglects environmental impacts. For example, in September 1998 it was found that illegal miners had dug holes that had almost penetrated the ventilation ducts of the Sawah Rasau V underground mine, a mine originally set up during the colonial era and now largely disused. If the ventilation ducts had been breached, then the carbon monoxide and methane gas in the ducts would very likely have exploded, causing a fire. And because the ventilation tunnel is linked to networks that run below the city of Sawahlunto, such a fire could easily have spread to disastrous effect.[3]

Local newspapers continually report the environmental problems caused by illegal mining operations.[4] For example, on 19 February 2000 a local newspaper, *Canang*, reported as one of its main stories that Sawahlunto was 'seriously damaged', and that because no rehabilitation work had been undertaken in the areas exploited by the illegal miners, the land in these areas resembled 'open wounds'. Illegal mining has created hundred of hectares of barren fields that can be subject to flooding. Such damage has occurred even in the areas that PTBA-UPO has replanted with acacia trees.

Illegal mining is a highly organised activity, often with close links to the criminal underworld. Each mining site is controlled by a group of *preman* (extortionists or standover criminals) headed by a 'boss' or mine leader. They hire miners to work the site, with the number of miners varying depending on the size of the area they control. The *preman* compete with other gangs for control of the best mining sites, and must protect their own mine from theft by other gangs. The *preman* also deal with the local authorities and the police, and ensure that the miners do not tell the general public about the mining operation.

Each mine leader maintains contact with or, more often, works for a *cukong*. A mine leader typically controls from two to 40 mine sites depending on the capital provided by his sponsoring *cukong*. Competition to obtain rich coalfields is fierce, and theft of coal from competing groups is commonplace. Thus these competing interests often lead to violence, with the law of the jungle ensuring that the boldest and strongest will prevail.

The *cukong*, who generally come from outside the region, provide all necessary equipment and cover the costs of mining operations. In return, mine leaders agree to sell their coal only to the *cukong*. Each *cukong* typically has a sales contract with one of the local coal distributors in Padang, which in turn has the connections to sell the coal to the state-owned companies, PT Semen Padang and PT Kereta Api Indonesia (PT KAI), or to export it to other countries, usually Malaysia and Singapore (*Singgalang*, 4 August 1998).

The activities of the illegal miners are not only well organised but also an open secret among many people, including the police. The coal the miners extract is transported from the coalmining areas by truck along public roads and stockpiled at various locations around Sawahlunto. It is then trucked to Padang, where it is stockpiled along the bypass roads. Finally, local coal distributors sell the coal to PT Semen Padang or ship it abroad through the Teluk Bayur harbour.

In 1998 mine leaders paid an average rate of Rp 10,000 per worker per day for coal digging. Per tonne of coal extracted, a worker received Rp 13,000–15,000. Workers were encouraged to work day and night without regard for their health or for the risks they were facing. Coalmining, besides being hard work, is very hazardous. In March 2000 the local media reported that 30 miners had died, and in February 2002 that the number had increased to 46.[5] The figures do not include the injured, many of whom would become permanently disabled. In many cases injured coalminers do not receive proper medical attention, and may not even be brought to a local health centre or hospital. Mine leaders threaten their miners to keep quiet about such accidents, preventing them from reporting cases to the local authorities.

Nevertheless, the local authorities' efforts to prevent illegal mining have come under strong challenge from the miners themselves. For example, in 1998 about 200 miners demonstrated in front of the office of the mayor of Sawahlunto to protest about the government's plan to stop illegal mining activities (*Haluan*, 12 September 1998). They argued that mining was a way of helping the common people to survive during the economic crisis (*Haluan*, 8 July 1998; *Kompas*, 28 September 1998).

Faced with this resistance, the local authorities' efforts shifted from trying to prohibit illegal mining activities to trying to prevent irresponsible mining activities. The mayor of Sawahlunto and the head of the district of Sawahlunto-Sijunjung decided to set up village unit cooperatives (KUDs) in their regions to provide financial support for small-scale mine activities and act as the agents for the sale of their coal. Under the KUD system, miners were given training by PTBA-UPO mining engineers in how to prevent mine accidents, and agreed not to mine in areas in which mining was prohibited. It was hoped that the KUD system would reduce the extent of illegal mining and put the *cukong* out of business. To prevent coal from being marketed outside the region, PTBA-UPO agreed to take the coal supplied by the KUDs, paying as much as Rp 55,000 per tonne to cover the costs of extraction and transportation to its stockpiles at Sawah Rasau V. PTBA-UPO would then sell the coal to PT Semen Padang in Padang or export it to Malaysia, Hong Kong or Japan. KUD Talawi was the first to sign an agreement with PTBA-UPO, on 11 November 1998. It was followed by the KUDs of Pincuran Batu, Sijantang and Kolok, all located in the city of Sawahlunto, and later by KUD V Koto in Bukit Bual in the district of Sawahlunto-Sijunjung (*Haluan*, 28 October 1998).

What is important to note about the establishment of these KUDs is that the new system legalised what had formerly been illegal coalmining activities in the Sawahlunto area. Although the KUD system could be considered an achievement in controlling illegal mining, in effect it created a new problem without really solving the old problems. The crux of the new problem was that the KUD system increased PTBA-UPO's coal production beyond the annual target. In 2000, PTBA-UPO exceeded its annual production target of 1.2 million tonnes, with about half of its coal in that year supplied by the KUDs (*Singgalang*, 12 January 2000). Unfortunately, however, PTBA-UPO was unable to pay for all the coal delivered by the KUDs because PT Semen Padang had bought the coal from PTBA-UPO on credit.

At the same time, the old problem of *preman* and *cukong* involvement in coalmining activities was not eliminated. Many *preman* became members of a KUD or even established a KUD to camouflage their illegal activities. When acting on behalf of a KUD, one of their tactics was to deliver coal mixed with dirt to PTBA-UPO, and force the company's staff to accept it. At a price of Rp 55,000 per tonne, this would clearly cause a substantial loss for PTBA-UPO. If the company succeeded in rejecting the delivery, then the coal was taken back to the mining site, replaced with the best quality coal and sold to a *cukong* in Padang, who was by now willing to pay a higher price than that offered by PTBA-UPO. There have also been cases of *preman* delivering a KUD's coal directly to *cukong* in Padang, in violation of the agreement with PTBA-UPO. The *cukong* would then either export the coal, even though this was forbidden by the regulations, or sell it on the domestic market. Hence the illegal coalmining business is still dominated by *preman* and *cukong* operating, according to the *Canang* newspaper, with police protection (*Canang*, 2–5 February 2000). The newspaper estimates that the police receive Rp 1–2 million per week from the *cukong*, much more than the Rp 100,000–200,000 per week offered by PTBA-UPO.

Illicit practices such as theft of coal and the mining of high-risk and prohibited areas also continue. PTBA-UPO has allocated more staff to deal with these problems, but many miners, supported and protected by *preman*, continue to steal other groups' coal and work in high-risk and prohibited areas.[6]

ACTORS BEHIND THE ACCESS

With the implementation of the regional autonomy law, Law 22/1999, in January 2001, cities, districts and provinces obtained the authority to issue mining permits (other than oil and gas-mining permits). Since then, local authorities have seized the opportunity to increase their own-source (PAD) revenue by issuing numerous mining permits. In West Sumatra, the district head (*bupati*) of Sawahlunto-Sijunjung and the governor of West Sumatra have proved to be no exception, issuing many coalmining permits. This section examines their role in providing access to the mines and in marketing the region's coal in greater detail.

The role of the *bupati*

The *bupati* of Sawahlunto-Sijunjung has used his power to encourage the formation of KUDs related to mining since 2000, a year before the effective implementation of the regional autonomy law. He has also become involved in the marketing of coal, the main topic of this section. This is an important issue, because the original intention of the local authorities in supporting the establishment of KUDs was to control illegal mining and reduce the number of mining accidents. But by becoming involved in coal marketing, the Sawahlunto-Sijunjung government has itself become part of the illegal mining business.

For the *bupati*, the decision to become a marketing agent was officially intended to increase the region's PAD revenue. The plan called for a newly established, locally owned company (*perusahaan daerah* or *perusda*), working together with KUD Muaro, an authorised mining operation, to sell 10,000 tonnes of coal to PT Koperasi Lingkar Mitra Mandiri (PT KLMM) located in Padang. PT KLMM would then export the coal to Malaysia. However, this plan was not well implemented. A few months after the establishment of the *perusda*, its stockpiles of coal increased significantly because PT KLMM did not take delivery of as much coal as had been expected, and the *perusda* was not able to find alternative buyers for its coal. About 300 miners complained to the local parliament, demanding permission to be able to sell their coal to other agencies (*Mimbar Minang*, 21 March 2000; *Padang Ekspress*, 21 March 2000).

The pros and cons of the *bupati*'s marketing policy became the subject of heated debate. The village heads of Salak and Sijantang, mine leaders, and coalminers who were members of KUD Talawi – all in the city of Sawahlunto – supported the policy and wanted the mayor and local parliament to establish a similar *perusda* with the right to sell coal from the Sawahlunto area (*Singgalang*, 29 March 2000). Their demand was supported by the provincial representatives of the Cooperative Ministry and the Indonesian Chamber of Commerce. However, the mayor and members of the local parliament held a different opinion, and refused to establish a new *perusda* in Sawahlunto (interview, 12 April 2000). Their decision was supported by the governor of West Sumatra and provincial representatives of the Ministry of Mining and Energy. A tug-of-war also arose between the provincial regional assembly (DPRD Propinsi) and the district regional assembly (DPRD Kabupaten), with most members of the provincial DPRD disagreeing with the *bupati*'s marketing policy and most members of the district DPRD supporting it (*Singgalang*, 19 June 2000).

With no agreement reached on the pros and cons of the *bupati*'s decision to become involved in marketing the district's coal, at the end of 2000 the governor of West Sumatra decided to prohibit all coal exports from the region. The governor hoped that this policy would put an end to the relationship between the Sawahlunto-Sijunjung *perusda* and PT KLMM – as an exporting company, PT KLMM would no longer be able to operate in the region (*Mimbar Minang*, 28 June 2000). However, just a few month after the export ban was introduced, it was reported that coal was being exported abroad without formal permission from the local authorities.

The governor and the case of PT Minang Malindo

In May 2001, five months after the regional autonomy law became effective, the governor of West Sumatra used his authority to issue coalmining permits (*kuasa penambangan*) and licences covering the transportation and marketing of coal to PT Minang Malindo, a local private company. One of the directors of the company was also a member of the provincial DPRD. Rumours indicated that the governor and his son were also involved in the company, but unofficially. The permit granted PT Minang Malindo coalmining rights over 500 hectares in the village of Bukit Bual. When forced to defend his decision, the governor argued that he had the right to issue such a permit because the coalfield was located on the border between Sawahlunto city and Sawahlunto-Sijunjung district, both of which came under his jurisdiction. Neither the mayor nor the *bupati* had the right to issue mining licences over border areas, he claimed.

The governor's decision to permit PT Minang Malindo to mine in Bukit Bual came under attack from several quarters. First, PTBA-UPO claimed that it held the sole authorisation to mine in the area, based on a permit issued to the company under a Soeharto-era presidential decree. The director of PTBA-UPO, Suhatri Arief,[7] refused to hand over the disputed land to PT Minang Malindo. He pointed out that PTBA-UPO was developing an underground mine in the area with financial support from China, and that the company had already dug tunnels of 400–600 metres in the area. He therefore requested the governor to recall the permit granted to PT Minang Malindo to mine in the Bukit Bual area (*Padang Ekspress*, 6 August 2001).

The governor and his allies in the provincial DPRD argued, however, that PTBA-UPO had never provided any compensation to local communities for mining in their area, and that the land in question was communal land that did not belong to PTBA-UPO. It was in the best interests of the local people, he said, to allow PT Minang Malindo to conduct coalmining in the area because the company was committed to providing training and capital to local people and paying compensation to the local community (*Padang Ekspress*, 9 August 2001).

The second layer of conflict was between the governor and the mayor of Sawahlunto as well as the *bupati* of Sawahlunto-Sijunjung. The regional autonomy law gives the city and district levels of government the authority to issue mining permits over the areas under their jurisdiction. Hence, the decision of the governor of West Sumatra to issue a coalmining permit to PT Minang Malindo was considered inappropriate. In addition, this decision was made without consultation with the mayor of Sawahlunto, the *bupati* of Sawahlunto-Sijunjung or even a competent agency such as the provincial Department of Mining and Energy. It was some time before the mayor and the *bupati* even found out that a coalmining permit had been issued to PT Minang Malindo (interview with Suhatri Arief, 12 October 2001). It is therefore not surprising that tensions arose between the governor on one side and the mayor, the *bupati* and representatives of the provincial Department of Mining and Energy on the other side.

The governor also came into conflict with local community leaders (*petinggi adat*) over his decision to issue a coalmining permit to PT Minang Malindo. It turned out that this decision was taken without consultation with local community leaders such as the *datuk*. What made the governor's conduct even more suspicious was that he had gone to the trouble of obtaining the approval of the various *datuk* of Koto Tinggi, a village in Sawahlunto-Sijunjung situated five kilometres from Bukit Bual. For some time the *datuk* of Bukit Bual remained blissfully unaware that their communal land had been handed over to PT Minang Malindo (interview with Suhatri Arief, 12 October 2001).

To make the matter even more complicated, only one week after obtaining its permit from the governor, PT Minang Malindo was selling coal to PT Semen Padang at a price of Rp 200,000 per tonne, the same price PTBA-UPO was receiving for its coal sold to the same company.[8] When members of the provincial parliament visited Bukit Bual to check on PT Minang Malindo's activities in July 2001, they found that in fact the company had not even begun to mine, but was simply acting as a distributor, buying coal from illegal miners. In other words, the company was acting as a new *cukong*, paying Rp 65,000–85,000 per tonne of coal, compared with Rp 55,000 per tonne for the coal PTBA-UPO was purchasing from the KUDs (*Singgalang*, 30 July 2001; *Haluan*, 10 August 2001). Without having to rehabilitate the exploited land or provide any social benefits to miners, PT Minang Malindo was able to make a significant profit (interview with Suhatri Arief, 12 October 2001)

The case of PT Minang Malindo was discussed several times in the provincial parliament between mid-2001 and the beginning of 2002. Since the matter could not be resolved at the regional level, it was finally referred to the national forum for mediation by the national parliament (DPR), the police and the Ministry of Internal Affairs, all in Jakarta. On 28 August 2002, after receiving heated representations from local leaders and local government agencies, the Ministry of Internal Affairs instructed the governor of West Sumatra to revoke the mining authorisation issued to PT Minang Malindo (*Padang Ekspress*, 21 August 2002).

FINAL REMARKS

The emergence of illegal mining in the city of Sawahlunto and the district of Sawahlunto-Sijunjung in West Sumatra cannot be separated from the economic crisis of 1997–98 and the political transformation from centralised to decentralised government. Coalmining was one of the few promising economic alternatives for unemployed people during and after the economic crisis of 1997–98.

Most illegal mining is conducted close to or even in the coalfields under the jurisdiction of PTBA-UPO and PT AIC. Illegal mining has damaged the environment and is very risky to humans, both miners and those living in the area. The operations of illegal mining were controlled by *preman*, supported by *cukong* in Padang, and protected by the local police.

The efforts of local authorities to control illegal mining by setting up KUDs did not prevent illegal miners from operating in prohibited areas or in the areas run by PTBA-UPO and PT AIC. Mining accidents continued to occur, and the *preman–cukong* networks continued to operate. Under the KUD system, PTBA-UPO agreed to buy all the coal supplied by the KUDs, but because of the quantity supplied, it ran out of cash. More importantly, the system actually 'legalised' the operation of illegal mining. To the extent that many formerly illegal miners have joined a KUD, it has become difficult to distinguish between legal and illegal mining. The situation has only been exacerbated by the decision of the *bupati* of Sawahlunto-Sijunjung to become involved in marketing the coal extracted by illegal miners, the decision of the governor of West Sumatra to issue a permit to PT Minang Malindo to mine an area already owned by PTBA-UPO, and the decision of PT Minang Malindo to buy coal from illegal miners. The involvement of the local authorities in such activities explicitly reveals the true extent of their involvement in the illegal coalmining business.

NOTES

1   Later on, some of these illegal miners were 'legalised' by the local authorities.
2   See PTBA-UPO (1998); and *Haluan*, 1 February 2000, 21 February 2000, 21 March 2000.
3   See *Singgalang*, 23 September 1998, 27 September 1998, 19 September 1998; and *Semangat*, 29 September 1998.
4   See, for example, *Canang*, 19 February 2000; *Mimbar Minang*, 22 February 2000; *Serambi Pos*, 22 July 2002, 28 July 2002; *Padang Ekspress*, 16 May 2002; and *Singgalang*, 2 October 2002.
5   See *Canang*, 18 March 2000, 22 March 2000, 8–11 June 2000; *Mimbar Minang*, 20 February 2001, 25 July 2001; and *Haluan*, 15 March 2000, 23 February 2002.
6   See *Merapi*, 29 December 1999; *Canang*, 7 January 2000, 29 January 2000; and *Padang Ekspress*, 26 January 2000.
7   Suhatri Arief, a local inhabitant (*putra daerah*) from a village in Sawahlunto-Sijunjung, was the new manager appointed during the reform era to replace Iwan Setiawan, a Javanese. It was hoped that because Arief was a *putra daerah*, he would have a good grasp of the issues of interest to the local community, and would be bet-

ter equipped to handle their requests with regard to communal land, illegal mining and so on (interview with Suhatri Arief, 6 October 2001).

8   This is actually much higher than the market price for coal or the price PT Semen Padang pays to other coal distributors in West Sumatra. PT Igasar, for example, is paid Rp 176,000 per tonne of coal (Zaiyardam et al. 2003).

14 LOCAL GOVERNMENT AND ENVIRONMENTAL CONSERVATION IN WEST JAVA

Joan Hardjono

INTRODUCTION

With regional autonomy now established in Indonesia, the implications of decentralisation for conservation of the land and water resources that are essential for human survival are frequently overlooked. This is particularly so in Java, where there is an urgent need to preserve the environment in such a way as to ensure a sustainable habitat for almost 60 per cent of the country's population. With some 130 million people living in Java in 2004 by comparison with 76 million in 1971, the prediction made by prominent economist Sumitro Djojohadikusumo more than a quarter of a century ago that Java would become an 'island city' is approaching reality (Djojohadikusumo 1977: 102). As pressure on sources of livelihood in the agricultural sector increases and more land is needed every year for expansion in housing and infrastructure in urban and rural areas alike, the rate of environmental deterioration is accelerating. To these factors can be added the demands of city residents for recreational facilities outside urban areas and the relatively recent efforts by local governments to derive more revenue from sources within their own administrative districts.

As human activities expand and intensify, environmental conservation becomes a question of appropriate decisions in situations where several land use options exist and the interests of quite different groups of people are involved. While environmental problems exist throughout Java (Hardjono 1994), they are particularly evident in the province of West Java, where there are extensive uplands and where plantation agriculture still plays a role in land use systems. This chapter looks at some recent concerns relating to land use in the district (*kabupaten*) and the city (*kota*) of Bandung and the district of Subang and at the attitudes to management of the environment displayed by local governments in these instances. The issues that have arisen in the Bandung–

Subang region, however, are by no means unique to West Java and are relevant to the utilisation of land and water resources throughout Java.

THE BACKGROUND

For many years the rate of environmental degradation on the slopes to the north of Bandung, the capital of West Java, has been growing. As the capacity of the uplands to retain water is reduced, this deterioration is manifest within the urban area in wet season floods and dry season water shortages. The extent of surface run-off can be judged from the torrents that flow down streets in the northern part of the city after every heavy fall of rain. Yet in the dry season rivers like the Cikapundung, which flows through the centre of the city, turn into unsightly and malodorous trickles. Meanwhile, the water table is becoming lower every year, as increasingly larger quantities of groundwater are drawn from aquifers below the city for domestic and industrial purposes. The shortage of water has, in the editorial opinion of West Java's major newspaper, already brought the whole Bandung area 'to the threshold of catastrophe' (*Pikiran Rakyat*, 7 August 2004).

A major factor that has encouraged deterioration of the environment in this and other parts of West Java has been the expansion of horticulture on steep slopes that used to be forested or else planted with perennials. The privately owned plantations that once covered slopes near Bandung and other cities such as Garut, however, have long disappeared (Hardjono 1991). Most of this land is now being cultivated by vegetable growers who have traditional usage rights to the land. These farmers cannot be prevented from selling horticultural land to 'developers', as has been happening for some years now. As developers convert arable fields into building sites, the rate of land deterioration increases. Meanwhile, there is very little evidence of the reforestation programs carried out by the government on state-owned land in past years, in part because local people have cut down trees for firewood but more because the state forestry company, Perhutani, continues to allow cultivators to intercrop vegetables between rows of newly planted trees, which as a consequence do not flourish (Hardjono 1994).

The Bandung metropolitan area has long extended beyond Kota Bandung into Kabupaten Bandung, in the same way that the Jakarta–Bogor metropolitan area has expanded into the mountainous Puncak region (Douglass 1991). The consequences for the environment are similarly negative. In the early 1980s the West Java provincial government attempted to control the spread of the built-up area on the slopes to the north of the city through a decree[1] that placed restrictions on development in the area known as Kawasan Bandung Utara (Northern Bandung).[2] The decree prohibited the construction of houses and other buildings on steeply sloping land above the 750-metre contour line and designated Northern Bandung as a conservation area that would function as a recharge zone for aquifers. Nothing was achieved, however, because the provincial government proved to be quite inconsistent in carrying out its own policy and allowed land within Northern Bandung to be built on. Since then, a series of government decrees (*surat keputusan*) and local regulations (*perda*) has failed to prevent further environmental degradation because enforcement measures have remained negligible.

DEVELOPMENT POLICIES IN ENVIRONMENTALLY SENSITIVE UPLANDS

In March 2004 the West Java provincial government announced that, in the interests of reducing traffic congestion on the existing road from the city of Bandung to the town of Lembang, a narrow rural road located on the slopes to the north of the city would be upgraded to provide an alternative route. The land through which the road passes lies geographically within Northern Bandung and administratively within Bandung District. To reach Lembang, which is located on the southern side of the volcanic Mount Tangkuban Prahu, the road in question would be extended through a part of the nature reserve known as Taman Hutan Raya Djuanda (Djuanda Recreational Forest) (*Pikiran Rakyat*, 7 May 2004).

Public reaction to the proposed upgrading of the road was quick, as its real purpose appeared to be to provide access to sites held by developers who had obtained location permits (*ijin lokasi*) for land development in past years.[3] Prior to 1996 the provincial government had handled the granting of these permits. Developers were able to obtain an *ijin lokasi* for land that suited their purpose without having to consult the regional spatial plan (RTRW) of the province or district, or other land use regulations. Using this *ijin* as a means of asserting an 'official' claim to the land, they then acquired it from local people at a low cost. Government authorities for their part issued permits without any reference to environmental implications. Before making an application for a building permit (*ijin mendirikan bangunan*) the developer had to prepare an environmental impact analysis (*amdal*) as stipulated in national-level legislation, but submission of the *amdal* was little more than a formality.

Despite the transfer of responsibility for the granting of *ijin lokasi* to the district-level government in 1996, the system has not changed and still makes it possible for developers to ignore local environmental conditions.[4] Some 85 development companies currently hold *ijin lokasi* for almost 4,000 hectares of land on steep slopes in Northern Bandung. According to the head of the district-level Regional Development Planning Board (Bappeda), however, the district government has given permits to only 15 of these companies, which control less than 10 per cent of the land (*Pikiran Rakyat*, 14 August 2004). The other 70 companies obtained their permits from the provincial government between 1991 and 1996, despite the fact that a provincial-level decree issued in 1994 (SK 660/1994) had stated that no more *ijin lokasi* were to be given for any part of Northern Bandung.

The basic reason for public opposition to the proposed road is environmental. Development of this kind is in clear contradiction to the provincial RTRW as described in Perda 2/2003, which reaffirms the basic argument of the 1982 legislation that the whole of Northern Bandung should function as a conservation area. Members of the public[5] pointed out that an upgraded road would encourage the construction of new buildings, which would lead to even greater damage to the environment. The deputy governor maintained that it would be a 'no access' road and that the surface would be elevated to make the construction of side roads impossible, while trees would be planted on either side to create a green belt and a provincial regulation would be issued prohibiting any kind of building along the road (*Pikiran Rakyat*, 7 May 2004). The public was sceptical, however, since there were already large, modern houses along the existing road, and side roads had already been constructed by developers. Furthermore, if there is a need for another road to Lembang, either of two other small rural roads leading to Lembang could be upgraded with less detrimental consequences for the environment.

In the face of the strong opposition that emerged, provincial authorities held a series of public consultations with those who had expressed concern about the road. In July 2004 the West Java Regional People's Representative Council (DPRD) formed a study team to examine the proposal, which had been prepared by the Research and Community Service Centre of the Bandung Institute of Technology in conjunction with the provincial-level Bappeda. After much internal disagreement as well as queries from the public about the vested interests of certain of its members, the DPRD announced shortly before the end of its period in office that it would recommend to the provincial government that the plan be dropped.

Issues relating to land use elsewhere in the district of Bandung, in particular the subdistrict of Lembang, which is within the Northern Bandung area, attracted public attention during this same period. The spread in the built-up area in Lembang since the 1970s has led to a loss not only of fertile land and agricultural employment but also of the very resources that originally made Lembang attractive as a rural holiday destination. At the same time the threat of landslides in many parts of the subdistrict has increased. Although the district government cannot be held responsible for development decisions prior to 1996, it has shown a tendency to continue earlier policies. In 2001, for example, it changed classifications in its own RTRW a few months after the RTRW was accepted as Perda 1/2001. Ratification of the revised RTRW as Perda 12/2001 enabled an *ijin lokasi* to be issued for a tourist resort in a hilly part of Lembang that had previously been defined as being within the Tangkuban Prahu conservation area. In fact, a 1998 decree of the Minister of the Environment had stated that no more *ijin lokasi* were to be issued for land in the Tangkuban Prahu section of Northern Bandung.[6]

The planned utilisation of 75 hectares of land for the establishment of a shopping mall and entertainment centre in Lembang likewise illustrates the prevailing attitude to the use of land. The land, which had been used as a dairy farm for almost a century, is adjacent to the Bosscha Observatory, which has protested over the proposal. In February and March 2004, observatory authorities explained through well-publicised public meetings and a widely reported seminar that the functioning of scientific equipment had already been seriously impaired by the glare of lights from buildings and would be even more affected by the presence of a recreational centre on the adjoining land. But despite protests the 'development' will almost certainly take place (*Pikiran Rakyat*, 25 May 2004).

LAND USE ON THE URBAN PERIPHERY

Similar concerns about land use within the city of Bandung were voiced by the urban public in 2004 when the city government announced that a development company would establish an 'integrated recreational area' consisting of a country club, hotel, restaurant and sports facilities on the Punclut hills. These hills take in 268 hectares to the north of the urban area but are within the boundaries and hence the jurisdiction of Bandung City. With its highest point reaching 927 metres, much of Punclut falls within the Northern Bandung conservation area.

Community reaction was even stronger than in the case of the alternative road to Lembang. Protests focused on a range of aspects, in particular the environmental implications and the need for a certain amount of open space to be retained within the urban area. As urbanisation continues, shopping malls, multistorey hotels and apartment blocks are becoming prominent features of the city landscape. Government Regulation 63/2003 urges city governments in all regions to keep at least 10 per cent of their territory free of buildings and to plant this land with trees in the interests of pollution control. So far, however, attempts to establish these so-called urban forests (*hutan kota*) in Bandung have been limited by the fact that city authorities continue to give priority to the proposals of investors.

Associated with this aspect is the special meaning that the Punclut hills have for many Bandung residents. As the only relatively large open space available within the urban area for cost-free recreation, Punclut is a popular place for camping and scouting activities, while on Sundays and public holidays the area is crowded with people who cannot afford to travel any further from the city to find suitable places for jogging, cross-country hiking and other outdoor sports. The editorial of *Pikiran Rakyat* on 23 June 2004 took up this theme in expressing its opposition to a development that was 'designed entirely to serve the interests and pastimes of the wealthy'. The suggestion, put forward by environmentalists, that the Punclut hills should be used for ecotourism was not acceptable to the city government, which sees greater advantages in recreational activities of a more commercial nature.

City residents living in the area adjacent to but lower than the Punclut hills stressed a third aspect, that is, the fact that more bricks and concrete on the hills would cause even greater surface water run-off in the wet season than occurs at present. They also argued that there would be a further reduction in the flow of water from springs and in the water level of wells, on which these households are dependent in the absence of piped water in this part of the city.

Many of the people living in the Punclut area have expressed concern about a fourth aspect, namely, the possibility of eviction. They feel that the status of land in the whole area should be clarified before any changes are made to current land use. Ambivalence on the part of the city government and its Bappeda about precisely which land would be built on and their unwillingness to make maps available to the public have further confused, if not antagonised, the local community. Some 18 per cent of the land is at present registered with the National Land Agency (BPN); the occupants of this land have certificates indicating private ownership. Approximately 39 per cent consists of land that once belonged to a Dutch plantation and that local people have been cultivating since the 1950s. In keeping with government policy concerning the conversion of rights to the land of small nationalised plantations, BPN had transferred ownership to these cultivators, but in 1997 cancelled their certificates while promising to issue new certificates after all claims had been re-examined.[7] The status of the remaining 43 per cent of the land is unclear. Some is occupied by low-income families who have lived there for many years but have no proof of any claim to the land, while the rest has been neglected and is in a degraded condition (*Pikiran Rakyat*, 13 July 2004).

In the midst of the debate about land utilisation in the Punclut hills, the community's confidence in its local government and in its representatives in the city-level DPRD was somewhat shaken when it was revealed that the former had manipulated land use classifications in the area (*Pikiran Rakyat*, 3 July 2004). In presenting the RTRW for 2004 to the DPRD for approval, the city-level Bappeda included a map on which the Punclut area was marked in yellow, thus indicating it to be an area of low population density that could be used for houses and other buildings. On the original map that had accompanied discussion of the draft RTRW, however, Punclut had been shown in green as a conservation area. The RTRW was adopted as Perda 2/2004, with no mention of the map. It has not subsequently been altered, despite allegations by certain DPRD members that they were unaware of the change and felt that they had been misled (*Pikiran Rakyat*, 3 July 2004). The alteration to the map suggests that, despite community opposition, the city government is keen to ensure that 'development' of the Punclut hills goes ahead.[8]

The provincial governor finally defused the issues of the road and the recreational area, at least temporarily, by announcing that the status quo in the whole Northern Bandung area, including the Punclut hills, would be maintained until a Bandung metropolitan master plan is prepared in 2005 to regulate spatial planning and land use in the Bandung basin as a whole.[9] This master plan will then constitute a point of reference for lower-level governments in drawing up their own RTRWs.[10] At the same time the governor stated that no new location, business or building permits are to be issued by the district government for sites in Northern Bandung and that ongoing building is to be suspended (*Kompas*, 5 August 2004).

PLANTATION OR GOLF COURSE?

In February 2004 a somewhat similar conflict of interests, again involving 'developers', arose over a proposed modification to land use on the northern slopes of Mount Tangkuban Prahu, which lie within the district of Subang and hence outside Northern Bandung. The modification involved the utilisation of some 850 hectares of land for a golf course, hotel and other tourist facilities of international standard. The proposal was not a new one. In 2002 the same foreign investor, in conjunction with a Jakarta company, was prepared to invest Rp 344 billion ($40 million) in the undertaking, at a time when Subang District's locally derived income (PAD) for 2001 amounted to only Rp 312 billion (*Kompas*, 7 May 2004). This proposal was rejected by the Minister of State for State Enterprises.

The basis of the conflict of interests lies in the fact that part of the land in question belongs to a government tea plantation (PTPN VIII), while the rest is classed as protection forest. The district receives very little revenue from plantation activities, whereas the taxes and levies (*retribusi*) from the proposed 'tourist development' could be expected to be much greater, especially since smaller commercial activities like shops, cafes and tourist services would most probably follow, all subject to *retribusi*. The golf course proposal was particularly attractive to the local government since Subang District has very little to offer to investors beyond mountain scenery, unpolluted air and hot water springs in its southern uplands, which the construction of new highways has placed within a two-hour journey of Jakarta.

Two major questions arose: does the district have the authority to transfer plantation and forested land to a private company, and what are the implications of a change in land use? On the first question, Law 22/1999 gives authority to regional governments in most spheres, yet two of the articles in this law are contradictory, as Resosudarmo (2003: 232) has pointed out. According to Article 7, the utilisation of natural resources and conservation of the environment are among the sectors for which authority remains with the national government, but Article 10 states that local governments have the authority to manage their own resources and are responsible for maintenance of environmental sustainability within their own regions. Local governments, meanwhile, are able to grant investment licences under Government Regulation 25/2000, although Clause 2.4 concerning forestry and plantations in the same regulation gives the provincial government authority to instruct district governments to reject an investor's proposal if it is inappropriate. It is perhaps the ambiguity in the existing legislation that led the Subang district government to attempt once again to have the golf course proposal accepted. The second attempt also appears to have been related to the fact that the district-level DPRD, which was favourably disposed to the proposal, was then approaching the end of its term in office.

On the question of land use implications, PTPN VIII's board of directors not surprisingly again refused to consider the golf course proposal. From the plantation's point of view, loss of land would mean a fall in production of tea, most of which is exported. This would be in obvious conflict with the national government's policy of promoting greater output of agricultural export commodities. The plantation management, however, has no objection to ecotourism of the type suggested by Soemarwoto (2003), since guided walking tours within the plantation would cause no damage to tea bushes. From the point of view of the Plantation Workers Union (SP-Bun), the proposal has always been unacceptable since loss of land would inevitably lead to a reduction in the number of plantation employees.[11] Meanwhile, there is another implication that the district government appears not to have considered. If the proposal were accepted, local authorities would almost certainly face social unrest stemming from the loss of jobs and from the fact that the investor would obtain control of the springs from which five villages obtain water (*Pikiran Rakyat*, 12 May 2004).

Environmentalists added their perspectives to the debate, arguing that a golf course does not offer the same protection to hilly land as tea bushes, which effectively break heavy falls of rain and thus minimise surface erosion.[12] They also stressed that the forested area included in plans for the golf course forms a buffer zone for an adjoining nature reserve. Research undertaken by Yayasan Pribumi Alam Lestari (Foundation for Preservation of Nature) has shown that the area provides a resting place for migratory birds travelling from Asia to Australia and is also the habitat of certain protected animals and endangered bird species, including the Java eagle (*Pikiran Rakyat*, 30 April 2004). Objections to the golf course were directed to the Minister of State for State Enterprises and also to the Ministers of Agriculture, of the Environment and of Home Affairs. The firm rejection of the proposal by these authorities has saved both the plantation and the forest and has indicated clearly that the national government intends to retain full control over what it regards as two of its own domains.

CONCLUSION

Decentralisation has put a different slant on the question of land use and environmental sustainability. Whereas in the past spatial planning was done at the national level and did not take micro-level implications into account (Hardjono 1986: 11), local governments at the *kota* and *kabupaten* levels now adopt the attitude that they have the full right to decide how land in their respective areas is to be used. In asserting this right, however, they tend to overlook the fact that their policies can have a negative impact on environmental conditions in their own local areas.

It would seem that in certain parts of West Java environmental considerations still tend to take second place to 'development' and that local governments are showing no greater regard for the conservation of land and water resources than the national government did in the past. These lower-level governments are frequently inconsistent in the application of their own policies, while political and related considerations can often persuade decision-makers to reverse their decisions. Meanwhile, ambiguity in existing legislation provides loopholes that can be used to justify decisions that work against preservation of the environment. Associated with this is a tendency for local governments to assume that environmental legislation ratified prior to 1999 no longer carries any legal weight.

The need for immediate measures to preserve the natural environment is obvious. Efforts to improve environmental conditions or at least to slow down the rate of deterioration are, however, handicapped by the extent of the damage done to the environment before the devolution of authority to lower levels. Much of the deforestation within Northern Bandung, for example, had occurred long before responsibility for conservation of the environment passed to the district government. Added to this is the fact that in the past 'developers' were allowed to build virtually wherever they pleased, making it extremely difficult for today's authorities to start enforcing regulations. Law enforcement as such, however, is not the only problem. Even with maximum good will on the part of government authorities, it would be difficult to apply many of the existing regulations because of the complicated way in which legislation has been phrased and drafted.

Quite clearly there must be control over the utilisation of natural resources. This will require a revision of the process by which changes in land use are allowed to take place. Instead of selecting a stretch of land or a water resource favourable to their plans and applying for an *ijin lokasi*, investors should first ascertain which areas can be 'developed' from the environmental point of view. Then when the development proposal is submitted to district-level authorities, *amdal* requirements as originally intended should be observed. If it is to have any meaning, the *amdal* must be a genuine on-the-ground analysis of the potential environmental impact of the proposed investment. Furthermore, the members of the *amdal* teams that evaluate requests for building permits should possess experience and competence in this work and 'not merely an easily falsified certificate from an [*amdal* evaluation training] course' (Soemarwoto 2004: 155). At the same time the public must have unimpeded access to *amdal* studies and approvals of investment proposals. Although Decree 8/2000 issued by the Environmental Impact Management Agency (Bapedal) provides for openness of information in the *amdal* process, its stipulations have been largely ignored by government authorities.

Despite the apparent disregard for the environment in local government circles, devolution of authority to district and city governments has encouraged the emergence of factors that are helping to reverse this tendency. Among these the most important is public opinion, which is expressed in particular through community forums and NGOs. Since the beginning of *reformasi* there has been growing community involvement in policy formation through public meetings and consultations, which in many instances are conducted by government agencies themselves. Open discussions are held in such diverse places as university research institutes and the editorial offices of regional newspapers. Meanwhile, NGOs have continued to play an important role in expressing community views and can no longer be dismissed by authorities as 'anti-government' or 'anti-development'. The culturally oriented groups are particularly important, as they view the natural environment as a part of the local heritage that they seek to preserve. As Soemarwoto (2004: 159) has observed, 'the distance between those who are watched, namely, the government and business elements, and those who do the watching is [now] close'.

Parallel with this is another factor in the form of the freedom now enjoyed by the media. Regional newspapers are able to give extensive publicity to environmental issues that the community would have known little about in previous times. Where once only the 'human tragedy' aspect of landslides, mud flows and floods was reported, journalists are now asking why the disaster happened and who is responsible. As a consequence, members of the public are increasingly questioning the procedure by which government bodies at provincial and district/city levels arrive at their policies, and there is far greater critical observation and more regular monitoring of the decisions adopted by individual government officials as well as by DPRDs at all levels. To these two factors, the community and the media, can be added a third in the shape of the political aspirations of certain government officials and members of the community who, with an eye on future local elections, are seeking to win favour among local communities by supporting popular causes.

Hopefully the combination of these factors will lead to greater accountability on the part of both local governments and the private individuals and businesses that benefit from the use of natural resources. With the rapid environmental degradation now taking place in the Bandung region, spatial planning can no longer be directed towards obtaining the maximum economic return from land and water resources but rather must be focused on ensuring environmental stability.

NOTES

*   I wish to thank Professor Otto Soemarwoto for the opportunity to discuss with him many of the points raised in this paper. The views expressed, however, are my own.

1   The decree (SK 181.1/SK.1624-Bapp/1982 concerning Land Use in the Northern Section of Greater Bandung) has never been revoked. It has been supported by Keppres 32/1990 concerning Management of Protection Areas.

2   Northern Bandung covers an area of 38,500 hectares bounded by the watersheds of Mount Burangrang, Mount Tangkuban Prahu and Mount Manglayang to the northwest, north and northeast of Bandung City; the southern boundary is the 750-metre contour line. It does not coincide with administrative boundaries.

3   The fact that developers have been able to extend *ijin lokasi* indefinitely while allowing local people to cultivate the land in question has given rise to widespread land speculation not only in Northern Bandung but throughout the region.

4   The *ijin lokasi* is now known as *ijin pemanfaatan tanah*, that is, a permit for the use of land.

5   The 'public' includes academics, community forums, environmental groups, cultural bodies and other NGOs. Among these, the most vocal were Komite Peduli Jawa Barat (Committee of Persons Concerned about West Java), Dewan Pemerhati Kehutanan dan Lingkungan Tatar Sunda (Board of Those Interested in the Forests and Environment of Sunda), Yayasan Pelestarian Alam dan Lingkungan Hidup (Foundation for Preservation of Nature and the Environment), Paguyuban Pelestarian Budaya Bandung (Bandung Society for Heritage Conservation) and Pusat Penelitian Sumber Daya Alam dan Lingkungan Universitas Padjadjaran (Padjadjaran University Centre for Research into Natural Resources and the Environment). Respected public figures, including Professor Otto Soemarwoto and former West Java governors Mashudi and Solihin, spoke publicly against the road and urged the provincial government to be consistent in its policies and decisions.

6   Kepmeneg LH/Kepala Bapedal 35/MENLH/12/1998.

7   The same issue of rights to former Dutch plantation land has arisen in Cimacan and

other parts of West Java, where conversion has favoured investors rather than cultivators (Bachriadi and Lucas 2001).

8 The head of the City Planning Office, quoted in *Pikiran Rakyat* on 13 July 2004, spoke of the continued existence of 'untouchables' whose vested interests cannot be challenged even by the local DPRD.

9 The Bandung basin takes in the city of Bandung, the adjacent city of Cimahi, a small part of the district of Sumedang and most of the district of Bandung, including the mountainous region to the south of the city. According to the Minister of the Environment, it is one of four basins in Java that will receive priority in groundwater conservation programs to be financed by the national government (*Kompas*, 16 August 2004).

10 Although Law 24/1992 concerning National Spatial Planning states that a district or city RTRW cannot be in conflict with the provincial RTRW, and that the provincial RTRW cannot contradict the national plan, there is disagreement between the West Java provincial RTRW on the one hand and the RTRWs of Bandung City, Cimahi City and Bandung District on the other. All refer to Northern Bandung as a conservation area and state that land use should be in accordance with the 1982 provincial legislation but they differ in their interpretations of the term 'conservation'. The district and city governments argue that the 1982 legislation provides only macro concepts and that they have the right to prepare their own detailed spatial plans.

11 Sugiarti and Novi (2002) give details of the extent of labour absorption on another PTPN VIII tea plantation in West Java.

12 The environmental aspects of golf courses are summed up in Bachriadi and Lucas (2001: 19–21).

PART V

Laws and Institutions

15 NEW LEGAL INITIATIVES FOR NATURAL RESOURCE MANAGEMENT IN A CHANGING INDONESIA: THE PROMISE, THE FEAR AND THE UNKNOWN

Jason M. Patlis

Much has been written about the effects of regional autonomy on natural resource management in Indonesia. While a survey of the literature generally will tout the benefits of decentralised management in the form of greater responsiveness, greater efficiency, greater transparency, greater accountability and so on, the literature on decentralisation in Indonesia – particularly as it relates to natural resource management – has been much less sanguine, portraying a system of governance that has moved rapidly towards greater exploitation at the regional level, with almost daily reports in local papers of corruption among regional parliaments, and little transparency among regional administrative offices (see, for example, Bünte 2004). At the same time, some districts and provinces (collectively referred to as regional governments) have undertaken some excellent initiatives and enacted some excellent regulations in order to better promote sustainable management, and clarify and enhance the administrative structure for more transparent natural resource management decisions. The question is now one of implementation of those regulations (Asia Foundation 2003).

Regardless of the direction, regional governments in Indonesia for the most part have fulfilled one universal truth of decentralisation: they have been much quicker and more responsive in exercising their newfound authorities than the central government has been in providing guidance or standards for those authorities. Only in 2004 – almost five years after the original decentralisation laws were enacted – did the central government enact revisions to those laws, and it is still developing a series of laws to better address natural resource management specifically. This new generation of laws includes a long list, including two newly enacted statutes on regional autonomy, one on developing new laws and one on fisheries, and pending bills not yet enacted on natural resource management, coastal resource management, maritime affairs, spatial planning, mining and agrarian reform. This chapter seeks to provide a background on regional autonomy, an analysis of natural resource management within the new framework, and an analysis of the systemic issues within the Indonesian legal system that are likely to determine the success or failure of the new generation of laws and bills currently in process. The chapter concludes that unless there are fundamental improvements in the systemic problems facing Indonesia's statutory structure, even this new generation of bills and laws will not improve the landscape, legally or ecologically.

NATURAL RESOURCE MANAGEMENT IN A DECENTRALISED FRAMEWORK

In one of the final acts of a 'lame-duck' legislature, the People's Representative Council (DPR) enacted two long-awaited statutes[1] that revised the decentralisation framework for Indonesia. These two statutes – Law 32/2004 and Law 33/2004 – supersede the original two statutes, Law 22/1999 and Law 25/1999. Many of the basic provisions in both the laws of 1999 and the laws of 2004 are similar, but there are also significant differences between them. Law 32/2004 sets out to correct the mistakes, and clarify the ambiguities, of Law 22/1999.

One of the biggest ambiguities in Law 22/1999 was the inherent conflict that it created with the pre-existing legal framework. Article 4 of Law 22/1999 gave districts and municipalities the authority to manage their affairs in accordance with their needs, goals and capacities. The central government, as stated in Article 7(1), maintained only certain reservations of authority, including foreign affairs, security, judiciary matters, national monetary and fiscal policy, and religion. Much has been written on decentralisation, but suffice it to say that this one law shifted the governmental power from the central government to the district, seeking to overturn a half-century of centrist, sectoral and exploitative laws. Relying on the amendments explicitly providing for regional autonomy in Articles 18, 18A and 18B of the Constitution, and applying general principles governing the interpretation of statutes (see Posner 1983), one can argue that Law 22/1999 held greater weight than other statutes. Bell (2001), for example, argued that Law 22/1999 was constitutional in nature, in that it regulated the functions and administration of government. However, Law 22/1999 was no higher in authority than other statutes, and its provisions did not transcend those of other statutes. Therefore, Law 22/1999 by itself could not – despite its broad premise and vision – undo the entire pre-existing framework. Furthermore, laws at the statutory level are studiously vague and broad, with specific direction to be given at the lower levels of the legal hierarchy (ADB 2002). The vagueness of Laws 22/1999 and 25/1999 was compounded by the fact that they went into effect a fast 19 months after enactment, with precious little guidance emerging during this period (Hofman and Kaiser 2002). Without such guidance, the interpretation of these laws was up for grabs, and districts won the early rounds by moving more quickly to implement their own vision.

In implementing their own vision of regional autonomy over the period 2000–04, districts exhibited ingenuity, guile and speed in enacting new regional laws, many of which took advantage of rent-seeking (or rent-harvesting) opportunities in the management of natural resources. A few examples will suffice. In the forestry sector, Regulation 6/1999 and implementing decrees by the Minister of Forestry provided for district-issued forestry permits to be limited to 100 hectares. Nevertheless, the district head in Malinau, East Kalimantan, issued permits that covered as many as 5,000 hectares and allowed for clear-felling and cutting of protected species of trees, all in violation of central law (Barr et al. 2001). Other districts in East and Central Kalimantan enacted regional laws that provided for a levy or tax on illegally transported timber passing through their jurisdictions (Casson 2001b; McCarthy 2001b). In the fisheries sector, the elucidation of Article 10 of Law 22/1999 provided that traditional fishing rights were not affected by the newly established regional maritime areas. However, a number of districts prohibited the entry of traditional fishing vessels into district waters even before those districts had formally declared their maritime boundaries (Kusumaatmadja 2000b). These – and many other – examples of illegalities and legal fictions have posed the greatest challenge to clear and consistent implementation of Law 22/1999 as well as to sustainable management, and have tested the central government's ability to respond to districts' *ultra vires* laws, that is, laws enacted outside their authority (Patlis 2002).

At the same time, however, some districts and municipalities have sought to develop a clear, meaningful legislative framework for management, especially where rent-seeking opportunities are not so readily available. In 2001, for example, the district of Minahasa in North Sulawesi enacted Regulation 2/2001 on Integrated Community-based Coastal Management, Indonesia's first coastal management regulation. It clarified the institutional responsibilities for integrated coastal management by assigning the District Fisheries Department as lead agency and establishing an advisory interagency council for coastal management. More importantly, it transferred the district's authority under Law 22/1999 for planning, management and regulation to the villages within the district, and allowed for formal authorisation and recognition of four village-based marine protected areas within the district's four-mile marine area (Patlis, Tangkilisan et al. 2003).

While districts were quick to take advantage of the broad premise and spirit of the regional autonomy laws, they generally ignored what one could consider the 'fine print' of Law 22/1999 and its implementing regulations. Under the original Law 22/1999, this fine print included Article 7(2), providing the central government with authority to devise policies, standards and guidelines for natural resource management and conservation; Article 9, providing provinces with a broad role in interjurisdictional issues and issues the district cannot or is not willing to manage; Article 10, authorising regional governments to manage natural resources in accordance with existing laws; and Articles 114–116, providing that the central government can review and reject regional laws that violated existing laws. Under Article 7 of the implementing regulation, Regulation 25/2000, the central government can take administrative action against a regional government for failures or violations in the enforcement of existing laws. Taken together, these provisions give regional governments the authority to manage resources, but with the responsibility to do so in a manner that is consistent with the existing framework. Moreover, they have an obligation to enforce that framework.

The central government has been slow to respond to controversial regional initiatives. As of 2003, the Ministry of Home Affairs had recommended that more than 200 regional regulations be rejected. Districts themselves had rescinded 123 regional regulations based on these recommendations (GTZ 2003). But this is a drop in the bucket. The ministry has reviewed only 1,528 regional regulations, but there are an estimated 7,000 that violate the law (GTZ 2003).

The newly enacted Law 32/2004 clarifies many of the questions, ambiguities and inconsistencies wrought by Law 22/1999. Much of the basic framework has been carried forth in the new law. Articles 2 and 10(1) of Law 32/2004 provide the broad authority for regional governments to manage their own affairs. The scope of this is covered in Article 13 for provinces and Article 14 for districts and municipalities, and includes spatial planning, community affairs, monitoring of the environment and a host of other subjects. Rights for regional governments (both provinces and districts) include developing revenues from natural resource management (Article 21), while responsibilities include protecting and conserving the environment (Article 22). Provinces maintain the ability to address interdistrict issues (Article 13), and the central government can still reject regional regulations that are inconsistent with central laws (Articles 136, 145). District heads are to be directly elected, and villages are given much greater responsibility in managing their affairs, although they still must answer to districts (Article 200 *et seq.*).

The new law does a better job than Law 22/1999 of incorporating the rhetoric of good governance. Traditional rights are to be respected and followed, consistent with the principles of the nation (Article 2). The principles of sound management, accountability and efficiency are to be the basis of government actions (Article 11). Natural resource management is to be done in a manner that is fair and harmonious (Article 2(6)). Communities have a right to be involved in the development of regional regulations (Article 139(1)). The law states in clear language that regional regulations must comply with the existing legal framework (Articles 139(2), 145).

The new law clarifies in Article 11(4) that the central government is responsible for developing minimum performance standards (SPMs). The Ministry of Home Affairs has engaged in a major effort to develop such standards (Ministry of Home Affairs 2003), but this is still strictly along sectoral lines, and there is still only a loose discussion about the need to link compliance with SPMs to regional financial distributions (Donor SPM Working Group 2002).[2] The significance of the SPMs for sustainable resource management cannot be overstated. This link between standards, funding and performance has been missing in Indonesia's decentralised governance, and is essential to the future success or failure of decentralised resource management. This was also the missing link between Law 22/1999 and Law 25/1999. If Law 22 was the vehicle for decentralisation, then Law 25 was the engine that made it run. In the same way, standards and performance *by* the districts should be tied to funding *for* the districts. A portion of the money that districts receive from natural resource revenues should be reinvested in those resources in order to maintain adequate levels of funding for sustainable management.

Vertically, there is now much greater emphasis on the *relationship* between central and regional governments, rather than on the *authority* of regional governments. This is a crucial, although as yet undefined, shift in the paradigm and epistemology of decentralised governance. For example, Article 2(4) of Law 32/2004 provides that, in conducting the affairs of government, regional governments have a connection (*hubungan*) with the central government and other regional governments. Article 2(5) elaborates that this connection covers such areas as spheres of authority, finance, general services and natural resource development. The elucidation of Law 32/2004 describes this relationship as a partnership (*kemitraan*). Specifically addressing natural resource management, Article 17 refers to these two sections in Article 2, and states that the connection between the governments includes authority, responsibility, development, conservation, monitoring and cultivation. Article 17 also specifically provides for cooperation among regional governments.

Specifically with respect to maritime issues, Law 32/2001 (Article 18) retains the regional sea delimitations established in Law 22/1999 (Articles 3 and 10), of 12 nautical miles[3] seaward from the shoreline for provincial waters, and four nautical miles seaward from the shoreline for district and municipality waters. The fact that this provision remains in the revised version, after four years of rumours and drafts to delete the provision (see, for example, Hoessein et al. 2001), is a victory for localised integrated coastal management. In fact, Law 32/2004 is a vast improvement on Law 22/1999 with respect to marine resource management. Under Law 32/2004, both provinces and districts are given broad and clear authority for management within their marine areas (*wilayah laut*) (Article 18(1)). Law 22/1999, in contrast, drew a very ambiguous distinction between the jurisdictional authority of the province (*wilayah daerah provinsi*) over its marine area, specified in Article 3, and the management authority of the district over its marine area (*kewewengan pengelolaan wilayah laut*), specified in Article 10. The new areas of authority under Law 32/2004 include exploration, exploitation, conservation and management of marine resources; spatial planning; and enforcement of laws (Article 18(3)). Regional governments will share in the benefits of management of the seabed in their marine areas (Article 18(2)). Guidelines are provided for cadastral marine boundary determination (Article 18(4) and (5)). Law 22/1999, in contrast, was silent on these issues: no provision was made for the use of the seabed, on the assumption that it would remain under central government control; furthermore, no provision was made for the designation of marine areas, cadastral determination, spatial planning and other aspects vital to determining the nature and scope of regional marine authority.

NATURAL RESOURCE MANAGEMENT IN A SECTORAL FRAMEWORK

Horizontally, natural resource management can be summed up as, in a word, sectoral. While this is a characteristic found universally, in Indonesia sectoral management is more deeply entrenched in the legislative process. Pursuant to the newly enacted statute on developing laws, Law 10/2004 on the Establishment of Laws, as well as its lower-level predecessor, Presidential Decree 188/ 1999, each agency essentially manages its own statute, from the initial scoping and drafting stages to the research and consultation stages, and finally to serving as the president's representative before the DPR as it considers the bill for enactment. Each agency thus champions its own statute, whether in fisheries, forestry, mining, tourism, agriculture or industry, so that rather than laws serving the national interest, they are developed to serve the administrative bureaucracy. There are more than 24 statutes governing natural resources, with several hundred implementing regulations involved. This has led to a framework that is replete with gaps, inconsistencies, redundancies and, generally, 'disconnects' (Patlis 2003a).

A few examples of these disconnects will suffice to underscore the magnitude of the problem. The examples will follow the structure of a law as provided in Law 10/2004 on the Establishment of Laws: general provisions (*ketentuan umum*); material to be regulated (*materi pokok yang diatur*); sanctions (*ketentuan pidana*); and transitional and closing provisions (*ketentuan peralihan dan penutup*).

Beginning with the general provisions, or definitions, one can find many inconsistencies. For example, there are two statutes that define 'natural resources' (*sumber daya alam*). In Law 5/1990 on the Conservation of Natural Living Resources, the definition includes living and non-living (*hayati* and *non-hayati*) resources, at the organism level. The definition in Law 5/1994, ratifying the Convention on Biological Diversity, has two differences: it does not include non-living elements and it does include genetic aspects. The term 'ecosystem' is defined in three statutes – Law 5/1990, Law 5/1994 and Law 23/1997 on Environmental Management. In the first two, it is defined as a functional system of biotic and abiotic elements. In Law 23/1997, however, it is defined in the subjective terms of a balanced, stable and productive human environment. It is unlikely that differences among definitions affect implementation, but they do confuse the legal framework.

In terms of management measures, the examples of disconnects are numerous. The most famous instance concerns the allowance of mining in national parks and other protected areas (Box 15.1). Pursuant to the Basic Mining Law, Law 11/1967, all lands within the Republic of Indonesia may be used for mining. However, a number of subsequent laws have regulated activities in national parks and protected areas, notably Law 5/1990 and Presidential Decree 132/1990. It was not until Law 41/1999 on forestry that open-cast mining in protection forests was explicitly prohibited by specific language (Article 37). This has since been undone by a special Government Regulation in Lieu of Legislation (Perpu) 1/2004 enacted in 2004. Coastal setbacks are another source of confusion. Under Article 50 of Law 41/1999, no harvesting may occur within an area 130 times the difference between the highest and the lowest tide, measured from the coastline, while tourism regulations provide a coastal 'green belt' of 100 metres from the coastline. Law 24/1992 on Spatial Planning contains no such provisions for coastal areas, and it is unclear how many provincial or district/municipal spatial plans provide for this greenbelt.

Provisions on sanctions perhaps present the greatest range of disconnects, in terms of standards of liability (strict, intentional, negligent) and in terms of fines. To be sure, one can generalise: earlier laws have lower fines, shorter sentences and more ambiguous standards of liability. Law 41/1999, for instance, provides for a sentence of 10–15 years and a fine of up to Rp 5 billion for intentionally destroying or burning forests, and five years and Rp 1.5 billion for negligent acts. The overarching and vague Law 23/1997 on Environmental Management has a full range of sanctions of 10–15 years or Rp 500–750 million for intentional destruction of the environment, and 3–5 years or Rp 100–150 million for negligent acts. Law 5/1990 on the Conservation of Natural Living Resources provides for a sentence of 5–10 years and a fine of Rp 100–200 million for intentional violations, and one year or Rp 50–100 million for negligent acts. The newly enacted fisheries statute provides for a sen-

BOX 15.1 MINING IN PROTECTION FORESTS

One major area of intersectoral conflict on resource utilisation relates to mining activities within protected forest areas. The legal basis for companies to mine in these areas is the Basic Mining Law (Law 11/1967), which implies that all lands within the Republic of Indonesia may be used for mining. Meanwhile, the Basic Forestry Law (Law 5/1967) did not specifically prohibit mining activities in protected forests. There has been a spate of subsequent laws and regulations instituting broad protection for natural resources and the environment, including specific regulations on activities in national parks and protected areas – notably Law 5/1990 on the Conservation of Living Resources, Law 23/1997 on Environmental Management, Regulation 68/1998 and Presidential Decree 132/1990. However, none of these have explicitly prohibited mining activities in protected forests. No regulatory or adjudicatory body of government attempted to resolve the conflict between the implicit allowance of mining under Law 11/1967 and the implicit prohibition of mining in protected areas under subsequent laws. Not until the issuance of the new forestry law (Law 41/1999) was the issue explicitly addressed, with mining allowed in protected forests, with the exception of open-pit mining, which was prohibited (Article 37). Implementation of Law 41/1999 would affect 150 mineral and coalmining companies that would no longer be able to carry out their operations.

The environmental argument
Indonesia's forests are classified into three categories according to their main functions: conservation, protection and production. Conservation areas have unique ecosystem functions and habitats, supporting specific fauna and flora, and these areas are intended to conserve the integral components of biodiversity. Production forests do not have critical ecological sensitivity, and are to be used to provide direct economic benefits through the development of both wood and non-wood products. Protection forests provide critical life and ecosystem support through watershed and other ecological functions, such as flood control, erosion control, coastal protection and soil nutrient maintenance. Currently, about 18 per cent of Indonesia's forest areas are classified as protection forests. Indonesia's protection forests are rich in biodiversity and ecologically important, also providing, indirectly if not directly, economic and social value. Converting the functions of protected forests into other functions such as open-pit mining is environmentally risky, with likely negative effects on the quality and function of the natural ecosystem.

The industry argument
The affected mining companies argue that they should be allowed to continue their operations in protection forests because they were granted their permits or contracts before the issuance of Law 41/1999. Retroactive application of the prohibition on open-pit mining would result in unlawful 'taking' of a private right to operate under existing licences, would further promote an unstable business climate and would create disincentives for future business investment. If the govern-

ment prohibits activities that were previously permitted, then these companies would, at a minimum, be entitled to compensatory damages to be paid by the government for the loss of their rights.

The outcome

The Ministry of Energy and Mining supported the claims of the mining companies, while the Ministry of Forestry supported the prohibition as stated in Law 41/1999. Finally, on 11 March 2004, due to 'non-technical' interventions, the president approved Perpu 1/2004, which exempts all mining permits or contracts granted before the issuance of Law 41/1999 from the prohibition. Subsequently, Presidential Decree 41/2004 has specifically allowed 13 mining companies to continue their activities on protected forest lands. This was followed by Ministry of Forestry Regulation 12/2004 on the use of protection forest areas for mining activities. It states that mining activities in protection forests shall be carried out through permits (*ijin pinjam pakai*, literally, 'borrowed use' permits) granted by the Ministry of Forestry, with compensation to be paid by the user. To minimise the environmental risks involved, the Ministry of Forestry may require companies to control and monitor the environmental, social and economic effects of their operations, from planning to closure.

End note

From a legal standpoint, both the original dispute and the nature of the resolution represent some of the systemic failures in the statutory framework. First, the dispute should never have languished as long as it did. Although Law 11/1967 implicitly makes all lands available for mining, subsequent laws and regulations explicitly set aside certain lands, including protected forest areas, for natural resource and environmental priorities (with expected implications for open-pit mining). Straightforward and consistent application of the canons of statutory construction and interpretation would have allowed for a decision on this issue by the regulatory or enforcement bodies of the government. Apart from that, an adjudicatory body could have reached a decision – one way or another – on how these various laws should be reconciled. Neither of these occurred. Instead, it was resolution through additional law-making (Law 41/1999) that addressed the conflict, but only in part, and once again, instead of turning to the courts, the parties sought resolution through yet another regulatory decision. As the parties are now contesting the emergency regulation, the legal dispute continues.

From an environmental standpoint, the utilisation of protection forests for mining activities represents a high risk for both human and non-human life. Although there are requirements for control and monitoring of mining operations, experience to date suggests that such requirements are rarely implemented or enforced, and rarely lead to improved practices in Indonesia.

Erwinsyah, Forestry Specialist, Natural Resources Management Project
Jason M. Patlis, Senior Legal Advisor, Coastal Resources Management Project
Jakarta

tence of up to 10 years and a fine of Rp 2 billion for intentionally damaging a fisheries habitat. These discrepancies allow for forum shopping and cherry picking among both defence attorneys and prosecutors as to what laws to use, what charges to lay and in what jurisdictions to file.

Because the statutes are so vague and broad, the majority of conflicts do not arise until the regulatory level, where there has been little analysis. There is a growing realisation – and concern – among all stakeholders as to the problematic consequences of these disconnects. Two years ago, the People's Consultative Assembly (MPR) adopted TAP MPR IX/2001, a decree that calls for integration and harmonisation of laws, public participation and transparency, a clearer legal hierarchy and a greater recognition of customary laws. This growing realisation of the need to harmonise laws is also evident in the spate of new bills relating to natural resource issues that are in various stages of development. These bills address natural resource management; coastal management; fisheries; maritime issues; environmental management; mining; spatial planning; and agrarian reform.

A NEW GENERATION OF LAWS FOR NATURAL RESOURCE MANAGEMENT

This section will look at only a few of the bills relating to natural resource management that are currently being developed. Most of the bills are too inchoate to offer any meaningful insights into their content. Only two, the coastal management bill and the natural resources management bill – together with the newly enacted fisheries law – have sufficient detail and have made sufficient progress in their development to warrant analysis at this point. This section will first look at the process of developing these bills, and then turn to their substance.

In general, the processes involved in developing the bills on natural resource management and coastal resource management have been quite impressive. In one of the most important developments, the executive branch is working more closely with the DPR, bringing in members informally and early on in the process. While each bill is still formally in the administrative stage of development, before its formal transmittal to the DPR, there has been greater interaction with the parliament than has been usual in the past. The Constitution provides for statutory law-making to be initiated either by the president (Article 5) or by the DPR (Article 20). This has resulted in the evolution of two very formal and independent tracks for law-making, the executive track (*hak eksekutif*) and the legislative track (*hak legislatif*). These two tracks, and the associated formal exchange of transmittals and hearings, have been maintained in Law 10/2004 (Article 17 *et seq.*). However, at least on an informal level, these tracks are finally beginning to converge during the early stages of negotiation and drafting. In the case of the bill on natural resource management, this has included informal meetings among DPR members and their attendance at workshops; in the case of the bill on coastal management, it has included the attendance of DPR members at public consultations as well as at workshops and conferences. These are major innovations in a system that had been characterised as being rigidly fixed on the legislative or executive tracks, with little interaction between the two until the very end of the process.

In terms of public engagement, the consultation processes for both the natural resources bill and the coastal management bill have been sophisticated in their design and extensive in their reach. Begun in 2000, the bill on natural resource management has seen a number of fits and starts coinciding with disputes between the NGO community and the leadership of the Ministry of the Environment. The National Development Planning Agency (Bappenas) is also integrally involved. The process has largely been driven by the NGO community, which has combined the best elements of grassroots support with funding and coordination shaped at the national level. The NGOs, largely through United Nations Development Programme (UNDP) and other grants, have put Rp 3.5 billion into the process thus far, and they are gelling into a strong collective voice (Kalmirah of Kehati (an NGO), personal communication, 2004). Bappenas, the Ministry of the Environment and NGOs collaborated in hiring and training regional facilitators, who worked with local NGOs to compile a record of 141 consultations over 26 provinces (Suwarno, Simarmata and Ahmad 2003). The close collaboration between the two government agencies has also worked to help keep the process somewhat transparent (Pokja PA PSDA 2004).

The bill on coastal management has also seen extensive consultations. Begun in late 2000, it was one of the early priorities of the newly established Ministry of Marine Affairs and Fisheries. The ministry first developed an academic study to justify the law. This is normally a perfunctory requirement in developing statutes, as provided originally by Presidential Decree 188/1999. The Ministry of Marine Affairs and Fisheries used the opportunity, however, to produce the first treatise on Indonesian coastal resources – their status, the threats to them, and the legal and institutional framework governing them (MMAF 2001b). It then embarked on a two-year consultation process designed by the NGOs and adopted by the ministry. This was a three-track approach that relied on formal consultations, informal meetings sponsored by NGOs to feed the formal process, and a mass media campaign (Idris et al. 2003). Since obtaining the president's permission to proceed with the bill (*ijin prakarsa*) in December 2003, the ministry has been hosting a series of interdepartmental meetings to obtain the approval of other departments. It then must seek final approval from the president (*amanat presiden*) before the bill can be transmitted to the

DPR. The development of the bill has been an example of a successful iterative process of drafting, public consultations, redrafting, interagency consultations and more redrafting (Patlis, Knight et al. 2003b). The Ministry of Marine Affairs and Fisheries has recently begun coordinating with staff of the DPR's Badan Legislatif (Legislation Board), an administrative body established in 1999 to provide technical expertise to DPR members. The bill has been officially included in the Priority List for the National Legislative Program (Prolegnas) of 2005 (*Kompas*, 8 February 2005: 8).

Coupled with this has been much greater information flow, in both directions. The groundwork in developing these laws has been stronger and more solid, with a detailed paper trail that creates a process of law-making that is significantly more accountable than in the past (Pokja PA PSDA 2004). Both bills have detailed minutes of all consultations, and NGOs, development projects and the ministries themselves have provided relatively good access to those minutes, making them available online, electronically on disk and, in some instances, on hardcopy.[4]

The fisheries law saw only a fraction of the effort towards transparency and consultation enjoyed by the other two bills. A series of consultations was sponsored by regional branches of the Ministry of Marine Affairs and Fisheries, but whether these were adequately documented, and how the documentation was utilised by the drafters of the bill, is unknown. While the Food and Agricultural Organization provided technical expertise on the drafting (Gillet 2001), none was provided on procedural safeguards.

In terms of substance, several general observations can be made about the fisheries law and the two bills. In terms of preamble or introductory language, there has been a marked increase in rhetoric on sustainability, coordination and integration, participation and transparency – the pillars of good governance – although little in the way of substantive provisions to support them. Institutionally, each of them sets up interagency bodies or councils to provide redress for the heavily sectoral nature of the legal framework. In terms of management, all have a strong emphasis on both permits and prohibitions as a means of management. Despite their emphasis on prohibitions against destroying or damaging natural resources, there is still a great deal of ambiguity as to what this means pending additional regulations. Community and traditional rights receive significant attention in each piece of legislation. In terms of enforcement, all contain a long litany of heavy fines and sanctions, and place a greater emphasis on adjudicatory processes and conflict resolution than has previously been the case, including clarification of the standing and authorisation of class action suits.

Now let us consider each one in a little more detail. The new fisheries law provides for an extensive system of permits. It sets up several councils to manage coastal areas, including fisheries, areas and species. It explicitly provides for Ministry of Marine Affairs and Fisheries management of protected marine habitats and species, including marine national parks, which had previously been under the Ministry of Forestry. This is a very significant step in consolidating authority and improving administrative decision-making for marine resource management. The law also sets up an administrative court to hear disputes; while this is a welcome alternative to a challenged judiciary, there is some question as to the legitimacy of this provision.

The bill for natural resource management is still being negotiated. At this point, however, it takes a bioregional approach to management, dividing Indonesia into seven bioregions (with the possibility that this will be doubled to 14) for purposes of species management. It establishes an extensive institutional network with a national council, bioregional councils and subcouncils. Recognition of traditional community rights is very prominent and very broad. The draft law also sets up a bioregion trust fund to ensure funding. However, it is worth noting that Law 23/1997 also set up a trust fund that has yet to come into existence.

The bill for coastal management seeks to establish an open, transparent and science-based process rather than focus on particular outcomes, which are likely to vary too much by region. It focuses on planning, providing for a relatively rigid hierarchy of strategy plans, management plans, spatial plans and action plans. It also recognises traditional rights, but the criteria are much stricter than in the draft law for natural resources. It provides for a system of management of protected areas. It authorises an interagency council without mandating it, leaving open the possibility that the existing Indonesian Maritime Board may fulfil this role, or that a new council may be established. The unique aspect of the draft law is that it sets up an accreditation program – a voluntary, incentives-based program under which provinces and districts that comply with the standards and criteria established by the central government will receive financial and technical assistance. Such a program would fulfil the vision of minimum performance standards mentioned earlier. Despite its good intentions, however, the draft law may not have significant reach in its ability to better integrate coastal management decisions, because the definition of 'coastal area' is extremely narrow, reaching inland only to the high-tide mark. This was a very deliberate political decision to avoid encroaching on other agencies' jurisdictions, which would jeopardise the law's likelihood of enactment.

DIAGNOSIS AND PROGNOSIS

Three developments – greater information flow, greater public involvement and greater legislative engagement with the executive branch – are creating a system of checks and balances within the law-making process that will improve the substance of the laws, and ultimately their implementation, enforcement and oversight. There is one caveat: the initiatives to enact a new natural resources law and a new coastal management law have received significant funding from the UNDP in the case of the natural resources bill and from the United States Agency for International Development (USAID) in the case of the coastal resources bill. This raises immediate questions about the sustainability of the efforts if the funding were to disappear, and about the replication of the process for other bills that might not have such funding and technical support. Nevertheless, the Asia Foundation (2004) observes a slow but steady general trend towards greater participation by NGOs and civil society in the regional law-making process.

In addition to this caveat, there are many problems with the bills themselves, and their place in the larger legal framework. The particular provisions of the bills need to be better coordinated. At this point, the new bills and the fisheries law have very similar, overlapping or even inconsistent provisions. For example, each one sets up a new interagency body for integrated, coordinated decision-making. These new bodies, even before they are established, trip all over themselves in setting up new councils sitting alongside the line ministries, as well as alongside the pre-existing coordinating councils. The treatment of traditional rights provides another example: in the natural resources bill there are very broad provisions for recognising traditional rights; in the coastal bill there is also a long chapter dedicated to recognising traditional rights, but the standards are more stringent; in the fisheries law there is community empowerment but no recognition of traditional rights. Despite their lofty rhetoric to the contrary, these laws – which are supposed to transcend sectoral management – are still very much sectoral in nature.

This is a function of both the particular processes used for each bill and the larger systemic foundation for law-making. It is the Ministry of the Environment that is championing the bills on natural resource and environmental management, and it is the Ministry of Marine Affairs and Fisheries that is championing the bills on coastal resource management, maritime affairs and fisheries. There is very little coordination in these efforts. One reason is institutional laziness, but the deeper reason is the systemic manner in which laws are developed. For example, it is a requirement in Law 10/2004 (Article 18), as well as its predecessors, that each bill be spearheaded by a specific line ministry, in drafting, in negotiation and even in representing the president before the DPR. This results in laws that serve the institution rather than the nation. ADB (2002) states that 'Regulations are more often issued and designed to empower the agency issuing them than to provide reliable and fair guidance to people or entities subject to the legislation', which is true enough, but what it does not state is that this is firmly rooted by design in the law-making requirements.

There is a host of systemic issues relating to law-making and statutory construction that further impede the implementation of laws once they are enacted. Only three are discussed here. First is the tradition of vagueness and overbreadth that plagues all laws at all levels in Indonesia. Much of this is a deliberate effort to obfuscate the corpus of laws so that they can be interpreted freely as necessary at that moment, which for a half-century has suited the autocratic government and corporate interests at the centre of Indonesian politics (ADB 2002). Much of it is a misplaced intention to maintain the characteristics of the legal hierarchy, and much of it is just plain poor drafting. Whatever the reason, even as the law-making process is being improved through greater transparency, vagueness and overbreadth remain stubborn aspects of legal drafting. The early drafts of the coastal resources bill contained detailed articles on programs, standards and management measures, but these have all but been deleted under pressure from both the public and other agencies who claimed that the language was too technical and administrative, and thus more suited to regulations. The Ministry of Marine Affairs and Fisheries agreed to delete them for reasons of political expediency. The results, whether deliberate or not, are devastating, creating a vast grey area within the law allowing for profound uncertainty or, worse, manipulation (Patlis 2002).

The second is the ubiquitous case of the 'implied repeal'. This is a legislative device by which one law supersedes another. An explicit repeal states that one law supersedes another specific law. An implied repeal states that all existing laws remain in full force and effect unless contradicted by the new law. The questions are immediate. What is a contradiction? Who decides? Through what process? In many jurisdictions throughout the world, implied repeals are narrowly construed and rarely used (Petroski 2004). In Indonesian statutes, however, they are the rule. Consider two examples in Law 41/1999. Article 83 explicitly repeals two laws, including the preceding forestry statute, by stating that 'at the time this Law takes effect, [Law 5/1967 on Basic Provisions on Forestry] shall be declared void'. On the other hand, Article 82 provides that 'All existing rules of implementation pertaining to forestry shall remain in effect, insofar as they do not conflict with this Law, until the issuance of the rules of implementation based on this Law'. The latter is an example of an implied repeal, and creates vast uncertainties in the legal system.

The third is the prevalent practice – again a vestige of the Soeharto era – of resolving conflicts between two laws by promulgating a third law. The judicial institutions of *stare decisis* and *res judicata* – essentially the use of precedent to guide decisions – are very weak. Even today, resolution of conflicts among laws is accomplished by additional law-making. Box 15.1 in this chapter discussed the conflict between mining and protection forests. The issue was not adjudicated; rather, the president issued an emergency regulation, Perpu

1/2004, allowing certain mines to continue their activities within protection parks, while other mines were required to comply with the prohibition.

CONCLUSION

This chapter has sought to identify some broad themes in the evolution of natural resource governance in a changing Indonesia and to provide some specific examples, especially with respect to the new generation of statutes currently being prepared. Participation by NGOs and regional governments is much greater than in the past. Parliamentary and administrative branches are working more closely together, albeit informally. With regard to processes, the doors into the process of law-making – the front end of law – have been thrown open in a significant way. This should bring a higher level of accountability as civil society takes a greater interest. In terms of substance, however, there is much that is still lacking in the new laws and bills. The enforcement and adjudication of laws – the back end of law – remains rife with intractable problems. The new generation of laws seeks to address these problems by promoting more integrated frameworks, more detailed provisions on standing and litigation, and heavier fines and penalties. However, there is no indication that heavier fines will lead to greater compliance. In addition, the new bills and laws need to be better coordinated themselves, even in the drafting stages. To ensure meaningful implementation at the local level, they need to establish the vital link between performance, standards and funding, and require the reinvestment of natural resource revenues in natural resource management.

This chapter suggests that it is the systemic issues in law-making, statutory construction and implementation that will be dispositive in the success or failure of the new laws and bills being developed. There needs to be an overhaul of how laws are drafted and how they are interpreted. Vagueness and overbreadth must be reduced as much as possible, and should be attacked explicitly in the implementing regulations to be prepared for Law 10/2004 on the Establishment of Laws. The use of implied repeals should be eliminated. There needs to be a more consistent means of statutory construction, with both an administrative procedure law and a freedom of information law to govern the administrative machinery of government. Two government bodies – the DPR's Legislation Board in the legislative branch of government, and the cabinet secretary, directly below the president, in the executive branch of government – could play a pivotal role in expediting and facilitating these improvements in law-making. These two bodies are able to provide expert advice on legislative drafting and are appropriately situated within their respective branches to review new laws within the existing framework. In addition, both would be able to transcend the sectoral nature of law-making, as the cabinet secretary is outside the individual line agencies within the executive branch, and the Legislation Board is independent of the individual committees within the DPR.

In sum, there are many positive aspects to the new generation of bills and laws governing natural resources, but there are also many reasons to expect that they will not fulfil their potential. The laws themselves may suffer from individual deficiencies or weaknesses, either in how they are drafted or in what they provide. Even if they are adequate in their own right, they are unlikely to fulfil their potential given the systemic failings of the Indonesian legal system. This new generation thus represents both the hopes and the fears for the future of natural resource management in Indonesia. How the laws will fare is entirely unknown, resting on the larger, deeper issues of law and governance reform. This will be a question of undertaking not merely a new generation of natural resources laws, but true legal reform.

NOTES

*   The author currently serves as senior legal advisor for the Coastal Resources Management Project (CRMP). The views expressed in this paper are the author's own personal views and do not reflect the positions of CRMP or any other institution. The author welcomes comments and can be reached at jason@yourearth.net.

1   A note on terminology: the author uses 'statute' to refer to laws enacted by the DPR, and 'regulation' to refer to administrative laws approved by the president. The legal hierarchy has shifted slightly over the years, as set out in MPR Decree III/2000 and revised in Law 10/2004 on the Establishment of Laws, but generally flows from the Constitution; followed by Decrees of the MPR (TAP MPR); Statutes or Laws (Undang-undang); Government Regulations (Peraturan Pemerintah or PP); Presidential Decrees (Keputusan Presiden or Keppres), although under Law 10/2004 they are now called Peraturan Presiden; Ministerial Decrees (Keputusan Menteri or Kepmen), although the status of ministerial decrees is subject to much change and debate; Regional Regulations (Peraturan Daerah or Perda) enacted by a regional people's assembly at either the provincial or the district/municipality level; and Regional Decrees enacted either by the governor (Surat Keputusan (SK) Gubernur) or by the district head/mayor (Surat Keputusan (SK) Bupati/Walikota).

2   The Donor SPM Working Group consists of the United States Agency for International Development (USAID), Deutsche Gesellschaft für Technische Zusammenarbeit (GTZ), the Canadian International Development Agency (CIDA), the Japanese International Cooperation Agency (JICA), the Australian Agency for International Development (AusAID), the World Bank, the Asian Development Bank (ADB) and the United Nations Development Programme (UNDP).

3   One nautical mile equals 1.9 kilometres.

4   Documentation on these legislative efforts is readily available at <www.dkp.go.id> for the Ministry of Marine Affairs and Fisheries and <www.menlh.go.id> for the Ministry of the Environment.

16 INSTITUTIONAL TRANSFORMATION FOR BETTER POLICY IMPLEMENTATION AND ENFORCEMENT

Isna Marifa

INTRODUCTION

Institutions play a central role in the success or failure of natural resource management. As the author and implementor of natural resource policies, government institutions with authority in this area are viewed as a source of hope as well as a source of constraints in relation to proper natural resource management. Today, the institutional challenges to Indonesia's natural resource policies consist of a combination of longstanding, unresolved issues from the New Order era and more recent issues that have emerged since the advent of the *reformasi* movement and the transition to regional autonomy. A wide range of institutional reforms is under way but will take considerable time to implement. Several studies have observed and analysed these recent institutional changes (World Bank 2001). Several chapters in this book also discuss the ongoing institutional changes in several natural resource sectors and their implications (see Chapter 6 by Fox, Adhuri and Resosudarmo, Chapter 9 by Gellert and Chapter 10 by Dutton).

This chapter works more on a conceptual level; the approach is general, intended to cover multiple natural resource sectors. It depicts the institutional issues currently surrounding natural resource policies and offers some ideas on the institutional transformations needed to ensure effective natural resource policy-making. The chapter points out that some provinces and districts are setting an example in achieving such transformations. However, since the main goal of the chapter is to convey a general concept of the kinds of institutional transformations needed, rather than how these should be implemented in practice, it does not cover practical implementation in any detail.

PORTRAIT OF NATURAL RESOURCE INSTITUTIONS

The New Order 'legacy'

During the New Order, inconsistent policies and weak cross-sectoral coordination were already seen as a problem for natural resource management. Several studies observed that natural resource and environmental management was dispersed over a large number of government ministries and specialised agencies. These studies also identified the need to define a comprehensive natural resource policy to coordinate sectoral policies.[1] In fact, the World Bank (1994: 31) argued that 'sectorally-oriented development planning seriously constrains interagency coordination' and that 'central government planning and implementation is increasingly ill-suited for dealing with emerging issues of environmental management at the provincial, municipal and village level'.

In the New Order period, sectoral departments at the national level were the source of policies on natural resources. There were at least nine key institutions at the central government level with authority to produce policies affecting natural resources. Table 16.1 summarises the institutional set-up and mandates of these agencies, with text in parentheses indicating institutional changes over time. The national-level institutions were massive bureaucracies, with authority to set policy, regulations and guidelines; develop and implement programs; supervise and monitor implementation of policies and regulations; and conduct research and development, training and capacity building. In short, they were multifunctional, with very grand responsibilities. Each department had a strongly hierarchical vertical structure. Problems in the field could take years to reach the top of the policy agenda, with several more years needed for study of the relevant issues. This made policy development a very slow process.

In the case of natural resource and environmental management, top-down management systems and poor internal coordination of line agency functions (such as research, planning, production, budgeting and development of regulations) meant that program and project implementation was at times inefficient. Field-level problems went unnoticed or unreported, and interventions were poorly designed or inappropriate for local needs, conditions and capabilities (USAID 1987; Bennett 2002; Kartodihardjo 2002).

Policy decisions involving more than one sector were dealt with in interministerial committees or coordination meetings. However, this mechanism did not work effectively, and endless meetings alone were not enough to ensure a common platform across sectors. In this setting, the line ministries continued to approach environmental management very much within their own traditional perspectives and programmatic approaches, making interministerial coordination of research and data gathering, analysis, policy formulation and mitigation programs extremely difficult. Decisions were, in the end, based more on polit-

*Table 16.1 National-level agencies involved in setting policies affecting
            natural resources*[a]

Institution	Mandate related to natural resources
Ministry of Forestry	Production forest, national parks and conservation areas, conversion forest, critical lands, hardwood plantations
Ministry of Mines and Energy (Energy and Mineral Resources)	Oil/gas, geothermal energy, mining, groundwater
Ministry of Public Works (Human Settlements and Regional Infrastructure)	Surface water, land conversion
Ministry of Agriculture	Agricultural land, plantations
Ministry of Trade and Industry	Wood processing, food processing, commodities trading
Department of Finance	Tax rates and import–export tariffs related to natural resources
Ministry of the Environment	Pollution control and prevention, climate change, biodiversity
Ministry of Marine Affairs and Fisheries (established in 2000)	Fisheries, shrimp farms, coastal management, coral reef conservation
Ministry of Transmigration (subsequently merged with the Department of Manpower)	Land conversion

a   Text in parentheses indicates institutional changes in the post-New Order era.

ical clout than on analysis and rational consideration of the issues, and policies were put in place despite inconsistencies with other policies (USAID 1987; Christanty and Atje 2004; see also Chapter 15 by Patlis in this book).

No institution played the role of referee, and conflicts were left to be played out in the field. The National Development Planning Agency, Bappenas, which held a mandate to produce a unified development plan and coordinate development programs and policies, in practice mainly compiled development plans from the sectors and organised budgets and project funding.

Sectoral agencies at the national level had scant interest in developing a robust local capacity for policy-making and planning (Turner et al. 2003). Provincial and district government institutions were mere implementers in the field:

Technically, these offices report to the governor, as well as to their own ministry, but their primary role is to implement the development programs of the respective central agencies (World Bank 1994).

As such, provincial and local agencies were unprepared for the greater autonomy that was to come in the ensuing years.

Regional autonomy and *reformasi*

The sudden and fundamental changes that occurred in 1997–2000 opened a new chapter in natural resource management. The national-level agencies, on paper, lost considerable power, while local agencies gained hitherto unimagined powers. Parliament and civil society also began to enjoy a significant role in policy-making – a marked turnaround from their role during the New Order period. Decentralisation offered potential benefits for improved resource outcomes and better governance (World Bank 2001). However, the improvements have not come automatically or with ease (see also Chapter 6 by Fox, Adhuri and Resosudarmo in this book).

At the national level, the institutional picture has not changed much at all. The same national-level institutions from the New Order era remain in place and still affect natural resource management – regardless of the fact that the authority for deciding what to do with natural resources has largely been decentralised to the districts. Although Government Regulation 25/2000 reallocates authority and responsibility to government institutions at all levels, this reassignment of duties has not been evident in how institutions operate, especially those at the national level.

Most departments have modified their structures – the Department of Energy and Mineral Resources abolished its Directorate General of General Mining, for example – or have reduced their direct operational activities in the districts to accommodate the changes in spheres of authority. But some ministries, such as forestry, have chosen not to decentralise (World Bank 2001). The national-level institutions are still the same massive bureaucracies, protective of their compartmentalised interests and relentless in their sectoral way of thinking. Major policy decisions continue to be made at the central level without consultation with local authorities, as was the case with Government Regulation in Lieu of Legislation (Perpu) 1/2004, for example. Perpu 1/2004 grants 13 mining companies permission to conduct open-pit mining in protection forest (*Kompas*, 22 July 2004), overriding certain articles in Law 41/1999 on forestry. Perpu 1/2004 has upset the district governments where the protection forests are located because it was, they claim, issued without prior consultation with them. Although the regulation was intended to re-establish the rights of companies holding mining concessions granted before 1999, it only under-scores the problem of oscillation and lack of thoroughness in central govern-ment policy-making (see also Box 15.1 in Chapter 15 by Patlis in this book).

At the provincial level, regional autonomy dissolved the powerful arms of the sectoral ministries (*kanwil*) and no longer placed the governor in a hier-archically superior position to the district head (*bupati*). The outcome observed in the field has been that the *bupati* no longer take much notice of the gover-nors, who feel left behind and powerless.[2] The *bupati*, who previously were only witnesses to natural resource exploitation, now have the authority to deter-mine the fate of the natural resources in their localities (with the exception of oil and gas). Driven by the desire to increase local revenues, most have opted for greater exploitation of resources. Districts are making and executing such decisions despite their lack of experience in decision-making. The reality remains that most district-level agencies, especially those outside Java, have limited information on the management options and short and long-term trade-offs associated with natural resources. They lack the capacity to undertake the analysis required for decision-making, or to encourage participation and public consultation in the decision-making process (Bappenas, NRM and LPEM-FEUI 2000b).

Current challenges

It is in this institutional setting that natural resource management finds itself today. At the central, provincial and district levels, there is much frustration and confusion about roles and responsibilities. If reorientation has occurred on paper, it has not manifested itself in institutional actions and improved deci-sions.

In effect there is policy chaos in natural resource management. With national policies that are inconsistent or even conflicting, districts feel free to follow the path of their choice. At the same time, sectoral institutions at the national level continue to be at odds with one another, and are busy trying to hold onto or retrieve authority from the districts. Law enforcement also contin-ues to lag because of the rate at which violations occur. Thus, the effective influence of national policies on natural resources is limited.

Very little effort is being made to integrate and improve consistency among natural resource policies, to make it clear to districts/cities that there are limits to natural resource exploitation and that a certain degree of resource conserva-tion and environmental protection is needed for long-term development. The lack of effort to integrate natural resource policies can be seen as unwillingness on the part of the sectoral institutions to relinquish their sectoral interests and powers, as well as failure by the non-sectoral institutions (Bappenas, the Coordinating Ministries, the Ministry of the Environment) to exert influence over the sectors. It can also be attributed to the fact that none of these institutions have been given a higher-order mandate to resolve policy differences and prevent them from occurring in the future.

Should this situation be allowed to continue, it is clear that the outcome will be imminent depletion of the natural resource base and an even more serious decline of the environment. Short-sighted districts and, indeed, provinces will continue to take advantage of the policy chaos, and the central government will be powerless to prevent them from doing so. At the same time, districts and provinces with a more enlightened vision will have difficulty in sifting through the plethora of policies to find those that support a more sustainable development path.

INSTITUTIONAL TRANSFORMATIONS: SOME THOUGHTS FOR THE WAY FORWARD

Regional autonomy and *reformasi* together offer a tremendous opportunity to improve natural resource policies. The legal and political framework established in the last six years is the kind of radical change that many Indonesians could only dream of in the 1980s and 1990s (Aspinall and Fealy 2003). The World Bank (2001) has said that regional autonomy 'offers an opportunity toward more local participation in resource allocation decisions, greater accountability by regional governments, a refocusing of central agencies on policy and oversight'. However, realisation of the opportunity will require institutional transformations that touch all levels of government.

To quote Turner et al. (2003: 96):

> Organizational structures define how organizations divide up work and then coordinate it. They are comprised of rules, roles and relationships that – if well designed – should enhance productivity.

In Indonesia, the regional autonomy law, Law 22/1999, offers the rules that now apply, but roles and relationships are still being redefined and reconfigured. At the national level, transformation is needed in the country's policy-making institutions. At the provincial level, there is a need to redefine the role of provincial institutions to support national policies. At the district level, much work is needed to strengthen capacity and accountability. Yet another essential transformation relates to how decisions are made.

The examples cited below were obtained by the author during discussions with individuals active at the provincial and district level, and through participation in various activities involving government institutions at all levels. Recall that the main goal of this chapter is to give a general overview of the kinds of institutional transformations required in Indonesia. This section therefore does not go into practical detail on exactly how these institutional transformations should be implemented.

Policy-making at the national level

Policy-making is a dynamic process. Economic and political conditions in any country are constantly changing. In Indonesia, with the new wave of decentralisation and democratisation, we can expect dramatic changes over the next 20 years until a new equilibrium is reached. Institutions with a mandate for policy analysis and policy issuance will have to be be agile and sharp. They must be able to read trends, respond to situations, analyse quickly what options are available and formulate the appropriate policies. They must be able to absorb the diversity of issues faced by the different regions and islands across Indonesia. With global interconnectedness in today's economy and politics, prompt reading of and response to international trends in, say, rubber prices, copper trading or global climate change are a must for our policy-making institutions. Policy-making is the spearhead of government – it defines where the entire nation is going and how it plans to get there. In the language of Osborne and Gaebler (1992), the 'steering function' of the government must be redesigned.

The massive sectoral departments at the national level are not agile or sharp, and they cannot keep up with the fast-paced analytics necessary for policy-making. The steering function cannot be compartmentalised into sectoral institutions, and must be unified to ensure that national rather than sectoral interests are protected. Given the current arrangement of the sectoral departments, a unit in the higher levels of government that takes a non-sectoral, integrated approach to policy-making is needed to spearhead the national development steering function.

Such a unit could be established in an existing non-sectoral institution such as Bappenas or the Coordinating Economic Ministry. It should be given the mandate and sufficient resources to undertake a comprehensive review of all policies affecting natural resources. It is important to emphasise that the main goal of the unit would be to integrate national policies on natural resources, not to take back authorities that have been decentralised to local governments.

The spearheading policy unit would analyse and make decisions on:

- national development goals, encompassing all elements of development and setting out short to long-term strategies and scenarios;
- how natural resources support these broader national development goals;
- how to balance exploitation for immediate economic gain, exploitation for

sustainable economic gain, conservation for future exploitation and conservation for ecological benefit; and
- recommended development models (plural) for consideration and adoption by the regions (provinces or district/cities).

The unit would start by analysing all policies affecting natural resources and seeing how they fit or do not fit together; revoking or revising policies that are out of step with other policies; and mapping the relations between spatial planning, exploitation permits, concessions, sustainable harvesting and so on.

Such a unit would create an opportunity to shift the dialogue on trade-offs away from chaotic interdepartmental or cross-sectoral coordination meetings and towards more rigorous analysis of the consequences of too much or too little exploitation; it would allow consideration of immediate needs today as well as future intergenerational and global issues. Such a unit would ensure that overarching policies affecting natural resources were consistent with each other, and that all supported the established development goals and strategies.

The unit would have the difficult role of communicating national policies on development and natural resources clearly and consistently to all levels of government. For the sectoral institutions located in Jakarta, this communication would be expected to ensure that lower-level sectoral policies maintained the intent and spirit of national policies. For the regional governments throughout the country, the task would be more challenging, and likely to be more of a two-way communication. With regional governments already having the authority to decide on most natural resource use, it is critical that they fully understand the national agenda and use it as the basis for developing their regional options on development and natural resource management. Likewise, it is important that the national spearheading policy unit also use information about the regions and their aspirations in analysing the options for, and deciding on, the national development agenda. An integrated yet diverse development and natural resource policy should be maintained at all times across sectors and regions.

The role of the provinces

In the context of regional autonomy, provincial-level institutions have authority for issues that concern more than one district/city. However, provincial agencies must find a new productive role for themselves rather than continue the tug-of-war with the district governments over spheres of authority. With limited capacity in the districts, provincial agencies could in fact play an important role. Provincial agencies have benefited from years of capacity-building programs, and through that have greater knowledge of and experience with development planning, decision-making and budgeting – including in the area of natural resource management. Such knowledge and experience are invaluable and should be utilised for the overall improvement of the regions.

Provincial agencies could serve as a bridge between national-level policies on natural resource management and local policies that take account of the regions' existing economic, social and environmental conditions. Provincial agencies should be able to assist in translating national-level policies on natural resource management into lower-level directives and guidelines; in analysing the options and approaches most appropriate for conditions in the field; and in guiding district government decision-making on natural resources. Provincial agencies are also in a strategic position to provide feedback to the national government institutions on policies that affect more than one district, to ensure that national policies sufficiently consider district and provincial-level aspirations and conditions.

One example of effective role redefinition concerns the Environmental Management Agency of the province of West Java. This agency handles management and restoration of forests, critical lands, and coastal and marine resources, in addition to pollution control and prevention. When the regional autonomy laws became effective, the agency immediately decided to play the role of 'think-tank'. Instead of getting in the way of the regions as they exercised their newfound authority, the Environmental Management Agency reoriented its programs and budgets towards preparing technical guidelines and conducting studies to be used by the district governments. It has also assisted the district governments to set up and strengthen their own institutions. Since 2001 the agency has prepared or is in the process of preparing guidelines on environmental impact assessment documentation, soil remediation and 'clean' development mechanisms – using its own provincial development funds. According to agency officials, the agency has found that by redefining its role and not getting drawn into a tug-of-war over decision-making authority, the district/city governments have become less reluctant to reveal their limited capacity and experience, and thus more willing to seek advice and counsel from the provincial government (Lex Laksamana and Setiawan Wangsaatmaja, personal communication, 2003).

Institutional adjustments in role and function are inevitable in this era of transition. Biting the bullet and directing energy to positive outcomes rather than negative battles would benefit the whole transition.

District-level decision-making

At the district level, decision-making on natural resources is now a daily reality. Many districts are continuing to seek advice or follow instructions from the central government. Some are making decisions considered unwise by other levels of government. Much has been said about the risk of further degradation of natural resources in the hands of the district governments, but it must also be recognised that some are genuinely concerned about the fate of development and natural resources in their regions. These districts are making headway in mobilising the available local resources to find solutions to local problems.

The city of Balikpapan is an example of a local government that has opened its doors to communicating with its civil society. The city government is now seen as progressive and efficient with a forward-looking leadership. It has established joint programs with NGOs and neighbouring districts on watershed management and conservation of Balikpapan Bay. More recently, confronted with a scarcity of fresh water, it opted to communicate horizontally with other elements of the community, namely NGOs and an oil/gas company operating in Balikpapan, to find a solution to this problem. Together they were able to exchange information and eventually locate a deep aquifer that could supply the municipality with sufficient water, at least in the medium term. The local water authority is now developing the wells and feeding them into the city's water treatment and distribution facilities (Niel Makinuddin, Mitra Pesisir, and Soufian, Bapedalda Kota Balikpapan, personal communication, 2004).[3]

Instead of crying out to the central government for assistance – the usual *modus operandi* before regional autonomy – Balikpapan was able to mobilise its own resources and ultimately solve its water problem. Problem solving has much greater immediacy at the district level: all those involved in finding a solution to Balikpapan's water shortage were also citizens of the city. Communication and the breaking down of traditional attitudes of distrust proved to be the key to finding a solution in this case. The lesson to be learned here is that good horizontal relations can create a collaborative energy among different stakeholders that exceeds any sense of urgency that vertical relations can offer.

CONCLUSION

Transforming institutions is a prerequisite for natural resource policies that are appropriate and consistent, and thus implementable and enforceable. First, the function of policy-making should be taken out of the sectoral departments and placed in a high-level policy unit responsible for spearheading a national development agenda that incorporates natural resources and balances short and long-term objectives. Second, provincial agencies should forge a positive role for themselves, particularly in bridging the gap between the national government and local governments. Third, district agencies should learn first to rely on their own constituencies in solving local problems, while still adhering to national policies.

Ensuring that policies are up to date and consistent with the development agenda will require institutions that have a positive energy; that have the ability to cross the traditional boundaries dividing technical and institutional sectors; that are quick to respond to changes in the global economy; and that clearly articulate the options for decision-makers at the lower levels of government. The process of transforming institutions (especially government) will require not just time but, more importantly, clarity of vision and consistency in translating this vision into new rules and procedures for the millions of employees working in these institutions. Leaders and managers will need to be persistent in communicating the overall vision and the new procedures. Employees will need to change their personal habits and reflexes in dealing with day-to-day tasks. Most of all, what is needed is a solid conviction that institutional transformation can be achieved in a lifetime – something that has become all too rare in the endless journey called development.

NOTES

1   See Katili (1983); USAID (1987); Patlis (2003b). The use of the dated references is intended to emphasise the reality that conditions and weaknesses identified in the late 1980s and early 1990s are still relevant today. There has not been sufficient progress to eliminate the institutional problems related to natural resource management.
2   This situation may be improved by revisions to the regional autonomy legislation. However, these had not been enacted at the time this paper was written.
3   Some are concerned, however, about the municipal government's plans for greater exploitation of the Sungai Wain protection forest, to produce more water for revenue and to supply the city as it continues to grow.

REFERENCES

Acemoglu, D., S. Johnson and J. Robinson (2002), 'An African success story: Botswana', *CEPR Discussion Papers No. 3219*, London: Centre for Economic Policy Research.

Acemoglu, D., S. Johnson and J. Robinson (2004), 'Institutions as the fundamental cause of long-run growth', *NBER Working Paper No. 10481*, Cambridge MA: National Bureau of Economic Research.

Adams, M. and S. Johnson (1998), 'Turmoil in Asian markets', *Tropical Forest Update*, 8.

ADB (Asian Development Bank) (2002), 'Draft country governance assessment report: Indonesia', Jakarta.

Aden, Jean (1992), 'Entrepreneurship and protection in the Indonesian oil service industry', in Ruth McVey (ed.), *Southeast Asian Capitalists*, Ithaca NY: SEAP, Cornell University.

Adhuri, Dedi Supriadi (2003), 'Does the sea divide or unite Indonesians? Ethnicity and regionalism from a maritime perspective', *Working Paper No. 48*, Canberra: Resource Management in Asian Pacific Program (RMAP), Australian National University.

Ahmad, M. (1992), 'Rente ekonomi dalam eksploitasi hutan', *Prisma*, 21: 3–18.

Alder, J., N.A. Sloan and H. Utolseya (1994), 'A comparison of management planning and implementation in three Indonesian marine protected areas', *Ocean and Coastal Management*, 24: 179–198.

Alisjahbana, Armida (1998), 'Desentralisasi fiskal dan tuntutan kebijakan perimbangan keuangan pusat daerah', *Orasi Ilmiah Pada Dies ke 41*, Bandung: Faculty of Economics, Padjadjaran University, October.

Alm, J., R.H. Aten and R. Bahl (2001), 'Can Indonesia decentralise successfully? Plans, problems, and prospects,' *Bulletin of Indonesian Economic Studies*, 37(1): 83–102.

Alqadrie, S.I., Ngusmanto, T. Manurung, T. Budiarto, Erdi and Herlan (2001), 'Desentralisasi pembuatan kebijakan dan administrasi kebijakan dalam mempengaruhi sektor kehutanan pada wilayah di luar Pulau Jawa: Hubungan antara otonomi dengan kelestarian hutan di Kabupaten Kapuas Hulu, Provinsi Kalimantan Barat', research report, Pontianak: Universitas Tanjungpura.

Andaya, Barbara Watson (1993), *To Live as Brothers: Southeast Sumatra in the Seventeenth and Eighteenth Centuries*, Honolulu: University of Hawai Press.

Arief, Sritua (1977), *Financial Analysis of the Indonesian Petroleum Industry*, Jakarta: Sritua Arief Associates.

Ascher, W. (1998), 'From oil to timber: The political economy of off-budget development financing in Indonesia', *Indonesia*, 65: 37–61.

Asfar, M. (2004), 'Di balik pergeseran suara NU-PKB', *Suara Merdeka*, 7 July.

Asia Foundation (2003), *Indonesia Rapid Decentralization Appraisal (IRDA): Third Report*, Jakarta, July.

Asia Foundation (2004), *Indonesia Rapid Decentralization Appraisal (IRDA)*: Fourth Report, Jakarta.

Aspinall, Clive (2001), 'Small-scale mining in Indonesia', report commissioned by Mining, Minerals and Sustainable Development, a project of the International Institute for Environment and Development, 79(September).

Aspinall, E. and G. Fealy (eds) (2003), *Local Power and Politics in Indonesia*, Singapore: Institute of Southeast Asian Studies.

Athukorala, P. (2003), 'Product fragmentation and trade patterns in East Asia', *Working Paper in Trade and Development No. 2003/21*, Canberra: Research School of Pacific and Asian Studies, Division of Economics, Australian National University.

Auty, R.M. (2001), 'The political economy of resource-driven growth', *European Economic Review*, 45(4–6): 839–846.

Awanohara, S. (1982), 'Jakarta trims the trees: Indonesia takes steps to restrict further – and eventually ban – log exports in favor of domestic processing', *Far Eastern Economic Review*, 115(12): 76–78.

Azis, I.J. (1990), 'Inpres's role in the reduction of interregional disparity', *Asian Economic Journal*, 4(2): 1–26.

Azis, I.J. (1992), 'Export performance and the employment effect', in Fu-Chen Lo and Narongchai Akrasanee (eds), *The Future of Asia-Pacific Economies*, New Delhi: Allied Publishers Limited, pp. 591–625.

Azis, I.J. (2000), 'Simulating economy-wide models to capture the transition from financial crisis to social crisis', *Annals of Regional Science*, 34: 251–278.

Azis, I.J. (2002), 'What would have happened in Indonesia if different economic policies had been implemented when the crisis started?', *Asian Economic Papers*, 1(2): 75–109.

Azis, I.J. and D. Roland-Holst (1999), 'Policy research for sustainable development: Notes on simulation modeling for Indonesia', in Fu-Chen Lo, K. Matsushita and H. Takagi (eds), *The Sustainable Future of the Global System II*, Tokyo: UN University-Institute of Advanced Studies and Institute for Global Environmental Strategies.

Bachriadi, D. and A. Lucas (2001), *Merampas Tanah Rakyat: Kasus Tapos dan Cimacan [Seizure of the Land of the People: The Tapos and Cimacan Cases]*, Jakarta: Kepustakaan Populer Gramedia.

Baharuddin, H. (1997), *Indonesian LNG: A Compilation of Presentation Papers*, Jakarta: Pertamina LNG Joint Management Group.

Bahl, Roy (2002), 'Revenue sharing in petroleum states', paper presented at a workshop on Petroleum Revenue Management organised by the Oil, Gas, Mining and Chemicals Department of the World Bank, Washington DC, October.

Bahl, Roy and Bayar Tumennason (2002), 'How should revenues from natural resources be shared in Indonesia?', paper presented at the Can Decentralization Help Rebuild Indonesia conference, International Studies Program, Andrew Young School of Policy Studies, Georgia State University, Atlanta, 1–3 May.

Bailey, Conner (1988), 'The political economy of marine fisheries development in Indonesia', *Indonesia*, 46(October): 25–38.

Bailey, C. and C. Zerner (1992), 'Community-based fisheries Management institutions in Indonesia', *Maritime Anthropological Studies*, 5(1): 1–17.

Balassa, Bela (1965), 'Trade liberalisation and "revealed" comparative advantage', *Manchester School*, 33: 99–123.

Ballard, J. and J. Platteau (1996), *Halting Degradation of Natural Resources: Is there a Role for Rural Communities?* New York: Oxford University Press.

Bappenas, NRM and LPEM-FEUI (National Development Planning Agency, Natural Resources Management and Institute for Economic and Social Research, Faculty of Economics, University of Indonesia) (2000a), 'Penerimaan daerah dari bagi hasil sumber daya alam', Jakarta, mimeo.

Bappenas, NRM and LPEM-FEUI (National Development Planning Agency, Natural Resources Management and Institute for Economic and Social Research, Faculty of Economics, University of Indonesia) (2000b), *Pengelolaan Sistem Informasi Sumber Daya Alam Daerah: Kebutuhan dan Permasalahannya*, Jakarta: NRM–USAID Project.

Barber, C.V. and K. Talbott (2003), 'The chainsaw and the gun: The role of the military in deforesting Indonesia', *Journal of Sustainable Forestry*, 16(3–4): 137–167.

Barber, C.V., N.C. Johnson and E. Hafild (1994), *Breaking the Logjam: Obstacles to Forest Policy Reform in Indonesia and the United States*, Washington DC: World Resources Institute.

Barbier, E.B. (1998), *The Economics of Environment and Development: Selected Essays*, Cheltenham: Edward Elgar Publishing Limited.

Barham, B., S.G. Bunker and D. O'Hearn (1994), 'Raw material industries in resource-rich regions', in B. Barham, S.G. Bunker, and D. O'Hearn (eds), *States, Firms and Raw Materials*, Madison WI: University of Wisconsin Press, pp. 3–38.

Barnes, Philip (1995), *Indonesia: The Political Economy of Energy*, Oxford: Oxford Institute for Energy Resources.

Barr, C. (1998), 'Bob Hasan, the rise of Apkindo, and the shifting dynamics of control in Indonesia's timber sector', *Indonesia*, 65(April): 1–36.

Barr, C. (1999), 'Discipline and accumulate: State practice and elite consolidation in Indonesia's timber sector, 1967–1998', MS thesis, Cornell University.

Barr, C. (2000), 'Profits on paper: The political economy of fiber, finance and debt in Indonesia's pulp and paper industries', Washington DC and Bogor: World Wildlife Fund and Center for International Forestry Research, mimeo.

Barr, C. (2001), 'Banking on sustainability: Structural adjustment and forestry reform in post-Suharto Indonesia', Washington DC and Bogor: World Wildlife Fund and Center for International Forestry Research, mimeo.

Barr, C. (2002), 'Timber concession reform: Questioning the "sustainable logging" paradigm', in C.J.P. Colfer and I.A.P. Resosudarmo (eds), *Which Way Forward? People, Forests, and Policymaking in Indonesia*, Washington DC: Resources for the Future, pp. 191–220.

Barr, C. and B. Setiono (2003a), 'CGI overlooks IBRA's forestry debt sales to Bank Mandiri', *Jakarta Post*, 6 June.

Barr, C. and B. Setiono (2003b), 'Writing off Indonesia's forestry debt: How the IMF, the Indonesian Bank Restructuring Agency and Bank Mandiri are financing forest destruction', *Multinational Monitor*, 24: 14–18.

Barr, C., D. Brown, A. Casson and D. Kaimowitz (2002), 'Corporate debt and the Indonesian forestry sector', in C.J.P. Colfer and I.A.P. Resosudarmo (eds), *Which Way Forward? People, Forests, and Policymaking in Indonesia*, Washington DC: Resources for the Future, pp. 277–292.

Barr, C., E. Wollenberg, G. Limberg, N. Anau, R. Iwan, I. M. Sudana, M. Moeliono and T. Djogo (2001), *The Impacts of Decentralization on Forests and Forest-dependent Communities in Malinau District, East Kalimantan: Case Study 3 on Decentralisation and Forests in Indonesia*, Bogor: Center for International Foresty Research.

Bartlett, A.G. III et al. (1972), *Pertamina: Indonesian National Oil*, Jakarta: Amerasian Ltd.

Basri, M. Chatib (2004), 'Gejala deindustrialisasi?' ['Symptoms of de-industrialisation?'], *Kompas*, 26 January.

Beeson, M. and R. Robison (2000), 'Introduction: Interpreting the crisis', in R. Robison, M. Beeson, K. Jayasuriya and H.-R. Kim (eds), *Politics and Markets in the Wake of the Asian Crisis*, New York: Routledge, pp. 3–24.

Bell, Gary F. (2001), 'The new Indonesian laws relating to regional autonomy: Good intentions, confusing laws', *Asian-Pacific Law and Policy Journal*, 2: 1–44.

Bengen, D. and I.M. Dutton (2004), 'Interactions: Mangroves, fisheries and forest management in Indonesia', in T. Northcote and G.F. Hartman (eds), *Fishes and Forestry: Worldwide Watershed Interactions and Management*, Oxford: Blackwell Science.

Bennett, C.P.A. (2002), 'Responsibility, accountability and national unity in village governance', in C.J.P. Colfer and I.A.P. Resosudarmo (eds), *Which Way Forward? People, Forests, and Policymaking in Indonesia*, Washington DC: Resources for the Future, pp. 60–80.

Bernard, M. and J. Ravenhill (1995), 'Beyond product cycles and flying geese: Regionalization, hierarchy, and the industrialisation of East Asia', *World Politics*, 47: 171–202.

Bertrand, J. (2004), *Nationalism and Ethnic Conflict in Indonesia*, Cambridge: Cambridge University Press.

BI (Bank Indonesia) (2004), 'BI tetap jaga stabilitas ekonomi: Tidak menutup kemungkinan suku bunga akan naik' ['BI continues to guard economic stability: Possible interest rate increase not ruled out'], Bank Indonesia press release No. 6/93/BGub/Humas, Jakarta.

Bohringer, C. (2001), 'Climate policies from Kyoto to Bonn: From little to nothing?', *ZEW Discussion Paper No. 01-49*, Mannheim: Zentrum für Europäische Wirtschaftsforschung.

Borsuk, Richard (1999), 'Markets: The limits of reforms', in Donald K. Emmerson (ed.), *Indonesia beyond Suharto: Polity, Economy, Society, Transition*, New York: Asia Society, pp. 136–167.

Boulan-Smit, M. Christine (2002), 'When the elephants fight, the grass suffers: Decentralization and the mining industry in Indonesia', *Antropologi Indonesia*, 68: 57–64.

Boyd, W., W.S. Prudham and R.A. Schurman (2001), 'Industrial dynamics and the problem of nature', *Society and Natural Resources*, 14: 555–570.

BPS (Badan Pusat Statistik) (2002), *Statistik Perusahaan Hak Pengusahaan Hutan, 2000*, Jakarta: BPS.

Brander, J.A. and M.S. Taylor (1997), 'International trade and open-access renewable resources: The small open economy case', *Canadian Journal of Economics*, 30(3): 526–552.

Broad, R. (1995), 'The political economy of natural resources: Case studies of the Indonesian and Philippine forest sectors', *Journal of Developing Areas*, 29: 317–340.

Brock, W.A. and S.N. Durlauf (2001), 'Growth empirics and reality', *World Bank Economic Review*, 15(2): 229–272.

Brodjonegoro, B. and J. Martinez-Vazquez (2002), 'An analysis of Indonesia's transfer system: Recent performance and future prospects', paper presented at the Can Decentralization Help Rebuild Indonesia conference, International Studies Program, Andrew Young School of Policy Studies, Georgia State University, Atlanta, 1–3 May.

Brown, D. (1999), 'Addicted to rent: Corporate and spatial distribution of forest resources in Indonesia; implications for forest sustainability and government policy', *Report No. PFM/EC/99/06*, Jakarta: Indonesia–UK Tropical Forest Management Programme.

Brown, D. (2001), 'Why governments fail to capture economic rent: The unofficial appropriation of rain forest rent by rulers in insular Southeast Asia between 1970 and 1999', PhD thesis, Department of Political Science, University of Washington.

Buchner B., C. Carraro and I. Cersosimo (2001), 'On the consequences of the U.S. withdrawal from the Kyoto/Bonn Protocol', *FEEM Working Paper No. 102.2001*, Trieste: Fondazione Eni Enrico Mattei.

Budiarto, T. (2003), 'Case study of illegal logging, livelihood security and conflict: The case of West Kalimantan', report for WWF-West Kalimantan, Pontianak.

Bunker, S.G. (1992), 'Natural resource extraction and power differentials in a global economy', in S. Oritz and S. Lees (eds), *Understanding Economic Process*, Monographs in Economic Anthropology No. 10, Lanham MD: University Press of America, pp. 61–84.

Bunker, S.G. (2003), 'Matter, space, energy, and political economy: The Amazon in the world-system', *Journal of World-Systems Research*, 9: 219–258.

Bünte, Marco (2004), 'Indonesia's decentralization: The big bang revisited', in Michael Nelson (ed.), *Thai Politics: Global and Local Perspectives; KPI Yearbook No. 2 (2002/2003)*, Bangkok: King Prajadhipok Institute (KPI).

Burke, L., E. Selig and M. Spalding (2002), *Reefs at risk in Southeast Asia*, Washington DC: World Resources Institute.

Butcher, J.G. (2004), *The Closing of the Frontier: A History of the Marine Fishery of Southeast Asia, c. 1850–2000*, Singapore: Institute of Southeast Asian Studies.

Carson, R. (1962), *Silent Spring*, Boston: Houghton Mifflin Co.

Casson, A. (2001a), 'Illegal tropical timber trade in Central Kalimantan', *Resource Management in Asia-Pacific Occasional Paper*, Canberra: Research School of Pacific and Asian Studies, Australian National University.

Casson, A. (2001b), *Decentralisation of Policies Affecting Forests and Estate Crops in Kotawaring in Timur District, Central Kalimantan: Case Study 5 on Decentralisation and Forests in Indonesia*, Bogor: Center for International Forestry Research.

Casson, A. and K. Obidzinski (2002), 'From New Order to regional autonomy: Shifting dynamics of "illegal logging" in Kalimantan, Indonesia', *World Development*, 30(12): 2,133–2,151.

CCSBT (Commission for the Conservation of Southern Bluefin Tuna) (2003), 'Report of the Indonesian Catch Monitoring Review Workshop', Queenstown, 10–11 April.

Cesar, H. (1996), 'Economic analysis of coral reefs', *Working Paper*, Washington DC: Environment Department, World Bank.

Cesar, H., C.G. Lundin, S. Bettencourt and J. Dixon (1997), 'Indonesian coral reefs: An economic analysis of a precious but threatened resource', *Ambio*, 26: 345–350.

Charoenpo, A. (2003), 'Illegal Thai fishing robbed Indonesia of billions of catches and cash', Southeast Asian Press Alliance, available at <http://www.seapabkk.org/fellowships/2002/anucha.html>.

Chomitz, K. and C. Griffiths (1996), 'Deforestation, shifting cultivation, and tree crops in Indonesia: Nationwide patterns of small holder agriculture at the forest frontier', *World Bank Working Paper*, available at <http://www.worldbank.org/research/peg/wps04/index.htm>.

Christanty, L. and R. Atje (2004), 'Policy and regulatory developments in the forestry sector since 1967', *CSIS Working Paper Series No. WPE077*, Jakarta: Centre for Strategic and International Studies.

Colfer, C.J.P. and I.A.P. Resosudarmo (eds) (2002), *Which Way Forward? People, Forests and Policymaking in Indonesia*, Washington DC: Resources for the Future.

Contreras-Hermosilla, A. (2001), 'Forest law compliance: An overview', Washington DC: World Bank.

Crawford, B.R., I.M. Dutton, C. Rotinsulu and L. Hale (1998), 'Community-based coastal resources management in Indonesia: Examples and initial lessons from North Sulawesi', in I. Dight, R. Kenchington and J. Baldwin (eds), *Proceedings of the International Tropical Marine Ecosystems Management Symposium (ITMEMS), Townsville, 23–26 November 1998*, Townsville: Great Barrier Reef Marine Park Authority, pp. 299–309.

Crawford, B.R., R.B. Pollnac, F. Sondita and L. Kusoy (1999), 'A comparison of level of development among coastal and non-coastal communities in North Sulawesi and South Sumatera', *Pesisir dan Lautan*, 2(1): 1–11.

Crawford, B., A. Siahainenia, C. Rotinsulu and A. Sukmara (2003), 'Compliance and enforcement of community-based coastal management regulations in North Sulawesi, Indonesia', *Coastal Management*, 32(39): 39–50.

Crouch, H. (1988), *The Army and Politics in Indonesia*, revised edition, Ithaca NY: Cornell University Press.

Crouch, H. (2003), 'Political update 2002: Megawati's holding operation', in E. Aspinall and G. Fealy (eds), *Local Power and Politics in Indonesia: Decentralisation and Democratisation*, Singapore: Institute of Southeast Asian Affairs, pp. 15–34.

Dahuri, R. (2001), 'Decentralising and delegating ICM to regional and local communities: A precarious balance of authority, capacity and consistency', UNESCO Oceans and Coasts Pre-World Summit on Sustainable Development Conference, Paris, 3–7 December.

Dahuri, R. and I.M. Dutton (2000), 'Integrated coastal and marine management enters a new era in Indonesia', *Integrated Coastal Zone Management*, 1: 11–16.

Dahuri, R., M.J. Sitepu and I.M. Dutton (1999), 'Building integrated coastal management capacity in Indonesia: The contribution of MREP', *Proceedings of the Oceanology International Conference (OI 99), 25–27 April 1999, Singapore*, pp. 223–237.

Daroesman, R. (1979), 'An economic survey of East Kalimantan', *Bulletin of Indonesian Economic Studies*, 15: 43–82.

Dauvergne, P. (1994), 'Politics of deforestation in Indonesia', *Pacific Affairs* 66(4): 497–518.

Dauvergne, P. (1997), *Shadows in the Forest: Japan and the Politics of Timber in Southeast Asia*, Cambridge MA: MIT Press.

David, Cecile T. (1995), 'The development of Indonesia's oil industry: Sectoral linkages and the rise of an indigenous capitalist class', MSc thesis, Madison WI: University of Wisconsin.

Dermawan, A. and I.A.P. Resosudarmo (2002), 'Forests and regional autonomy: The challenge of sharing the profits and pains', in C.J.P. Colfer and I.A.P. Resosudarmo (eds), *Which Way Forward? People, Forests, and Policymaking in Indonesia*, Washington DC: Resources for the Future, pp. 325–357.

Dienst van het Boswezen (1949), 'Productie van Hout in 1948', *Economisch Weekblad voor Indonesie*, 2: 23–27.

Dijk, L.J. van (1938), 'Aanteekeningen over Boschexplotatie en Boschwezen in Britsch en Nederlandsch Noord-Oost Borneo', *Tectona*, 31: 442–514.

Dinas Kehutanan Kalimantan Timur (2000), *Dinas Kehutanan Dalam Angka 1999/2000*, Samarinda.

Djojohadikusumo, Sumitro (1977), *Science, Resources and Development: Selected Essays*, Jakarta: LP3ES, pp. 95–128.

Donor SPM Working Group (2002), 'Local government obligatory functions and minimum service standards: A proposal for conceptual development and implementation', unpublished draft, June.

Dooley, M., D. Folkerts-Landau and P. Garber (2003), 'An essay on the revived Bretton Woods system', *NBER Working Paper No. 9971*, Cambridge MA: National Bureau of Economic Research, September.

Douglass, M. (1991), 'Planning for environmental sustainability in the extended Jakarta metropolitan region', in N. Ginsburg, B. Koppel and T.G. McGee (eds), *The Extended Metropolis: Settlement Transition in Asia*, Honolulu: University of Hawaii Press, pp. 239–273.

DTE (Down to Earth) (2004), 'BRIK: A flawed approach', *Down to Earth Newsletter*, 60(February), available at <http://dte.gn.apc.org/news.htm>.

Durlauf, S. and P.A. Johnson (1995), 'Multiple regimes and cross-country growth behaviour', *Journal of Applied Econometrics*, 10(4): 365–384.

Dutton, I.M. and D.G. Bengen (2001), 'The significance of coastal resources to food security in Indonesia', *InterCoast*, 38: 4–5.

Dutton, I.M. and K. Hotta (1995), 'Introduction', in K. Hotta and I.M. Dutton (eds), *Coastal Management in the Asia–Pacific Region*, Tokyo: Japan International Marine Science and Technology Foundation, pp. 1–18.

Dutton, I.M. and P. Saenger (eds) (1990), *Environmental Management of Tourism in Coastal Areas*, volumes I and II, Bogor: SEAMEO Biotrop and UNESCO.

Dutton, I.M., D.G. Bengen and J.J. Tulungen (2001), 'The challenges of coral reef management in Indonesia', in E. Wolanski (ed.), *Oceanographic Processes of Coral Reefs: Physics–Biology Links in the Great Barrier Reef*, London: CRC Press, pp. 315–330.

Dutton, I.M., D. Storey, K. Hidayat, T. Gunawan, J. Steffen, F. Sondita, R. Merrill and D. Sylvianita (2001), 'Sikap dan persepsi masyarakat mengenai sumberdaya pesisir dan laut di Indonesia', *Pesisir dan Lautan*, 3(3): 46–52.

Edinger, E.N. and M.J. Risk (2000), 'Reef classification by coral reef morphology predicts coral reef conservation value', *Biological Conservation*, 92: 1–13.

EIA–Telapak (Environmental Investigation Agency and Telapak) (1999), 'The final cut: "Illegal logging" in Indonesia's orangutan parks', London and Jakarta.

EIA–Telapak (Environmental Investigation Agency and Telapak) (2000), 'Illegal logging in Tanjung Puting National Park: An update on the "Final Cut" report', London and Jakarta.

EIA–Telapak (Environmental Investigation Agency and Telapak) (2002a), *Di Atas Jangkauan Hukum: Korupsi, Kolusi, Nepotisme (KKN) dan Nasib Hutan Indonesia* [*Above the Law: Corruption, Collusion, Nepotism and the Fate of Indonesia's Forests*], London, Washington DC and Bogor.

EIA–Telapak (Environmental Investigation Agency and Telapak) (2002b), 'Timber trafficking: Illegal logging in Indonesia, Southeast Asia and international consumption of illegally sourced timber', London and Bogor.

EIR (Extractive Industries Review) (2003), 'Striking a better balance: The extractive industries review', executive summary of EIR final report, Washington DC: World Bank Group.

Erdmann, M.V. (1999), 'An account of the first living coelacanth known to scientists in Indonesian waters', *Environmental Biology of Fishes*, 54: 439–443.

Erman, Erwiza (2004), 'Deregulation of tin and the emergence of local shadow state: Case study of Bangka', paper presented at the Renegotiating Boundaries workshop, Jakarta: LIPI-KITLV, 20–22 December.

Fane, George (1998), 'The role of prudential regulation', in Ross H. McLeod and Ross Garnaut (eds), *East Asia in Crisis: From Being a Miracle to Needing One?* London and New York: Routledge, pp. 287–303.

FAO (Food and Agriculture Organization) (1997), 'Review of the state of the world fishery resources: Marine resources', *FAO Fisheries Circular No. 920/FIRM/C920*, Rome.

FAO (Food and Agriculture Organization) (2000), 'Fishery country profile: The Republic of Indonesia', May, available at <http://www.fao.org/fi/fcp/en/IDN/profile.htm>.

FAO–GOI (Food and Agriculture Organization and Government of Indonesia) (1990), *Situation and Outlook of the Forestry Sector in Indonesia*, Jakarta: FAO and Directorate General of Forest Utilisation, GOI.

Fatchurrochman, Agam (2000), 'Gurita KKN dan restrukturisasi Pertamina', unpublished manuscript, Jakarta.

Fealy, G. (2001), 'Creating "total Muslims": The Tarbiyah movement and Islamic neo-revivalism in Indonesia', paper presented to Indonesia Council Open Conference, Melbourne University, 10–11 July.

Fegan, B. (2003), 'Plundering the sea', *Inside Indonesia*, 73(Jan–Mar); also available at <http://www.insideindonesia.org/edit73/Fegan per cent20fishing.htm>.

Firman, Tommy (1999), 'Indonesian timber-based industry at a crossroad: Efficiency, international market and local development', *Canadian Journal of Development Studies*, 20(1): 105–126.

Fitrani, F., B. Hofman and K. Kaiser (2005), 'Unity in diversity? The creation of new local governments in a decentralising Indonesia', *Bulletin of Indonesian Economic Studies*, 41(1): 51–74.

Fox, James J. and Grahame Applegate (2000), 'Issues and forest use policies and strategies in Indonesia: A need for change. Part I: Directions for sustainable management', paper prepared for the World Bank, Jakarta.

Frécaut, Olivier (2004), 'Indonesia's banking crisis: A new perspective on $50 billion of losses', *Bulletin of Indonesian Economic Studies*, 40(1): 37–57.

Fried, S.G. (2003), 'Writing for their lives: Bentian Dayak authors and Indonesian development discourse', in C. Zerner (ed.), *Culture and the Question of Rights: Forests, Coasts and Seas in Southeast Asia*, Durham NC: Duke University Press, pp. 142–183.

Furkon, A.M (2004), *Partai Keadilan Sejahtera: Ideologi dan Praksis Politik Kaum Muda Muslim Indonesia Kontemporer*, Jakarta Selatan; Teraju.

FWI–GFW (Forest Watch Indonesia and Global Forest Watch) (2002), 'The state of the forest: Indonesia', Bogor and Washington DC.

GEF (Global Environment Facility) (1998), 'Republic of Indonesia: Coral Reef Rehabilitation and Management Project', project document, Washington DC: World Bank.

Gelb, A. (1988), *Oil Windfalls: Blessing or Curse?* Oxford: Oxford University Press.

Gellert, P.K. (1998a), 'The limits of capacity: The political economy and ecology of Indonesia's timber industry, 1967–1995', PhD dissertation, Madison WI: University of Wisconsin.

Gellert, P.K. (1998b), 'A brief history and analysis of Indonesia's forest fire crisis', *Indonesia*, 65(April): 63–85.

Gellert, P.K. (2003), 'Renegotiating a timber commodity chain: The politics of the Indonesia–Japan plywood link', *Sociological Forum*, 18: 53–84.

Gillet, Robert (2001), 'Revising fisheries legislation in Indonesia: Fisheries management considerations', *FISHCODE Mission Report, GCP/INT/648/NOR*, Rome: Food and Agriculture Organization.

Goldstone, Anthony (1974), 'Indonesia: Asia's timber giant', *Far Eastern Economic Review*, 85(26): 57–58.

Goodland, R. and H. Daly (1996), 'If tropical log export bans are so perverse, why are there so many?', *Ecological Economics*, 18: 189–196.

GTZ (Deutche Gesellschaft für Technische Zusammenarbeit) (2003), 'Project support for decentralization measures (SfDM)', *Decentralization News Issues No. 48*, August, available at <http://www.gtzsfdm.or.id>.

Guerin, Bill (2004a), 'Managing Indonesia's state assets', *Asia Times Online*, 27 March.

Guerin, Bill (2004b), 'New worries for Indonesian bank sector', *Asia Times Online*, 17 April.

Gylfason, T. (2001), 'Natural resources, education, and economic development', *European Economic Review*, 45: 847–859.

Hadiz, V.R. (2003), 'Power and politics in North Sumatra: The uncompleted *reformasi*', in E. Aspinall and G. Fealy (eds), *Local Power and Politics in Indonesia: Decentralisation and Democratisation*, Singapore: Institute of Southeast Asian Studies, pp. 119–131.

Hadiz, V.R. (2004), 'Decentralization and democracy in Indonesia: A critique of neo-institutional perspectives', *Development and Change*, 35(4): 697–718.

Halpern, B.S. and R.P. Warner (2002), 'Marine reserves have rapid and lasting effects', *Ecology Letters*, 5: 361–366.

Hardjono, J. (1986), 'Environmental crisis in Java' [English version], *Prisma*, 39: 3–13.

Hardjono, J. (1991), 'Environment or employment: Vegetable cultivation in West Java', in J. Hardjono (ed.), *Indonesia: Resources, Ecology, and Environment*, Singapore: Oxford University Press, pp. 133–153.

Hardjono, J. (1994), 'Resource utilisation and the environment', in H. Hill (ed.), *Indonesia's New Order: The Dynamics of Socio-economic Transformation*, Sydney: Allen & Unwin, pp. 179–215.

Hausmann, R. and R. Rigobon (2002), 'An alternative interpretation of the "resource curse": Theory and policy implications', *NBER Working Paper No. 9424*, Cambridge MA: National Bureau of Economic Research.

Het Bosch (1935a), 'De Bevolkingskap in Borneo', volume 3, pp. 169–178.

Het Bosch (1935b), 'De Houtaankap op Noenoekan', volume 3, pp. 146–151.

Hill, H. (2000), *The Indonesian Economy*, second edition, Cambridge: Cambridge University Press.

Hill, H. (2002), 'Spatial disparities in developing East Asia: A survey', *Asian-Pacific Economic Literature*, 16(1): 10–35.

Hoessein, Bhenyamin S.H. et al. (2001), *Pemikiran Filosofis, Yuridis Dan Sosiologis Revisi UU No. 22 Tahun 1999 Dan UU No. 25 Tahun 1999*, Jakarta: Sekretariat Jenderal Dewan Perwalikilan Rakyat, Republik Indonesia and United Nations Development Programme.

Hofman, Bert and Kai Kaiser (2002), 'The making of the big bang and its aftermath: A political economy perspective', paper presented at the Can Decentralization Help Rebuild Indonesia conference, International Studies Program, Andrew Young School of Policy Studies, Georgia State University, Atlanta, 1–3 May.

Holmes, D. (2000), *Deforestation in Indonesia: A View of the Situation in 1999*, Jakarta: World Bank.

Hopley, D. (1999), 'Geological and geomorphological input to tropical coastal management with special reference to Balikpapan Bay, East Kalimantan', *Proyek Pesisir Technical Report TE/99/01/E*, Jakarta: Coastal Resources Center, University of Rhode Island.

Hopley, D. and Suharsono (2000), *The Status and Management of Coral Reefs in Eastern Indonesia*, Townsville: David and Lucille Packard Foundation USA and Australian Institute of Marine Science (ID 2989).

Hugo, G. (2000), 'The impact of the crisis on internal population movement in Indonesia', *Bulletin of Indonesian Economic Studies*, 36(2): 115–138.

Human Rights Watch (2003), 'Without remedy: Human rights abuses and Indonesia's pulp and paper industry', New York: Human Rights Watch, available at <http://www.hrw.org/reports/2003/indon0103/Indon0103.pdf>.

Hunt, L.J., I.M. Dutton and J.P. Duff (1998), *Integrated Coastal Zone Planning and Management Manual*, Jakarta: Vaughn International, Canora and BCEOM, CD-ROM (bilingual).

Ianchovichina, E. and W. Martin (2004), 'Economic impacts of China's accession to the WTO', in D. Bhattasali, S. Li and W. Martin (eds), *China and the WTO: Accession, Policy Reform and Poverty Reduction Strategies*, Washington DC: Oxford University Press and World Bank, pp. 211–236.

Ianchovichina, E. and T. Walmsley (2003), 'The impact of China's WTO accession on East Asia', *World Bank Policy Research Working Paper No. 3109*, Washington DC: World Bank, August.

IBRA (Indonesian Bank Restructuring Agency) (2003), *Monthly Report*, December.

ICG (International Crisis Group) (2004a), 'Indonesia: Violence erupts again in Ambon', *Asia Briefing*, Jakarta/Brussels, 17 May.

ICG (International Crisis Group) (2004b), 'Why Salafism and terrorism mostly don't mix', *Asia Report*, 83, 13 September.

Idris, I. et al. (2003), 'Studi kasus konsultasi publik dalam penyusunan rancangan undang-undang', in M. Knight and S. Tighe (eds), *Koleksi Dokumen Proyek Pesisir 1997–2003*, Seri Reformasi Hukum, Narragansett RI: Coastal Resources Center, University of Rhode Island.

IEA (International Energy Agency) (2004), *Analysis of the Impact of High Oil Prices on the Global Economy*, Paris, May.

IMF (International Monetary Fund) (2004), *World Economic Outlook*, Washington DC, September.

IPCC (Intergovernmental Panel on Climate Change) (2001), *Climate Change 2001*, three volumes, Cambridge: Cambridge University Press.

Ishihara, Yoichiro and Daan Marks (2004), 'Capacity utilization in Indonesia: Time to invest', Jakarta: World Bank, mimeo.

ITTO (International Tropical Timber Organization) (1999), 'Annual review and assessment of the world timber situation 1998', Yokohama, available at <http://www.itto.or.jp>.

ITTO (International Tropical Timber Organization) (2001), 'Achieving sustainable forest management in Indonesia', Yokohama, available at <http://www.itto.or.jp>.

ITTO (International Tropical Timber Organization) (2004), 'Annual review and assessment of the world timber situation 2003', Yokohama, available at <http://www.itto.or.jp>.

ITTO MIS (International Tropical Timber Organization Market Information Service) (2004), 'Tropical timber market report', 16–31 October, available at <http://www.itto.or.jp>.

270 REFERENCES

James, W.E., D.J. Ray and P.J. Minor (2003), 'Indonesia's textiles and apparel: The challenges ahead', *Bulletin of Indonesian Economic Studies*, 39(1): 93–103.

Jarvie, J., M. Malley, N.A. Manembu, D. Raharjo and T. Roule (2003), 'Conflict timber: Dimensions of the problem in Asia and Africa: Indonesia case study', ARD report submitted to the United States Agency for International Development, May.

Jaya, Wihana Kirana and Howard Dick (2001), 'The latest crisis of regional autonomy in historical perspective', in G. Lloyd and S. Smith (eds), *Indonesia Today: Challenges of History*, Singapore: Institute of Southeast Asian Studies, pp. 216–228.

Jenkins, D. (1980), 'Military budgets: The military's secret cache', *Far Eastern Economic Review*, 107(6): 70–73.

Jentoft, Svein (1989), 'Fisheries co-management: Delegating government responsibility to fishermen's organizations', *Marine Policy*, 13: 137–154.

Jentoft, Svein, Bonnie J. McCay and Douglas C. Wilson (1998), 'Social theory and fisheries co-management', *Marine Policy*, 22 (4–5): 423–436.

Jones, S. (2004), 'Political update 2003: Terrorism, nationalism and disillusionment with reform', in M.C. Basri and P. van der Eng (eds), *Business in Indonesia: New Challenges, Old Problems*, Singapore: Institute of Southeast Asian Affairs, pp. 23–38.

Kahn, B. (2003), *Conservation, Socio-economic and Policy Benefits of Indonesia's Protected Marine Mammal Fisheries Area (Pmmfa): A National Conservation and Management Initiative for Indonesia's Marine Mammals*, Jakarta: Nature Conservancy.

Karl, Terry Lynn (1997), *The Paradox of Plenty: Oil Booms and Petro-states*, Berkeley CA: University of California Press.

Kartodihardjo, H. (2002), 'Structural problems in implementing new forestry policies', in C.J.P. Colfer and I.A.P. Resosudarmo (eds), *Which Way Forward? People, Forests, and Policymaking in Indonesia*, Washington DC: Resources for the Future, pp. 144–160.

Katili, J.A. (1983), *Sumberdaya Alam untuk Pembangunan Nasional*, Jakarta: Ghalia Indonesia.

Kato, G. (2005), 'Forestry sector reform and distributional change of natural resource rent in Indonesia', *Developing Economies*, 43(1): 149–170.

Kemfert, C. (2001), 'Economic effects of alternative climate policy strategies', *FEEM Working Paper 85.01*, Trieste: Fondazione Eni Enrico Mattei. Also mimeo, University of Oldenburg.

Kenward, Lloyd (2004), 'Survey of recent developments', *Bulletin of Indonesian Economic Studies*, 40(1): 9–35.

Khan, A. (2001), 'Preliminary review on illegal logging in Kalimantan', paper presented at the Resource Management in Asia-Pacific Conference on Resource Tenure, Forest Management and Conflict Resolution: Perspectives form Borneo and New Guinea, 9–11 April, Australian National University, Canberra.

King, Dwight Y. (2000), 'Corruption in Indonesia: A curable cancer?', *Journal of International Affairs*, 53(2): 603–624.

Knight, M. and S. Tighe (eds) (2003), *Learning from the World of Coastal Management in Indonesia*, CD-ROM Collection, Narragansett RI: Coastal Resources Center, University of Rhode Island.

Koehler, K.G. (1972), 'Wood processing in East Kalimantan: A case study of industrialisation and foreign investment in Indonesia', *Bulletin of Indonesian Economic Studies*, 8(3): 93–129.

Krugman, Paul (2000), *The Return of Depression Economics*, New York: Norton.

Krumm K. and H. Kharas (2003), *East Asia Integrates: A Trade Policy Agenda for Shared Growth*, Washington DC: World Bank.

Kuncoro, A. and B.P. Resosudarmo (2004), 'Understanding Indonesian economic reforms: 1983–2000', report for the Understanding Reforms Project, New Delhi: Global Development Network.

Kusumaatmadja, S. (2000a), 'Coastal and marine management enters a new era in Indonesia', presentation by the Indonesian Minister of Marine Affairs and Fisheries, Hart Senate Building, Washington DC, 14 September.

Kusumaatmadja, S. (2000b), 'National marine exploration and fisheries policy: Statement by the Minister', Washington DC, 14 February.

Kwan, Chi Hung (2002), 'The rise of China and Asia's flying-geese pattern of economic development: An empirical analysis based on US import statistics', *NRI Papers No. 52*, Tokyo: Nomura Institute, August.

LATIN (Lembaga Alam Tropika Indonesia) (1998), *Kehutanan Indonesia Pasca Soeharto: Reformasi tanpa Perubahan* [*Post-Soeharto Indonesian Forestry: Reform without Change*], Bogor, Indonesia: Penerbit Pustaka Latin.

Lee J.W., W.J. McKibbin and Y. Park (2004), 'Transpacific trade imbalance: Causes and cures', *Issues Brief*, Sydney: Lowy Institute, September.

Lembaga Pionir Bulungan (2003), 'Dampak desentralisasi terhadap sektor kehutanan dan kesejahteraan masyarakat, studi kasus pengelolaan hutan di Kabupaten Bulungan', draft.

Lewis, Blane D. (2001), 'The new Indonesian equalisation transfer', *Bulletin of Indonesian Economic Studies*, 37(3): 325–343.

Lewis, Blane D. and Jasmin Chakeri (2004), 'Decentralized local government budget in Indonesia: What explains the large stock of reserves?', World Bank Jakarta Office, mimeo.

Li, Muqun and I. Coxhead (2004), 'The natural resource curse: An annotated bibliography', unpublished manuscript, Madison WI: University of Wisconsin.

Lindblad, J.T. (1988), *Between Dayak and Dutch: The Economic History of Southeast Kalimantan 1880–1942*, Dordrecht: Foris Publications.

Löschel, A. and Z.X. Zhang (2002), 'The economic and environmental implications of the US repudiation of the Kyoto Protocol and the subsequent deals in Bonn and Marrakech', *Weltwirtschaftliches Archiv*, 138(4): 711–746.

Machmud, Tengku Nathan (2000), *The Indonesian Production Sharing Contract: An Investor's Perspective*, The Hague: Kluwer Law International.

Mackie, J. (1962), 'Indonesia's government estates and their masters', *Pacific Affairs*, 34(4): 337–360.

Malley, M.S. (2003), 'New rules, old structures and the limits of democratic decentralisation', in E. Aspinall and G. Fealy (eds), *Local Power and Politics in Indonesia: Decentralisation and Democratisation,* Singapore: Institute of Southeast Asian Studies, pp. 102–116.

Manning, C. (1971), 'The timber boom with special reference to East Kalimantan', *Bulletin of Indonesian Economic Studies*, 7(3): 30–60.

Manning, C. (2000), 'Labour market adjustment to Indonesia's economic crisis: Context, trends and implications', *Bulletin of Indonesian Economic Studies*, 36(1): 105–136.

Manzano, O. and R. Rigobon (2001), 'Resource curse or debt overhang?' *NBER Working Paper No. 8390*, Cambridge MA: National Bureau of Economic Research.

Marks, Stephen V. (2004a), 'Fiscal sustainability and solvency: Theory and recent experience in Indonesia', *Bulletin of Indonesian Economic Studies*, 40(2): 227–242.

Marks, Stephen V. (2004b), 'Survey of recent developments', *Bulletin of Indonesian Economic Studies*, 40(2): 151–175.

Matthew, E. and J.W. van Gelder (2001), *Paper Tiger, Hidden Dragons: The Responsibility of International Financial Institutions for Indonesian Forest Destruction, Social Conflict and the Financial Crisis of Asia Pulp and Paper*, London: Friends of the Earth.

McCarthy, J.F. (2000), '"Wild logging": The rise and fall of logging networks and biodiversity conservation projects on Sumatra's rainforest frontier', *Occasional Paper No. 31*, Bogor: Center for International Forestry Research.

McCarthy, J.F. (2001a), *Decentralization and Forest Management in Kapuas District, Central Kalimantan, Case Study 2*, Bogor: Center for International Forestry Research.

McCarthy, J.F. (2001b), *Decentralisation, Local Communities and Forest Management in Barito Selatan District, Central Kalimantan: Case Study 1 on Decentralisation and Forests in Indonesia*, Bogor: Center for International Forestry Research.

McCarthy, J.F. (2002), 'Power and interest on Sumatra's rainforest frontier: Clientelist coalitions, illegal logging and conservation in the Alas Valley', *Journal of Southeast Asian Studies*, 33(1): 77–106.

McCawley, Peter (1978), 'Some consequences of the Pertamina crisis in Indonesia', *Journal of Southeast Asian Studies*, 9(1): 1–27.

McKibbin, W.J. and A. Stoeckel (2004a), 'China: The implications of the policy tightening', *Economic Scenarios*, Issue 8, February, available at <www.Economic Scenarios.com>.

McKibbin, W.J. and A. Stoeckel (2004b), 'Oil price scenarios and the global economy', *Economic Scenarios*, Issue 9, October, available at <www.EconomicScenarios.com>.

McKibbin W.J. and P. Wilcoxen (1997), 'A better way to slow global climate change', *Brookings Policy Brief No. 17*, Washington DC: Brookings Institution, June.

McKibbin, W.J. and P.J. Wilcoxen (2002a), *Climate Change Policy after Kyoto: A Blueprint for a Realistic Aapproach*, Washington DC: Brookings Institution.

McKibbin, W.J. and P.J. Wilcoxen (2002b), 'The role of economics in climate change policy', *Journal of Economic Perspectives*, 16(2): 107–130.

McKibbin, W.J. and P.J. Wilcoxen (2004), 'Estimates of the costs of Kyoto–Marrakesh versus the McKibbin–Wilcoxen blueprint', *Energy Policy*, 32(4): 467–479.

McKibbin, W.J., D. Pearce and A. Stegman (2004), 'Long run projections for climate change scenarios', *Working Paper in International Economics*, Sydney: Lowy Institute for International Policy, 5 May.

McLeod, Ross H. (1997), 'Policy conflicts in Indonesia: The impact of the current account deficit target on growth, equity and stability', *ASEAN Economic Bulletin*, 14(1): 32–45.

McLeod, Ross H. (2000), 'Survey of recent developments', *Bulletin of Indonesian Economic Studies*, 36(2): 5–40.

McLeod, Ross H. (2004), 'Dealing with bank system failure: Indonesia, 1997–2003', *Bulletin of Indonesian Economic Studies*, 40(1): 95–116.

Ministry of Finance (2002), 'Summary workshop report: Evaluasi DAU TA 2002 dan usulan penyempurnaannya untuk TA 2003', Jakarta, mimeo.

Ministry of Home Affairs (2003), 'Statement of the Republic of Indonesia on Progress of Decentralization in Indonesia', Working Group on Decentralization, 12th Meeting of the Consultative Group on Indonesia, Bali, 21–22 January.

Miraza, M.E. (1973), 'Development of Indonesian timber', *Economic Review*, 57: 33–36.

MMAF (Ministry of Marine Affairs and Fisheries) (2001a), *Pengkajian Stok Ikan di Perairan Indonesia 2001*, Jakarta.

MMAF (Ministry of Marine Affairs and Fisheries) (2001b), *Naskah Akademik Pengelolaan Wilayah Pesisir*, Jakarta.

MMAF (Ministry of Marine Affairs and Fisheries) (2002a), 'Capture fisheries in Indonesia: The main prospective capture fisheries in Indonesia', brochure, Jakarta.

MMAF (Ministry of Marine Affairs and Fisheries) (2002b), *Pedoman Umum Pengelolaan Pesisir Terpadu Kep.10/Men/2002* [*General Guidelines for Integrated Coastal Management*], Jakarta.

Monografi Kaltim (1968), *Monografi Daerah Propinsi Kalimantan Timur Tahun 1967*, Kantor Gubernur Kepala Daerah Propinsi Kal. Timur, Samarinda.

Monografi Kaltim (1969), *Monografi Daerah Propinsi Kalimantan Timur Tahun 1968*, Kantor Gubernur Kepala Daerah Propinsi Kal. Timur, Samarinda.

Monografi Kaltim (1970), *Monografi Daerah Propinsi Kalimantan Timur Tahun 1969*, Kantor Gubernur Kepala Daerah Propinsi Kal. Timur, Samarinda.

Moreau, R. (2001), 'Saving the coral reefs', *Newsweek*, 12 November, available at <http://www.msnbc.com/news/652494.asp>.

MOSE (Ministry of State for Environment) (1996), *Indonesia's Marine Environment : A Summary of Policies, Strategies, Actions and Issues*, Jakarta.

Muhtadi, D. (1999), 'HPH, Hak Pembabatan Hutan', *Kompas*, 30 August.

Murniati, S. and Djamaludin Suryohadikusumo (2004), *Hidup Tetap Bermakna*, Jakarta: Yayasan Surya Andana Asih.

Nadjamuddin (1960), 'Hasil Hutan Sebagai Penghasil Devisen Penting Bagi Negara', *Warta Ekonomi*, 13(26/27/28): 479.

Ng, F. and A. Yeats (2003), 'Major trade trends in East Asia: What are their implications for regional cooperation and growth?', *World Bank Policy Research Working Paper No. 3084*, Washington DC: World Bank.

Obidzinski, K. and A. Andrianto (2004), 'Illegal forestry activities in Berau and East Kutai Districts, East Kalimantan: Impacts on economy, environment and society', draft report for Nature Conservancy and Center for International Forestry Research.

Obidzinski, K. and C. Palmer (2002), '"How much do you wanna buy?" A methodology for estimating the level of illegal logging in East Kalimantan', Bogor: Center for

International Forestry Research (forthcoming in the *Bulletin of Indonesian Economic Studies*).

Obidzinski, K., I. Suramenggala and P. Levang (2001), 'L'exploitation forestière illégale en Indonésie: Un inquiétant processus de legalisation', *Bois et Forêts des Tropiques*, 270(4): 85–97.

Osborne, David and Ted Gaebler (1992), *Reinventing Government: How the Entrepreneurial Spirit Is Transforming the Public Sector*, Sydney: Addison-Wesley.

Palmer, C. and K. Obidzinski (2002), 'Higher international standards or rent-seeking race to the bottom? The impacts of forest trade liberalisation of forest governance in Indonesia', report for the Food and Agriculture Organization and the International Institute for Environment and Development (Project GCP/INT/775/JPN), mimeo, Bonn: Center for Development Research.

Parks, John E., Ghislaine Llewellyn, Ian M. Dutton and Robert S. Pomeroy (2001), 'Learning networks called for by conservation practitioners', *InterCoast*, 39: 18–19.

Patlis, J. (2002), 'Mapping Indonesia's forest estate from the lawyer's perspective: Laws, legal fictions, illegal activities, and the gray area', unpublished preliminary assessment prepared for the World Bank–World Wildlife Fund Alliance, Jakarta.

Patlis, J. (2003a), 'The role of law in promoting the sustainability of integrated coastal resource management', *Indonesian Journal for Coastal and Marine Affairs: Special Volume*, 1, Bogor: Institute Petanian Bogor.

Patlis, J. (2003b), 'A rough guide to developing local laws for natural resources', in B.P. Resosudarmo, A. Alisjahbana and B.P.S. Brodjonegoro (eds), *Decentralization, Natural Resources and Regional Development in Indonesia*, Jakarta: Indonesian Regional Science Association.

Patlis, J., M. Knight, D. Silalahi, S.P. Ginting, W. Siahaan, G. Hendrarsa and A. Wiyana (2003a), 'The process of developing coastal resource management laws', in M. Knight and S. Tighe (eds), *Coastal Legal Reform Series*, Narragansett RI: Coastal Resources Center, University of Rhode Island.

Patlis, J., M. Knight, S.P. Ginting, A. Wiyana, G. Hendrarsa and W. Siahaan (2003b), 'Case study: Developing a national law on coastal management', in M. Knight and S. Tighe (eds), *Koleksi Dokumen Proyek Pesisir 1997–2003*, Seri Reformasi Hukum, Narragansett RI: Coastal Resources Center, University of Rhode Island.

Patlis, J., N.A. Tangkilisan, D. Karwur, M.E. Ering, J. Tulungen, R. Titahelu and M. Knight (2003), 'Case study: Developing a district law', in M. Knight and S. Tighe (eds), *Koleksi Dokumen Proyek Pesisir 1997–2003*, Seri Reformasi Hukum, Narragansett RI: Coastal Resources Center, University of Rhode Island.

Patter de, C. and P. Visser (1979), *Kalimantan in de Houtgreep*, Vakgroep Boshuishoudkunde, Wageningen University.

Pauker, Guy (1961), 'Indonesia's eight-year development plan', *Pacific Affairs*, 34(2): 115–130.

PCI (Pacific Consultants International) (2001), *Study on Fisheries Development Policy Formulation*, Jakarta: Directorate General of Capture Fisheries, Ministry of Marine Affairs and Fisheries.

Peluso, N.L. (1983), 'Markets and merchants: The forest products trade of East Kalimantan in Historical Perspective', MA thesis, Ithaca NY: Cornell University Press.

Pertamina (1985), *Hands across the Sea: The Story of Indonesian LNG*, Jakarta: Pertamina.

Petebang, E. (2000a), 'Tracing large-scale illegal logging business in Kalimantan', *Jakarta Post*, 23 May: 23.

Petebang, E. (2000b), 'Illegal logging rampant along Indonesian–Malaysian border', *Jakarta Post*, 23 May: 23.

Petroski, Karen (2004), 'Retheorizing the presumption against implied repeals', *California Law Review*, 92(2): 487–540.

Pet-Soede, C., H.S.J. Cesar and J.S. Pet (1999), 'An economic analysis of blast fishing on Indonesian coral reefs', *Environmental Conservation*, 26(2): 83–93.

Pet-Soede, C., W.L.T. van Densen, J.S. Pet and M.A.M. Machiels (2001), 'Impact of Indonesian coral reef fisheries on fish community structure and resultant catch composition', *Fisheries Research*, 51: 35–51.

Pezzey, J. (2003), 'Emission taxes and tradable permits: A comparison of views on long run efficiency', *Environmental and Resource Economics*, 26(2): 329–342.

Pizer, William A. (1997), 'Prices vs. quantities revisited: The case of climate change', *RFF Discussion Paper 98-02*, Washington DC: Resources for the Future.

Pokja PA PSDA (Working Group for Agrarian and Natural Resources Management Reform) (2004), 'Merangkai keragaman: Proses dan hasil konsultasi publik rancangan undang-undang PSDA', unpublished draft, Jakarta.

Pomeroy, Robert S. and Fikret Berkes (1997), 'Two to tango: The role of government in fisheries co-management', *Marine Policy*, 21(5): 465–480.

Posner, Richard (1983), 'Statutory construction: In the classroom and in the courtroom', *University of Chicago Law Review*, 50: 800–822.

Post, P. (1993), 'Japan and the integration of the Netherlands East Indies into the world economy, 1868–1942', *Review of Indonesian and Malaysian Affairs*, 27: 134–165.

Potter, L. (1988), 'Indigenes and colonisers: Dutch forest policy in South and East Borneo (Kalimantan) 1900 to 1950', in J. Dargavel, K. Dixon and N. Semple (eds), *Changing Tropical Forests: Historical Perspectives on Today's Challenges in Asia, Australasia and Oceania*, Canberra: Centre for Resource and Environmental Studies, Australian National University, pp. 127–153.

Prawiro, Radius (1998), *Indonesia's Struggle for Economic Development: Pragmatism in Action*, Kuala Lumpur: Oxford University Press.

Prebisch, R. (1959), 'Commercial policies in underdeveloped countries', *American Economic Review*, 49: 252–273.

PTBA-UPO (1998), *Report of the PTBA-UPO*, Sawahlunto, August.

Purnama, B.M. (2003), *Sustainable Forest Management as the Basis for Improving the Role of the Forestry Sector*, Jakarta: Forest Planning Agency, Department of Forestry.

Purwaka, T.H. (1995), 'Policy on marine and coastal resource development planning', *Occasional Paper Series No. 8*, Bandung: Center for Archipelago, Law and Development Studies.

Raharjo, M.D. (1972), 'Kedudukan dan peranan sektor kehutanan dalam pembangunan daerah Kalimantan Timur', *Prisma*, 2: 27–33.

Rais, J., I.M. Dutton, J. Plouffe, L. Pantimena and R. Dahuri (eds) (1998), *Proceedings of the International Symposium on Integrated Coastal and Marine Resources Man-*

agement, Malang, 25–27 November 1997, Malang: Proyek Pesisir Bakosurtanal and ITN.

Ray, David (2003), 'Survey of recent developments', *Bulletin of Indonesian Economic Studies*, 39(3): 245–270.

Resosudarmo, B.P. (2001), 'The economy-wide impact of integrated food crop pest management in Indonesia', *Research Report Monograph*, Ottawa: Economy and Environment Program for Southeast Asia.

Resosudarmo, B.P. and N.I.L. Subiman (2003), 'The management of biodiversity in Indonesia at a sustainable level', *Indonesian Quarterly*, 31(1): 73–87.

Resosudarmo, B.P. and O. Tanujaya (2002), 'Energy demand in Indonesia: Past and future trends', *Indonesian Quarterly*, 30(2): 158–174.

Resosudarmo, B.P., N.I. Subiman and B. Rahayu (2000), 'The Indonesian marine resources: An overview of their problems and challenges', *Indonesian Quarterly*, 28(3): 336–355.

Resosudarmo, I.A.P. (2003), 'Shifting power to the periphery: The impact of decentralisation on forests and forest people', in E. Aspinall and G. Fealy (eds), *Local Power and Politics in Indonesia: Decentralisation and Democratisation*, Singapore: Institute of Southeast Asian Studies, pp. 230–244.

Resosudarmo, I.A.P. (2004a), 'Closer to people and trees: Will decentralization work for the people and forests of Indonesia?', *European Journal of Development Research*, 16(1): 110–132.

Resosudarmo, I.A.P. (2004b), 'Preliminary observations of forestry dynamics in decentralizing Indonesia: Case study of Bulungan and Kutai Barat districts of East Kalimantan', draft.

Rhee, S. (2000), 'De facto decentralisation and the management of natural resources in East Kalimantan during a period of transition', *Asia-Pacific Community Forestry Newsletter*, 13(2): 34–38.

Ribot, J.C. (2002), *Democratic Decentralisation of Natural Resources: Institutionalising Popular Participation*, Washington DC: World Resources Institute.

Roberts, C.M., J.A. Bohnsack, F. Gell, J.P. Hawkins and R. Goodridge (2001), 'Effects of marine reserves on adjacent fisheries', *Science*, 294: 1,920–1,923.

Roberts, M.J. and A.M. Spence (1976), 'Effluent charges and licenses under uncertainty', *Journal of Public Economics*, 5: 193–208.

Robison, R. (1986), *Indonesia: The Rise of Capital*, North Sydney: Allen & Unwin.

Robison, R. and V.R. Hadiz (2004), *Reorganising Power in Indonesia: The Politics of Oligarchy in an Age of Markets*, volume 4, New York: Routledge Curzon.

Robison, R. and A. Rosser (2000), 'Surviving the meltdown: Liberal reform and political oligarchy in Indonesia', in R. Robison, M. Beeson, K. Jayasuriya and H.-R. Kim (eds), *Politics and Markets in the Wake of the Asian Crisis*, New York: Routledge, pp. 171–191.

Rocamora, J.E. (1970), 'The Partai Nasional Indonesia 1963–1965', *Indonesia*, 10: 143–181.

Rodriguez, F. and D. Rodrik (1999), 'Trade policy and economic growth: A skeptic's guide to the cross-national evidence', *NBER Working Paper No. 7081*, Cambridge MA: National Bureau of Economic Research.

Roeder, O.G. (1973a), 'Timber: The magic word', *Far Eastern Economic Review*, 79(9): 43.

Roeder, O.G. (1973b), 'Indonesian timber boom', *Far Eastern Economic Review*, 82(40): 60.

Rola, Agnes C. and Ian Coxhead (2005), 'Economic development and environmental policy in the uplands of Southeast Asia: Challenges for policy and institutional development', in D. Colman and N. Vink (eds), *Reshaping Agriculture's Contribution to Society: Proceedings of the Twenty-fifth International Conference of Agricultural Economists*, Malden MA and Oxford UK: Blackwell, pp. 243–256.

Ross, M.L. (1996), 'The political economy of boom-and-bust logging in Indonesia, the Philippines, and East Malaysia 1950–1994', PhD dissertation, Princeton NJ: Department of Politics, Princeton University.

Ross, M.L. (1999), 'The political economy of the resource curse', *World Politics*, 51: 297–322.

Ross, M.L. (2001), *Timber Booms and Institutional Breakdowns in Southeast Asia*, Cambridge: Cambridge University Press.

Ruddle, Kenneth (1999), 'The role of local management and knowledge systems in small-scale fisheries', *Journal of Policy Studies*, 7: 1,001–1,107.

Rumphius, G.E. (1705), *The Ambonese Curiosity Cabinet*, English edition translated by E.M. Beekman and republished (1999) by Yale University Press, New Haven.

Rutten, L. and S.H. Tan (2004), 'Reviving tropical plywood: How increasing transparency and cooperation in the tropical hardwood plywood trade could reduce market fluctuations and price volatility and reinvigorate the trade', *Technical Series Report No. 20*, Yokohama: International Tropical Timber Organization.

Ruzicka, I. (1979), 'Rent appropriation in Indonesia logging: East Kalimantan 1972/73–1976/77', *Bulletin of Indonesian Economic Studies*, 15: 45–74.

Rytkönen, A. (2003), 'Market access of tropical timber', report submitted to the International Tropical Timber Organization, Yokohama.

Sacerdoti, G. (1979), 'Where timber is booty: Complex swindles demand open official collusion', *Far Eastern Economic Review*, 106(48): 64–65.

Sachs, J. and A. Warner (1995), 'Natural resource abundance and economic growth', *NBER Working Paper No. 5398*, Cambridge MA: National Bureau of Economic Research.

Sachs, J. and A. Warner (2001), 'Natural resources and economic development: The curse of natural resources', *European Economic Review*, 45(4–6): 827–838.

Salim, E. (1993), *Lingkungan Hidup dan Pembangunan*, Jakarta: Mutiara Sumber Widya.

Salim, E. (2004), 'World Bank must reform on extractive industries', *Financial Times*, 16 June.

Salm R.V., S. Smith and G. Llewellyn (2001), 'Mitigating the impact of coral bleaching through marine protected area design', in H. Schuttenberg (ed.), *Coral Bleaching: Causes, Consequences and Response*, Coastal Management Report No. 2230, Narragansett RI: Coastal Resources Center, University of Rhode Island, pp. 81–88.

Sangkoyo, Hendro (2003), 'Indonesia: The coming decline of a ludicrous carbocracy', paper presented at the Workshop on Human Rights and Oil in Southeast Asia and Africa, Berkeley Center for African Studies and Southeast Asia Studies, 31 January.

Sarjono (1961), 'Mempelajari Politik Kehutanan di Indonesia Dewasa Ini', *Madjalah Kehutanan*, 1: 5–27.

Satria, Arif, Yoshiaki Matsuda and Masaaki Sano (2004), 'Multilevel conflicts in community based coral reef management systems: Case study in West Lombok, Indonesia', paper presented at the IIFET2004 conference, Tokyo, July.

Schuttenberg, H.Z. (2001), 'A national perspective on community-based marine sanctuaries: Opportunities and challenges for establishing a network of community sanctuaries in Indonesia', *Proyek Pesisir Working Paper*, Jakarta: Coastal Resources Center, University of Rhode Island.

Schwartz, A. (1990), 'A sawpoint for ecology', *Far Eastern Economic Review*, 148(16): 60.

Schwarz, A. (2000), *Nation in Waiting: Indonesia's Search for Stability*, Sydney: Allen & Unwin.

Silver, C., I.J. Azis and L. Schroeder (2001), 'Intergovernmental transfers and decentralisation in Indonesia', *Bulletin of Indonesian Economic Studies*, 37(3): 345–362.

Simangunsong, B.C.H. (2004), 'The economic performance of Indonesia's forest sector in the period 1980–2002', *GTZ-SMCP Briefing Paper # 4*, Jakarta: GTZ-SMCP, July.

Simangunsong, B.C.H. and B. Setiono (2004), *Study on Debt Restructuring of Forest Industries under Indonesian Bank Restructuring Agency (IBRA)*, Jakarta: Indonesian Working Group on Forest Finance.

Slamet, M. (1971), '"Green gold" Kalimantan Timur', *Warta Pertanian*, 6-7-8: 17–19.

Sloan, N.A. and A. Sughandy (1994), 'An overview of Indonesian coastal environmental management', *Coastal Management*, 22: 215–233.

Soemarwoto, O. (2004), *Atur-Diri-Sendiri: Paradigma Baru Pengelolaan Lingkungan Hidup [Self-regulation: A New Paradigm in Environmental Management]*, third edition, Yogyakarta: Gadjah Mada University Press.

Soemarwoto, O. (ed.) (2003), *Towards Jogja, The Eco-province: The Regional Agenda 21 for the Sustainable Tourism Development of the Special Province of Yogyakarta*, Yogyakarta: UNDP/Yogyakarta Provincial Government.

Soepardi, R. (1972), 'Sekedar perbandingan: Pengusahaan hutan dulu dan kini', *Indonesia Commodity Review*, 2(1): 23–25.

Sofa, F. (1998), 'Coastal management projects in Indonesia 1987–1998', *Proyek Pesisir Working Paper*, Jakarta: Coastal Resources Center, University of Rhode Island.

Storey, D. (2000), 'Sikap-sikap dan perilaku mengenai pengelolaan lokal sumberdaya terumbu karang: Model-model dari survei masyarakat di Riau, Sulawesi Selatan dan Papua Utara' ['Attitudes and behaviours related to local management of coral reef resources: Models from a survey of the public in Riau, South Sulawesi and Papua'], presentation to the Second National Coastal Conference (Konas II), Makassar, 15–17 May.

Streets, D. (2004), 'Black smoke in China and its climate effects', paper presented to the Asian Economic Panel, Columbia University, New York, October.

Streets, D.G., T.C. Bond, G.R. Carmichael et al. (2003), 'An inventory of gaseous and primary aerosol emissions in Asia in the year 2000', *Journal of Geophysical Research*, 108(D21): 8,809.

Strutt, A. and K. Anderson (2000), 'Will trade liberalisation harm the environment? The case of Indonesia to 2020', *Environment and Resource Economics*, 17: 203–232.

Sugiarti, K.L. and S. Novi (2002), 'Bentuk dan dinamika hubungan buruh-majikan: Studi kasus di perkebunan teh negara PTPN VIII Rancabali dan perkebunan teh rakyat Ciwidey' ['The form and dynamics of labour relationships: A case study of the PTPN VIII tea plantation at Rancabali and smallholder tea in Ciwidey'], *Working Paper Series 11*, Bandung: Akatiga.

Sun, X., E. Katsigris and A. White (2004), 'Meeting China's demand for forest products', Forest Trends, Chinese Center for Agricultural Policy, and Center for International Forestry Research, available at <www.forest-trends.org>.

Sunderlin, W.D. (2002), 'Effects of crisis and political change, 1997–1999', in C.J.P. Colfer and I.A.P. Resosudarmo (eds), *Which Way Forward? People, Forests, and Policymaking in Indonesia*, Washington DC: Resources for the Future, pp. 246–276.

Sunderlin, W.D., I.A.P. Resosudarmo, E. Rianto and A. Angelsen (2000), 'The effect of Indonesia's economic crisis on small farmers and natural forest cover in the Outer Islands', *CIFOR Occasional Paper. No. 28(E)*, Bogor: Center for International Forestry Research.

Suryahadi, Asep, Wenefrida Widyanti, Daniel Perwira and Sudarno Sumarto (2003), 'Minimum wage policy and its impact on employment in the urban formal sector', *Bulletin of Indonesian Economic Studies*, 39(1): 29–50.

Suwarno, R. Simarmata and R. Ahmad (eds) (2003), *Di Bawah Satu Payung: Hasil Konsultasi Publik RUU Pengelolaan Sumberdaya Alam*, Jakarta: eKADAKA.

Tacconi, L. and I. Kurniawan (2004), 'Forest cover, deforestation and forest degradation in Indonesia, 2002', Bogor: Center for International Forestry Research.

Tacconi, L., K. Obidzinski and F. Agung (2004), 'Learning lessons to promote forest certification and control of illegal logging in Indonesia', Bogor: Center for International Forestry Research.

Thee Kian Wie (2000), 'The Soeharto era and after: Stability, development and crisis, 1966–2000', in Howard Dick, Vincent J.H. Houben, J. Thomas Lindblad and Thee Kian Wie (eds), *The Emergence of a National Economy*, Honolulu: Allen & Unwin and University of Hawaii Press.

Thorbecke, E. (1992), 'Adjustment, growth and income distribution in Indonesia', Paris: OECD Development Centre.

Thorburn, C.C. (1998), 'Sasi lola (*Trochus niloticus*) in the Kei Islands: An endangered coastal resource management tradition', *Pesisir dan Lautan*, 1(2): 15–29.

Tomascik, T., A.J. Mah, A. Nontji and M.K. Moosa (1997), *The Ecology of the Indonesian Seas*, Parts 1 and 2, Singapore: EMDI and Periplus.

Trihadi, A. (1964), 'Ekonomi kehutanan nasional, tugas dalam rangka realisasi ekonomi sosialis', *Rasionalisasi Bulletin Bulanan Kehutanan*, 1(1-2): 2–11 and *Rasionalisasi Bulletin Bulanan Kehutanan* 1(3-4): 42–66.

Tulungen, J.J., P. Kusoy and B. Crawford (1998), 'Community-based coastal management in Indonesia: North Sulawesi early stage experience', Convention on Integrated Coastal Management Practitioners, Davao City, 10–12 November.

Turner, Mark and Owen Podger, with Maria Sumardjono and Wayan K. Tirthayasa (2003), *Decentralisation in Indonesia: Redesigning the State*, Canberra: Asia Pacific Press.

UNIDO (United Nations Industrial Development Organization) (2004), Statistical data-
    bases, available at <http://www.unido.org/regions.cfm?TY=R&RID=02>, accessed
    5 November 2004.
Universitas Tanjungpura and Yayasan Konservasi Borneo (2004), 'Analisis kebijakan
    sektor kehutanan dalam era otonomi daerah di Kabupaten Sintang, Pontianak: Kali-
    mantan Barat', draft.
USAID (United States Agency for International Development) (1987), *Natural
    Resources and Environmental Management in Indonesia: Annexes.*
USAID (United States Agency for International Development) (2004), 'Strategic
    approaches to job creation and employment in Indonesia', report prepared for
    USAID, Jakarta Mission, 4 February, mimeo.
Usman, Syaikhu (2003), *Politik Lokal di Era Decentralisasi: Menuju ke Otonomi
    Rakyat*, Jakarta: SMERU Publication.
Usui, Norio and Armida S. Alisjahbana (2003), 'Local development planning and bud-
    geting in decentralized Indonesia', paper presented at the International Symposium
    on Indonesia's Decentralization Policy: Problems and Policy Directions, LPEM-
    FEUI and Hitotsubashi University, Jakarta.
Vincent, J.R., J. Aden, G. Dore, M. Adriani, V. Rambe and T. Walton (2002), 'Public
    environmental expenditures in Indonesia', *Bulletin of Indonesian Economic Studies*,
    38(1): 61–74.
Vous, Reinout (1990), 'Koopman en Koning: De VOC en de Maleise Tin Handel, 1740–
    1800', PhD dissertation, Utrecht: University of Utrecht.
WALHI (Wahana Lingkungan Hidup) (1995), *Hutan Tanaman Industri: Blunder Kedua
    Kebijakan Kehutanan Indonesia* [*Industrial Tree Plantations: The Second Blunder
    of Indonesian Forestry Policy*], Jakarta.
Walters, C. and J.J. Maguire (1996), 'Lessons for stock assessment from the northern
    cod collapse', *Review of Fish Biology and Fisheries*, 6: 145–159.
Walton, A.A. (2004), 'Mining a sacred land', *Human Rights Dialogue*, 2(11): 24–25.
Warta FKKM (2004), 'Modus operandi korupsi kehutanan,' *Warta FKKM*, 7(9): 6–8.
WCED (World Commission on Environment and Development) (1987), *Our Common
    Future*, Oxford: Oxford University Press.
Weiss, J. and S. Gao (2002), 'People's Republic of China export threat to ASEAN: Com-
    petition in the US and Japanese markets', *ADB Institute Discussion Paper No. 2*,
    Manila: Asian Development Bank.
Weitzman, M.L. (1974), 'Prices vs. quantities', *Review of Economic Studies*, 41:
    477–491.
Weyant, John (ed.) (1999), 'The costs of the Kyoto Protocol: A multi-model evaluation',
    Energy Journal, Special Issue.
Wilkinson, C.W. (2000), 'The 1997–1998 mass bleaching event around the world', in C.
    Wilkinson (ed.), *Status of Coral Reefs of the World*, Global Reef Monitoring Net-
    work, Australian Institute of Marine Science, pp. 15–38.
Winters, J. (1996), *Power in Motion: Capital Mobility and the Indonesian State*, Ithaca
    NY: Cornell University Press.
Woo, W.T., B. Glassburner and A. Nasution (1994), *Macroeconomic Policies, Crises
    and Long-run Growth: The Case of Indonesia*, Washington DC: World Bank.

World Bank (1993), *The East Asian Miracle: Economic Growth and Public Policy*, New York: Oxford University Press.

World Bank (1994), *Indonesia: Environment and Development*, Washington DC.

World Bank (2000), *Greening Industry: New Roles for Communities, Markets and Governments*, Washington DC.

World Bank (2001), *Indonesia: Environment and Natural Resource Management in a Time of Transition*, Washington DC.

World Bank (2003), 'Decentralizing Indonesia: A regional public expenditure review', *Report No. 26191-IND*, Jakarta: Poverty Reduction and Economic Management Unit, East Asia and Pacific Region, World Bank.

World Bank (2004), *Averting an Infrastructure Crisis: A Framework for Policy and Action*, Washington DC.

WRI (World Resources Institute) (2004), *World Resources 2002–2004*, Washington DC.

Wrighter, S. (2005), 'Questions of judgement', *Inside Indonesia*, 81: 23–24.

Yowono, F.D.H. (1998), 'Community-based fishery management', in D. Bengen (ed.), *Proceedings of the First National Coastal Conference, 19–20 March 1998*, Bogor: Institut Pertanian Bogor, C68–C85.

Zaiyardam Zubir et al. (2003), *Seputar Kasus Mark-up PT Minang Malindo*, Padang, September.

INDEX

Abdurrahman Wahid, 17, 19, 20, 49n, 94, 154,172
Aceh, 27–9, 30n, 115
adat (customary) law, 1, 7, 86, 94, 240
Africa, 152
Agreement on Textiles and Clothing (ATC), 76, 90n
agriculture, xxi, 4, 38, 39, 40, 78, 80, 88, 90n, 123, 124, 127
airplane factory, 128, 150
Alaska, 122
Ambon, 27
Amien Rais, 24, 30n
Apkindo, 149, 151, 157, 200, 202
Armed Forces Bill, 26–7
armed forces
    see military
ASEAN, 71, 75, 76, 78, 154, 171, 186
Asia, 54, 55
    see also Southeast Asia
Asia Foundation, 244
Asian Development Bank, 171, 247n
Australia, 3, 54, 69, 165
Australian Agency for International Development (AusAID), xiii, 171, 247n
Australian embassy bombing, 29

Bali bombings, 25, 29
Bali tourism, 170
Bandung
    see West Java
Bank Indonesia (BI), 32, 34, 43, 181
Bank Mandiri, 156
banking system, 43–4, 44–6, 50n, 187–8
    collapse, 45, 46
    deposits, geographical distribution, 47–8
    lending, 44–5, 46
    non-performing loans, 43
bankruptcy, 156
Bappenas, 163, 171, 176, 183, 185, 241, 250
biodiversity, 85, 133
    forests, 129, 136, 141–2n, 238
    marine, 2, 164, 176, 177–8
biological resources, xxi, 128–9, 133, 135, 237
bombings, 29, 37
    see also Australian embassy bombing; Bali bombings; Marriott Hotel bombing
BRIK, 145, 155–7
bupati (district head), 23, 99, 107n, 155, 199, 210–12, 213
business involvement in development, xxiv, xxv

Cambodia, 79
carbon dioxide emissions
    see greenhouse gas emissions
carbon emissions
    see greenhouse gas emissions
Center for Coastal and Marine Resources
    Studies, Bogor Agricultural Univer-
    sity, 163
Center for Research on Fish Capture, 96
CGE model, 131–41
    definition, 142n
Chile, 3, 122
China, 3, 5–6, 64, 71–91, 152–4, 168,
    194, 200, 202, 203, 213
    exports, 6, 39, 41, 42, 49n, 153
    imports, 76, 79, 84, 87, 145
        forest products, 102–3, 153
    logging ban, 253
    pollution, 62, 91n
    rapid growth, 6, 41, 54–5, 102
    trade with, 41–2
civil society, xxii, xxiv–xxv, 131, 187,
    203, 244
Clean Development Mechanism (CDM),
    62, 63, 68
climate change, 53, 54, 62–8, 69, 167,
    177, 254
    see also greenhouse gas emissions
clothing/textiles, 6, 71, 72, 78, 79, 87, 88
    see also manufacturing
coal
    energy consumption, 60, 62
    gas emission, 60, 61, 64
    illegal mining, 206–15
    prices, 213, 215n
    theft, 210
    thermal, 3
    village unit cooperatives (KUDs),
        209–10, 214
Commission for the Conservation of
    Southern Bluefin Tuna, 164
comparative advantage, 78–9, 84, 87
compensation, 127, 168
conflicts, 4
    coalmining, 206, 212–13
    forestry sector, 150

governments, 6–7
    land use, 218, 220
    local community fisheries, 94, 106n,
        162
    local communities and logging per-
        mits, 98–9
    mining sector, 103, 104, 108n, 206,
        212–13
    party politics, 22
    revenue-sharing arrangements, 3–4,
        114, 115
    see also violence
Consultative Group on Indonesia, xxv,
    151
contracts of work (CoWs), 104, 126, 183,
    189, 190n
Coral Reef Rehabilitation and Manage-
    ment Program (Coremap), 171
coral reefs, 2, 95, 174
corruption, xxiv, 1, 14, 16, 22–3, 25, 49,
    146, 157
    bribe collection system, 7
    legal system, 46
    local, 7, 8, 16, 19, 22–3, 155
    New Order era, 186–8
    Pertamina, 181, 182, 189
    reforestation, 102, 107n
Council of Regional Representatives
    (DPD), 14
customary law
    see *adat*

decentralisation, 1, 4–5, 6–8
    and democracy, 46–9, 85, 92
    and forests, 154–5
    and land use, 224–6
    and resource management, 72, 84–7,
        92–108, 231–47, 251–2
    effects of, 6–8, 37, 47–9, 104–5
    fiscal disparity, 109–24
    goal, 4–5
democracy/democratisation, 1, 4, 13, 26,
    37, 131, 146, 188, 198–200
    and decentralisation, 46–9
    see also reformasi

deregulation of state enterprises
  see privatisation
deterioration, environment
  see environmental degradation
development, 125–42, 218–24, 226n
  environmentally sensitive uplands,
    218–20
  history, xxi–xiv, 126–31
  link with environment, xxi, xxii, 224
  regional, 118–22
  strategy, oil and gas industry, 183–6
  triple-track, xxiv
Dutch disease, 72, 73, 127
  definition, 141n

Earth summit, xxii–xxiii, xxv, 62
economic crisis
  see financial crisis
economy, 31–50, 129
  central government budget, 111
  CPI, 32
  depreciation, 32–4, 34, 49n
  domestic savings, 36
  current account deficit, 135–6
  exchange rate, 32, 49n
    floating, 34
  fiscal policy, 5, 34–5, 86–7
  GDP, 5, 31–2, 33, 34, 36, 38, 49n, 59,
    61, 87, 130, 131, 132, 164, 181
    effect on, based on forecasts to
    2020, 132–40
  Gini index, 137
  global, 5–6
  growth, 3, 140
  inflation, 5, 32–4, 49n, 135
  interest rates, 33, 49n
  international reserves, 5, 34
  investment, 35–7, 39, 45, 49n, 57–8,
    67
  JSX index, 32, 33
  labour market, 37–40
  monetary policy, 32–4, 49n
  per capita income, 5, 31–2
  price index, 135
  public sector debt, 49n
  recession, 31, 33

education, 8, 16, 19, 35, 110, 115, 120,
  122, 123, 171, 175
Egypt, 19
elections, 4, 13–30
  1999 and 2004 DPR results, 15, 17
  1999, 15, 17, 22
  April 2004, xxiv, 4, 13, 14, 22, 27
  communal voting, 23–4
  presidential, 4, 13, 14, 16, 17, 21, 188
    percentage of votes, 17
  vote-buying, 17, 22–3
employment
  female, 38
  fisheries, 2, 162, 162–3
  forecasts to 2020, 138
  forests, 2, 128
  illegal mining sector, 207, 208–9
  incomes, 39
  low-skilled labour, 42
  manufacturing, 38, 39, 42, 79
  minimum wages, 39–40, 49n
energy
  consumption, 59–60, 62
  renewable, 60
  systems, 64–5
environmental
  conservation, land and water
    resources, 216–27
  degradation, 3, 53, 62, 63, 68, 86,
    102–3, 127–8, 128–9, 136, 140, 146,
    150, 152, 155, 167, 168, 174, 194,
    201
  disasters, 88
  expenditure, 86–7
  indicators, xxiii, xxiv
  pollution, 5, 53, 60, 61, 62–9, 91n,
    167–8
Environmental Defense Fund, xxii
ESE triangle, 125, 129–30, 131, 141,
  141n
Europe/European Union, 54, 58, 65, 76,
  126, 156
exports, 3, 62, 76, 185
  competition with China, 6, 39, 77, 78
  during 1990s, 3
  fish, 163

liquefied natural gas, 3, 181–2, 185
log export ban, 35, 128, 147, 198
non-oil, 42
oil, 5, 60, 185
potential, 136
trade with China, 77, 153
wood products, 3, 6, 42, 128, 147,
148, 151, 152, 157, 160n, 197
Extractive Industries Review, 127

financial crisis, xxiii–xxiv, xxiv, 4, 16,
31, 45, 46, 48, 102, 110, 123, 151,
164, 166, 188
financial market deregulation, xxii
fiscal capacity, 115–18, 123n, 124n
development expenditures, 118–20
variation per capita, 118
fisheries, 5, 93–7, 162–78
aquaculture production, 133, 165
conflict within local communities,
94–6, 106n, 162
employment, 2, 162, 162–3
exports, 163
fish stocks, 2, 96–7
fishing ground violations, 94–5
future of, 96–7
illegal, 163, 168, 169, 178n, 193–205
legislation, 93–4, 94
marine jurisdiction zones, 93, 97,
106n, 235, 237
overfishing, 167, 168, 174
penalties, 97
production, 164–5
reforms, 173
revenues, 115
surveillance, 94
traditional fishing, 93–4, 94, 106n
trawl technology, 106n
vessel limits, 164
food
sector, 129
security, 165–6
Food and Agriculture Organization
(FAO), 151, 162, 165
foreign aid, xxi–xxii, 174, 177
see also Australian Agency for Inter-

national Development (AusAID); US
Agency for International Development (USAID)
foreign direct investment (FDI), 68, 74,
75, 76, 79
foreign exchange earnings, 128
foreign investment, 2, 3, 6, 9, 68, 75,
126, 127
foreign portfolio investment, 33
forests/forestry, 97–103, 127–8, 145–61,
193–205
biological diversity, 129, 141–2n
degradation/depletion/deforestation,
53, 62, 63, 68, 86, 102–3, 127–8,
128–9, 136, 146, 150, 152, 155, 194,
201
employment, 2, 128
exports, 3, 6, 42, 128, 147, 148, 151,
152, 157, 160n, 197
financing plantations, 156
fires, 62, 102, 159n
foreign firms, 200–1
forest products, 3, 6, 79, 84, 148,
151–2
future, 102–3
HPH concessions, 197–8, 199–200
illegal logging, 128, 152, 153, 154,
156, 157, 158, 193–205
ways to control, 203–4
Law 5/1967 (basic forestry law), 2, 9,
85, 245
Law 22/1999 (defines forestry jurisdiction), 4, 23, 92, 92–3, 93–4, 98,
172, 199, 210, 212, 232–6, 253
Law 41/1999 (revised forestry law),
98, 99, 102, 237, 238, 239, 245
log export ban, 35, 128, 147, 198
log export tariff, 158, 160n
logging permits, 98–100, 107n, 199
payments, 98–9, 107n
manual logging ban, 148, 197
overproduction, 151–2
plywood industry, 149, 151, 152,
159n, 198, 202, 205n
protected forests, mining, 238–9,
251–2

rainforests, location, 2
reforestation, 102, 107n, 128, 150, 157, 158
revenues, 100–2, 115, 150
sawn-wood, 148, 152, 153, 158, 159n, 160n, 198
smuggling, volume of timber, 42, 200–1
spatial planning, 107n, 226n
timber extraction permits, 154
timber plantation licence revocation, 158
taxes, 100–2, 157
20-year forest concessions, 147
fossil fuels, 59–62, 64–5, 69
Freeport McMoRan Copper & Gold, 126–7
Friends of the Earth, xxii
fuel, 179–90
    domestic demand, 5
    government subsidies, 5, 65
    see also gas; oil
furniture, 42, 78, 81, 88, 148
    see also manufacturing

GAM (Free Aceh Movement), 20, 27–9
garments
    see clothing; see also manufacturing
gas, 61, 179–90
    exports, 42, 181–2, 185
    liquefied natural (LNG), 3, 181–2, 190n
    location, 2
    revenue, 86, 110, 111, 114, 115, 116–17, 150, 183
general purpose funds (DAU), 86, 100, 108n, 114, 115, 116, 117, 122, 124n
Global Trade Analysis Project (GTAP), 90n
globalisation, 8, 53–70, 84
golf course, 222–4, 227n
governance, xxiv, 6, 131, 234, 242
greenhouse gas emissions, 5, 53, 60, 61, 62–9
    black carbon emissions, 62
    climate change, 62–8

McKibbin–Wilcoxen blueprint, emission permit trading, 67–8, 70n
    tax on, 65–6

Habibie, President B.J., 46–7, 49n, 92, 150, 154, 184
Hasan, Bob, 149, 158, 159n, 187
health, 4, 8, 35, 62, 110, 115, 120, 123, 124n, 126
Hong Kong, 54, 55, 57, 159n, 209
human development index, xxiv
human rights, 25, 26

illegal resource extraction, xxiv, 7, 35, 42, 104, 128, 152, 153, 154, 156, 157, 158, 163, 168, 169, 178n, 193–205
imports, 41–2, 49, 184
    oil, 35
India, 55
Indonesia, description, 1–2, 125–6, 164
Indonesian Bank Restructuring Agency (IBRA), 145, 156, 159
    legal foundation, 49n
    winding up, 43–4
Indonesian Association of Forest Concessionaires (APHI), 157, 200
Indonesian Forestry Society (MPI), 155, 157
Indonesian Institute of Sciences (LIPI) Research and Development Centre for Oceanography, 96
Indonesian National Army (TNI), 26–7, 28
Indonesia–UK Tropical Forest Management Programme, 158
industrial production, 55
infrastructure, xxi, xxiv, 37, 49n, 57, 115, 120, 122, 123, 124n, 126, 127, 169–70, 183–4
Inpres program, xxii, 110, 123n
institutions, 244, 248–58
Inter-Governmental Group on Indonesia, xxiii, 141n
international aid, xxi–xxii
    see foreign aid

international conferences, xxi
International Energy Agency, 55
International Monetary Fund, 31, 54,
    145n, 151, 159n
International Rice Research Institute
    (IRRI), 129
Islam, 2, 18, 19, 23–4
    Jemaah Islamiyah network, 29
    see also Nahdlatul Ulama (NU)

Japan, 54, 56, 58, 65, 71, 74, 90n, 149,
    152, 154, 165, 168, 190n, 195, 196,
    202, 203, 209, 247n
    effect of world oil price, 56
    forestry products, 149, 152, 154
    GDP growth, 54
    reduced trade barriers, 71
Japanese International Cooperation
    Agency (JICA), 247
Jemaah Islamiyah, 29
judiciary/judicial system, 14, 24–5
    corruption, 25, 46
    need for reform, 46
    scope of court authority, 25
Jusuf Kalla, 4, 14, 19, 20, 21

kabupaten, 111, 116
Komodo National Park, 165
Kyoto Protocol, 54, 61, 62, 63, 64, 65,
    68, 69, 70n

labour force, 39–40, 42, 72
    mining sector, 104
    mobility, 90n
    see also employment
land and water resources, 216–27
    environmental degradation, 217, 22
land
    speculation, 226n
    tenure, 1, 6
    use, 9, 218–24
Latin America, 73, 152
law enforcement, xxiv, 1, 6, 224, 242
legal and institutional framework, 85–6

legal system
    see judiciary/judicial system; see also
    adat law; legislation
legislation, 1, 6, 231–47
    ambiguity, 7, 105, 245, 246
    Anti Money Laundering, 203
    Armed Forces Bill, 26–7
    draft coastal management, 241, 243
    draft fisheries, 242–3
    draft natural resources, 105, 240–3
    draft oil and gas industry, 189
    environmental, xxiii
    Government Regulation in Lieu of
    Legislation (Perpu) 1/2004, 237, 239,
    251–2
    implied repeal, 245
    Law 5/1960 on agrarian law, 9n, 85,
    105
    Law 1/1967 on foreign investment, 2,
    147
    Law 5/1967 on forestry, 2, 9n, 85,
    147, 238, 245
    Law 11/1967 on mining, 2, 104, 237,
    238–9
    Law 8/1971 on Pertamina, 180
    Law 9/1985 on fisheries, 94
    Law 5/1990 on conservation, 237,
    238
    Law 24/1992 on spatial planning,
    227n, 237
    Law 5/1994 on environmental man-
    agement, 237
    Law 23/1997 on environmental man-
    agement, 237, 238, 243
    Law 2/1999 on political parties, 4
    Law 3/1999 on elections, 4
    Law 22/1999 on local government, 4,
    23, 92–5, 98, 154, 172, 199, 210,
    212, 223, 232–6, 253
    Law 25/1999 on fiscal decentralisa-
    tion, 4, 86, 92, 100, 101, 103, 114,
    121, 124n, 172, 199, 232, 235
    Law 41/1999 on forestry (revised),
    98, 99, 102, 237, 238–9, 245
    Law 34/2000 on regional taxes and
    levies, 124n

Law 22/2001 on mining, 104
Law 31/2002 on political parties, 4
Law 12/2003 on elections, 4
Law 15/2003 on terrorism, 25
Law 10/2004 on developing laws, 236, 240, 244, 246, 247n
Law 24/2004 on deposit insurance, 45
Law 31/2004 on fisheries, 97
Law 32/2004 on regional local/government, 105, 232, 234–6
Law 33/2004 on fiscal balancing between the central government and regional governments, 232
legal hierarchy, 107n
natural resources, gaps/inconsistencies, 236–40
precedents, 245–6
revision/reform, 47, 105, 156, 243–6
special autonomy laws, Aceh and Papua, 115, 121, 122
local government, 4–5, 6–7, 7–8
fiscal policies, 86–7
legal and institutional frameworks, 85–6
see also decentralisation

Malaysia, 55, 58, 74, 77, 78, 79, 81, 84, 88, 89, 153, 194, 200, 202, 208
mangrove forests, 2, 170
manufacturing, 6, 37–8, 39, 42, 71, 72, 74–5, 76, 78, 79, 84, 87, 88, 90n, 148, 184
map of Indonesia, xxvi
Marine and Fisheries Research Agency, 163
Marine Resources Evaluation and Planning (MREP) Project, 171, 173
marine resources, 93–7, 162–78, 235–6
coastal development, 163, 166–70
decentralisation, 172
depletion, 96–7, 163
diversity, 2
draft coastal management act, 173
employment, 2, 164
future of, 96–7

history, 170–4
legislation, 172, 233
maximum sustainable yield, 173
pollution, 167–8
post-*reformasi*, 172–4
pre-*reformasi*, 170–2
protected areas (MPAs), 170, 176–7
reefs, 2, 95, 174
scientific knowledge, 175
threats to, 166–70
tourism, 169–70
sustainable management, 174–7
see also fisheries
Marine Sciences Education Project, 171
Marriott Hotel bombing, 25, 29
media reporting
deforestation debate, 201
freedom, 25, 225–6
illegal mining, 207, 208
politics, 20–3
violence, 29
Megawati Sukarnoputri, 14, 15, 16, 17, 19, 20, 21–2, 24, 31, 97, 105
and economy, 31, 34–5
and forestry, 154–5
husband, 16
2004 election loss, 16
military, 14, 25–6, 27–8
decoupling from political system, 26
forestry connections, 148–9, 158
oil and gas industry, 179, 183
politics, 19, 20
mineral ores, 103–4, 108n
location, 2
mining sector, 1, 2–3, 103–4
conflicts, 103, 104, 108n
distribution of revenues, 103, 108n, 115
employment, 208–9
illegal, xxiv, 104, 206–15
legislation, 104
in protected areas, 237, 238–9
Ministry of Agriculture, 94, 106n
Ministry of Energy and Mining, 239
Ministry of Finance, 101, 102, 103

Ministry of Forestry, 96, 99, 101, 102,
107n, 128, 157–8, 198, 201, 243
Ministry of Home Affairs and National
Development Planning Agency, 102,
234
Ministry of Trade and Industry, 157–8,
185
Ministry of Marine Affairs and Fisheries,
94, 96, 97, 162, 163, 169, 241, 242,
244
Ministry of the Environment, xxiii, 241,
244
establishment, xxii
Mobil Oil, 190n
money politics, xxiv, 22–3
Multifibre Arrangement (MFA), 71, 76
multinational companies, 3
Muslim Brotherhood, 19
see also Islam

Nahdlatul Ulama (NU), 15, 16, 18, 24
National Committee on Indonesia's
Marine Conservation, 176
National Movement of Forest and land
Rehabilitation, 107n
natural resource 'curse', 71–91
abundance v. dependence, discussion,
73–4
definition, 71
discussion of, 72–5
natural resources, 2
after decentralisation, 114–15
agencies, 230
before decentralisation, 110–14
border disputes, 7
distribution of benefits/sharing of
revenue, 4, 5, 8, 47, 109–24
comparison, before and after
decentralisation, 112–13
extraction licences/rights, 1, 3, 7
future policies, 253–7
district, 256–7
national, 254–5
provincial, 255–6
legislative gaps/inconsistencies,
236–40

revenues, 86
unsustainable rate of extraction, 4, 6,
8, 53
forecasts resource depletion to
2020, 132–40
see also forests/forestry; gas; oil;
marine resources; mining sector
Nature Conservancy, 165
nepotism, 16, 131
New Order period, 17, 19, 26, 85–6, 100,
104, 146, 147–50, 151, 156, 184,
193, 196–8, 199, 206–7, 249–51
endemic corruption, 186–8
see also Soeharto, President
New Zealand, 54
newly industrialised countries (NICs), 56,
57
see also Hong Kong; Singapore;
South Korea; Taiwan
Nippindo, 149
non-government organisations (NGOs),
xxii, 151, 154, 155, 158, 171, 189,
193, 225, 241, 244, 246
activists, 26, 30n
non-natural resource-based sector, 3
non-renewable resources, xxi
see also fossil fuels; mining sector
Norway, 122

OECD countries, 54, 59
oil, 34–5, 61, 179–90
boom, 1970s, 126, 127
energy consumption, 60
export commodity, 3, 5
location, 2
pollution, 167–8
revenue, xxii, 86, 110, 111, 114, 115,
150
taxes, 141n
world price of, 5, 54, 55–6, 185
'Old Order' period, 195–6
oligarchy, 145–61
Organization of the Petroleum Exporting
Countries (OPEC), 53

parliament, 4

patronage, 146, 147
People's Representative Council (DPR),
    14
Pertamina, 126, 141n, 179–8
    bankruptcy, 181
    corruption, 181
    establishment, 179, 190n
    history, 179–80
petroleum, 179–90
    see also fuel; oil
Philippines, 54, 55, 75, 76, 77, 78, 81,
    84, 147, 166
Plaza Accord, 74
police, 7, 15, 25, 26, 27, 28, 29, 37, 208
political parties, 4, 9, 15, 14–24
    1999 and 2004 election results, 15
    Democratic Party (PD), 15, 18, 19
    Golkar, 9n, 14, 17, 18, 19, 20–1, 24,
    157
    Indonesian Democracy Party (PDI),
    9n
    Indonesian Democratic Party of
    Struggle (PDI-P), 15, 16, 17, 18, 23
    Koalisi Kebangsaan (Nationhood
    Coalition), 18, 20
    National Mandate Party (PAN), 15,
    24
    National Awakening Party (PKB), 15,
    17, 23, 24
    Prosperous Justice Party (PKS), 15,
    18, 19, 23
politics, 13–30
    personality as key to success, 13,
    20–1
    Soeharto-era elite, 14
population, 1–2, 5, 31
    surrounding forest areas, 127, 147
poverty
    alleviation, xxii, xxiv, 35, 36, 39, 42,
    196
    forecasts, 138–40, 142n
    proportion of population, 3
    and workforce, 38–9
privatisation, xxii, 183, 186
production-sharing contracts (PSCs),
    182–3, 190n

Propatria, 26
property rights, 46, 53, 66, 68, 69, 89,
    128
PT Minang Malindo, 212–13
public sector reform, xxiv

rainforests
    location, 2
recentralisation (resentralisasi), 154,
    160n
Reforestation Fund, 150, 151
reformasi, 4, 5, 6–8, 16, 20, 24, 26, 114,
    145, 170, 198–200, 251–2
regional autonomy laws
    see Law 22/1999; Law 25/1999; Law
    32/2004; Law 33/2004
regional disparity, 109–24
religion, 2, 9
renewable resources, xxi, 60
    see also water; fisheries;
    forests/forestry; biological resources
Repelita, 130, 171
resource depletion, xxiv
revealed comparative advantage (RCA),
    76, 78, 80–1, 82, 83, 84
    definition, 90n
revenue
    intergenerational issues, 122
    natural resource transfers, 121–2
    own-source (PAD), 100, 104, 115,
    117, 210, 211, 222
    sharing, 4, 5, 8, 47, 109–24
        comparison, before and after
        decentralisation, 112–13, 116, 117,
        121
Rio conference, xxii–xxiii, xxv, 62
riots, 1998, 4
ruling elite, xxiv
Russia, 63, 65, 79, 153, 154, 202
Ryamisard Ryacudu, General, 26

sanctions, 97, 237–8
Santiago summit, xxiii–xxiv
SDO scheme, 110, 116
shariah law, 23
Singapore, 55, 78, 159n, 208

social development, xxii, xxiv
Soeharto, President, 2, 19, 20, 46, 131,
    146, 245
  corruption, 187–8
  development policy, 2–3, 9, 184–6
  fall, 1, 4, 13, 92, 102, 146, 188, 189,
    193, 198
  forestry, 147
  nepotism, 16, 131, 148, 179
  nostalgia, 17, 20
  oil and gas industry, 179, 180–2, 183,
    187–8, 189, 190n
  patronage, 3, 146, 147, 148, 148, 187
  political elite, 14, 19
South Africa, 3
South Korea, 54, 55, 57, 58, 159n, 168,
    198, 203
Southeast Asia
  economy, 74–5, 87, 88
  trade with China, 75–84
spatial planning, 107n, 226n, 227n, 237
specific allocation funds (DAK), 100,
    124n
Stockholm conference, xxi, 130
subsidies
  fuel, 5, 35, 56, 60, 65
  state enterprises, 184
Sukarno, President, 16, 24, 180, 195–6
Susilo Bambang Yudhoyono, xxiv, 4, 13,
    14, 19–20, 30
  background, 19
  personality, 20, 21
  2004 election, proportion of vote, 16
sustainable development/management, 5,
    125–42
  future, 131–40, 253–7
  community-based small island man-
    agement (Decree 41/2000), 94
  marine resources, 163, 174–7
  Rio conference, xxiii
Sutowo, Ibnu, 180, 181, 182, 183, 184,
    188, 190n

Taiwan, 54, 55, 57, 160n, 168, 198
TAP MPR IX/2001, 240

taxes, 115–17
  before decentralisation, 111
  concessions, foreign companies, 2
  forestry sector, 100–2, 157
  gas emission, 65–6
  local, 1, 7–8, 47, 104
  mining sector, 104
  personal, 114
  revenue, comparison, before and after
    decentralisation, 112–13
terrorism, 25, 29, 30n, 37
Thailand, 54, 55, 57, 58, 59, 74, 77, 78,
    79, 81, 84, 89
timber
  see forests/forestry
tourism, 95, 124n, 169–70
trade, 40–2
  balances, 5–6
  barriers, 71
  imbalances, 53, 56–8, 68
  intra-East Asia, 75
trade, hotels, restaurants, and services,
    38, 39
tsunami, 28–9

ulama, 24
unemployment, xxiv, 165
UNESCO, 171
United Development Party (PPP), 9
United Nations
  Conference on the Human Environ-
    ment (Stockholm), xxi, 130
  Convention on the Law of the Sea,
    171
  Development Programme (UNDP),
    241, 244, 247n
  Earth Summit, Rio de Janeiro, 62
  trade balance with Asia, 5–6
United Nations Framework Convention
  on Climate Change, 54
United States of America, 3, 41–2, 76,
    156, 160n, 165
  anti-dumping ruling, 153
  current account deficit, 56, 69n
  fiscal balance, 56–7
  GDP growth, 54

investment, 57–8
and Kyoto Protocol, 63, 65, 69
trade restrictions, 90–1
US Agency for International Development (USAID), 163, 171, 176, 244, 247n

Vietnam, 79, 81, 83, 84, 87, 88, 89, 90
violence
Aceh, 27
Ambon, 27
immediate post-Soeharto area, 13
politics, 27–9
see also terrorism

wages
see employment
Washington Consensus, xxii–xiii, xxiv
water, xxi, 37, 87, 127, 129, 136–7, 167, 216–17, 221–7, 257–8, 238
water conservation
see land and water resources

wealthy community, 35, 36
West Java, 216–27
Environmental Management Agency, 256
West Sumatra, 206–15
governor, 212–13
Wiranto, General, 18, 20, 24
wood industry
see forests/forestry
Wood Industry Revitalisation Agency
see BRIK
World Bank, xxii, xxiii, 72, 74, 127, 146, 247
world economy, 53–70
climate change, 62–8
competition, 76–8
GDP growth, 54
interest rates, 58
longer term issues, 58–62
short-term outlook, 54–8
World Trade Organization (WTO), 71, 75, 76, 90n

INDONESIA UPDATE SERIES

Indonesia Assessment 1988 (Regional Development)
edited by Hal Hill and Jamie Mackie

Indonesia Assessment 1990 (Ownership)
edited by Hal Hill and Terry Hull

Indonesia Assessment 1991 (Education)
edited by Hal Hill

Indonesia Assessment 1992 (Political Perspectives)
edited by Harold Crouch

Indonesia Assessment 1993 (Labour)
edited by Chris Manning and Joan Hardjono

Finance as a Key Sector in Indonesia's Development
(Indonesia Assessment 1994)
edited by Ross McLeod

Development in Eastern Indonesia
(Indonesia Assessment 1995)
edited by Colin Barlow and Joan Hardjono

Population and Human Resources
(Indonesia Assessment 1996)
edited by Gavin W. Jones and Terence H. Hull

Indonesia's Technological Challenge
(Indonesia Assessment 1997)
edited by Hal Hill and Thee Kian Wie

Post-Soeharto Indonesia: Renewal or Chaos?
(Indonesia Assessment 1998)
edited by Geoff Forrester

Indonesia in Transition: Social Aspects of Reformasi and Crisis
(Indonesia Assessment 1999)
edited by Chris Manning and Peter van Diermen

Indonesia Today: Challenges of History
(Indonesia Assessment 2000)
edited by Grayson J. Lloyd and Shannon L. Smith

Women in Indonesia: Gender, Equity and Development
(Indonesia Assessment 2001)
edited by Kathryn Robinson and Sharon Bessell

Local Power and Politics in Indonesia: Decentralisation and Democratisation
(Indonesia Assessment 2002)
edited by Edward Aspinall and Greg Fealy

Business in Indonesia: New Challenges, Old Problems
(Indonesia Assessment 2003)
edited by M. Chatib Basri and Pierre van der Eng

The Politics and Economics of Indonesia's Natural Resources
(Indonesia Assessment 2004)
edited by Budy P. Resosudarmo

Printed in the United States
52308LVS00003B/1-90